An Internment Odyssey

An Internment Odyssey
Haisho Tenten

Suikei Furuya

Translated by
Tatsumi Hayashi

With a Foreword by
Gary Y. Okihiro

Japanese Cultural Center of Hawai'i
Honolulu, Hawai'i

22 21 20 19 18 17   1 2 3 4 5 6

Library of Congress Cataloging-in-Publication Data

Names: Furuya, Suikei, 1889–1977, author.
Title: An Internment Odyssey = Haisho Tenten / by Suikei Furuya ; translated
by Tatsumi Hayashi ; with a foreword by Gary Y. Okihiro.
Other titles: Haisho tenten. English
Description: Honolulu, Hawai'i : Japanese Cultural Center of Hawai'i, 2016. |
"Originally published as Haisho tenten, ? Suikei Furuya, Honolulu,
1964"—Title page verso. | Includes bibliographical references and index.
Identifiers: LCCN 2016023394 | ISBN 9780976149330 (pbk. : alk. paper)
Subjects: LCSH: Furuya, Suikei, 1889–1977. | Japanese Americans--Evacuation
and relocation, 1942–1945. | World War, 1939–1945—Personal narratives,
Japanese American. | World War, 1939–1945—Concentration camps—United
States. | Concentration camps—United States—History—20th century. |
Japanese Americans—Hawaii—Biography. | Concentration camp
inmates—United States—Biography.
Classification: LCC D769.8.A6 F87 2016 | DDC 940.53/1773092 [B]—dc23
LC record available at https://lccn.loc.gov/2016023394

Originally published as *Haisho Tenten*, © Suikei Furuya, Honolulu, 1964

The poems "I went east to Asia," "For the sake of the mouth," and "A thousand sorrows" are
from Lai, Him Mark, Genny Lim, and Judy Yung, eds., *Island: Poetry and History of Chinese
Immigrants on Angel Island, 1910–1940*, © 1991, reprinted with the permission of the University of Washington Press.

The poem "Trusting the Buddha" is from D. T. Suzuki, *Buddha of Infinite Light: The Teachings
of Shin Buddhism, the Japanese Way of Wisdom and Compassion*, © 1989 by The American Buddhist Academy, reprinted by arrangement with The Permissions Company, Inc., on behalf of
Shambhala Publications Inc., Boston, Massachusetts, www.shambhala.com.

The translation of Soga's description of the death of Shoichi Asami is used with the permission of Emi and George Oshiro.

The photographs of the Missoula Internment Camp that appear in this book are used with
the permission of the Historical Museum at Fort Missoula.

The Japanese Cultural Center of Hawai'i gratefully acknowledges the generous contribution
of the Hanzo Furuya family for the translation of this book.

The opinions contained in the body of this work are those of Kumaji Suikei Furuya and do
not necessarily reflect those of the translator or the Japanese Cultural Center of Hawai'i.

This book is printed on acid-free paper and meets the guidelines for
permanence and durability of the Council on Library Resources.

Design and composition by Wanda China

This translation is published in memory of

Shige Yoshitake
Kihei Hirai
Janet Kanja
and
Hanzo Furuya

Contents

List of Illustrations   ix

Foreword to the Translation by Gary Y. Okihiro   xi

Acknowledgments   xv

Translator's Note by Tatsumi Hayashi   xvii

About the Translation   xix

Introduction to the Translation by Brian Niiya and Sheila Chun   xxiii

Kumaji Furuya's Internment History   xliii

Haisho Tenten   1

Forewords
   Joei Oi: A Chronicle with Poetic Artistry   3
   Masahiro Himeno: History is Alive   4
   Totaro Matsui: Joy and Hope   6

1.   The Outbreak of War   7

2.   Sand Island Camp   11

3.   Back to the INS Office   20

4.   Life at Sand Island   24

5.   Embarking on a Wanderer's Journey   43

6.   Angel Island   52

7.   To the Interior of the Mainland   58

8.   Camp McCoy   64

9.   Camp Forrest   88

10. Camp Livingston   98

11. Fort Missoula   128

12. Santa Fe Internment Camp   185

13. On Our Way Back to Hawai'i   263

Postscript   274

Author's Profile   276

Appendix A: In the Case of Kumaji Furuya   279
Appendix B: The Mott Bill   292
Appendix C: Letter from Ivan Williams, Officer-in-Charge   293
Appendix D: Excerpt from "A Note to Roosevelt"   297
Notes   299
Bibliography   345
Index   353

List of Illustrations

Figures

Hōryū Asaeda with military police at the Honolulu
Immigration Station   167

Rev. Hōryū Asaeda photographed at the Honolulu
Immigration Station   167

Internees carrying gas masks at the Honolulu Immigration Station   168

Charles Ichitarō Hasebe being interviewed at the Honolulu
Immigration Station   168

Sand Island Internment Camp, January 1942   169

Double rows of barbed wire fence, Sand Island Internment
Camp, January 1942   169

Internees putting up tents, Sand Island Internment Camp,
February 1942   170

Internee tents and barracks near completion, Sand Island
Internment Camp   170

The Army-run INS station on Angel Island   171

Re-creation of the bunk beds on the second floor of the
Angel Island INS station   171

Poem carved into the wooden walls of the Angel Island
detention barracks   172

Furuya at funeral for Masao Sogawa   173

Internees at Fort Missoula nine-hole golf course   174

Tournament-winning Hawaiʻi internee softball team,
Missoula, c. 1943   174

Painted reproduction of Santa Fe Internment Camp   175

The Santa Fe camp internee News Broadcasting Department   175

Attendees at an exhibit of internee art   176

Internees in the mess hall to celebrate a special event   177

Watercolor of the Santa Fe Internment Camp by
Bannosuke Yoshida   178

Hawai'i internees in the Santa Fe Internment Camp, January 1945   179

The Santa Fe camp cast and crew of "Hiroshima miyage to
Tamazo" performed March, 1945   180

Cover illustration for the original *Haisho Tenten*   181

Furuya's return to Honolulu on November 13, 1945   181

Relatives and friends gather at Honolulu Harbor on
December 10, 1945, to greet Hawai'i internees being
brought back to the islands   182

Koichi Iida disembarks at Honolulu Harbor, November 13, 1945   182

Akio Robert Kimura upon his return to Honolulu,
December 10, 1945   183

The Furuya family several years after the war   183

Kumaji Suikei Furuya, 1964   184

Maps

Furuya's Interment Odyssey Map   xlii

Sand Island Internment Camp by Chikashi Nakayama   12

Santa Fe Internment Camp by Chikashi Nakayama   186

Foreword to the Translation

Gary Y. Okihiro

Pu'uloa, later called Pearl Harbor by foreigners, emerged from Pele's fires as a haven for life. In morning light, its waters appear so still they mirror perfectly the bordering lands and immense skies. Ripples on its surface betray the fecund life below—corals, shellfish, *limu* (seaweed), and fishes. Pu'uloa's crystal-clear waters, fed by fresh water springs, were a source of abundance for the people who settled, fished, and farmed along its shores. Its violation, its militarization by foreigners, defiled that gift of the ancestors to their people—the Hawaiians.

"When I was asked to write a foreword for this book, I was so surprised that I was unable to reply," confessed Masahiro Himeno, a Honolulu Christian minister, in the original issue of this book in 1964. "I should have responded, but the request was so weighty that words failed me." Like Himeno, I feel the gravity of gratitude and responsibility in this foreword to the English translation of that book, *Haisho Tenten*.

I write from my subject positions as a boy who came of age in the Honolulu Plantation's camp overlooking Pu'uloa. I fished its forbidden waters, which the U.S. Navy had fenced off and pinned "KAPU" signs around; like the nation's border, barbed wire encircled the bay. My grandparents and mother watched with astonishment, when on December 7, 1941, warplanes with Japan's rising sun painted on their fuselage, bombed and strafed that U.S. military installation.

Since my small kid time, I have grown into a historian of the U.S. and the world, or at least I make those claims. From those standpoints, I see Pu'uloa, Hawai'i, and Oceania not as backwaters of U.S. and world history, but as their mainland. The U.S. islands formed an armed flotilla pointed at Japan, essential for the nation's strategic interests in the Pacific and the world. The origin of that historical formation rests in Europe's search for Asia.

When Spain's Christopher Columbus stumbled onto lands Europeans called "America," he was on his way to India. In fact, Columbus, upon making landfall, thought he had found islands just off the coast of Japan and christened the peoples "Indians." Spanish conquest of their "New World" gave them a base of operations and, just as critically, resources—gold and silver—extracted at great cost by Indians that enabled their trade with Asia, once having crossed the ocean they called the South Seas and, later, the Pacific.

The English company that established a foothold in America at Jamestown, Virginia, in 1607 directed its settlers to find a road to Asia. After independence, the new nation's invasive expansion across the continent, called "manifest destiny" by some of its leaders, from sea to shining sea was in large part a thrust toward Asia. Wealth, they believed like their European forebears, could be gotten for the taking in Asia. That "manifest destiny" shows that the U.S. arises from and occupies both the Atlantic and Pacific worlds.

Hawai'i is central to that global strategy. The illegal U.S. takeover of the Hawaiian kingdom was accomplished with the force of arms and juridical doctrine, terminating Hawaiian sovereignty. The deed followed from earlier erosions of the Hawaiian nation through ideology and the material conditions, including the waters of Pu'uloa, which the U.S. secretly surveyed in 1873. Disguised as a tourist, Major General John M. Schofield reported Pu'uloa offered an excellent anchorage for U.S. military and commercial vessels. An emerging world power, the U.S. was intent on converting Oceania, like the Caribbean, into "an American lake."

That U.S. ambition to dominate the world was a European patrimony, which began in the fifteenth century and lasted for about four hundred years. In 1900, African American scholar W. E. B. Du Bois called that spread and occupation "the problem of the twentieth century." The color line, Du Bois noted, justified the imperialism that encompassed the earth. Japan challenged that white supremacy with its defeat of Russia in 1905, the first victory of a nonwhite over a white nation in modern times, and its expansion into Korea, China, and Asia broadly followed the European formula for national greatness.

Japan's attack on the U.S.'s Pearl Harbor was a part of that problem of the twentieth century. In that sense, U.S. entry into World War II was as much a defense of white global supremacy as a declaration of national sovereignty, even as the U.S. ignored its own lawless transgression of Hawaiian sovereignty. Within that context, Du Bois understood the unconstitutional infringement of Japanese American rights in the people's forced removal and confinement during that war as indicative of the racial cast of the war.

Not a solitary witness, Kumaji (Suikei) Furuya's *Haisho Tenten* bespeaks U.S. and world history. In his detailed account, as Masahiro Himeno observes, history comes alive. Furuya's testimony of lives broken under coercion and abuse tracks a veritable archipelago of hatred, from Honolulu's INS station to Sand Island; Angel Island in San Francisco Bay; Camp McCoy, Wisconsin; Camp Forrest, Tennessee; Camp Livingston, Louisiana; Fort Missoula, Montana; and Santa Fe, New Mexico. Furuya's historical narrative, Himeno offers, sparkles with "sentiment, compassion, and wisdom," imparting humanity to the objects of inhumanity.

Other witnesses will surely come forward to testify to the strength and resilience of the human spirit. Although mute to inattentive ears, the ground speaks volumes. Pele's creation, despite its desecration and pollution, continues to sustain life abundant. Human-designated sites of remembrance populate the earth's lands and waters. Our lives form connections with one another, with history, and with our planet. We forget those to our poverty and at our peril.

Acknowledgments

This book would not have been possible without the generous help and support of so many people. The idea of translating for publication the memoirs of Hawai'i Issei internees was the inspiration of Brian Niiya, Jane Kurahara, and Betsy Young of the Japanese Cultural Center of Hawai'i and Professor Dennis M. Ogawa of the University of Hawai'i. Their support and enthusiasm has guided the JCCH Resource Center's production of three such publications: Yasutaro Soga's *Life behind Barbed Wire*; *Family Torn Apart: The Internment Story of the Otokichi Muin Ozaki Family*; and now Kumaji Furuya's *Haisho Tenten*.

At the Resource Center, Sheila Chun, Florence Sugimoto, Yaeko Harbin, and the late Shige Yoshitake provided thoughtful and careful editorial input. Nicki Garces, former Resource Center coordinator, has remained a kind friend, providing library help even after her departure.

Warren Nishimoto and Michiko Kodama-Nishimoto of the University of Hawai'i's Center for Oral History graciously made available oral histories by the Furuya family. Alan Rosenfeld, assistant professor of history at the University of Hawai'i-West O'ahu, generously shared his knowledge of the German internment in Hawai'i and provided help in locating internment-related documents. Doris Berg Nye and Arthur Jacobs also kindly aided in the search for material important to the translation. Jean Toyama, University of Hawai'i professor emerita, lent her talents as a poet to help with the rendering of Furuya's haiku.

At the University of Hawai'i's Hamilton Library, Tokiko Yamamoto Bazzell, Japanese Studies librarian, and Minako Ito-Song, retired librarian, kindly shared their expertise and time. Government Documents librarian Mabel K. Suzuki provided much needed help in tracking down several hard-to-find documents that were critical to the work. Her generosity and persistence proved invaluable.

We are grateful to Emi Oshiro and her husband, the late George Oshiro, Japanese history professor at J. F. Oberlin University in Tokyo, for providing the translation of Soga's description of the death of Shoichi Asami.

We thank the following organizations for sharing their resources: the Japanese American National Museum in Los Angeles for camp directories, the Historical Museum at Fort Missoula for the Missoula internment photographs that appear in this book, Judith Bowman and the staff of the U.S. Army Museum of Hawai'i for their friendship and generous sharing of photographs, and the U.S. Naval Academy Museum in Annapolis for the Japanese and English versions of the Ichimaru Toshinosuke (Rinosuke) letter to FDR.

Members of the Angel Island Immigration Station Foundation have given generously of their time and unstintingly of their support. We especially thank Grant Din for sharing so selflessly his insights and resources, for taking us to Angel Island, and for helping us locate the Chinese poem that appears in Furuya's book. Thank you to Benjamin Fenkell of the U.S. Immigration Station, Angel Island State Park. We also owe appreciation to Charles Egan, professor of Chinese at San Francisco State University, for his efforts in identifying Issei internee writings left on the island.

The translator gratefully acknowledges the generosity of Mike Nakayama for his sharing of the maps of Sand Island and Santa Fe that were sketched by his father, Chikashi Nakayama. Many thanks go to George Okuhara for his fine work on the maps that appear in this book. His patience and attention to detail have produced valuable aids in furthering our understanding of the internment.

Hanzo Furuya and the Furuya family have given generously in support of the publication of this book. They have been very patient, and for this we are grateful.

Brian Niiya, editor of the online *Densho Encyclopedia*, has been a source of constant encouragement and unfaltering goodwill. We have turned to him often for his expansive knowledge and wise counsel.

Lastly, a big *mahalo* goes to my wife, Masako. Her support has not wavered through the more than ten years that it has taken to see this book to completion.

Translator's Note

When I began volunteering at the Japanese Cultural Center of Hawai'i a year after I retired, I was assigned to translate Otokichi Ozaki's radio scripts about his World War II internment experiences, which were broadcast on local Japanese radio stations after the war. Translating these scripts was my first encounter with the Japanese internment in Hawai'i. At the time, I had no idea that Hawai'i Japanese had been incarcerated during the war, although I had some knowledge about the mass relocation on the West Coast. My interest in this subject grew as I continued to work on Ozaki's camp news scripts. A few years later, I discovered *Haisho Tenten* in the JCCH collection and decided to translate it. By the time the translation was done, I had learned a lot about this subject.

Although Hawai'i Issei had written their first-hand wartime accounts in Japanese, not many of them had been translated for publication. One of the few exceptions was *Tessaku Seikatsu* by Yasutaro Soga, who had been interned in the Mainland camps. The late Kihei Hirai translated Soga's book, which was published in 2008 as *Life behind Barbed Wire*. Both Furuya and Soga were detained by the FBI on the day of the Pearl Harbor attack and were sent to the Mainland camps—Furuya with the first group that left Honolulu in February 1942 and Soga with the fifth group that left in August 1942. Each had his own unique and severe experience of being transferred from camp to camp. The two were reunited in Santa Fe in 1944, two years after they had been separated at the Sand Island Detention Camp.

It was my intention to translate this account of one of the most unforgettable events in the history of Hawai'i's Japanese in order to give the younger generations a chance to learn about what their ancestors had experienced. However, when I finished the preliminary translation in 2002, I never expected that it would be published. Rather, I expected that someone would just look at the translation one day.

I am honored that this book is being published as part of JCCH's series on the Hawai'i internment experience. The other books are *Life behind Barbed Wire* by Yasutaro Soga and *Family Torn Apart*, edited by Gail Honda.

While in the final phase of preparing this manuscript for publication, I received the sad news of the passing of the author's eldest son, Hanzo Furuya, at the age of ninety-one. I regret that he was not able to see this book in print.

Last but not least, this book would not have been published without the persevering assistance of my fellow volunteers. I would like to express my special appreciation to Sheila Chun, editor.

May 2016

About the Translation

Kumaji Furuya, writing under the pen name Suikei Furuya, published his Japanese-language internment memoir, *Haisho Tenten*, more than fifty years ago. In producing this translation of *Haisho Tenten*, care has been taken to remain as true to the original work as possible.

The sub-chapters of *Haisho Tenten* originally appeared as a series of articles that Furuya wrote for *The Hawaii Times*, a Japanese-language newspaper published in Honolulu. Some 196 articles appeared in the paper over a period of two years, from September 29, 1961 to September 21, 1963. However, the last three sections of the book's final chapter—"Haiku From Santa Fe," "The Rest of Our Group Returns," and "The Family Camp"— were not part of the original series and, therefore, were most likely written for the book.

The poem "At Angel Island" and the song "Moon over the Camp," which bookend *An Internment Odyssey*, originally appeared on the book jacket of *Haisho Tenten*.

The maps of the Sand Island and Santa Fe internment camps are based on the sketches of internee Chikashi Nakayama, a Japanese language teacher at Chuo Gakuin in Honolulu. Sent to the mainland with Group 5, Nakayama left Honolulu on August 6, 1942, and was in the Santa Fe Internment Camp when the war ended. The sketches were part of Nakayama's unfinished memoir and were given to the translator with the permission of the artist's son, Mike Nakayama. They represent the only known internee renderings of the layouts of these two confinement sites and are published here for the first time.

In the body of *An Internment Odyssey*—the translation of *Haisho Tenten*—parentheses enclose text as it appears in the original work; brackets enclose information added by the translator.

All footnotes were added during the translation and are not part of the original text.

In several instances, Furuya includes in his book passages taken from English-language sources, which he has condensed and translated into Japanese. When Furuya's version of these passages differs substantially enough from its English original, we have retranslated Furuya's version into English and, where possible, either provided the previously unpublished original or cited its published version. Otherwise, the original English version is provided.

In later chapters, most notably that on Santa Fe, Furuya frequently makes use of information from other sources. Attempts have been made to verify this information, with a citation of a source provided when possible.

Some mention must be made of Furuya's camp vocabulary. (For a list and description of the different types of World War II confinement sites, see the online *Densho Encyclopedia*, "Sites of incarceration," http://encyclopedia .densho.org/Sites%20of%20incarceration/.) Furuya uses several Japanese terms to identify the various confinement sites. For temporary detention facilities, like the Immigration and Naturalization Service station in Honolulu or the Sand Island camp, he uses the term *shūyōsho* 収容所. Although formally a U.S. Army internment camp, Sand Island functioned for fifteen months as a temporary holding site from where internees were either transferred to Mainland camps or to the inland Honouliuli facility.

For internment camps, i.e., those camps administered by the U.S. Army or the Department of Justice, in which Japanese nationals as well as German and Italian enemy aliens and Japanese Latin Americans were confined, Furuya uses the term *yokuryūsho* 抑留所. It is worthwhile noting that other Japanese language sources use the term *shūyōsho* to identify this category of confinement site. For example, see the Santa Fe Camp directories.

Most of the Hawai'i Issei internees (Japanese nationals) were transferred to Mainland internment camps. Hawai'i Nisei internees (U.S. citizens)—most of whom were Kibei, that is, Americans who had been educated in Japan—were sent to Honouliuli Internment Camp after the Sand Island facility was closed in late February 1943. At the end of the war, the Santa Fe Internment Camp in New Mexico and the Crystal City Family Internment Camp in Texas were the major facilities for Hawai'i Issei internees on the Mainland.

Camps administered by the War Relocation Authority are identified by Furuya as *tenjūsho* 転住所. These were primarily facilities for Nikkei living on the West Coast. About three hundred Hawai'i Issei were granted transfers from internment camps to relocation centers in order to live with family members who had voluntarily entered the Mainland internment system. There were no relocation centers in Hawaiʻi.

An attempt has been made to retain the contemporaneous usage of terminology. For example, "incarceration center" is widely used today to refer to those camps run by the War Relocation Authority. During the internment and at the time when Furuya was writing, however, these were usually called "relocation camps" and internment itself was often referred to as "detention." The translator has attempted to retain this usage.

Establishing a correct and uniform transliteration of the names of the Hawaiʻi internees also has been a goal of the translation. In romanizing the internees' names, the translator has relied on the Japanese Cultural Center of Hawaiʻi's Hawaiʻi Internee Database, which to date provides the most accurate rendering of the names of the Hawaiʻi internees. See below for further discussion of this database.

In some cases, a discrepancy may exist between the transliteration of a name as it appears here and in other sources, for example, Yasutaro Soga's *Life behind Barbed Wire*. These discrepancies are sometimes caused by the differences in the Japanese readings of the *kanji* (Chinese characters) used for the names. Most *kanji* have at least two kinds of Japanese readings: an *on* reading (based on its Chinese pronunciation) and a *kun* reading (a native Japanese pronunciation). Names are usually read according to the native *kun* pronunciation, although there are many exceptions, for example, literary and priest names, which can be read according to the Chinese pronunciation. Occasionally, Japanese also will unofficially use the *on* reading of a name because it is shorter and easier to pronounce, for example, Ko (*on*) versus Miyuki (*kun*). In extreme cases, there may be several ways of reading a *kanji* name. The variant renderings of the names of the Hawaiʻi internees who appear in Furuya's book can be found in the Index and in the JCCH Hawaiʻi Internee Database.

Throughout the text, the names of Japanese Americans, including that of the Issei, are given in Western style, with given name first, followed by family name. Otherwise, Japanese names are rendered traditionally, family name first.

Furuya often identifies internees only by their family name. In the case of Hawaiʻi internees, first names are provided by the translator only when an accurate, full identification can be made. Those remaining men who are referred to only by their family name were very likely from the Mainland or Latin America.

Many internees were active in poetry clubs and wrote under a pen name. Furuya often refers to these individuals by their poetry name; for example, Shoichi Asami, the editor of the *Nippu Jiji*, appears as Seiha

Asami. Also, Furuya himself used his pen name, Suikei, as the author of this book. This convention has been retained in the translation. Refer to the Index for the internees by their given and pen names.

Brief biographical footnotes are provided for individuals who appear prominently or frequently and for whom published information is available. For other internees who are mentioned in passing or for whom there is little published information, basic biographical data is available from the JCCH Hawai'i Internee Database. Basic personal information in the footnotes is from the JCCH Hawai'i Internee Database, *Nippu Jiji Hawai nenkan* directories, or camp directories, as identified in the Bibliography.

A Hawai'i internee list appears at the end of Furuya's original book, as well as a tally of the number of Hawai'i internees, some 702 individuals. Internees were categorized by their group at the time of their transfer to the Mainland camps. Lists of female internees and Honouliuli internees also were provided. These lists and the tally have not been reproduced in this English-language translation. Similar lists have been published in Patsy Sumie Saiki's *Ganbare* and Soga's *Life behind Barbed Wire*.

Moreover, since the publication of the original *Haisho Tenten* in 1964, new sources of information have become available to the researcher. These include internment-related files released by the National Archives and Records Administration, as well as primary Japanese-language sources, such as those archived at the JCCH Resource Center. Taken together, these new sources provide a more accurate list of the Hawai'i internees, which is available as the JCCH Hawai'i Internee Database and can be accessed at http://hawaiiinternment.org/internee_list.

According to the JCCH Hawai'i Internee Database, to date the approximate number of Hawai'i internees is as follows:

Internees	1,320
Family members	950 (from 270 families)
Total	2,270

Introduction to the Translation

Brian Niiya and Sheila Chun

This translation of Kumaji Furuya's *Haisho Tenten* is an unusual work in the enormous canon on the wartime internment and incarceration of Japanese Americans. In this introduction, we will examine three different types of contexts for understanding this book. First, we will provide a brief background on the Japanese American internment and incarceration, noting the difference between the two, both generally and specifically in Hawai'i. Second, we will provide a brief biography of Furuya's entire life as immigrant, businessman, poet, and community leader, since the account in this book essentially begins on December 7, 1941, and ends nearly four years later with his return to Honolulu. And third, we will look at the historiography of wartime incarceration and where Furuya's internment memoir fits in.

Internment and Incarceration

It has become fairly well known today that during World War II, many thousands of Japanese Americans were removed from their homes and sent to barbed-wire ringed concentration camps purely on the basis of their Japanese ancestry.[1] But for many, this newfound general knowledge is a bit murky on specifics. To begin with, there were really two distinct programs that involved the apprehension and detention of Japanese Americans during World War II. Though the roots of these two programs—which might broadly be referred to as "enemy alien internment" and "mass incarceration"—generally came from the same place and though there was ultimately a fair amount of overlap between the two, the end results of the two programs were dramatically different, with the first resulting in the limited internment of 7,000 or so mostly Issei (Japanese immigrant) male commu-

nity leaders and the second ending with the forced removal and incarceration of some 120,000 Japanese Americans from the West Coast states. The
first also included at least the pretense of fairness—there was at least some
"evidence" for the arrest of these detainees and each had a hearing in which
he could clarify his actions and call character witnesses—while the second
incarcerated with the broadest of racial brushes.

The roots of the enemy alien internment program sprang from a
decade of surveillance of the Japanese American community by various federal intelligence operations prior to the attack on Pearl Harbor. As detailed
in Tetsuden Kashima's introduction to the first book in this series, Yasutaro
Soga's *Life behind Barbed Wire*, the Federal Bureau of Investigation (FBI),
Office of Naval Intelligence (ONI), Military Intelligence Division (MID),
and a separate investigative team commissioned by President Roosevelt all
both competed and collaborated to investigate Japanese Americans as tensions between Japan and the United States increased in the 1930s.[2]

By the 1930s, there were approximately three hundred thousand Japanese Americans in well-established communities more or less equally
divided between the Hawaiian Islands and the continental United States.
Large-scale migration from Japan, mostly of sugar plantation laborers to
Hawai'i, had begun in the 1880s and increased through the 1890s. Inev-
itably, these early immigrants faced intense race-based agitation due to
perceived competition, nativism, and anti-Asian sentiment inherited from
the Chinese immigrants who had preceded them. This anti-Japanese sentiment was harshest in California, where the largest number of Japanese
Americans in the continental United States ended up, and spread through
all sectors of society and to the federal government as well. As a result of a
wide array of federal and state/local measures, the lives of Japanese immigrants were severely circumscribed: their further migration from Japan was
limited and then cut off completely, they were prohibited from becoming
naturalized American citizens, and they were not allowed to purchase land
in Western states, among many other restrictions.[3]

As a result of this discrimination, which climaxed in the early 1920s,
many Japanese migrants left the United States, whether to return to Japan
or to seek their fortune in other parts of the world. But by this time, many
had married and begun families with American-born children. Despite
the restrictions, most decided to stay on in the United States. They found
economic niches where they were allowed. In Hawai'i, many remained
as sugar plantation laborers, but others became independent farmers or
started small businesses. On the West Coast, roughly half were farmers
who devised a variety of means to evade the so-called alien land laws; much
of the other half supported the farmers, starting small businesses that

served them. In both places, there was a sizable second generation—the Nisei—whom the Issei parents had high hopes for, since they were native-born American citizens and thus presumably immune from the citizenship based restrictions the Issei faced. By the 1930s, this American born group had passed the Japan-born group in population.[4]

In both Hawai'i and the continental United States, Japanese Americans, like other immigrant groups, formed ethnic communities, both in response to racism and out of the greater comfort they felt around others with a common language and culture. Colloquially referred to as Japan (or J-) towns and Little Tokyos, these ethnic enclaves became gathering places for the broader ethnic community where Japanese American restaurants and markets, churches, newspapers, and many other institutions could be found.[5] Issei and Nisei enjoyed a range of community organizations. For the older generation, there were the Japanese Associations, a loosely organized political organization which originated to mediate relations between the immigrants and Japan; *kenjinkai*, organizations of Japanese Americans who hailed from the common regions in Japan; various occupation-based organizations; and culturally oriented organizations such as poetry clubs, among many others. For the younger generation—Nisei were for the most part still children and teenagers in the 1930s—there were a wide range of social clubs that often focused on sports, along with fledgling political organizations among the minority of Nisei who were already young adults.[6]

Against this backdrop of what was in many ways a pattern of immigration and settlement not unlike that of many other ethnic groups that had come to the United States in generally the same time period were the international developments of the 1930s. With its invasion of Manchuria in 1931, an increasingly militaristic Japan began what would become an ill-fated imperial campaign to bring East Asia under its influence. As was the case with other immigrant groups, Japanese immigrants often retained a sentimental attachment to the country of their birth even if they had spent most of their lives in the U.S., had American-citizen children, and intended to spend the rest of their lives in their adopted country. But there were several factors that drew Japanese immigrants closer to Japan in the 1930s. One was their rejection by the United States. Rampant and codified discrimination meant they could never become American citizens or enjoy the rights that other Americans—including other immigrants—took for granted. That rejection no doubt encouraged a greater valuing of their Japanese citizenship, the only one they would ever have.[7]

A second factor was a continuing relationship with the Japanese government that was partially a result of racism and strained ties between the U.S. and Japan. When the Japanese government voluntarily agreed to restrict immigration to the U.S. under pressure from the U.S. government, the Japanese government turned to immigrant community leaders to perform the bureaucratic functions necessary to enforce the restrictions. Though the subsequent prohibition of all Japanese immigration in 1924 ended the need for this particular function, Issei leaders continued to serve in a go-between role between the Japanese government and Japanese immigrant communities. In the Hawaiian Islands, there was just one Japanese consulate office located in Honolulu to serve a Japanese population spread throughout Oʻahu and among the various other islands. A large network of *torisuginin* (consular agents) located in Japanese communities throughout the islands assisted community members with a wide range of bureaucratic tasks: filing necessary papers for visits to Japan, making sure newborns were added to family registries in home prefectures, or registering Nisei as citizens of Japan as well as the U.S., among many other tasks. The consular agents were generally respected and literate Issei community leaders: educators, Buddhist and Christian clergymen, journalists, and the like.[8]

A third factor was the active embrace of immigrants by the Japanese government as part of its colonial ambitions and the immigrant response. Once largely disdained, immigrants were now recast a "pioneers of racial development" (*minzoku hatten no senkusha*), the vanguards of Japanese expansion. Since Hawaiʻi was the first place that saw large-scale migration from Japan, Hawaiʻi Issei enjoyed a special status as the pioneers among the pioneers, so to speak. Having felt rejected by both their old and new countries, many Issei eagerly embraced their new status and took pride in Japanese military exploits in Asia. Issei raised money for these exploits, sent comfort bags (*imonbukuro*) to Japanese soldiers, and flocked to welcome Japanese naval vessels on their visits to Hawaiʻi and West Coast ports.[9] At a November 1940 conference in Tokyo for overseas Nikkei ostensibly commemorating the 2,600th anniversary of the Japanese imperial line, some five hundred delegates from Hawaiʻi and the continental U.S. attended and enjoyed special status as the first group of pioneers. Many older Nisei also embraced Japanese imperialism at this time as well; one-quarter of the Tokyo delegates from Hawaiʻi were Nisei.[10] Popular among Nisei intelligentsia was the "bridge of understanding" concept, the idea that a future role of Nisei would be that of an ambassador of sorts who could help interpret each country to the other. Many Nisei writers took that role to heart in defending Japanese expansionism in the 1930s to other Americans.[11]

A fourth factor were the Kibei, American born Nisei who had been sent to Japan for some portion of their education. Issei had several reasons to sending children away. For some who were not able to raise all their children due to cost or other factors, sending children back to Japan was purely an economic or logistical decision. For those who did so for ideological reasons, it represented both a hedging of bets by Issei still considering a return to Japan and a recognition that better job opportunities might be available to Nisei who were bilingual/bicultural. Thus, thousands of Nisei children were sent to grandparents and other relatives to be educated in Japan. Upon their return to the U.S., Kibei came to be considered a distinct sub-group of the Nisei, since, depending on how long they had spent in Japan, they sometimes spoke limited or accented English and were culturally more Japanese. In addition to the Kibei, there were also a good number of older Nisei young adults who went to Japan in the 1930s on their own for further educational or occupational opportunities. At the outbreak of the war, several thousand Kibei or Nisei were caught in Japan, unable to return to the U.S.

One could view these connections between Japanese American communities and Japan in different ways. While seemingly ominous in hindsight, it should be understood that many Japanese Americans who expressed support for Japan or sent their children to be educated there saw no conflict with also being good law-abiding Americans at a time when the two countries were not at war. But for those with pre-existing racial biases or beliefs in innate racial characteristics, these factors induced notions of divided loyalties should war break out between the U.S. and Japan in a way that pro-Nazi sentiment in German American communities, for example, did not.

The various investigators of the Japanese American community were aware of all of these groups and dynamics. Based on their investigations, they complied custodial detention lists of those who would be rounded up in the event of war. Those who greeted Japanese naval ships, sent relief funds to Japan, or belonged to organizations that were believed to have a pro-Japan slant were put on the list, as where those who attended the 2600th anniversary commemoration in Japan or smaller local commemorations. Consular agents made the list, as did some Kibei and Nisei who had ties to Japan. Thus, when war did come to the U.S. in the form of the Japanese attack on Pearl Harbor on December 7, 1941, the authorities were ready. In the islands, aided by local police, the FBI went into action, and by December 10, some 1,291 Japanese nationals were in custody, including one Kumaji Furuya.

An Immigrant Leader and Poet

Furuya was born in 1889, the second son of a farmer in a village nestled at the base of Mount Fuji in Yamanashi Prefecture. He graduated from the government's agricultural school, intending to carry on the family work of farming, but when heavy flooding in the region devastated his village, he set his sights on America. He encountered difficulty in securing permission to travel to the continental United States, receiving approval to go to the Hawaiian Islands instead. Deciding that Hawai'i could serve as a stepping stone to the Mainland, Furuya boarded a steamship out of Yokohama bound for Honolulu. It was March 1907, and he had just turned eighteen.[12]

From the pier at Honolulu Harbor, Furuya was sent to the Immigration Station on Sand Island, where he underwent a medical inspection. That night, he stayed at the Kobayashi Ryokan, one of a number of Japanese-run hotels located in the burgeoning immigrant enclave of 'A'ala. It was then that he learned of the conclusion, just that February, of the so-called Gentlemen's Agreement effectively ending Japanese immigration to the continent. With his Mainland plans stymied, Furuya went instead to Hawai'i Island where he worked for five months on the Wainaku Sugar Plantation near the town of Hilo. He then went to the island of Maui, where he labored for nearly three years at the Ka'elekū Plantation in the Hāna district.[13]

In 1910, with two hundred dollars saved from his work in the cane fields, Furuya moved to Honolulu. He worked as a clerk at a Japanese mercantile in 'A'ala and learned the ways of running a business in Hawai'i. In the evenings, he attended English-language classes at the Anglican St. Andrew's Cathedral a half-a-mile away on Queen Emma Street. A few years later, partnering with a fellow Yamanashi immigrant, he opened Fuji Store, named for the mountain of his youth. The store was located at the tip of King and Beretania streets in the heart of 'A'ala, the bustling Japanese commercial center of the island.[14]

In October 1921, Furuya married Jun Kitagawa, the daughter of a minor Japanese government official. At the age of eighteen, despite her parents' opposition, Jun had ventured to Hawai'i in search of a world outside the strict confines of her traditional samurai upbringing. In Honolulu, she lived with and did domestic work for her cousin, Sei Soga, whose husband, Yasutaro Soga, was the publisher of the *Nippu Jiji*, then the largest Japanese newspaper outside of the empire. Friends of the Sogas introduced Furuya and Jun, who upon meeting Kumaji for the first time thought him "a real country bumpkin." But, she noted, "I heard that he had many interests, like writing haiku."[15] The couple were married at the Makiki Christian Church by the prominent Honolulu minister Takie Okumura. Jun wore a kimono borrowed from Sei, with a new *obi* ordered from Japan. Furuya wore a tuxedo. The reception was simple, with cake and ice cream.

Before long, Furuya moved his business several blocks east to the area between Fort Street and Nuʻuanu Avenue. The new store, Fuji Furniture, offered Western-style home furnishings made in Mainland factories, while jockeying with bookstores, dry goods shops, and appliance vendors for the attention of its immigrant customers. Dominating the Japanese commercial scene in the 1920s and '30s was the ʻAʻala Rengo (ʻAʻala Union), a combine of more than a dozen businesses, which together with neighboring ʻAʻala Market, made up a retail shopping center of green grocers, dry goods shops, drug stores, fishmongers, and tofu-sellers. To compete against ʻAʻala Rengo and the similar Honolulu Ginza, Furuya and several other merchants organized as the Chuo Rengo (Central Union). In a further effort to increase business, Furuya expanded the inventory of his furniture store, selling small household items such as kitchen appliances, brooms, mops, furniture polish, and radios.[16]

In 1922, the U.S. Department of Commerce had assigned the call letters KGU to the first and only, and at that time exclusively English-language, radio station in the territory. Realizing that interest in radio within the Japanese community would need to be developed if sales of the novel product were to expand, Furuya conceived of a plan to introduce Japanese-language radio broadcasting to the islands. In 1929, from KGU's tiny studio on the second floor of the Advertiser newspaper building, Furuya called out greetings, "To all radio fans throughout the Hawaiian Islands…." and with that his became the first Japanese voice in the territory to be heard over the air waves. The program was sponsored by Fuji Furniture and several other radio sellers. It marked the beginning of Japanese-language commercial broadcasting in the islands.[17]

A weekly thirty-minute program on Sunday evenings soon followed. By the mid-1930s, the KGU program had achieved great popularity within the Japanese community, although finding engaging entertainers to volunteer their talents remained a challenge. With this in mind, Furuya organized the bosses and employees of the Chuo Rengo businesses into an amateur troupe, producing live broadcasts of traditional Japanese dramas and well-known historical tales. They gathered frequently at the Furuya home to practice, with Furuya taking on the characters of packhorse driver, manservant, or old lady. Sometimes he provided the background animal sounds. In all, the Chuo Rengo troupe performed in some fifty productions.[18]

While his furniture store remained modestly successful, Furuya himself was rising as a leader within the immigrant Japanese business community. He was elected head of the Honolulu Japanese Merchants' Association, which in 1939, through a merger that he helped negotiate, became part of a reorganized and more powerful Honolulu Japanese Chamber of Commerce. The HJCC's origins could be traced to a protection and advocacy association established by Japanese merchants quarantined during the bubonic plague crisis that had terrified Honolulu at the turn of the century. Several decades later, the HJCC had become the most powerful coalition of Japanese commercial interests in the territory, and its members included the wealthy and successful within the Nikkei business community. Furuya was considered "one of the mainstays of the organization" and on the eve of the war had become an HJCC vice president. Other officers included his Chuo Rengo associate and drama troupe partner, Koichi Iida; 'A'ala merchant Taichi Sato of Sato Clothiers; and prominent Honolulu banker Totaro Matsui.[19]

Furuya also was playing a leading role in what was then the largest Japanese organization in the islands, the Honolulu United Japanese Society. The society served as an umbrella agency for business groups and fraternal associations with ties to Japan and Hawai'i's Nikkei population. The HJCC was a member organization of the United Japanese Society, and officers in the former frequently served in a similar capacity in the latter. Thus, by 1941, Furuya was also vice president of the UJS.[20]

Although a profile of Furuya written by a contemporary in 1936 noted, "There is no question at all that he is one of the favorites in business circles," Furuya himself professed that his true passions remained elsewhere. His wife, Jun, observed that throughout his life, Furuya was really more interested in the arts than in commerce: he dabbled in acting; enjoyed *go*, a scholarly game akin to chess; tried his hand at drawing; and loved haiku.[21]

Furuya had arrived in the islands during what has been called "the golden age of haiku in Hawai'i."[22] The period saw the emergence of haiku societies throughout the territory, one of the earliest being the 'Ewa Saturday Club (Ewa Doyō-kai). It had ten members, mostly laborers on the 'Ewa Sugar Plantation, who met on Saturday nights to compose and share haiku. The club lasted for more than eight years but was eventually eclipsed by Honolulu societies like the June Club (Minazuki-kai), the Village Rain Club (Son'u-kai), and the Young Buddhists Haiku Club. On the Big Island, the center of the haiku world was in the town of Hilo, where the leading society was the Rain on Banana Leaves Club (Sho-u-kai). Kaua'i Island had the Green Frog Club in Līhu'e, as well as a society in Kekaha. On Maui, a club formed in Wailuku.[23]

Poets also began publishing magazines dedicated to haiku. The first edition of the journal *Kasei* [Mars] came out in October 1909, inviting readers to submit original compositions for publication. Hundreds of submissions were received, and although the publication ceased the following summer, its appearance invigorated existing clubs and spurred the creation of new societies and publications throughout the islands.[24]

In 1912, a friend gave Furuya a copy of a brand new journal from Japan called *Sōun* [Layered clouds], published by a poet named Ogiwara Seisensui, who was quickly becoming the leading voice of a new, progressive type of haiku. Over the course of the decade, Seisensui would shock the poetry world with his abandonment of haiku's defining characteristics of seasonal themes and fixed meter in favor of a freer style of composition. In the islands, far from the four seasons and the traditional literary resonances of Japan, this new style of haiku, and the Hawai'i-influenced language that it allowed, proved very appealing. Furuya was thrilled, and with his discovery of *Sōun*, he became a student of Seisensui.[25]

Furuya had long been submitting haiku to the poetry columns of Japanese-language periodicals in Honolulu, very likely already writing under his pen name, Suikei (Green Valley). One newspaper in particular, the *Hawai'i Shimpō*, ran a column every Sunday and Monday, to which Furuya frequently proffered compositions. The paper's editor, Kyoshu Aoki, became Furuya's mentor, and before long they, along with another Honolulu poet, Chumu Mita, established a new society named South Club, devoted to the composition of *Sōun*-style haiku. South Club's members numbered more than eighteen and included the up-and-coming of Honolulu's Japanese community. They produced the magazine, *No no tori* [Wild birds], and many South poets, Furuya included, saw their compositions published under their society's banner in Seisensui's journal. After a few years, South Club disappeared from the pages of *Sōun*, but some of its poets, like Furuya and *Nippu Jiji* journalist Bunshiro Furukawa, continued to see their haiku published independently in the journal under the imprimatur, "selected by Ogiwara Seisensui."[26]

In 1926, poets from South and several other clubs of freestyle haiku came together to establish the Hawai'i Haiku Club. They were led by Bunshiro Furukawa, Chumu Mita, and Suikei Furuya. Calling themselves a branch of the *Sōun* school, Hawai'i Haiku boasted more than twenty members and their poems were published regularly in *Sōun*. Seisensui himself was said to have supported them "most enthusiastically."[27] The poet master traveled to Hawai'i in 1937, his approval inspiring Furuya to pursue all the more earnestly the writing of haiku. Furuya took his teacher on a tour of the Big Island, where they both marveled at the expanse of Kamuela, its rolling foothills verdant below Mauna Kea's snowy peak—a reminder, perhaps, of the mountain that had stirred Furuya in his youth.[28]

But fate would bring the life Furuya had built for himself in his adopted country to a halt.

Internment

Furuya was arrested on the afternoon on December 7, 1941, joining an illustrious list of Japanese immigrant leaders in Hawai'i and across the continental United States. The vast majority were Issei male community leaders, though there were some Nisei and Kibei and a smattering of women. A smaller number of German and Italian immigrants and some of their American citizen children were also detained. Most were held for a few days in local jails or prisons until they could be brought to internment camps run by the army. In the case of those arrested on O'ahu, like Furuya, the U.S. Immigration Station building in downtown Honolulu was the first site of their detention. After two nights, they were transferred to a detention camp built on Sand Island, the man-made island in Honolulu Harbor that was at the time accessible only by boat. Sand Island became the main camp holding the Hawai'i internees, Japanese as well as those of European descent. Internees on the neighbor islands were held at various sites including Kilauea Military Camp on Hawai'i Island, Haiku Camp on Maui, and Kalaheo Stockade on Kaua'i. As space allowed, they were gradually brought to Sand Island for their hearings and for further internment if so decreed.

Though the specifics differed, the detainees in both Hawai'i and in the continental United States received at least token hearings to determine whether they would be interned for the duration of the war. On the mainland, the Alien Enemy Hearing Boards were set up and run by the U.S. Department of Justice's Alien Enemy Control Unit. In Hawai'i, the military government under martial law set up Boards of Officers and Civilians that were made up of three civilians and one military officer. In both cases, the boards were made up of prominent civilians who heard the case against the internee and were allowed to question him about topics such as his general attitudes toward the U.S. and Japan, his associations, who he wanted to win the war, and about specific items in his files. The board then recommended either release, parole, or internment, with the final decision made by higher ups, the Alien Enemy Control Unit and attorney general on the mainland, and the heads of the local intelligence agencies and the military governor in Hawai'i. The main difference was that in Hawai'i, detainees could have a lawyer and call character witnesses, though in both places, they could not cross-examine government witnesses nor question the charges brought against them.[29]

Hearings for the Hawai'i internees held on Sand Island took place back at the Immigration Station building starting in January of 1942. Furuya's hearing took place on January 24. The case against him was fairly straightforward: he held leadership positions in the United Japanese Society and in the Honolulu Japanese Chamber of Commerce, organizations that were broadly characterized as "pro-Japanese," and had been part of a welcoming committee for a visiting Japanese naval ship a few years before. The committee briefly questioned him and also heard from three character witnesses, business associate Eugene Valentine, prominent Nisei attorney Masaji Marumoto, and Nisei employee Beatrice Matsui Arita. But because of his leadership in the two organizations, his case was a simple one, and he was recommended for internment, which was approved by both the local heads of the intelligence agencies and by the military governor's office. His entire hearing took less than forty-five minutes.[30]

While Issei leaders like Furuya were languishing in internment, further trouble was brewing on the West Coast and in Washington, D.C. Despite the fact that all those deemed suspect enough to make the custodial detention lists had been detained, calls for forcibly removing all Japanese Americans from the West Coast began to gain momentum in early 1942. It was a perfect storm: a combination of powerful West Coast interests—mainly agricultural groups who stood to gain from the eviction of Japanese farmers and politicians looking to exploit racial hatreds—a famously racist and insecure general in charge of the Western Defense Command, smart and ambitious figures who supported mass removal in the War Department, and a president willing to go along with it all. Despite opposition from Attorney General Francis Biddle and others in the Justice Department, President Roosevelt issued Executive Order 9066 on February 19, 1942, which ultimately allowed General John L. DeWitt to order the mass removal and subsequent incarceration of over 110,000 Japanese Americans from California, the western halves of Oregon and Washington, and the southern portion of Arizona. Despite being 2,500 miles closer to the front, no such mass removal of Hawai'i's 160,000 Japanese Americans took place, though some in the administration, including FDR himself, supported it. A new civilian agency, the War Relocation Authority (WRA), was created to administer ten concentration camps to hold these new wards of the government: Manzanar, Tule Lake, Heart Mountain—names that would become part of infamy.[31]

While the enemy alien internment program run by the Justice Department and army and the massive concentration camp system run by the WRA were completely separate programs, there were some intersections. In many cases, Issei internees had wives and children caught up the mass West Coast incarceration. Much bureaucratic wrangling was sometimes necessary to reunite families in these cases.[32] In many cases, Hawai'i Issei internees held on the mainland were later granted parole because they had sons serving in the U.S. Army. But the new parolees were not allowed to return to Hawai'i during the war and often did not know anyone in the inland regions of the continental U.S. Thus, they were "paroled" to WRA concentration camps. In some cases, the family members of Hawai'i internees were held in the WRA camps as well. And finally, over five thousand embittered Nisei renounced their U.S. citizenship and declared a desire to go to Japan after the war. Some of these new "native American aliens" were later sent to the Santa Fe internment camp to join the foreign-born aliens already there.[33]

Back in Hawai'i, the detainees designated for internment after their hearings were returned to Sand Island, then taken to a variety of internment camps. Generally Issei were assigned to mainland camps, while American-citizen Kibei and Nisei remained at Sand Island and its successor, Honouliuli. (The rationale for keeping the Nisei in Hawai'i was that authorities wanted to preclude the possibility of habeas corpus suits, which would be possible once interned American citizens reached the continental U.S. Since the courts had been shut down under martial law in Hawai'i, there was no possibility of such suits there.) The first of ten shipments of Hawai'i Issei to the mainland left Honolulu on February 21, 1942. Furuya was among the one hundred and seventy aboard.

The group landed in San Francisco, where they were held for a few days at Fort McDowell on Angel Island for processing. From there Furuya went to a series of five different internment camps where he remained for the next three-and-a-half years. The first three—Camp McCoy in Wisconsin; Camp Forrest, Tennessee; and Camp Livingston in Louisiana—were enemy alien and POW camps run by the U.S. Army. The army and Department of Justice had previously agreed that the former would hold alien enemy internees after the latter ran their hearings. Livingston was one of two main camps that held Japanese internees (the other was in Lordsburg, New Mexico), so it seems likely that the army was trying to consolidate Japanese internees at those camps and moved Furuya there after short stays at camps McCoy and Forrest (less than four months total).

But in the spring of 1943, an increasing number of Axis POWs began to strain the army's capacity to hold them and the internees, leading the army to request that the Justice Department now hold the internees. As part of this shift, Furuya was transferred after eleven months at Livingston to two camps run by the Justice Department for the remainder of his internment, first to Fort Missoula, Montana, and then to Santa Fe, New Mexico, just prior to Missoula's closing in May 1944. He remained at Santa Fe for the remainder of his internment, just under eighteen months. *Haisho Tenten* devotes a chapter to each of these camps, describing the geography, administration, and population at each. This translation represents virtually the only English-language descriptions of some of these camps from the perspective of an internee.

Family Life Under Martial Law

While Furuya and four hundred other Issei remained under armed guard in the offices of the Immigration Station during the first few days after arrest, Hanzo Furuya, Kumaji's eldest son, was defending strategic sites in the city against sabotage by the Japanese. He was in his first year at the University of Hawai'i and was a member of the Reserve Officers' Training Corps, so when the call went out shortly after the Japanese attack for cadets to help with the guarding of sites around Honolulu, he immediately volunteered.

"I was assigned to guard Farrington High School, which was converted to a hospital," Hanzo recalled more than fifty years later. "The following night, I was assigned to guard in front of Farrington Hall, [at the] university, because of rumors that Japanese paratroopers had landed on the mountains there. Now, Tuesday, I got my first pass. I went home, at which time I found out that on Sunday, about two o'clock, some people came and they talked to my father a short while, and they took him away someplace."[34] Furuya's arrest altered significantly the family's circumstances. He had been the sole income earner and, besides eighteen-year-old Hanzo, there were four more children in the Furuya household: Seizo, sixteen; Robert Keiichi, thirteen; Albert, eleven; and Florence Yoko, the youngest at four. Hanzo now stopped attending the university and went to work at Fuji Furniture fulltime.

With the store's owners having been declared "enemy aliens," the business came under the control of the federal government through the offices of Price Administration and Alien Property Custodian. The Office of the Alien Property Custodian, established by Roosevelt in the spring of 1942, held the power to seize, control, and sell off all assets owned by individuals deemed by the president to be enemies of the United States. This control extended to real property, bank assets, and ships, as well as patents, copyrights, and trademarks, and, of course, businesses, like Fuji Furniture. "(T)hey would come frequently and check your operation. Any of the things, every decision we had to make, we had to get their approval," Hanzo explained. "They'd come in and first of all, they'd check the books. Periodically, they'd ask different employees any kind of questions for whatever purpose they had in mind. But definitely, [we were] fully controlled by them."[35]

The store also was required to abide by regulations imposed by the Office of Price Administration. Roosevelt had established this office a year earlier, in April 1941. Its intent was to prevent the inflation and profiteering that officials worried would plague the nation as consumer resources were diverted to the war effort. The office was invested with the power to fix prices and regulate the supply of consumer goods. Fuji Furniture was required to obtain approval from the OPA regarding the price of all merchandise offered for sale.[36]

Returning to Hawai'i

On November 13, 1945, after nearly four years of incarceration, Furuya was returned home. "Trying to express in words the kinds of feelings at a moment like that—I felt completely relieved," Jun recalled of the day when the family went to the pier to greet Furuya. "I was just so relieved—both body and soul."[37]

Furuya spent the next several months recuperating. In the spring, he was able to fully return to running the business, and so Hanzo contacted his draft board to fulfill the military obligation that he had deferred while his father had been interned. In May 1946, Hanzo entered the U.S. Army. After two years of service, he returned to the University of Hawai'i to complete the education that had been interrupted more than seven years earlier.[38]

Though internment ruined the lives of no small number of Issei community leaders, Furuya was able to reestablish himself after the war, no doubt due to his relative youth (fifty-seven at war's end) and good health. After the war, Furuya again became active in business and community organizations. In 1951, he was elected president of the Honolulu Japanese Chamber of Commerce. With a peace settlement yet to be completed between Japan and the United States, the Japanese consulate in Honolulu remained shuttered, and it would be several years before the United Japanese Society would be re-established. This made the HJCC the leading representative organization in the Japanese community and Furuya its highest executive officer. Thus, in March, he was among a delegation that welcomed U.S. Envoy John Foster Dulles, who had stopped over in the islands while engaging in peace negotiations with Japan. Five months later, a twenty-one-member delegation of Japanese officials, including Prime Minister Yoshida Shigeru, cabinet ministers, and members of the Diet, arrived in Honolulu at the completion of the San Francisco peace talks. Furuya oversaw a grand, formal reception at the Queen's Surf Hotel in Waikiki, attended by more than six hundred guests, including the territorial governor, the Honolulu mayor, representatives of the U.S. Army and U.S. Navy, as well as prominent members of the Japanese community. Displayed beside the American flag was the Hinomaru, the flag of Japan. It was the first time in ten years that the flags of the two nations had been exhibited side-by-side—a sight, it was reported, that moved many Issei to tears. Writing in *The Hawaii Times*, Furuya reflected on having met Yoshida, calling 1951 "the most splendid year of my life."[39]

Furuya continued to operate Fuji Furniture into the mid-1950s, until controlling shares of the company were bought by other investors, and Furuya ended his participation in the business he had begun forty years earlier. He purchased another corporation and became involved in the leasing of commercial property. Despite the interruptions of the war years, Furuya had arrived at the pinnacle of business success. Together with long-time acquaintances Koichi Iida and Daizo Sumida, of Honolulu Sake Brewery, he had come to be known as one of the "outstanding elders" of Honolulu, "titans" of the business community.[40]

All the while, Furuya continued his literary pursuits. In 1958, a retrospective of his haiku was published by Seisensui. The book, *Ruten* [Vicissitudes], represented a lifetime of haiku composition. Writing in the book's introduction, Seisensui described Furuya as a true poet, for whom haiku had remained constant, throughout the ebb and flow of his life. Equally telling was the focus of *Ruten*—the internment—a period characterized by Seisensui as Furuya's most productive and soulful. The master wrote, "Amid the wretchedness of a lonely and remote imprisonment, where one is treated as a criminal although he has committed no crime, turning to haiku as a comfort is like nourishment for the heart." And then, a few years later, to commemorate fifty years since the inauguration of his groundbreaking journal, Seisensui's publishing house issued a collection of haiku by *Sōun* writers from across Japan, California, and Hawai'i. Among the more than 250 poets included in the book were a dozen from the islands, including Suikei Furuya, Chumu Mita, and Bunshiro Furukawa.[41]

In 1964, when Furuya was seventy-five years old, *Haisho Tenten* was published. His decades-old haiku companion, Bunshiro Furukawa, provided the illustrations for the book. Furuya's last work, *Imin no Rakugaki* [The scribblings of an immigrant], came out in 1968, in conjunction with the one hundredth anniversary of Japanese immigration to Hawai'i. Once again, Seisensui wrote the introduction. A collection of more than one hundred and fifty articles on a variety of topics, many of which had been previously published in Japanese newspapers and magazines, *Rakugaki* spans some thirty years and covers subjects ranging from the variety of orchids in Hawai'i to the tranquility of old age and a life lived well.

Remembering Interment

As the title of an insightful late 1945 article by University of Hawai'i sociologist John Rademaker read, "Hawai'i Will Never Be Quite the Same Again." Indeed Furuya and the other internees returned home to a Hawai'i that had been dramatically changed by World War II and that would change even more dramatically over the next decade or two. As tourism gradually replaced the sugar plantations as the main economic driver of the islands, Japanese Americans in particular found themselves well positioned to take advantage of the postwar economic boom and the opening up of formerly closed occupations and opportunities. Returning Nisei war veterans, armed with college degrees through the G.I. Bill, led this change, asserting that they would no longer stand for second-class citizenship after their wartime service. Within a decade after the end of the war, young Nisei leaders such as Daniel Inouye, Spark Matsunaga, and George Ariyoshi were among members of the previously moribund Democratic Party that took control of the territorial legislature with the support of the large number of new Nisei voters—as well as even more numerous American-born Filipino, Chinese, and Puerto Rican offspring of plantation workers—in what was dubbed "the Revolution of 1954." By the end of the decade, Hawai'i had become the fiftieth state and an apparent symbol of racial tolerance and racial minority achievement, with Japanese Americans standing at the head of the line, an emerging "model minority."[42]

It was in this context that Furuya—who by then had successfully reclaimed his prewar status as one of the leaders of Hawai'i's Japanese American community—first began publishing the newspaper articles that would become *Haisho Tenten* in *The Hawaii Times* nearly sixteen years after his return to Hawai'i. Over a two-year period—September 29, 1961 to September 21, 1963—Furuya produced 196 short articles about his internment experience. Apparently well received—for instance, a week after the series concluded, *The Hawaii Times* columnist Seigai Shinjo called it "a great piece of mainland internment literature," adding that completing it left him "filled with satisfaction, as if I myself had written it"—Furuya then sought to turn the articles into a book, adding additional pieces to fill in gaps in the story.[43] The book was published in Honolulu by *The Hawaii Times* in 1964.

Furuya's book was hardly the first Issei internment memoir. Some fifteen years earlier, *Nippu Jiji* publisher Yasutaro Soga authored a similar book that was also based on serialized newspaper accounts from *The Hawaii Times*. A translation of that book, *Tessaku Seikatsu*, was published in 2008 as *Life behind Barbed Wire*, the first book in the Japanese Cultural

Center of Hawai'i/University of Hawai'i internment trilogy. A bibliography by pioneering historian Yuji Ichioka lists no less than eleven other Japanese language memoirs that cover the internment/incarceration period that were published between the end of the war and 1970, a period often characterized as one of Japanese American silence regarding that experience. There were other accounts in Japanese American vernacular newspapers that didn't become books, as well as discussions of the topic in other Japanese-language media, such as in the radio programs of Otokichi Ozaki, whose scripts make up part of the second JCCH/UH book, *Family Torn Apart*. These accounts were written by Issei and Kibei for other Issei and Kibei, and they have mostly not been read by anyone else both for reasons of language and access. In a 2000 article, Ichioka laments the fact that these Issei/Kibei autobiographical accounts "have never been incorporated into the wartime internment studies" and represent a "glaring omission." These statements largely still hold true nearly fifteen years later.[44]

Related to the lack of Issei voices is the relative lack of studies that look at enemy alien internment (as opposed to mass incarceration), especially with regard to Hawai'i, though things are a bit better here. Patsy Saiki's *Ganbare! An Example of Japanese Spirit* (Honolulu: Kisaku, Inc., 1982; Honolulu: Mutual Publishing, 2004), based largely on interviews with Hawai'i internees, was the first book specifically on their internment, though it was marred by a lack of documentation. More recently, Tetsuden Kashima's *Judgment Without Trial* (Seattle: University of Washington Press, 2003) is perhaps the first overview study to explore internment in a significant manner, and Gary Okihiro's *Cane Fires* (Philadelphia: Temple University Press, 1991) spends three chapters on the internment of Japanese Americans from Hawai'i, drawing heavily on Soga's memoir. Louis Fiset's *Imprisoned Apart* (Seattle: University of Washington Press, 1997) is an edited volume of letters between an Issei husband and wife, the former interned in army and INS camps, the other incarcerated in WRA camps and also includes a detailed introduction on the mechanics of internment. George and Tamae Hoshida's *Taken from the Paradise Isle: The Hoshida Family Story*, edited by Heidi Kim (Boulder: University of Colorado Press, 2015) is an atypical Hawai'i enemy alien internment story, in that George, while technically Issei, had been raised in Hawai'i since age four and thus wrote his memoir, on which this book was largely based, in English. There are also two studies of specific internment camps, Carol Van Valkenberg's *An Alien Place: The Fort Missoula, Montana, Detention Camp, 1941–1944* (Missoula, Mont.: Pictorial Histories Publishing Company, Inc., 1996) and Priscilla Wegars *Imprisoned in Paradise: Japanese Internee Road Workers at the World War II Kooskia Internment Camp*

(Moscow, Idaho: Asian American Comparative Collection, 2010). Various widely distributed publications by the National Park Service having to do with the current status of the various confinement site—most notably Jeff Burton, et al.'s *Confinement and Ethnicity* (Western Archeological and Conservation Center, National Park Service, 1999, 2000; Seattle: University of Washington Press, 2002)—generally treat the various internment camp sites in more or less the same way as the WRA camp sites, no doubt increasing knowledge about the former.

While the "silent" characterization of the '50s and '60s with regard to Japanese-language material might be questionable, it is no doubt true when it comes to English-language material written by Japanese Americans. After just a handful of mostly non-threatening memoirs by Japanese Americans in this period, a great many more began to appear in the '70s and '80s, with a steady stream appearing to the present day. The most widely read has no doubt been Jeannie Wakatsuki Houston and James Houston's *Farewell to Manzanar* (Boston: Houghton Mifflin, Co., 1973), first published in 1973, which has become a fixture on middle and high school reading lists. While most descriptions are by Nisei, there are a few Issei accounts that originated at least in part from Japanese language writings. These include Kiyo Hirano's *Enemy Alien* (translated by George Hirano and Yuri Kageyama; San Francisco: Japantown Art and Media Workshop, 1984), Minoru Kiyota's *Beyond Loyalty: The Story of a Kibei* (translated from Japanese by Linda Klepinger Keenan; Honolulu: University of Hawai'i Press, 1997), and Noboru Shirai's *Tule Lake: An Issei Memoir* (translated by Ray Hosoda and edited by Eucaly Shirai and Valerie Sampson; Sacramento, Calif.: Muteki Press, 2001). There is also a volume of poems by Hawai'i internees that have been translated into English by Jiro and Kay Nakano, *Poets Behind Barbed Wire* (Honolulu: Bamboo Ridge Press, 1983). There are also many more Japanese language autobiographical accounts by Issei and Kibei that have been published since 1970 that have not been translated.

In the last twenty years, we've also seen technological changes that have made more Japanese American internment/incarceration accounts available. The ease of self-publishing has led to many self-published autobiographies that in most cases are distributed just to family members. The rise of the Internet has also led to a number of websites that feature streaming oral histories, most notably Densho.org. Since these technologies have largely become available just in the last fifteen or twenty years, these autobiographical accounts tend to be overwhelmingly Nisei.

So despite the flood of material on internment/incarceration we've seen in recent years, there is still relatively little that represents the perspective of Issei and that focuses on enemy alien internment, especially with regard to Hawai'i. With this book—as well as the entire JCCH/UH internment series—we hope to contribute in a small way to the broader story of internment/incarceration by making a few Issei voices widely available and accessible in the hope that the "glaring omission" will one day be routinely filled.

Furuya's Internment Odyssey

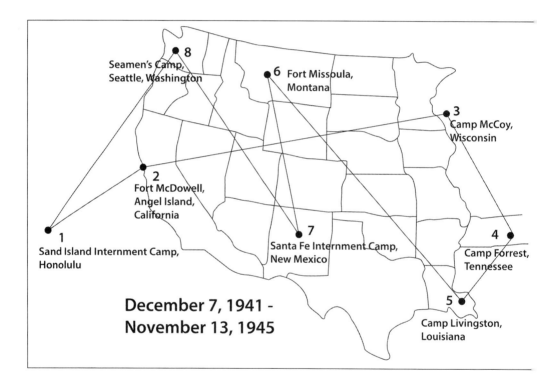

8 Seamen's Camp, Seattle, Washington

6 Fort Missoula, Montana

3 Camp McCoy, Wisconsin

2 Fort McDowell, Angel Island, California

1 Sand Island Internment Camp, Honolulu

7 Santa Fe Internment Camp, New Mexico

4 Camp Forrest, Tennessee

5 Camp Livingston, Louisiana

December 7, 1941 - November 13, 1945

Kumaji Furuya's Internment History

From	To	No. of Days	Location
Dec. 7, 1941	Dec. 9, 1941	3	INS Station, Honolulu, T.H.
Dec. 9, 1941	Feb. 18, 1942	72	Sand Island Internment Camp, Honolulu, T.H.
Feb. 18, 1942	Feb. 20, 1942*	3	INS Station, Honolulu, T.H.
Mar. 1, 1942	Mar. 6, 1942	6	Angel Island, California (in transit)†
Mar. 9, 1942	May 25, 1942	78	Camp McCoy, Wisconsin
May 28, 1942	Jun. 29, 1942	33	Camp Forrest, Tennessee
Jun. 30, 1942	Jun. 2, 1943	337	Camp Livingston, Louisiana
Jun. 5, 1943	Apr. 3, 1944	303	Fort Missoula, Montana
Apr. 6, 1944	Oct. 30, 1945	572	Santa Fe Internment Camp, New Mexico
Nov. 2, 1945	Nov. 7, 1945	6	Seamen's Club, Seattle, Washington (in transit)
Nov. 13, 1945	Arrival in Honolulu onboard USS *Yarmouth*		

Total: 3 years, 11 months

---

* Overnight onboard the USS *Grant*; left Honolulu on February 21, 1942.

† Incarcerated at the former INS detention facility on the island.

At Angel Island

Nine days across the ocean without sun,
A frightful life in a convoy ship's hold
Pitching and rolling, we finally reach
Cold San Francisco in early spring

Seagulls and plovers cry as the evening fog
Rolls into golden gate bay
Thinking of dear Hawaii, my family there,
Despair envelopes me.

A large crimson moon rises

エンゼル島にて

湖路ここのか陽の目も見ずに
こわいコンボイ船底くらし
ゆられゆられて漸く着いた
加州フリスコ春寒い
夕霧せまる金門湾
啼くはかもめか磯千鳥
妻子残したなつかしの
ハワイ思えば眼がくらむ
赤い大きなお月さま

An Internment Odyssey

Haisho Tenten

Forewords

A Chronicle with Poetic Artistry
Joei Oi[1]

I thought he had started something strange when I first saw Mr. Furuya's series of newspaper articles, *"Haisho Tenten."*[2] Generally speaking, this type of writing tends to be formal, pedantic, and, therefore, prosaic. I assumed Mr. Furuya's work would follow a similar path. As the series progressed, however, I became more interested and found myself longing to read the coming articles. I even began to wonder how he would write about particular incidents and worried that he might have forgotten some.

Since we had lived together under the same roof and eaten from the same pot of rice during the four years of war, we shared the same experiences. Accordingly, I supplemented what Mr. Furuya had forgotten or, in other cases, often reminisced about the old days when reading episodes that I had forgotten, and this triggered additional memories.

I recall a particular incident involving Mr. Furuya. While we were still at Sand Island,[3] Mr. Furuya came to our tent to spend the night. He snored all through the night—very quietly, of course—but it annoyed us. The next morning, we politely asked him to leave. I do not find this episode in his writings; I think Mr. Furuya may have forgotten about it.

Mr. Furuya is regarded as a "pioneer" in our internee community. In the late afternoon of December 7, as fires continued to rage at Pearl Harbor and Hickam Air Force Base, FBI agents came to my house to arrest me. Mr. Furuya was already in the car when I got in. In this sense, he is my predecessor in our internment experience. Together, we were taken to the Immigration and Naturalization Service office. From that day on, he and I shared four years of joy and hardship, until Japan's unimaginable defeat brought us back to Hawai'i.

3

This book is a compilation of Mr. Furuya's internment experiences. Although he has depended on the memories of others for the latter part of his book, I am, nevertheless, impressed that he still remembers those days so vividly. Noteworthy is his depiction of Fort Missoula in Montana, one of the highlights of this book. I can still see Mr. Furuya's frustrated expression when he failed to land a fish or how he looked when he caught a cold—dressed in thick layers of clothing, with a towel around his neck, plodding wearily along in the snow.

Mr. Furuya has already published a book of haiku, which were written during his internment.[4] I envy him, as he has a gift for composing poems, many of which you will find in *Haisho Tenten*.

I will never forget the night of December 7. Lying beside me in the dark of the second-floor INS room, amidst all of the tension and anxiety, Mr. Furuya whispered, "I've composed a haiku."

In the pitch darkness
Familiar voices
We have all been captured
真暗み
知り人の声もして
囚われている[5]

I admired and envied his gift for poetry then. I am sure that his amiable nature and rich life experiences, in addition to his talent, have borne fruit in this book.

In a sense, this is a part of World War II history as told by an amateur historian. This also is a part of the history of the Japanese living in Hawai'i.

I dedicate this foreword to Mr. Furuya in celebration of the publication of his book, *Haisho Tenten*.

Late autumn 1963

History is Alive

Masahiro Himeno[6]

When I was asked to write a foreword for this book, I was so surprised that I was unable to reply. I should have responded, but the request was so weighty that words failed me.

I wonder what Mr. Furuya wants to say with this book. Is it merely a day-to-day account of the lives of the internees? No, the scope of the book extends far beyond that. Mr. Furuya has deeper insight. An account of internment life is merely like the branches, leaves, and flowers of a tree. One is hard-pressed to find the core of the tree—the trunk—that brings life to it. After all, there is nothing especially colorful or showy about internment life. In this historical narrative, the author looks beyond the obvious as he writes in retrospect. The book, replete with personal observations, avoids the cold facts while incorporating sentiment, compassion, and wisdom. His breath is like the dewdrops that sparkle here and there throughout the book.

In recent times, history has become a popular topic of discussion among intellectuals, who are calling for a review of its meaning. They urge that history is alive, not just to be repeated. Moreover, the concept of history must be reinterpreted. Each time a history is studied, revisions must be made, enabling one to view an event in a new way.

What is depicted in this book happened twenty years ago. When we compare the history of Hawai'i, including that of the internment as it was seen by Mr. Furuya, with the postwar history of the last twenty years, we can see that history is alive. An enumeration of incidents, one after another, cannot be called a history. There are many lives connected to each event, and these lives are too precious to be glossed over and forgotten. These lives are at the core of history, which is why history is alive. Because history is alive, we must interpret it as correctly as possible. This book is being published in an effort to help us to interpret history correctly. Please allow me to be repetitious: History is alive.

The discussion of any event should be accompanied by an explanation and understanding of the significance of the event. How, then, will the history of the period covered in this book be interpreted? What is the meaning of this book? This war and we, who suffered the effects of it, and our sons, who sacrificed their lives, now whisper to all the meaning of this history. And when it becomes our grandchildren's generation, this history must be rewritten once again. It will surely be done. When that day comes to rewrite this history, will the meaning that we now give to these events still be valid? I doubt that anyone would deny this.

If they were to, it would be disastrous—the sufferings of the internment would be meaningless. Why, then, did our sons risk their lives on the battlefields? Why did they sacrifice their precious lives? Their deaths would be meaningless—they would have died in vain. God would never allow this to happen. It is the duty of us, as internees, and of our descendants to see to it that those who lost their lives did not die in vain. It is because of the significance of history that we try to make the best use of our experiences. History lives on in this book.

Early October 1963

Joy and Hope
Totaro Matsui[7]

After having been featured in *The Hawaii Times* newspaper as a continuing series of articles, *"Haisho Tenten"* is being published in book form. I was asked by the author to write a foreword, having shared as barracks mates the joys and hardships of the internment camps. Although this role is out of character for me and I risk embarrassing myself, I take pen in hand.

On the evening of the Pearl Harbor attack, with the city blanketed in the ash of the smoky fires that still raged in the aftermath of the bombing, I was taken prisoner. Without being given a clear reason or explanation of the charges, I was incarcerated for four years. It was not until December 10, 1945, after the war had ended, that I was released from the Mainland and returned to my beloved Hawai'i. Eighteen years have passed since then.

Many have cited the need for a record of the internment experience, particularly the emotional and psychological impact on its victims. In addition to these stories, however, many have called for a recording of the painful ordeal suffered by alien internees, who were treated as hostiles in an enemy country. Periodically, fragmented episodes of personal accounts have appeared in newspapers and magazines, but to my knowledge, the late Keiho Soga's *Tessaku Seikatsu* is the only complete work to have addressed this need.[8]

Not fully satisfied with the portrayals thus far, I am delighted about the publication of this book based on Mr. Furuya's series of articles. The author, who is a writer, has painstakingly recorded the internees' ordinary activities, making extensive use of material provided by his barracks mates. A few discrepancies in the details notwithstanding, I am confident that this book will serve as an outstanding reference for its faithfully recorded and thorough explanations of daily internment life. I am very grateful to him and respectfully recognize his hard work.

If I am allowed to ask a little more, I would like to see the publication of: the experiences of internees at the three detention camps in Hawai'i,[9] the Honouliuli Internment Camp, the Tule Lake Internment Camp, and the Crystal City Family Camp; the women internees' stories of patience and forbearance; and articles written by internees which have appeared in the newspaper from time to time. Such books would complete the history of the internment experience for the present. I personally hope that the author will assume the leadership role of editor. It would add luster to what is already brilliant. This is my fervent wish.

November 3, 1963

| 1 |

The Outbreak of War

December 7, the Day of Destiny

Even in Hawai'i, once called the Paradise of the Pacific, the situation was becoming increasingly unstable. No one could predict what would happen in the near future.

December 7 was a Sunday, and the ceremony to mark the completion of the emergency rescue class was going on at the Kokusai Theater[1] when two police officers appeared and ordered us to go home immediately. They said that Japanese military aircraft had bombed Pearl Harbor and that the United States was now at war with Japan.

We could not believe that such a thing had happened, and there was no alternative but to go home. When I got back home, I told my wife that war had broken out, and I went to turn on my shortwave radio to see if I could catch a broadcast from Japan. As it was daytime, it was very difficult to catch a transmission. Despite this I could clearly hear the words, "went to see the emperor." I could not help but acknowledge that war had indeed broken out. I was overcome with emotion and did not know what to do.

Caught by the Authorities

Local radio stations were continuously broadcasting all sorts of orders: "Do not use the telephone!" "Do not go outside!" "Go home quickly!"

As I listened, there came an announcement directing University of Hawai'i ROTC students to report to the college campus. Since Hanzo, our eldest son, was in the ROTC, he immediately dressed and headed for the university in my car.[2]

After he left, two officers—probably a policeman and an FBI agent—arrived at my house asking for "Kumaji Furuya."[3]

I went out to the veranda and was told, "We need to ask you some questions, so we want you to come with us." I knew I had not done anything wrong, so I readily followed. I was leaving my house in just a shirt, when my wife said, "Why don't you wear your jacket?"

I went to our bedroom to get it, and an officer followed me. When I pulled out a dresser drawer to remove a handkerchief, he pointed a revolver at me.

"What you do?" I asked in English.

"Just watching you," he answered.

I put a handkerchief in my pocket and left. In the car, I felt uneasy hearing the continuous stream of instructions coming over the radio. Naturally, I thought I would be taken to police headquarters. Instead the car headed toward Shafter. Fearing that I was being taken to a military base, my whole body turned cold.[4]

I was relieved when the car instead headed toward the mountains on Kamehameha IV Road. As I wondered where we were going, men such as George Otani; vice president of the United Japanese Society Osuke Shigemoto;[5] and the reverends Joei Oi and Hanzo Shimoda, Shinto priests at the Kato Shrine,[6] were put into the car with me. We were told not to speak, so we could only look at each other in silence. As the car headed out of Kalihi Valley, Mr. Otani patted my shoulder and pointed toward Pearl Harbor. There I could see columns of heavy smoke rising in the dusk. It truly was a frightening scene.

The sun had already set and there was no one on the streets. The only traffic was that of military vehicles with blue headlights. Honolulu felt like a ghost town. Our car sped toward the Immigration and Naturalization Service office.[7] At the gate, two MPs stood guard, armed with bayonets. As our car approached, they yelled, "Halt!" and pointed their guns toward us. When the officer told them that we were "prisoners," they let us through. The word "prisoners" really shook us.

Detained at the INS Office

Seven or eight soldiers wearing helmets stood at the entrance of the INS office and conducted body searches of us as we entered the building. They led us by flashlight to a dark room on the upper floor and locked the iron door behind us. I could sense that twenty or thirty people were already in the room. When I heard a voice I could identify, I understood for the first time what had happened to me.

I groped around in the dark and finally found the upper bunk of a bed to lie down on, although I did not feel like sleeping. I sat on the bed and watched man after man join us. By midnight, the room was so crowded we could barely move.

I occasionally heard loud noises outside and felt the increasing tension. Mr. Kojima, owner of Kojima Book Store, who was occupying an adjacent bed, softly recited the *Hokke-kyō*.[8] It made me feel like I was dying.

After a while, the elderly Mr. Miyotsuchi Komeya, whom we heard had been ill for a long time, was carried into the room. We thought he would not be able to sleep on a bunk bed, so we piled a few mattresses on the floor and laid him down. An MP came in and tried to pull Mr. Komeya off the mattresses.

"Goddamn!" he said.

In spite of our explanation that Mr. Komeya was ill, the MP dragged him off the mattresses. As much as I wanted to attack the MP for such an inhumane act, I held myself back, taking the situation into account. But I shook with anger.

As we whispered in the dark, I learned that those being detained were Japanese community leaders such as heads of organizations, teachers at Japanese language schools, and priests. When the U.S. government began freezing the assets of Japanese citizens, the United Japanese Society conducted several meetings with influential people in Honolulu to discuss ways to protect us and our property.[9] Among those at the meetings were the territorial governor, the mayor, FBI Chief Robert Shivers, Commander Samuel King, General Wells of the Hawaiian Sugar Planters' Association, the president of the Caucasian Chamber of Commerce, and the head of U.S. Customs in Honolulu.[10] At the time, every one of them said that the Japanese were law-abiding citizens and that no permanent resident alien in Hawai'i would ever be detained, even if war were to break out. However, in times of war, the military has absolute power and no one can interfere.

Day Two at the INS Office

The hard night of imprisonment had passed. I had not been able to sleep for most of the night.

It was now already after nine in the morning, and there was no indication that we were going to be given breakfast. Although we had no appetite, we all still wondered if they were going to feed us. Finally, at about ten o'clock, breakfast was announced, and we were all taken from the room. When I stepped out, MPs carrying rifles with bayonets, and looking like they had just arrived from the Mainland, lined both sides of the hallway. As we walked down the corridor, they would thrust their rifles out toward us whenever someone got close to them. I thought they were scared, too.

At the foot of the stairs, we were given coffee, a piece of bread, boiled sausage, and sauerkraut. We went out to the yard and ate squatting down. As soon as we finished eating, we were hustled back to the upstairs room. All this occurred in less than ten minutes. I had expected some kind of hearing, but nothing happened.

We all felt sick from the stuffiness of the dark room full of people. As the minutes went by, some of us began to wonder out loud about certain acquaintances who should have been detained but were not among us. Tetsuo Toyama of Toyama Enterprises said loudly in his unique accent, "I bet they slipped through the net."[11] Everyone chuckled and the tension seemed to be slightly eased by his funny comment. After that, "slipped through the net" became a popular phrase among us.

The next day was the ninth. While I was standing in line for breakfast, someone in the back called my name. As I turned to look, an MP came to me with a bag.

"Your son brought this bag," he said. I quickly took it to our room and then returned to the line. After breakfast, I opened the bag and found handkerchiefs, underwear, a shaving kit, and Camel cigarettes. It was such a surprise. I was happy that my family knew where I was.

At about nine o'clock, the names of fifty or sixty people were called. Mine was among them. We were lined up and roll was called. We were then taken from Pier 6 to Sand Island in a heavily guarded scow. At Sand Island, we were taken deep inside the *kiawe*[12] forest. No one uttered a word. I had the sudden thought that this might be a death march, and I broke into a cold sweat, fearing we were about to be executed.

It was December 9, 1941, two days after the Pearl Harbor bombing. I had no idea what was going on in the outside world.

| 2 |

Sand Island Camp

They Tell Us We Are Prisoners of War

I heard that there once had been a quarantine facility on Sand Island known as "*sennin goya*," meaning a shack for a thousand people.[1] Now the island was under the jurisdiction of the U.S. Army, and the 35th Regiment guarded the area. When we arrived, the commander, Captain John G. Coughlin, addressed us.

"You are not criminals, but nationals of the enemy country," he said. "Your human rights will be recognized, and you will be treated fairly according to military regulations governing prisoners of war." We were a little relieved to hear that we were not going to be killed.

I looked around, wondering where they were going to put us. I could see some structures that looked like a mess hall and latrines in a large field surrounded by barbed wire. We were told to go into the fenced area, put up tents, assemble army cots, and set them up eight to a tent according to the soldiers' instructions. These were to be our temporary accommodations. Although each of us got a pillow and a blanket, we were not given pajamas. We were expected to lie down on the cots as we were dressed.

At five o'clock we were confined to our tents. It was still sunny. We were bored, and since there were no women around, we shared bawdy stories. Before long, we caught the attention of the guards, who struck our tents with their truncheons, saying we were too loud. It was quite annoying. The latrines were at the edge of the campsite. We hated to go there at night, for we were required to stop and say "prisoner" when the guards ordered, "Halt!" If we did not stop, we would be shot and killed.

Morning roll call was conducted while it was still dark. Our tent was located at the farthest end of the camp. In the space between our tent and

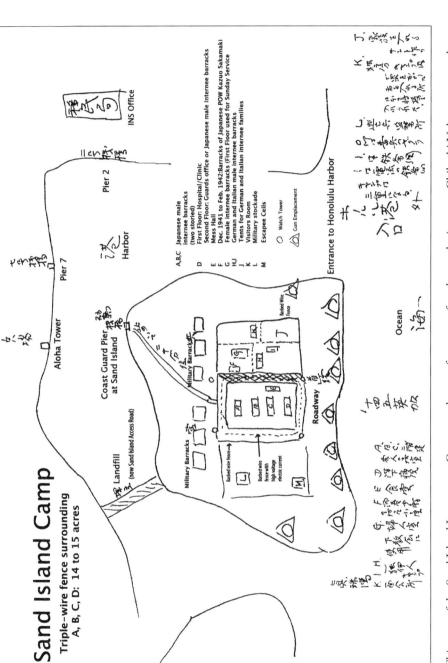

Sand Island Camp

Triple–wire fence surrounding
A, B, C, D: 14 to 15 acres

Landfill

(now Sand Island Access Road)

Military Barracks

Coast Guard Pier
at Sand Island

Military Barracks

Aloha Tower

Pier 7

Harbor

Pier 2

INS Office

A,B,C   Japanese male
         internee barracks
         (two storied)
D   First Floor: Hospital/Clinic
         Second Floor: Guards office or Japanese male internee barracks
E   Mess Hall
         Dec. 1941 to Feb. 1942:Barracks of Japanese POW Kazuo Sakamaki
F   Female internee barracks (First Floor used for Sunday Service
G   German and Italian male internee barracks
H,I   Tents for German and Italian internee families
K   Visitors Room
L   Military stockade
M   Escapee Cells

○ Watch Tower
◇ Gun Emplacement

Barbed wire fence→

Barbed wire
fence with
high voltage
electric current

Barbed Wire
fence

Roadway

Ocean

Entrance to Honolulu Harbor

This map of the Sand Island Internment Camp was drawn a few years after the war by internee Chikashi Nakayama, a teacher at the Chuo Gakuin Japanese Language School in Honolulu. The map along with the translation of its accompanying notes appear here in publication for the first time. *Courtesy of the Nakayama Family* the adjacent one, there were many stakes in the ground to hold the tent ropes. If you were absent-minded, you could trip over them.

One morning, I was about ten seconds late to respond to the roll call whistle. I was ordered to drop out of line. I was reprimanded and ordered to work as a dishwasher. Just as Ensign Sakamaki was the first Japanese POW of this war,[2] I became the first KP. But I was not alone. Mr. Iida of Iida Suisando; Reverend Kubokawa of the Jodo Mission; and Mr. Kimura, branch manager of Nippon Yusen, were my colleagues.[3]

KP was the abbreviation for Kitchen Police, which is what we called it to make fun of whoever had dishwashing and kitchen-cleaning duties at a time when the others were taking a break. KP duty was one of the lightest punishments we could be given during our camp life. Later in our internment, even after we were allowed to manage our daily life, we took turns doing KP once every ten days. Thanks to this assignment, even the most arrogant of us came to appreciate our wives and often helped in the kitchen later on. Some good did come out of the internment.

A Shortage of Cigarettes

After we had settled in at Sand Island, the first problem we encountered was a shortage of cigarettes. Among the items I had received from my family was a carton of Camel cigarettes, so I had no problem for the next four or five days. I still had five or six packs left after giving a pack to each of my close friends. Smokers miss cigarettes all the more when they realize there won't be any available. Some dared to make recycled cigarettes by collecting butts that had been thrown away by the guards. Others dried used tea leaves and rolled them with toilet paper.

As the rumor spread that I had cigarettes, my smoker friends came to me and begged, "Come on, give me one." Since my stock was very limited, they began to gather at my tent to smoke just one puff each after every meal. Some greedy guys took two or three puffs, so one cigarette was not enough to go around. Naturally, smokers who could not get a puff complained. As a result, we agreed to behave like gentlemen and to smoke only one puff each, but this left us somewhat dissatisfied. Eventually, we decided on two puffs each. I can still remember the happy faces as we puffed on the cigarettes.

"You are the only one of us one-hundred-plus prisoners who has been sent anything by his wife," said Mr. K, who was good at flattery. "Your wife is the best wife in Hawai'i. She must be the modern-day version of the wife of Yamanouchi Kazutoyo."[4] Upon hearing this empty compliment, everyone burst out laughing.

As I learned later, this gift from my wife was the result of information from Mrs. Koichi Iida, who had somehow learned that I was being detained at the INS office. Mrs. Iida had also notified Mrs. Soga[5] and others, but it was too late. When the Iidas, the Sogas, and the Sumidas brought bags of items to the INS office for their family members, they were turned away.

The guards at the Sand Island camp were ROTC students at the University of Hawai'i. Among them were two Portuguese students who had lost their older brothers at Pearl Harbor. They glared at us and picked on us every time we met. On the other hand, boys like the son of territorial Senator William Heen purposely dropped the cigarettes they hadn't smoked on the ground. Senator Heen's son might have done this because his father and Mr. Otani of 'A'ala Market were acquaintances.[6] The many smokers very much appreciated this gesture.

Speaking of dropping things, what we appreciated most was that they also delivered newspapers to us—by dropping them on the ground. Without newspapers, we had no information about the outside world. So desperate were we that we were willing to steal them from the back pockets of the guards' pants. Some ROTC guards knowingly dropped newspapers on the ground and left them there. They made us happy.

War Hysteria

The attack on Pearl Harbor was like a bolt out of the blue, and the governor, as well as the military, FBI, and police, were in a state of hysteria. Besides us, they apprehended anyone on the streets who was thought to be Japanese. A few Japanese fishermen were killed by machine gun fire as they returned to port on the evening of December 7, and Japanese who were gathering around the Kewalo Basin area were all arrested.[7]

All Nikkei[8] and Japanese ham radio operators or radio technicians were also apprehended. Among them was Tokio Kobayashi, a friend's son, who was attending the University of Hawai'i. He volunteered to work in the vegetable garden outside the fence at Sand Island. One day when he arrived at the camp gate, he was caught by the guards, who also were UH students. His sweatshirt was ripped off of him, and he was beaten and humiliated and accused of being a disloyal citizen. The reason for the attack was his sweatshirt, which bore a large "H," the logo of the University of Hawai'i. This young man was soon released from the camp, as the authorities concluded he did not fall into the category of internee.

There is a sequel to this story. I later received a note from him with a list of people to whom he had sent some candy. I passed on the word at once. We waited a long time, but the candy never arrived. I grew impatient and asked Lieutenant Springer[9] about it. He replied that he had seized the candy because regulations required that each and every candy be unwrapped and inspected, but he had lacked the manpower to do this. We felt like betrayed sweethearts, for we had been so longing for this gift.

Later, when we were allowed to correspond with people on the outside, we were each given a postcard and a pencil. If we could not finish writing our card by the end of the day, we were required to turn it in and retrieve it the next morning. The cards were then taken to the administration office. Access to writing materials and communication with the outside world were strictly controlled.

Internee representatives and group leaders became quite agitated and enforced strict control over our communications, as they would be held responsible for the loss of even one missing pencil or postcard. Our internee representative at the time was George Otani, and Rev. Kazoe Kawasaki was the secretary. Group leaders included Heigo Fuchino, Sadasuke Hamamoto, Kensaku Tsunoda, Kenji Kimura of Nihon Yūsen, and principal Yoshinobu Sasaki.

Victims of War Hysteria

In the detention camp, everyone started to call the outside world *"shaba."*[10] We jokingly passed judgment on the seriousness of our crimes based on the extent of our contribution to society. We became inclined to think that "serious criminals" were destined to be detained. There were some detainees, however, who had done nothing significant. These unfortunate people were accidentally apprehended and detained for four years.

Among them was Yuki Miyao, the wife of Rev. Shigemaru Miyao.[11] She was apparently mistaken for Reverend Miyao's mother, Yoshiye, since the name of both women began with the letter "Y." In the Miyao family, mother, son, and son's wife were all detained, leaving behind three young children, the eldest only five years old. At her hearing, Yuki explained that she was just a housewife, but still she was not released.

Incidentally, I had a heart-stopping experience related to Mrs. Miyao. It happened while I was still being held at the INS office. Someone told me that as he stared out from a barred window, he could see my wife outside. I was shocked and rushed to the window to see if she was, in fact, in the courtyard. After a while, a tall lady came into view. When I looked closely, I saw that it was Mrs. Miyao. Frankly, I was very relieved.

Another episode concerning women detainees involved the wife of Seigi Yamane, who rented out houses on Pauoa Road. When officials came to apprehend him, presumably because he had visited Japan right before the war broke out, Mrs. Yamane vigorously protested, speaking in English. The officials told her to file a complaint at their office and took her away with Mr. Yamane. The two were not released until the end of the war.[12]

About two weeks into our detention, elderly Rev. Shuntaro Ikezawa joined us. We had assumed that Christian ministers, except for those working for the Japanese Consulate as *toritsuginin*,[13] would not be arrested. When we asked him why an old minister like him had been brought in, Reverend Ikezawa said he had been arrested when he went to see Vice Consul Otojiro Okuda, his close friend, who had been under house arrest at the time.

There were others who were mistakenly detained because of the similarity of their names. One of them was Rev. Shushin Matsubayashi. He had been stationed at 'Ōla'a, but was transferred to the main temple in Honolulu just a few days before the war broke out. The FBI came for him, and an agent asked if he was Shoten Matsubayashi.[14]

"You are mistaken," he answered. "My name is Shushin."

"But you, too, are a priest, aren't you?" the agent asked.

As soon as he replied, "yes," he was arrested and taken into custody. Of course, I realized that Reverend Matsubayashi would have been apprehended sooner or later.

Commander Eifler

The first thing we worried about after being detained at Sand Island was that we could be attacked by Japanese bombers since the island was located at the neck of Pearl Harbor. Some prudent detainees secretly dug holes under their cots that were large enough to accommodate themselves. They then filled them up. The detainees figured they could easily dig out the holes again when it became necessary to hide. Another man suggested we spread out our white sheets to signal that we were there. Most of us thought a small shelter underneath our bed was more practical, so when a detainee started digging, everyone followed. Digging became very popular everywhere in the camp. We can laugh about it now, but we were quite serious about it then.

Once, there was an emergency air raid drill. As instructed, as soon as we heard the warning siren, we all hid in our tents, and the whole camp became very quiet. Our tent was at the farthest end of the camp. I was watching outside the tent, when I heard a gunshot. The loud sound surprised Commander Eifler, who was near the water tank. He ran for cover behind the tank and quickly drew his pistol. He probably thought that Japanese forces had landed. I was very happy to see the pompous commander so frightened and panicked.[15]

Apparently, a soldier had mistakenly fired his gun. In a fit of anger, Commander Eifler yelled at the corporal and yanked off his stripes. Although he was mean and old, Eifler sometimes acted childishly. He often inspected the garbage cans. If he found even a small piece of bread in the garbage, he would immediately whistle for all of the detainees, gather us together, and scold us for wasting food. When we saw him coming, swinging his chain of keys, we immediately retreated into our tents, fearing a reprimand.

One day, after learning about our holes in the ground, he came to our tent. When he saw the holes neatly covered, he could only leave in frustration, shouting that we were not to dig holes again.

The Okano Incident

Commander Eifler, a former customs officer who was given the rank of captain upon his enlistment, had replaced our first commander, the man who had spoken on our first day at Sand Island about treating us fairly. As I have written before, Eifler was a mean, tough guy, and all of us were afraid of him. I admit that it was his duty to enforce the rules, but he seemed to enjoy picking on us for trivial matters.

According to the rules governing POWs and detainees, we were not allowed to carry any item that could be considered a weapon, no matter how small—that meant not only small knives, scissors, and razor blades, but nails and tie pins, as well. In other words, all metal items were considered potential weapons. However, some among us secretly made knives and toothpicks from metal strapping ties left on the ground. They ground them with coral fragments. Others used thick paper to make pieces for *shōgi*.[16]

One day, as the detainees who had worked outside the fence were being searched upon their return, Reverend Okano was found to be in possession of a flimsy knife made from a strapping tie.[17] All of the detainees were immediately called to the field. We were ordered to stand in a line and remove all of our clothing. We took off our shirts, but not our pants, although there were only men among us. The guards demanded that we take off our pants, so we reluctantly stripped off all our clothes. Our impulse was to cover ourselves with our hands, but this was not allowed. We all felt so awkward, standing naked in the field, with our hands by our sides. I had heard that recruits must take off everything when they go through the military draft examination in Japan, but it takes place inside a small room and among a small number of people. In our case, nearly two hundred detainees stood naked in an open field.

There were elderly men, such as Bishop Kubokawa, Bishop Kuchiba, president Soga, and principal Inokuchi,[18] as well as Daizo Sumida, Koichi Iida, Taichi Sato,[19] Osuke Shigemoto, Tetsuo Toyama, Nisshu Kobayashi, and Tokuye Takahashi; also middle-aged and younger men like Kensaku Tsunoda (our group leader), Takeo Kagawa, Tomoaki Nakamura, Hiroshi Motoshige, Norizane Tsuha,[20] Soichi Obata, Kenkichi Fujimoto, and Shinzaburo Sumida. It was a most unusual sight, both pathetic and comical that a group of men, young and old, would be left standing completely naked. As they searched our tents, we were required to remain standing in the cold December wind. It was already night when the guards completed a thorough search of our tents. I cannot recall ever having been more offended. Among ourselves, we called this the "Okano Incident." Everyone was angry at the commander, not at Reverend Okano. Because of this incident, Mr. Tsunoda was discharged from his post as group leader.

Another time, while I was being interrogated by the FBI at the INS office, the same kind of thing happened when two forks went missing from the mess hall.

Wishful Thinking

As the days passed, internees who had previously worried about their future now became more settled and wanted to be interrogated right away. Because we had done nothing wrong, we were sure we would be released after the interrogations.

This was when Rev. Josen Deme of Waipahu was called by the authorities. It created a big sensation among us detainees. Someone said, rather sarcastically, that the reverend was probably leaving the camp because, being very smart, he was always flattering the sugar plantation owners, who were now obtaining his release. Later we learned that he had been sent to the German camp, as the officers had mistakenly read his name as Josef Deme.

On Christmas day, Rev. Shinpei Goto, a Christian minister from Windward Oʻahu, was released. A few days later, Totaro Matsui, chairman of Pacific Bank; Osuke Shigemoto, vice chairman of the United Japanese Society; Sadato Morifuji, vice chairman of the Japanese Chamber of Commerce; and I were summoned by the authorities. The rest of the detainees were very envious because they thought we were going to be released. I gave away my underwear and soap box, which my wife had sent me, to friends who wanted them, like Dr. Iga Mori; Yasutaro Soga, publisher of the *Nippu Jiji* newspaper; and Seiha Asami.[21] I left the camp cheerfully.

We arrived at the pier, escorted by two gentle-looking Caucasian officers. We were taken from Sand Island aboard a scow under armed guard. This time, we boarded a pretty little steamer that stopped at Pier 12. The pier had been painted in a camouflage pattern, and I could see that machine guns had been installed on the roof of the building. The luxury ship, the SS *Lurline*, once painted white, was now a dark gray, like all of the other ships in the harbor.[22] Barriers blocked the harbor entrance. I could not help but feel the tension in the air.

No car was waiting for us at Pier 12. I wondered what they would do to us. They told us to walk, so we walked on the street that went along the shore until we got to the Dillingham Building.[23] At Sand Island, we had never been without guards, so now to be unexpectedly walking to downtown without guards made me feel like a bird released from its cage.

At the Dillingham Building, uniformed University of Hawai'i ROTC boys were on guard duty. In the hallway, I was shocked to see a boy who looked very much like my son. Actually, he was Chinese, and I had mixed feelings of disappointment and relief.

The atmosphere here made me begin to doubt that our hopes for release would be realized.

| 3 |

Back to the INS Office

Taken to the FBI Office

When I was brought into the FBI office, I noticed that all of the windows had been covered with a makeshift roofing-paper-like material that had been nailed onto the window frames. The office looked quite dreary. Investigator Tillman[1] was a husky man, but he appeared gentle in manner. Calmly, he began to question me.

"What is your profession?"

"I manage a store."

"The furniture business is interesting. I once worked at a furniture store in Los Angeles." I had never expected to be making small talk like this at the FBI office, so I was rather at a loss for words. I did feel more comfortable, however.

"By the way, do you know about the Yamanashi Club?" he asked.[2]

This put me on guard, and I felt that I should choose my words carefully.

"Yes, I know of it."

"Is Seiji Yoda the club president?"

"That's right."

"What does Mr. Yoda do?"

"He runs City Grill."

"You were the president last year, weren't you? Who was your predecessor?"

"I don't remember clearly whether it was Mr. Norimasa Horiuchi or Mr. Toshisuke Komeiji. The position does not mean very much, as the club is strictly for social purposes, and we just take turns as president."

"I don't think so."

"When the club was first organized, we elected the president, but since then he has become a mere figurehead. It's mostly the secretary, Mr. Nakamura,[3] and I who manage the organization. Mr. Yoda, this year's president, refused to assume this position at first, saying he could not spare the time since his store is open at night. He finally consented when we told him he would not need to do anything other than to let us use his name."

"What does Secretary Nakamura do?"

"He is the general manager of Hakubundo Store, but he is at Sand Island now."

"Is that so? Has the club ever raised funds for the Japanese military forces?"

I was startled to hear the question. I suddenly recalled that a receipt from the Japanese Consulate for a donation had been left in a desk drawer at the store.

"We once did donate some money. It was not for war funds, but for war relief."

"What does that mean?"

"The funds were to entertain the wounded soldiers."

"When did you send the donation to Japan?"

"I believe we sent it when I was the president." I became more tense and began to stammer. I feared that Mr. Horiuchi, Mr. Komeiji, Mr. Yoda, and others would be arrested for their part in the fundraising activities.

A Clever Interrogation by an FBI Agent

When the agent noticed that I was becoming nervous, he suddenly changed the subject and started asking me about the fighting in Manila.

"The Japanese army is doing quite well in Manila, isn't it?"

"I don't know. I've had no opportunity to read the paper."

"That's true. Look at this." He showed me a morning edition of *The Honolulu Advertiser*. Although I really wanted to read it, I did not feel like taking it from him.

Mr. Tillman appeared to notice the time.

"Oh, it's noon. Let's have lunch at the restaurant downstairs."

"I don't have any money," I said, being at a loss as to what to say.

"It's on the house," he responded.

We had lunch at the restaurant, but I was not hungry and did not enjoy it. We went back upstairs, and he started questioning me again.

"You were vice chairman of the United Japanese Society's board of directors, weren't you?"

"Yes, I was."

"I understand Mr. Yoda is a member of the board."

"No, he's not."

"Oh, you're right. That's Mr. Koichiro Nakamura of the Restaurant Association. Am I correct?"

"I don't know exactly."

"The board members of the United Japanese Society were quite eager to welcome Japanese warships, weren't they?"

"It was not the board members but the officers."

"Who are the people that you know who often visited the Japanese Consulate?"

"There are too many to remember, but most of them are being detained now."

"You live in the Kalihi area, so you must know Mr. Goichi Yamane. He must be a big shot in your community."

"He is rich but not a big shot. He does not donate money for warship receptions and community-related activities, so Japanese call him a Jew behind his back."

I was relieved when Mr. Tillman stopped his questioning. I was afraid he would ask me about Mr. Yamane's relationship with the Kalihi Japanese School, and I certainly could not say that I knew nothing about it since I was the president of the Kalihi Education Foundation.

Mr. Matsui had been the first in our group to be questioned, and it had taken more than an hour. During that time, we had waited in the hall, feeling very anxious. In my case, the interrogation was considerably shorter—about thirty minutes.

It was now evening, and as we were wondering what was to happen to us, we arrived back at the INS office. We were surprised to see Reverend Deme there, for we thought he had been released. There were also some from "the slipped through the net" group, like Katsuichi Kawamoto, Norikazu Nakano, Kyoichi Miyata, and Dr. Akio Kimura. These men, along with the four of us, were detained at the INS office, and for the first time in our lives, we greeted a miserable New Year's Day from inside a prison cell.

New Year's Day *Mochi* at the INS Office

All four of us were officers in organizations: Mr. Shigemoto, United Japanese Society vice chairman; Mr. Morifuji, Japanese Chamber of Commerce vice chairman; Mr. Matsui, Japanese Chamber of Commerce secretary; and myself, United Japanese Society vice chairman. It appeared that the purpose of questioning us was to identify those to be placed under arrest.

However, a day later, four gentlemen, namely Rev. Joei Oi; Rev. Shigemaru Miyao; and the Motoshige brothers, Hiroshi and Tatsuo, were called in for questioning. Reverend Oi was a reserve officer in the Japanese army, and the Motoshige brothers were both in the U.S. Army Reserve. Reverend Miyao was a Shinto priest. At the time, military authorities suspected Shintoists of spying. As we feared, their interrogations were very severe. I was told the men were treated like criminals.

At one point, Reverend Oi lost his temper with the agent.

"We are not criminals," he said. "I will not answer questions that assume that I have committed a crime."

The agent's attitude then changed, and he became a little more pleasant.

I guess it was not Mr. Tillman who had done the questioning. As I've mentioned earlier, Tillman was very clever and had even bought us lunch at the restaurant downstairs. The agent on this day did nothing of the kind. Rather he said, "Yesterday's bunch ate a lot, and it was a big expense."

When the four men arrived at the INS office, it was already past dinnertime, so their only meal that day was breakfast. It seems the questions they were asked were similar to the ones we had been asked.

On New Year's Day, we enjoyed a special treat of *mochi*,[4] sweet roasted chestnuts, and dried persimmons. Since Dr. Kimura, our spokesman, had instructed all of us to share all the gifts we received, everyone was able to enjoy an equal share of the treats.

Before the end of the year, Reverend Deme's wife had sent him some *mochi*, which he had not mentioned at the time. But he now offered it to us, saying, "Everyone, let's have some New Year's Day *mochi*."

Dr. Kimura, who was the spokesman for our group and also a physician, was allowed to carry a knife. He took out his large knife and cut each *mochi* into four pieces. All of the *mochi*, together with the persimmons and chestnuts, were distributed equally among the forty-eight detainees. We were all very grateful to Reverend and Mrs. Deme and to Dr. Kimura for this unexpected feast.

| 4 |
Life at Sand Island

Unfortunate Mr. Tsunoda

If I were to categorize the people who had been detained immediately after the war broke out, I would say that some had been active in community affairs, while others had been blacklisted by military intelligence and the FBI.[1] Otto Kuehn, a German, was the only person known to have engaged in espionage for Japan during the war.[2] However, there were one or two Japanese who the authorities suspected of being spies. They were given a hard time, their houses searched, and their photographs and rolls of film seized.

Among those who had committed so-called "serious crimes" were gentlemen like Mr. Makino, editor of the Japanese newspaper *Hawaii Hochi*; Rev. Zenkyo Komagata, a temple bishop; Mr. Oi, United Japanese Society executive director; and Mr. Tsuchiya, *Shōgyō Jihō* newspaper president. They were among those who had "slipped through the net."[3]

On the other hand, Kensaku Tsunoda, an administrator of the Japanese Hospital, was detained.[4] Mr. Tsunoda's arrest was a surprise to us. He had been an officer of the United Japanese Society a few years earlier. I asked him why he thought he had been detained, because I thought it strange that Tetsuo Oi, a current officer, had not been. He said that it was most likely because the U.S. Navy intelligence had blacklisted him.

Mr. Tsunoda had been an officer of the United Japanese Society at the time of the so-called "Consul General Fukuma Photo Incident."[5] Because he had gone to visit a Japanese navy special duty ship with staff members of the Japanese Consulate and other United Japanese Society officers, he happened to be there when the incident occurred.

Special duty ships often made port calls in those days. Whenever they docked at the pier, someone was always there to take pictures of the greeters. When Consul General Fukuma noticed that someone had taken his picture, he became very upset and insisted that the police arrest the man. He then instructed Takaichi Sakai[6] of the Consulate staff to take the man to police headquarters and asked Mr. Tsunoda to go with them as a witness. So, Mr. Tsunoda felt obliged to go.

The consul general told Mr. Sakai to demand that the man who had taken the picture apologize and give up the exposed film. However, the man claimed he had not taken a picture of the consul general, only of the ship. He also insisted that the consul general had infringed on his rights by grabbing his shoulder. Unfortunately, for Mr. Tsunoda, the man happened to be a U.S. Navy intelligence officer. The police determined that the man was only performing his duty and the case was closed. Although the consul general had made a big fuss, no one was punished. As the Japanese proverb goes, "Although the entire mountain shook and rattled, it brought forth just a single mouse."

In those days, as relations between Japan and the United States grew increasingly strained, U.S. military intelligence watched every move of the consul general, members of the United Japanese Society, and others like them. Naturally, rank-and-file agents tended to dislike the people at the Consulate and the United Japanese Society.

Mr. Tsunoda, of course, was blacklisted. One day, he received a threatening letter demanding that three thousand dollars be left in three separate thousand-dollar bundles at one-hundred-step intervals along Sheridan Street at a date and time to be specified. He was told to follow the instructions if he did not want to be reported to the authorities as a spy. But Mr. Tsunoda reported the incident to the police, who used it as an opportunity to check into his background. The police told him to follow the letter's instructions and to use counterfeit bills when he dropped the bundles in the dark along Sheridan Street. They said they would position detectives along the route. Mr. Tsunoda dropped the bundles as instructed, but no one came to pick them up.

The entire incident was probably perpetrated by the FBI to test Mr. Tsunoda. If he had not notified the police, it would have meant that he had something to hide. Mr. Tsunoda himself suggested that the FBI might have instigated the plan so that it could conduct a full investigation into his activities. Because of this incident, he was blacklisted and had to spend his four-year internment alone, even though he had only recently gotten married.

Tent Assignment Troubles

As the four of us were being taken back to Sand Island with the other detainees, I noticed a group of people at the Sand Island pier. They were Takeo

Akizaki, Kazuma Araki, Tamaki Arita, Shoichi Asami, Noriaki Atsuumi, Tokuji Baba, and Heigo Fuchino. They were on their way to the INS office aboard the boat that had carried us to attend those hearings that we had been so eagerly awaiting. This was the first group of detainees to be summoned in alphabetical order. Their hearings became the cause of tent assignment troubles for me. This terrible experience came about when I replaced Mr. Fuchino, our group leader, who had left the camp to attend his hearing.

It is said that humans possess at least seven characteristic habits and that, without fail, we each have our own peculiarities. With three hundred people living together, there were many problems related to these idiosyncrasies. Eight people, each with their own peculiarities, all sleeping in one tent meant detainees complained about tent mates snoring, or grinding teeth, or talking in their sleep. Among eight tent mates, only one or two did not snore or grind their teeth, in my experience, and among those who did, noise levels differed. Naturally, those who snored loudly became the targets of criticism, but they knew that no one could evict them from their tents.

Someone came up with the idea that the group should leave the loud snorers behind and move to tents that had been vacated by the detainees who had left for their hearings. They actually carried out the plan, and the loud snorers were left alone in their tents. When the detainees returned from their hearings, they saw others occupying their tents. They all came to me and complained. I was completely at a loss. After many twists and turns, those who could not live together with their original tent mates gathered together in a tent and formed their own group. It was called "the *pupule* tent."[7]

One day when the hearings were almost halfway through, Dr. Kazuo Miyamoto[8] was left alone in his tent, as all of his tent mates had been summoned for their hearings. An *aikāne*[9] came to his tent and asked to be allowed to stay, explaining that he could not sleep because one of his tent mates ground his teeth loudly. Dr. Miyamoto consented and let him in. That night, the friend started snoring very loudly and it was Dr. Miyamoto who could hardly sleep. He could not tell his friend to leave, so Dr. Miyamoto had to endure the snoring until he was summoned for his hearing. This is a true story that I heard from the doctor himself.

There is a Japanese proverb that says that people laugh at others' shortcomings without noticing their own. Based on this incident, I find the proverb to be true.

Ensign Sakamaki, the First Japanese POW

About three days after the one hundred and fifty or so of us arrived at Sand Island, rumors spread that a Japanese naval officer who had participated in the Pearl Harbor attack had been captured and that the sound of someone being tortured had been heard coming from an INS cell. The captured man was believed to be Ensign Sakamaki of Ehime Prefecture. I wondered how any of us could know this, as military authorities would have kept his captivity strictly confidential. Nevertheless, it turned out to be true when he was sent to Sand Island several days later and held in a small, newly built cottage at the mountainside of the camp entrance.

Being an officer, he was allowed an attendant. Recruited for this duty from among the detainee volunteers was Aisuke Shigekuni of Windward Oʻahu. Because Second Lieutenant Spillner[10] and a guard were assigned to carry all of Sakamaki's meals to his cottage, Mr. Shigekuni hardly had anything to do. We hoped to hear about the ensign from Mr. Shigekuni, but we learned nothing, for he told us that Sakamaki seemed unwilling to say anything. Moreover, Mr. Shigekuni was not allowed to converse with him.

Later we learned that the POW was, in fact, Kazuo Sakamaki, a Japanese navy ensign who had been captured after having navigated his mini-submarine into Kāneʻohe Bay.[11] Although he was an ensign, we always called him "Lieutenant Junior Grade Sakamaki." I knew that servicemen who died in action might have their rank upgraded, but in his case, we promoted him even though he had only been captured. I think we wanted to show our respect for someone who had performed such a heroic act.

In our camp, we did not have the opportunity to read newspapers, but we did get some news about Japan's victories from those detainees who came after us. We were surprised to hear that Japanese forces had won battles so quickly, and we wanted to somehow inform Ensign Sakamaki of this. We avoided asking Mr. Shigekuni, fearing he would be punished. Instead, as we passed the ensign's cottage, we intentionally spoke amongst ourselves in loud voices and sang songs with the lyrics modified to convey the news.

When I had a chance to talk with him later at Camp Forrest in Tennessee, I asked him whether he understood our messages. He replied that he had been very encouraged to hear the news. Ensign Kazuo Sakamaki was a young man in his early twenties with a boyish face. Looking at him, I could hardly believe that he had committed such a brave act.

The stories of Ensign Sakamaki and the rumors of the arrest of Otto Kuehn, the only spy for Japan in Hawaiʻi, spread quickly. It seems that it is absolutely impossible to keep a secret. As the Chinese proverb goes, "The sky knows, the earth knows, and people know."

Unfortunate People Are Forced to Work

The fences surrounding Sand Island Camp were built during the days when the area was a quarantine station known as "the shack for a thousand people." The fences were about six feet high and simple in design. When the island was to be converted into a camp for detainees and POWs, orders called for a contractor to build two rows of barbed wire fencing, six feet apart, so that guards could patrol between them. One morning, I noticed that no laborers had reported to work. This caused much trouble for a dozen detainees.

The workers had gone on strike because they were angry at the commander, who always complained about their slow progress. The commander ordered some of us to work in their place. He should have chosen young detainees to work, but instead he assigned us at random, including elderly men like Mr. Soga of the *Nippu Jiji* newspaper and Mr. Matsuda of Yokohama Specie Bank.[12] Luckily, a young man offered to replace Mr. Soga. Their jobs were to carry nine-foot-long fence posts and to push wheelbarrows full of concrete. With many younger people among us, I could not understand why elderly detainees had been selected, when clearly the commander was not choosing the elderly as punishment.

The job site was nearby, although it was outside the fence, and I could see them working. The area was slightly hilly and the ground uneven with buried stones. Mr. Matsuda was struggling to push a wheelbarrow, and it was apparent that he was having great difficulty doing it. Commander Eifler came over and showed him how to do it. But with Mr. Matsuda's small frame it was an impossible task. I wondered how the commander could have ordered such a man to perform such a task.

Teams of two had to carry posts from the entrance gate to the other end of the camp, a distance of more than five hundred feet. It must have hurt them to carry the posts on their shoulders. Seiha Asami, the editor-in-chief of the *Nippu Jiji* newspaper, was assigned this duty. Fortunately, his counterpart happened to be a strong young man. Lifting it in the middle, the young man carried the whole post, while Mr. Asami looked like an attachment at the end of it.

After about two days, the regular workers returned to their jobs. I heard that the commander had to give in to the workers, who insisted that he had violated their right to strike.

Entertainment Relieves Our Tensions

Most of the detainees had lived in Hawai'i for a long time. Up until their arrest, of course they had been good, law-abiding residents, working very hard and educating their children to be one hundred percent American citizens. So, they were shocked when they were taken away with only the clothes on their backs. Some of them became emotionally disturbed or went mad with anguish. These were mainly middle-aged people. Elderly men like Rev. Kyokujo Kubokawa, Rev. Ninryo Nago, Rev. Gikyo Kuchiba, president Soga of *Nippu Jiji*, contractor Mankichi Goto, Rev. Kametaro Maeda, Sadasuke Hamamoto, and Rev. Hanzo Shimoda, as well as a relatively younger group of people like Shinzaburo Sumida, the Motoshige brothers, Shoho Fujiie, Umeo Wada, Jikyo Masaki, Suijo Kabashima, and Kazoe Kawasaki were fairly calm and high-spirited. Those who were middle-aged, after all, had more responsibilities and concerns about their families and their financial situation. I could well understand that they were very worried.

Preventing the detainees and POWs from becoming unstable or going insane was a top priority for the authorities and the Red Cross. They often moved us from one camp to another and encouraged such activities as athletics, entertainment, and handicrafts. The most unusual of gifts were *hanafuda* playing cards and wooden *go* board game pieces that had been made by the Red Cross. The *go* pieces, which should have been made of stones or shells, were instead half-ball-like objects made of wood. They sat well on the board, but were very hard to collect after the game.

One of my friends, a Mr. T, had a nervous breakdown and became depressed. He began to speak incoherently. His friends were very worried and tried to cheer him up. He eventually recovered and got hooked on handicraft work after he moved to a Mainland camp. He was one of the richest Japanese in Hawai'i. Under stressful circumstances like ours, the rich are more likely to suffer than the poor.

Mr. T was later transferred to Camp Livingston in Louisiana, where he met Mr. Takatsuka, a furniture craftsman, who was originally from Shizuoka. Mr. Takatsuka had been interned earlier in Panama[13] and was teaching a craft-making class using tools borrowed from the U.S. Army. Mr. T was a hard worker, who labored on his small nude statues. Later, he completed a fairly large model of a Shinto shrine. By this time, he had completely recovered from his illness and was able to socialize again.

Among the internees, those who played sports, *go*, or *shōgi* were able to forget their miseries. However, a few internees became addicted to card games, which brought tragic results. In the early days of our detention, we used to tell obscene stories in our tents every night. According to the doctor, it proved that we had already become mentally abnormal.

The Commander Enjoys Giving Us a Hard Time

As I wrote earlier, the commander was unreasonable in assigning duties, like working on the fences. There is another story that I think shows how unreasonable he was. We called it the "Digging Out a Blind Shell Incident."

On the day of the Pearl Harbor attack, American anti-aircraft guns fired many rounds at Japanese planes. Some of the shells failed to detonate in the air and fell to the ground, causing fires and injuring people. One of the blind shells happened to fall on Sand Island. Things like this do happen, and something like unearthing a blind shell really did happen to us.

Motoichi Matsuda, branch manager of Yokohama Specie Bank, was an unfortunate man. Previously, he had been assigned to push a wheelbarrow. This time, he was ordered to dig out a blind shell. It was the punishment for his violating a camp regulation about gathering and talking in a group. He was ordered to carry out this dangerous assignment along with Rev. Gikyo Kuchiba of the Hongwanji Mission and a few others. This assignment was not only heavy labor and a dangerous task, but it could have killed him if the shell had exploded when he struck it with his pick. Mr. Matsuda told us later that he could not keep from trembling and was hardly able to use the pick. I thought this was quite natural.

I, too, experienced an incident that made me a victim of the unreasonable conduct of the commander. It involved using the latrine. The commander was very strict about keeping the latrines clean. Inspectors never gave their okay unless we cleaned the white tile floor so well that we could lick it. When an inspector was ready to start checking, we would take him first to the latrines. When we passed this inspection, we would smile at each other and feel proud of ourselves. Those who received this assignment remained very nervous until the inspection was successfully completed. In the early days, everyone hated this assignment and no one wanted it.

But one day, Soichi Obata of the *Nippu Jiji* newspaper volunteered for this assignment together with some other detainees. After they had finished cleaning the tile floor and toilet seats in the early hours of the morning, they were able to relax for the whole day, while others were assigned to pull weeds in the yard all day long, bending over the ground where no weeds grew. Soon, everyone wanted to be assigned to this duty. As a result, Mr. Obata was appointed to make the volunteer assignments.

One morning, I happened to have a bout of diarrhea while Seiha Asami and Ryou Adachi[14] were on duty. I could hardly wait for the inspection to be over. Since Asami and Adachi were my close friends, I asked them to give me a break and let me use the latrine. They flatly refused, even after I promised to mop the floor after I used the toilet. Although I was angry and embarrassed, there was nothing I could do. I sat in the shade of my tent and waited patiently, determined to accept the consequence of staining my pants. I can never forget that hardship.

Group Leader Otani Is Confined to a Cell

It was around January 5, 1942, after the difficult month of December had passed, when eight of us, together with several new detainees, were returning to Sand Island after the hearing at the INS office. George Genji Otani, our spokesman, who was supposed to be at Sand Island at that time, joined us on the boat, accompanied by guards. His hair was disheveled, he was unshaven, and he looked totally down and out. He looked exhausted, and I imagined that something very serious had happened to this brazen-faced man.

Commander Eifler and the wardens always called him by his nickname, "Admiral." And so, someone asked him, "What's happened, Admiral?" He only waved his hand and did not utter a word. We thought that perhaps he was not allowed to speak. I had never seen him so dispirited, he who was always so assertive.

Later, we heard that he had used some insulting words to one of Commander Eifler's subordinates and had been ordered to one week of solitary confinement in a cell at Fort Shafter. There, he was fed only hard crackers and water. I imagined that a gourmet such as he must have suffered a great hardship. He was discharged from his post by the commander and Dr. Kazuo Miyamoto was elected the new spokesman.

Mr. Otani was a unique individual. Once, there appeared in a newspaper, a letter he had written and directed at Consul Arita,[15] accusing the consul general of arrogance. In the early days of our Sand Island life, when no one wanted to be the spokesman and represent the detainees, Mr. Otani willingly accepted the post and took very good care of us. I later heard that after returning to Japan on the first exchange ship, he died in the South Pacific while working as a civilian employee of the Japanese armed forces. He was a skillful man and volunteered for chimney cleaning while interned at Camp McCoy. He worked very hard, climbing the snow-covered roofs, his face blackened by soot. I still remember how energetically he spoke to us.

The Services of Those with Particular Skills

At Sand Island, we received no provisions whatsoever from the government, except for a blanket and a pillow. We lived for more than a month with only the clothes we had been wearing at the time we were arrested. We all looked like beggars in worn clothes, our hair ungroomed. To overcome this difficult situation, we negotiated with the administration for some implements. We expected that those possessing professional skills would volunteer their services. Kazuo Tomita of Tomita Store in Waipahu offered haircuts, as he had previously been engaged in that business. Taichi

Sato of Sato Clothiers agreed to mend our underwear and shirts. We were happy indeed that they volunteered their skills.

We felt confident that we would receive medical care, as there were three doctors among us, namely Motokazu Mori, Kazuo Miyamoto, and Tokuye Takahashi. But we had no dentist. Someone said that Dr. Zensuke Kanashiro might also have been detained, for he knew that Dr. Kanashiro had been active in community work. After a while, Dr. Kanashiro was, in fact, "successfully" detained. We all welcomed his arrival, as if we had been expecting him. Later, when many of us were to be sent to Mainland camps, he asked the authorities to allow him to go with us. They denied his request because no other dentist was available among those remaining at Sand Island. He was eventually sent to Honouliuli Camp, where he remained until the war ended.[16] By the way, Dr. Kanashiro was the only naturalized citizen in Hawai'i to be invited to President Kennedy's inauguration ceremony.

At first, the chief of the mess hall cooks was a German. Later, men like Tokuji Baba, Masao Sakamoto, Masayuki Iwata, Tomoichi Hayashi, and Shigemi Isobe took over the job. At the time, we were extremely short on vegetables. Someone once asked a kitchen worker for a piece of onion. He passed on the word to his boss, but he was turned down because onions were the only ingredient available for flavoring food. I had never before known onion to be that important as a flavoring agent.

Aware that the supply of vegetables was limited, we started growing some in the space outside the fence. Joei Oi, Tomoaki Nakamura, Miyuki Sokabe, Ryoshin Okano, Kakujiro Nishiki, Keisei Kuroda, Jikyo Masaki, and Rev. Kyokujo Kubokawa volunteered to care for the garden. Reverend Kubokawa wore a white Buddhist outfit and went to the field with only the tail of his garment tucked into his pants. It did not look good at all, even though I tried to evaluate his style favorably.

Because of the volunteers' tireless efforts, the vegetables were ready for harvesting by February. We were delighted with the few chances we had to enjoy them, for soon the time would come when we would be sent to the Mainland. A group of about one hundred and sixty of us would leave Honolulu on the first ship, finding it very hard to tear ourselves away from our families.

Attorney Marumoto Comes to See Us

Although Sand Island was very close to our homes in Honolulu, we had no information about what was happening in *shaba* or how our families were doing. We felt as if we had drifted off to a faraway island. Soon after we were detained, someone built a sundial so that we could tell the time of day.

We did not have calendars, so we had to keep a count of the days as they went by. Soon it became very confusing, as it was difficult for us to keep track of the exact date.

One morning, a mess hall worker told us that we were going to have a Christmas meal the following day, which is how we learned exactly what the date was. Everyone talked about the dishes that might be served on Christmas Day.

On the same day, attorney Masaji Marumoto came to see Soga, Sumida, and a few others, including myself. A civilian had never visited us before, so I expected that, as a friend and our store's legal advisor, he would be bringing us good news. When I got to the mess hall, I found Mr. Marumoto looking pale, his face stiff with tension. Instinctively, I knew the news was bad, and I was a little disappointed. But fortunately, he did not bring bad news. I later learned that what had upset him was what he had seen— our dreadful surroundings, our wan appearance, our anxious behavior. He had come to get our signatures on power-of-attorney letters, but we knew it had been just an excuse to see us. Thanks to his visit, I was able to learn how my business and my family were doing.[17]

The next day was Christmas and we had turkey and other delicious treats for lunch. Professor Tauber, a detainee who had been teaching at the University of Hawai'i, presented a lecture.[18] In the mess hall was a crudely decorated Christmas tree that the German detainees had put together. The lunch we had for Christmas was as good as those served in our homes.

A little more than a month later, in February, we were again served the same menu, which left us wondering why. Someone told us that the army had sent a meal just like the one we had received at Christmas to its troops in the Philippines. Unfortunately, before the supplies could reach their destination, Japanese forces had occupied Manila, and the supplies had to be rerouted. We became the lucky recipients. For us detainees, it was quite an unexpected treat, like *botamochi* falling from the shelf.[19]

The Hearings We Had Been Waiting For

Every detainee prayed that a hearing summons would lead, ultimately, to his release. The hearings began in January. When I spoke with detainees who had already been summoned, they told me not to expect much, as it was just a hearing and seemed more like a formality to recognize us as internees. It was clear, however, that no one was giving up hope. We tried to get our most influential Caucasian acquaintances to testify on our behalf.

I had missed my turn earlier because I had been away at the FBI office, so my hearing was postponed. Finally, I was summoned to the INS office in early February. My witnesses were Mrs. Arita, the bookkeeper at my store, and Mr. Valentine, with whom I had business dealings. The hearing was conducted by a five-man committee made up of civilians and military personnel. I was the second person to be questioned that day.[20]

As I waited for my turn in the hallway on the second floor of the main building, I saw Mrs. Arita coming to testify on my behalf. She carried a gas mask that looked like a big canteen slung over her shoulder. I wanted very much to ask her how my family and my business were doing. However, an MP was beside her, so I had no choice but to keep quiet. It was as if I was very thirsty but could not drink water from a fountain right before me.

After a little while, the MP was called away.

"Now's the time," I thought. When I realized I could talk to her, I suddenly became very emotional and my eyes filled with tears. I did not hear even half of her story, however, for the MP returned in no time.

When my turn came, I entered the hearing room and saw the committee members seated at a big table. I could recognize only Senator Akana and Mr. Sylva. The rest were Caucasians, whom I did not know, and an army captain, who was acting as the prosecutor.

My hearing started with the usual questions: What is your name? Where do you live? How old are you? Also, there were questions regarding my family, my profession, organizations I belonged to, and my trips to Japan. Then they asked me three main questions: "Who do you wish to win the war?" "What do you think of Japan having attacked Pearl Harbor without a declaration of war?" "What would you do if Japanese military forces were to land in Hawai'i?"

These questions were asked of most of us, and we had a hard time answering the first question. Since we were Japanese, we hated to say that we wanted Japan to lose. On the other hand, we did not wish for the United States to lose either, because we had lived in this country for many years. And, above all, our children were Americans. Favor one and you betray the other. We were all at a loss as to how to answer the question. The hearing committee had come up with very embarrassing questions, I thought.

"I wish this unfortunate war would end as soon as possible," I answered to the first question. I thought I had done a good job of avoiding the question, but, in truth, it was exactly how I felt at that time.

To the second question, I answered that I did not know anything about strategy. And, finally, to the third question, I replied, "I would watch the situation calmly."

My character witnesses were asked the following sorts of questions: What is your relationship with Mr. Furuya? How long have you known him? Don't you think Mr. Furuya is pro-Japanese? They were relatively simple and ordinary questions. The witnesses' responses were all favorable to me, but I thought none of them would be helpful in securing my release.

At the conclusion, a Caucasian man who looked like the chief judge asked me if I had anything to say. I decided to speak out.

"We Japanese in Hawai'i have been living for many years in this democratic country and have been contributing to business in Hawai'i," I said. "We have educated our children in such a way that they can be proud of themselves as Americans. Now they have grown up and have become loyal U.S. citizens. However, when the war broke out, the government detained the parents of these loyal and good citizens. I fear that such actions will cause them to reconsider their loyalty to this country."

My statement seemed to interest some of the committee members, especially the army captain who was acting as prosecutor. He repeatedly asked for clarification from the Christian minister who was translating my statement. The translator asked me to speak in simpler language.

My hearing ended and I was taken back to the detention facilities. While I was chatting with other detainees after lunch, I was called again.

The Captain's Penetrating Questions

I headed to the main building with the faint hope that I might be freed. I was directed to the captain's office. Seated beside the captain's desk in the large room were George Sakamaki and Katsutoshi Yanaga. They had me sit in between them in front of the captain's large desk, and they offered me a cigarette. I wondered if my wishful thinking had come true.

The captain's questions shattered my expectations when he again started questioning me about my last statement.

"Are you saying that the children of detained Japanese have waivered in their loyalty toward our country because their parents were detained?" he asked.

I was stunned by this question.

"No, I didn't say that. I just wondered if their absolute loyalty might be diminished because of what's happened," I said.

"If so, then how does *your* son feel?"

I was shocked that he had turned the focus on me. I thought it best to not give him the wrong impression, and, wanting to protect my son and my other children, as well, I was confused about how to answer.

"I have not spoken to, nor even corresponded with, my children since my detention. Hanzo, my eldest son, volunteered for the Hawai'i Territorial Guard and is now in service.[21] I may have been overly anxious on the loyalty issue," I said.

The questions had hit a sensitive area and I had become uncomfortable. Fortunately, the captain seemed satisfied, and he became friendlier and offered me a cigarette. I felt he had asked everything he had wanted to. I felt relieved, at last.

Finally, We Become Internees with Serial Numbers

The hearing that had held our hopes for release ended with no results. We had asked witnesses to testify, planned strategies, reminded one another about dos and don'ts, and had gone through so much stress, only to receive a long serial number. The authorities had never intended to release those of us who were on the FBI's blacklist.

The serial number I got was ISN-HJ-188-CI, which stood for Internee Serial Number, Hawai'i Japanese, 188, Civilian Internee. The number seemed to have been given according to my turn in the order of the hearing. If it had been based on arrest order, I should have been lower than number thirty. When I was summoned by the FBI, my hearing was delayed, which must have been the reason my number was in the one-hundred-eighties. Actually, the number itself was not important, but it suggests that the FBI blacklist probably did not include these serial numbers.

When I think of serial numbers, I recall an episode that I would like to share. Since there was no laundry facility at Sand Island, we washed our underwear when we took our showers. Because of this, the shower room became so congested that we were finally given permission to send our underwear to the military laundry. Every piece of underwear had to be labeled with the owner's serial number. Group leaders were responsible for liaising with the soldiers, who took care of sending out and delivering the laundry. But, the soldiers often made mistakes. To prevent this, the internee group secretary came up with a complicated procedure and notified the group leader about it. Mr. Kimura of Nippon Yūsen, a group leader who was slightly neurotic at the time, told secretary Kazoe Kawasaki that he could not comply with such a ridiculous procedure. He insisted that the procedure was a violation of the Geneva Convention and that Mr. Kawasaki should study the convention's clauses.

We can laugh about such incidents now, but at the time, we were all on edge, and the atmosphere of the camp was very tense.

Ordinary Men Forced to Move from One Place to Another

None of those on the FBI's blacklist were released after their hearings, even though they hired top-ranking attorneys and asked influential men to take the witness stand. On the other hand, ordinary people who had done nothing significant and those who had been mistakenly captured were released without a hearing.

Employees of Yokohama Specie Bank, unaware of the unfolding war, had been playing golf at the Moanalua Golf Course in the early morning hours of December 7. All of them were arrested on the spot.[22] Among them, Motoichi Matsuda, general manager; Nihei Miyamoto, assistant general manager; and Toraichi Uyeda were sent to Mainland camps. Isamu Yonemura was interned at Honouliuli, but was later released. Masayuki Adachi, Moritsugu Motoki, Toshikazu Kotake, and Mitsuru Nakamura were freed.

Other men released without hearings included Matsutaro Kamioka, Tokuzo Matsuoka, and Usuke Seri. Among radio station-related people, I believe several were released, namely Fukuo Tarumoto, Mr. Morioka, Mr. Shibata, Tokio Kobayashi, and a few others. Dr. Iga Mori, Miyotsuchi Komeya, Shinkichi Yamamoto of ʻEwa Plantation, and Kyuichi Hamada of Waipahu were released due to their health conditions. Rev. Shinpei Goto, a Christian minister, was freed with the mission to inform the families of our situation. There was a man named Hanaoka, an amateur magician, who was inexplicably arrested and later released.

On the morning of the Pearl Harbor attack, Japanese fishermen on their way back to port were hit by U.S. machine gun fire. Some of them were killed and the others were arrested. People seen around Kewalo Basin also were caught. Among them was an elderly man named Tachibana. At Sand Island, he made *zōri* slippers from morning until night and gave them away to his fellow detainees. Everyone appreciated his gift. There was also Mr. Nakanishi, who had been detained with his fifteen-year-old son. The fishermen were all released, eventually.[23]

There is one interesting episode, if I may be permitted to call it "interesting." It is about a man who made a round trip from Sand Island and the INS office between December 7 and March of the next year due to a lack of communication among the authorities.

One of my friends, Toraichi Yasutake, had gone fishing early on the morning of December 7 and was arrested. Although he was not on the FBI's list, he was taken to Sand Island because an MP had told him, "You have to go."

He followed the other detainees to the INS office for their hearings. Of course, he was not called and was sent back to Sand Island. As time went by, some detainees were released and others were sent to the Mainland. Yet, Mr. Yasutake had not heard anything. After running out of patience, he finally asked Commander Eifler what they intended to do with him.

The commander, who knew Mr. Yasutake fairly well by this time, checked the records and found that he was not on the FBI's list. As a result, Mr. Yasutake was released after a detention of more than ninety days. During that time, he volunteered to work outside the fence and collected cigarette butts dropped by the soldiers and guards, passing them on to the smokers. After our regular barber, Kazuo Tomita, was sent to the Mainland on the first ship, Mr. Yasutake volunteered to give haircuts, despite his lack of experience. After his release, Mr. Yasutake called on the families of detainees to report on how the men were doing.

The Ones Who "Slipped through the Net" and Those Who Were Mishandled

The FBI and military intelligence had begun paying careful attention to the Japanese community as the relationship between Japan and the United States grew increasingly tense. They apparently took pictures of those who welcomed Japanese naval ships and recorded the names of people who visited the Japanese Consulate. That is why they were able to arrest more than one hundred Japanese immediately after the war broke out. However, as I said earlier, many mistakes were made in the confusion.

What we found strange at Sand Island was roll call. The authorities would line us up in the clearing in front of the camp administration office and call the names of people who had not been detained. One of those called was Yaroku Tanaka, president of the *Kazan Shinbun* in Hilo. I wondered why they were calling the name of a Hilo resident. When his name was called again and again, I assumed it was because he had not been in Hilo at the time of his arrest.[24]

One day, they called the name of Rev. Genshin Tatsutani, principal of the Hawaii Japanese Language Middle School. My guess was that he was one of those who had "slipped through the net." His name was called several times, but he was not there. Several days later, principal Tatsutani, looking thin and worn out, came to join us. We asked him what had happened to him and he told us this story: A few days before the war began, he had moved out of the house he had been living in and a young *kibei*[25] man named Toguchi had moved in. Believing that he was Reverend Tatsutani, the FBI arrested Toguchi. At Sand Island, Reverend Tatsutani was nowhere to be found. The young man, of course, insisted that he was not Reverend Tatsutani and did not even know the principal. Finally, convinced that Toguchi was too young and did not appear to be a principal, the authorities conducted a long search and found Reverend Tatsutani. Although he had not gone into hiding, he did have the feeling that someone would eventually come for him, since such Betsuin[26] priests as Reverends Kuchiba, Shinri Sarashina, Suijo Kabashima, and Shushin Matsubayashi had been detained. He had been feeling insecure the whole time and had even grown to fear the sounds of automobiles and telephones.

Zenyu Aoki, a minister with the administrative staff of the Hongwanji Temple in Hilo, was a lucky man who was never taken into custody, since he had just been transferred from Canada and none of his records were in Hawai'i. By the way, he was promoted to bishop of the Honolulu temple after the war.

Most of those who had "slipped through the net" were detained eventually, but they were lucky in that they missed nasty Commander Eifler and all the other hardships, like the toilet shortage on the ship to the Mainland. They also were fortunate that they were later able to see their families.

Among the "lucky" (?) were such friends of mine as Nobutaro Harada, Shigeru Horita, Masao Idemoto, Masao Iwamoto, Takuzo Kawamoto, Zen'ichi Kawazoe, Zenkyo Komagata, Shikatsu Kagesa, Yoshiharu Kodama, Tomomichi Kuraishi, Masao Koga, Iwao Oki, Ryuzo Hirai, Shinjiro Fukutomi, Yasumasa Murata, Kaname Murakami, Seiichi Shimamoto, Giichi Wakamoto, Minoru Urata, Shigeyuki Uemori, Shozo Takahashi, Seiichi Tsuchiya, Kyuzo Terada, Tokuichi Tsuji, and Takeo Yamamoto.

Women Detainees

I do not know much about the women who were detained in the early days. Initially, several were assigned to a wooden two-story house adjacent to the German part of the camp. They were Ishiko Mori; Yoshiye Miyao, the widowed mother of Reverend Miyao; Yuki Miyao, Reverend Miyao's wife; Haru Tanaka, principal of the Wahiawa Japanese Language School; Tsuta Yamane; and others. They were treated nicely in the camp, for this country respects women. Unlike her husband, Mrs. Eifler,[27] who was in charge of the women, was especially nice to them. Not only did she allow them to see their husbands once a week, but she also let them have lunch together. We have a saying, "The wife of a devil is like a Buddha."[28]

One day, Dr. Mori returned to his tent after seeing his wife.[29]

"How was it?" I asked, jokingly. "You look so happy."

"Not bad," he grinned. "Mrs. Eifler is very open-minded and knows what the love between husband and wife is. Commander Eifler does not deserve her."

He confirmed my guess that the other women in captivity were happy with her, too. He said that all the ladies were very appreciative of her and had asked him to petition the Japanese commander to assure her release in the event that the Japanese army were to successfully land in Hawai'i and capture Commander Eifler and his wife. He said this with a smile on his face.

Mrs. Mori was a correspondent for the newspaper the *Yomiuri Shimbun* and had received a telephone call from its Tokyo head office a few days before the war. Thus, the investigation of her was quite intensive.[30] Haru Tanaka was the widow of the late Tekisui Tanaka and was a *toritsuginin* for the Japanese Consulate. She also greeted Japanese training ships, taking with her many of her female students from faraway Wahiawā. She must have been detained for these reasons.[31]

As I mentioned earlier, Mrs. Miyao and Mrs. Yamane were detained accidentally.

Shizuyo Takechi was a young lady who lived near my house and worked for the *Nippu Jiji*. I was so surprised to see her in the camp. She must have been caught because she was a fervent believer in the Konkōkyō religion and wanted to become a missionary.[32] Shizuyo had just married a man named Yoshioka and was expecting a child. She was later released because of her pregnancy. I suppose Mrs. Miyao and Mrs. Yamane might have been freed, as well, had they been pregnant. Ladies interned later were the nun Shinsho Hirai, the wife of Kosaku Horibe, the nun Kanzen Ito, Miyuki Kawasaki, Ryuto Tsuda, Haruko Takahashi, Yasuye Takahashi, Masako Fujimura, widow Umeno Harada of the Ni'ihau Incident, and the Nisei minstrel Teruchiyo Suzuki.[33]

My Fourth Visit to the INS Office

Tent life at Sand Island was not at all hygienic. We placed low canvas cots on the damp soil and slept on blankets, just like dogs. However, hardly anyone became sick, perhaps because we were constantly on edge. In time, four two-story barracks were built in a clearing on the 'Ewa side[34] of the camp. We were soon able to harvest vegetables from our farm, so we were happy to see that our life was improving.

On the afternoon of February 17, the sound of a whistle ripped through the air, and everyone was ordered to line up in the clearing in front of the administration office. We feared there had been another incident. The commander took out a list and said that those whose names he called were to gather with their belongings and go to a designated area. At first we thought that they were going to release us, and a roar came up from us. As the commander called out our names in alphabetical order, mine came up quickly. I was very excited and rushed to the designated area with my belongings. It felt somewhat strange to see so many people assembling. About 170 people gathered, leaving only twenty or thirty behind. I felt sorry for them when I saw them waving at us as we left the camp in high spirits. We were taken to the INS office and placed in the detention facilities that I had already been in three times before.

The following morning, February 18, we were called, in alphabetical order, to the main building. When I got to the building, several MPs were there. One by one, we were instructed to stand in a specific position in front of a white background. A plate with large numbers on it was at my side, and my picture was taken from various angles. I felt uncomfortable as they photographed me, just as they would a prisoner. But my wishful thinking still led me to believe that I was going to be released, perhaps on the condition that I would be watched.

Then, used military boots and overcoats were distributed to everyone. I wondered what had brought this about, since we had never been given anything before. I slowly came to realize that our chances of being released were almost none. But, I must confess that somewhere in my mind, I held on to a glimmer of hope that I would be released.

When we got back to the detention facilities, we all felt uneasy and began talking about what was going to happen to us. Some were still optimistic, but most of us had already become quite despairing.

Notified We Are Being Sent to the Mainland

As we were discussing our fate, attorney Masaji Marumoto entered the room.

"I am very sorry to tell you this, but the army has decided to send all of you to the Mainland," he said. "We, the members of the Emergency Service Committee,[35] will tell your families of your transfer. You will be allowed to take one suitcase with you, and you may ask your families to send you up to fifty dollars. We will gladly pass on your messages to your families if you wish."

The shocking news left us speechless. We knew it had been merely a hope that we would be released, but once clearly informed to the contrary, we were so disappointed. Committee members Masaji Marumoto, Masatoshi Katagiri, Isao Murai, Katsumi Kometani, Yasuo Goto, and Shigeo Yoshida kindly helped us.[36]

When it came time to give them my message to my family, tears welled up, and I could hardly utter a word. Some of us began to cry.

We tried on the overcoats that we had been given. They turned out to be very heavy. Someone complained that he did not want to wear his. The shoes, all big, were not of much use to people with small feet. The shoes I had been given were originally for an officer and were made of softer and lighter leather, so everyone envied me.

Our families had a hard time buying things like overcoats, socks, handkerchiefs, sweaters, and underwear for us, for we were allowed to carry only one suitcase each. Besides, they had to work hastily to sew name labels on all of these items within the limited time before our departure. In the end, their efforts went unrewarded. Our baggage was not loaded onto the ship that we boarded, but rather was delivered to us at Camp McCoy on April 24, by which time the snow had melted and the weather had become much warmer.

Likewise, the money our families sent us through the army reached us about a year later, on February 1, 1943. In the meantime, we tried many times to request delivery of our money as soon as possible, but our efforts were in vain. The reason for the delay was that with all of our families sending money to a central location, the total amount became so large that the account was frozen, in accordance with regulations governing the assets of hostile nationals. Although it seems unthinkable now, such unreasonable incidents did actually occur. Because our money was frozen, we could not afford to buy even airmail postage stamps to send letters to our families after we had reached Camp McCoy.

At the INS office in Honolulu, there was a group of detainees who had been arrested after us. Among them, Dr. Akio Kimura, Dr. Yukihide Kohatsu, Rev. Jikai Yamasato, and Koichiro Nakamura joined us on the first ship to the Mainland.

From the window of a separate second-floor room, Takuzo Kawamoto, Seigo Miwa, and several others watched us as we left.

| 5 |

Embarking on a Wanderer's Journey

Like a Funeral Procession

It is hard to describe the atmosphere at the INS office the night before our departure for the Mainland—a kind of tragic scene, you might say. Some of us were quiet, some sang sad songs and talked in an attempt to be cheerful, while still others wept.

After roll call the next morning, 172 internees were loaded onto more than a dozen military trucks. Guarded by cars armed front and back with machine guns, the convoy departed from the oceanside of the INS office. It was nine o'clock in the morning on February 20, 1942. The convoy looked like a motorcade for a military funeral. We stared out from the trucks, hoping to see our families. But we saw no one as the trucks sped their way to Pier 27.

At the pier, the USS *Grant* was waiting for us. We walked down to the hold through a narrow passage, carrying over our shoulder a large *'āhina*[1] duffel bag that had been distributed to each of us. After we were all on board, Matsujiro Otani of 'A'ala Market and Yoshihiko Ozu, a teacher at the Hawai'i Japanese Language Middle School, were called off the ship. We talked about the possible reasons for their removal. The rumor was that Mr. Otani had been released because he was close to William Heen, and Mr. Ozu because he was a brother-in-law of attorney Marumoto. However, we learned later that our assumptions were wrong. Mr. Otani was removed because he was ill, and Mr. Ozu because the condition of his sick father had worsened. Both of them were later sent to the Mainland.

As we entered the hold, each of us was given a life jacket and instructed on how to wear it. After drilling us on the use of the life jacket, the guards locked the iron doors and went away. We felt very insecure as we thought about how we might sink with the ship if it were attacked by a submarine and the guards failed to open the doors.

We knew nothing about what was going on, for we were kept in the hold the entire time. The ship did not sail out that day. It left port at five o'clock the next afternoon, February 21.

Although Dr. Akio Kimura seemed tired after our two-month detention at the INS office, we asked him to continue as our spokesman.

At Least the Meals Are as Good as a Passenger Ship's

We were kept in the hold in the bow of the ship. My roommates were Josen Deme, Heigo Fuchino, Seiichi Fujii, Shoho Fujiie, Kenkichi Fujimoto, Hideo Fujisawa, Utanosuke Fujishiro, Teiichiro Fukuda, and Kyoichi Hamamura.

Meals were served in the galley at the stern, so we walked there with our life jackets on, as instructed. It was a strange sight to see so many men standing in a long line wearing life jackets. The galley was very large and grand. The food, served cafeteria-style, was very good.

Our ship appeared to be part of a convoy made up of five or six ships, all carrying civilians and military families returning to the Mainland. As we were lining up for our meal one day, we noticed a newspaper that had been left on a table nearby. The headline read, "Japs Smashed Near Bali." We did not think much of it, since none of us knew where Bali was, although the word "smashed" shocked us. Some people became angry, thinking that some mean-spirited serviceman had placed it there intentionally.

Toilet Hell

Since our arrest, although we had experienced many difficulties, using the toilet had been trouble free. But now on this ship, we were permitted to go to the toilet only once every three hours. We could do nothing but wait until the time came, for the iron door was kept locked. Mr. Hattori,[2] the assistant general manager of Sumitomo Bank, who was always gentle and looked rather noble, once kept calling for a guard while banging on the door more than a dozen times because he could wait no longer. We were all surprised and wondered if he had gone insane.

When the time came, long lines formed instantly. We had to wait a long time for our turn. To solve this problem, Dr. Kimura suggested that garbage cans be placed in the hallway leading to the toilets so we could urinate in the cans. The cans filled up quickly, and we had to empty them somehow. Finally, we asked the younger internees to carry them to the toilet. This solved the urine problem, but not the feces issue. The ones waiting their turn urged those inside to get out quickly, but the men inside could not act very fast under such pressure. It was no laughing matter for those who waited patiently, all the while massaging their bellies and groaning in pain.

Troubles Aboard Ship

Although I enjoyed cruises, I had never before experienced as dreary and unpleasant a voyage as this one. Of course, I hadn't expected it to be an enjoyable one, but it was much worse than I had imagined. As many as fourteen internees were cooped up in a small cabin in the hold. Bunk beds filled most of the cabin space. There were no tables or chairs, and we had no space to move around. The cabin was dark, for the lighting was poor, and we had no books to read. All we could do was talk amongst ourselves. But, because of our fear of a possible submarine attack, no one felt like telling bawdy stories like we used to. Playing solitaire was the only entertainment we had to divert us from feeling scared.

On the third day or so, we were given a typhoid vaccine for the second time. When we received the first shot at the INS office, some people became sick and others were unable to lift their arm, so many did not welcome it. One of them, Mr. Sanko Harada,[3] had the misfortune of receiving one-and-a-half shots the second time around. This happened when the syringe needle inserted by the apparently inexperienced corpsman broke midway. It was finally removed, but Mr. Harada had to be given another injection. The experience must have made him irritable, for he picked on Reverend Fujisawa, whose cot was next to his. We were embarrassed by his behavior, but felt some pity for him.

It was Reverend Fujiie of the Hongwanji Mission who brightened up the atmosphere by talking to others cheerfully and singing songs with somewhat off-color lyrics. By contrast, Reverend Fujishiro, a Christian minister who may have been feeling sick, looked depressed and kept quiet the whole time. His attitude made all of us feel gloomy.

The Ship Stops Suddenly

Sometime around eleven o'clock on the morning of the fifth day, the ship suddenly stopped, and an emergency call was made through the PA system to all the crew and servicemen aboard. We were instructed to put on our life jackets. I realized that even with our life jackets on, we would barely reach shore in the lifeboats if our ship were sunk, for it seemed that we were at the halfway point between Hawai'i and the Mainland. The sea appeared very calm, and the waves that lapped at the belly of the stalled ship were gentle. Nonetheless, the quiet felt like the calm before a storm, and it gave us an eerie feeling.

TWO HAIKU

An alarm sounds
Ship engines stop
Pounding waves in the silence
Lonely and empty the sound
信号に船はぴったり止まりて船腹を打つ波音わびし

I wonder, will my compatriots board later?
Should I leave writings
On the walls of this ship's hold?
同胞がまた乗ることのありやなしや船壁にもの書きて置かまし

The ship was stopped for about one-and-a-half hours, but nothing happened. We then resumed our journey. We were all relieved when we were told to take off our life jackets, but even after I had gone to bed, I could not fall asleep for a long time.

Memories of Sand Island

In the monotony of daily life on the ship, I thought back on my seventy days at Sand Island and realized that life there had not been so bad. I even found myself rather missing those days. Sand Island Camp was located very close to downtown Honolulu, and yet we had felt as if we were living in another world, for the island was covered with trees and in total darkness at night.

Late one night, as I headed to the latrines located near the edge of the camp, I heard no sounds from the tents. It was a full moon, and the moonlight shining so peacefully made it feel like it was peacetime. The line of tents cast long shadows on the ground, as if a large *sumi-e*[4] had been painted there. For a while, I indulged myself in this scene, forgetting about my circumstances. Internment, if I may say so, helped me rediscover the beauty of the stars, something I had forgotten about for so many years.

In a blacked-out camp, with only a wide-open sky, we had nothing to do but stare at the heavens. On clear nights, I watched the stars to console myself about the wasting of time. I had never watched the Southern

Cross before, although I was intrigued by its romantic name. Listening to Dr. Tokuye Takahashi's lectures on such solar satellites as Mercury, Venus, Mars, Jupiter, Saturn, and the Milky Way became my entertainment. He taught us that the Southern Cross is visible before dawn, just above the southern horizon. One morning, I got up early and watched the southern sky from the field. The sky was very clear, and I could see four stars shining brightly in a cross-like pattern. They were so beautiful and overwhelmingly brighter than any other stars nearby. After that, I made a point of getting up early so I could enjoy watching the Southern Cross and breathe in deeply the early morning air.

I used to be a late riser, but I found it worthwhile to get up earlier, for Mr. Hamamoto, our group leader, would come to each tent while it was still dark, offering a fire to light our cigarettes. Thanks to him, I woke up and enjoyed a cigarette every morning. I still remember and miss his ringing voice.

On the other hand, there were some things that really bothered us. We were quite annoyed by the noises of the dredging boats working all night long at Kalihi Basin. We did not mind them so much during the day, but they made us feel anxious at night, even though their noise was not very loud. Another thing that bothered us were the fighter planes—a dozen or so of them would fly over us every morning as they headed toward Moloka'i. It felt as if they were threatening us. It was not frightening, but it did always remind us that we were at war, and that was depressing.

In the Mainland camps, we rarely heard any aircraft noise, but while living in Kalihi after my return to Hawai'i at the end of the war, whenever I heard an airplane flying overhead, I would feel as though I was back at Sand Island. It always reminded me of those days.

Haiku Written at the Beginning of My Detention

Has war begun?
They've come to arrest me
So quickly
戦争になったのかもう私を捕へに来た

Aware of his pistol
My hands move
To put on my coat
ピストルを感じている手がコートを着る

So war is like this
I tell myself
As I am hauled away
戦争とはこうしたものか引かれて行く

Forced to ride this car of destiny
Instructions blare from the radio
乗せられてる運命の車ラジオの命令が鳴りつめる

Words uttered in the pitch darkness
So, my friends are imprisoned too
真っ暗闇知り人の声もして囚われている[5]

Marched through the *kiawe*
Surrounded
By soldiers with bayonets
キアベの茂る中銃剣にかこまれて行く

Under the winter sky
The silence broken
Only by our footsteps
冬空声なしわれらの足音ばかり

After a meal
The taste of a cigarette
My only pleasure
たのしみは食後の一本の煙草の味

Lined up in rows
Stark naked
The evening darkness draws near
はだかにされて並んでいる夕暮せまる

Throughout the moonlit camp
One after another
The shadows of tents
テントのかげがかげへつづくキャンプが月夜で

The moon turns full
For the first time
Since our detention
捕えられてからのキャンプの月が満月になる

Stars light my way
Into the pitch dark tent
星明りでまっくらなテントへはいる

HAIKU WRITTEN AT THE INS OFFICE:

Beyond the barred windows
Of the detention room
The moon should be rising now
監禁室の鉄窓いま月が昇るらしい

Guarded by cars with machine guns
We depart in a motorcade
Like a funeral
機関銃にかこまれ葬列の如く我等行く

From inside the truck
We strain for a glimpse
But see no family
護送車から見ても見ても家族は見えない

The duffel bag on my shoulder
Bumps me many times
As we force our way into the hold
肩の振分け荷物がごつごつ船艙へ追い込まれる

My cabin in the hold
Lit by a dim lamp
So this is home for now
ここがしばしのすまいか船底電燈が赤い

Our Arrival in San Francisco

Ten days had passed since we had been put in the ship's hold with no chance to see daylight. We were relieved to see crewmen joyfully polishing their shoes, for we thought it meant that we would soon be arriving at our destination and disembarking. Both crewmen and servicemen were busily going back and forth. The activity onboard picked up, and even we became a little excited.

At four o'clock in the afternoon on March 1, our ship docked in San

Francisco. We were allowed to go on deck and take in the fresh air. It was like drinking water when one is very thirsty.

THREE HAIKU:

Fresh air at last
All is bathed in violet
やっと空気へ出た空気がむらさき色だ

On the ship's deck
I brave the bright glare
Inhaling my fill of air
まばゆくデッキで空気をたくさん吸う

Ten long days
Our life in the hold
Without sunlight
数へて十日陽のない船底のくらしも

All of us disembarked carrying our duffel bags over our shoulders. I cannot say that we had finally landed on Mainland soil, for the whole area was covered with concrete.

As usual, it took a long time to finish roll call. Contrary to my expectation that we would be going inland, we were ordered onto a small boat, and after we had all gotten on board, it headed northward. Very close by, to our left, we could see Alcatraz Island, where Al Capone had been imprisoned. We did not think that we would be taken there, but we were worried nonetheless, not knowing exactly where we were heading. Soon the boat passed Alcatraz and sailed into San Francisco Bay. Far to the left, we saw the famous Golden Gate Bridge. A big red moon was rising in the sky over Alameda. It was very dramatic and impressive.

The boat turned left and approached a rather large island. We learned later that it was called Angel Island. It was already dark when we landed at the pier. We walked up the hill to an old, wooden building. A former INS facility, it contained many bunk beds. After dinner, we went through the usual physical examination, but this time it was very thorough. We were told to strip naked and get down on all fours so that our anuses could be checked. They even confiscated our aftershave lotion, which had passed all previous inspections. Naturally, our first impression of the Mainland was very negative. It was almost midnight when they were done examining us, and we took to the bunk beds to dream our first dream of the Mainland.

The next morning, March 2, was cold, but comfortable. We walked to the adjacent building for breakfast. There I saw Ensign Sakamaki in clothing marked with the large letters "PW." I had seen him only from a distance at Sand Island and had thought he looked like a fearless young man. But seeing him now at close range, he appeared to me gentle, and even humble, as I watched him get his meal from the kitchen workers.[6]

| 6 |

Angel Island

Hummingbirds among the Green Leaves

Although the physical examination was very severe, the officers, noncommissioned officers, and guards were nice to us. Angel Island turned out to be better than I had expected. In the morning, mist covered the entire bay area, while sirens and alarms sounded in unison. They were very loud, but somehow did not seem noisy. Instead, they created a rather lively and cheerful atmosphere.

Behind the building was a small field on a hill. Bushes grew around the field, and I happened to find apricot flowers blooming among the green leaves. Birds were singing, and it felt as if spring were here. Then, I saw a bird hovering among the green leaves. It looked just like a hanging *orizuru*,[1] floating motionlessly in the air. It reminded me of the hummingbirds I had read about during my school days. As I was watching the hummingbird, I heard the voices of children walking along a road in the middle of the woods beyond. It was the first time I had heard children's voices since being taken from my home just three months earlier, but it felt as if I had not heard this sound for years. I thought of my own children and, for a moment, I was filled with emotion.

As I was standing there lost in thought, a gentleman walked up to me. Brought back to reality, I began a conversation. The gentleman was Hisashi Tominaga, who had come originally from Kagoshima. He had been caught in Pago Pago, Samoa, and sent all alone to this camp. He had been working for the Dollar Steamship Company there and had married a chief's daughter, who was said to be quite passionate and attractive. At Camp McCoy, he offered his support at a time when we were experiencing some hardship. I will tell you more about this later.

From the hill, I could see the Alameda, Oakland, Berkeley, and Richmond areas, with the famous Bay Bridge in the foreground. It looked like a *hako-niwa*[2] on a huge scale.

Since I had nothing to do, I took my underwear, which I had crammed into my duffel bag, and washed them with plenty of soap, not minding how much time I spent. All my stained underwear became so clean and white. As I hung them out to dry in the backyard, the mist cleared, as if it had been waiting for me to finish my laundry. It was so pleasant under the sun that I began whistling, something I had not done for a long time.

The Poems of Chinese Immigrants

Even though I enjoyed the area's scenery, with nothing much to do, I became bored. I was walking aimlessly around a big hall when I noticed the walls were covered with graffiti. I was surprised to see that the marks had been engraved, most likely with knives. There were many kinds of graffiti, and I assumed they had been made by Chinese immigrants long ago. They were all written in Chinese, and there were many characters that I did not completely understand. I found the following poem to be in a typical seven-character format.[3]

> A thousand sorrows and a hatred ten-thousand-fold burns between my brows.
> Hoping to step ashore the American continent is the most difficult of difficulties.
> The barbarians imprison me in this place.
> Even a martyr or a hero would change countenance.
> 千秋萬恨燃眉間
> 望登美洲難上難
> 番奴把我囚困此
> 烈士英雄亦失顏

One can deduce from this poem that Chinese immigrants must have been treated inhumanely in the early days. The guards must have humiliated them, ignoring their human rights. But it seemed to me that the poem used exaggeration, as is typical in Chinese writing. I admired the way they translated English terms with appropriate Chinese characters. I thought the choice of characters for "guards" 番奴 was admirably appropriate—"guys on watch."[4] By the way, America is written in Chinese characters as "beautiful states" 美洲.

I went east to Asia; I went west to Europe.
I came to the South, to North America, where the harsh exclusion
    laws cause me worry.
Allowing you to enter the place of imprisonment,
Even if you don't shed tears, you will lower your head.

東走亜兮西走歐
南來北美苛禁愁
任君入到囚困此
若不流涕也低頭

For the sake of the mouth, I rushed about and must tolerate
    humiliation.
I gritted my teeth, clutched the brush, and recorded the circumstances.
The day my compatriots become prosperous and return to China,
They should once more outfit battleships to punish America.

為口奔馳須忍辱
咬牙秉筆録情由
同胞発達回唐日
再整戦艦伐美洲

    It appears that the man who wrote the first poem was eventually allowed to land. But the man who worked on the second poem must have been rejected and sent back to his country.[5] He was probably very patriotic. I had no idea when it was written, as it had no date. The last two lines might give the impression that the poet was a megalomaniac, but China is a huge country with a long and glorious history, so perhaps he was simply expressing his pride as a Chinese citizen. Generally speaking, graffiti is considered nonsense, but I think these poems carry serious messages. Although they may have been engraved one hundred, or even one hundred and fifty, years earlier, I can understand how the two Chinese immigrants may have felt.

Our Exercises Surprise the Soldiers

Captain Eifler, the commander at Sand Island Camp, was a mean fellow, but he considered the health of the internees to be a top priority, and he encouraged us to perform physical exercises. Rev. Suijo Kabashima was appointed the instructor, and he always shouted orders vigorously in a rich and ringing voice. Thanks to his leadership, even the elderly joined his exercise sessions every day. It made us feel healthy.

Since leaving Sand Island, we had not exercised at all. Many intern-ees wanted to participate in some sort of exercise, so we decided to hold sessions in the field on the hill. Reverend Kabashima was a well-built man and held a fifth-grade black belt in judo. Having served in the Jap-anese army, he gave orders in a very loud voice. Soldiers in the barracks on the hill beyond must have thought something had happened because many of them gathered on the hill to watch us. Someone apparently made a telephone call to our guards because two soldiers came hurrying to the field. Upon seeing what we were doing, they left quickly, smiling bemusedly.

Every morning, the mist never failed to rise up over San Francisco Bay, always vanishing at around ten o'clock. It was so refreshing to see the fuel tanks on the other side of the bay, in Richmond—pure white, as if they had been cleansed by the mist.

It had not rained at all since our arrival. According to a guard, resi-dents of the area rarely experienced this kind of weather.

"It's probably because the Japanese were sent here," this friendly man said. We laughed at his joke. He also told us that those sirens and alarms we had been hearing were set to sound automatically when a thick fog covered the area. We were very curious as to why so many soldiers were stationed here. He replied that an army reception center was located on the island and that servicemen from various parts of the United States assembled there before deploying to the Pacific theater.

HAIKU WRITTEN AT ANGEL ISLAND

On a small boat
We head to an island
A red moon rises
島へ送らるる小蒸汽へ赤い月が出た

Moonlight on my back
My shadow lands
On an unknown island
月を背に知らぬ島へ上陸するわが影

When fog covers the bay
Sirens blare
Alarms ring
湾を霧が覆うと鳴り出す警笛や警鐘

Birds are free and sing at dawn
We feel only envy
In captivity
あかつきをさえずる小鳥ら捕われのわれら

Hummingbirds among the shrubs
Hover motionless
Leaves tremble
青葉がゆるる蜂雀はうごかず青葉のなか

At long last!
My chance to do laundry
A thorough washing
洗濯するチャンスを得たきれいに洗う

Under the bright sunlight
I dry my fresh white underwear
朝日へまっ白になった洗濯を干す

Although we had not yet received any notice, we nevertheless felt
that our departure was near at hand. I wanted to write to my family, but
I could not buy the five-cent postage stamp for I had no money at all.
Someone who had carried prepaid postcards gave them to Dr. Kimura, saying, "Please distribute these to those who need them." I was fortunate to
receive one and wrote a note crammed with small lettering. I was relieved
that I had been able to write to my family and felt ready to be interned
anywhere on the continent.

Unintentional Abuse of the Elderly

On our fifth day at Angel Island, just as we were expecting new orders, there
came a call to gather at the field on the hill. The area was so small that we
had to form in three lines. The commander and his lieutenant studied our
faces. Then, they called a group of people and had them line up in a separate area. In this group were elderly men like Reverend Kubokawa; Reverend Kuchiba; principal Inokuchi; Reverend Ikezawa; Reverend Nago;
Reverend Shimoda; and Mr. Toyama, a company president. We wondered
why they had been selected. Someone in our group suggested that these
elderly men were probably going to be given sleeping berths on the train.
This made enough sense that the rest of the elderly people waited eagerly
for their names to be called.

After the oldest-looking man had been called, it was the next older generation's turn. Kyoichi Hamamura, who was fluent in English, and George Otani left their places in line and went to speak with the commander. But Mr. Hamamura looked younger than he really was, and he was rejected. The next group was made up of balding or gray-haired men like Mr. Kawamoto of the *Nippu Jiji*,[6] Sanko Harada, Kusuro Ishida, Takeo Miyagi, principal Nada,[7] Kichitaro Sekiya, engineer Takinosuke Toyama, Mr. Hattori of Sumitomo Bank, and Aisuke Shigekuni. Again, Hamamura and Otani patiently negotiated with the commander and were finally accepted. Thus was formed a group of forty to fifty detainees who were supposed to board the sleeper cars.

We, the younger group, would end up having a hard time, for we had to remain seated in the cars for the entire three-night and four-day trip. After we arrived at Camp McCoy, we asked the elderly group how they had fared during the journey. They said it had been agonizing to spend the entire trip in upright seats with no reclining mechanism—like traveling in a third-class car in old Japan. In our cars, the windows had been covered with wire screens, but the seats could recline, so we were better off. Their only advantage was that their windows had no wire screens, so they had an unobstructed view of the outside. We wondered why they had selected such an elderly group to ride in such a junky car. We theorized that these elderly men could not have escaped through the windows, and even if they had, they would have been easily identified by their balding heads or silver hair. Later, we found out that our theory was correct.

Those unlucky people who had expected better treatment not only experienced hardship, but also lived bitter lives afterward. I say this because most of them were assigned to the same barracks. Many were argumentative, critical, or eccentric, so there was constant dissension. Mr. Sumida was nominated barracks captain, but he declined. No one wanted the post, which was quite embarrassing. We nominated Mr. Kawamoto, but he declined, although eventually the good-natured man was forced to accept. I lived in the barracks next to theirs and often heard people arguing in loud voices.

I know the meaning of the word "godsend," but it was quite the opposite of that in this case. It was like expecting to hold in your hand a precious jewel, but receiving a lump of mud instead. I really felt sorry for this unfortunate elderly group. This was yet another example of how incidents of tragicomedy are often born of our indulgence in wishful thinking.

| 7 |

To the Interior of the Mainland

The Snowy Sierra Nevadas

We had enjoyed fairly well our five-day stay at Angel Island, but the morning had now come when we were to be moved farther inland. At around ten, the mist that had covered San Francisco Bay cleared to reveal a cloudless sky. The waters of the bay were very calm and peaceful, looking exactly like a spring sea.

Our boat sailed out of Angel Island, past San Francisco on our right and Richmond on our left. We passed Treasure Island, where the Exhibition had been held,[1] sailed under the Bay Bridge, and docked past noon at a pier in Oakland. We underwent roll call again, as usual, and boarded a train that was waiting for us. The train cars were old and run-down and seemed to not have been used for many years. We wanted to wipe away the dust from the windows, but wire screens had been installed on the front of them, so our hands could not reach through to clean the glass surfaces. We had no choice but to poke our handkerchiefs through the mesh, and in this way, we cleaned the windows enough to get a dim view of the outside.

The train proceeded north along the Sacramento River. As we passed over a bridge, a wide plain came into sight. It appeared to be a ranch, for we could see herds of sheep. After a while, we passed beautiful blooming trees of cherry or, perhaps, peach. It was a large orchard, and it looked as if a cloud of pink flowers was trailing behind us.

At about five o'clock, we arrived at Sacramento Station. Curious, I looked through the window at a neon sign that read "Euro Saloon." The area looked like the suburbs of a city, and it reminded me of the Shibuya district of Tokyo in the early days. The snow-capped Sierra Nevada range could be seen in the distance.

We had our dinner while stopped at this station. For the first time during our detention, we did not have to line up for our meal. Instead, we were served in our seats by polite Negro waiters. This we appreciated very much.

At about six-thirty, the train stopped again at a station that we did not know. The sun had already set, so we pulled our window shades down and spent some time playing cards. At nine-thirty or so, we reclined our seats and went to sleep. As the night grew deeper, it became colder and I woke up several times.

When I awoke the next morning, everything outside was covered in snow. The cattle in the pasture looked cold as they huddled together. I had no idea how far the train had traveled while we had been asleep. Somehow, however, I was sure that we were somewhere in Nevada. An army major, accompanied by an army surgeon, came to conduct an inspection, so I asked them where we were. They just smiled and said nothing.

FOUR HAIKU

The plains stretch beyond the horizon
We pass tree after tree, house after house
野は地平線まで果なく樹があると家ある

A fruit orchard
A compatriot's, perhaps
Its blooms like cherry blossoms
同胞の果樹園か花が桜のような

A snowy plain before sunrise
Cattle huddle together
日の出まえの雪野牛等かたまっている

Our train rumbles across the snowy plain
As the sun breaks through
雪野走る我等の汽車へお日さまが出た

We traveled over plain after plain. Then a huge lake that looked like an ocean became visible in the distance. We were sure it was the Great Salt Lake. At the fairly large Alta Station, the dining car was replaced, and we were given better meals. Caucasian waiters served us, and the food tasted better than before. It may have been just a coincidence, but it seemed that the farther east we traveled, the better we were treated.

There, the time changed to Mountain Standard Time, so we advanced our watches one hour ahead of California time. On the mountain-side of the train, we could see Salt Lake City, but we would not have a chance to see the famous Mormon Temple because the train windows were so dirty.

Over the Rockies

As our train traveled through the Rockies, we enjoyed seeing the steep mountains and frozen waterfalls. We watched with great curiosity until finally the beautiful scenery vanished in the twilight. The slow-moving train climbed slope after slope, groaning all night long. When I awoke the next morning, the train was still climbing the central Rockies at an altitude of more than ten thousand feet.

After a while, the train entered a tunnel, and it took us about ten minutes to go through it. We were then fed breakfast, the third of this trip. This meal, eaten at an altitude of ten thousand feet, was even more delicious—especially the coffee. As we entered Colorado, we saw many Christmas trees with gracefully shaped branches growing splendidly in the snowy fields. We passed through many short tunnels, and I was reminded of the experience of traveling the Chūō Railway Line. At about eight o'clock, we came out of a tunnel and were greeted by the lovely sight of a great snowy field reflecting the morning sunlight.

The train finally crossed the Great Rockies, and we arrived in Denver at nine-thirty. The size of the train station was staggering. I learned that the city was a transfer hub for all of the western and central railway routes. Here, again, our dining car and waiters changed, and so did the food that we were given. It took two hours to change tracks at Denver, going back and forth in the station yard. It was one-thirty when the train finally left, headed in a northwesterly direction. Nothing but desert-like plains continued endlessly, with no woods or rivers. Even though snow could barely be seen, it was still cold. At about five-thirty, the train stopped at a station, where we advanced our watches an hour to adjust to Central Standard Time. At night, we passed a pretty town where neon lights glowed. I guessed it was Sidney and asked a guard if this was correct, but he did not answer.

By then, we had been sitting for three days and two nights. Our bodies were very stiff, and it was extremely painful to remain in the same position. A few people lay down with their legs across the seats and their head sticking out into the aisle. We passed through hilly areas between the mountains, and the train took sharp turns as it went up and down the slopes. Because I was extremely tired, I fell into a state of semi-consciousness and dozed, as though I were roaming a wonderland.

FOUR HAIKU

Looking down on a vast snowy land
The morning sun shines
Through my train window
見下ろせて大雪原朝日さす車窓

While snow falls
The train speeds headlong
Through snow-covered fields
汽車は雪の中を雪野へまっ下りに下る

Passing through desolate fields
For how many days
Have we traveled on this continent?
枯野が続く大陸や走り走りていくにち

Over the desolate fields
Nothing but the faraway horizon
なんにも無い枯野地平線は遥かにある

The Interesting Scenery of the Northern States

We traveled through the mountains all night long. When we finally reached the plains, we were given breakfast. Many trees grew here and large fields came into view, one after another. Roofs were pentagon-shaped, and silos stood like towers beside the houses. They stood in nice contrast to each other. The whole scene was well composed, as if it were a painting. This kind of scenery was characteristic of America's northern region, and all of us stared out at it with curiosity. In Japan, too, one can see such scenery in Hokkaidō. The pentagonal shape of the roofs makes it easy to remove the snow when it piles up. The silos are used to store fodder during the wintertime so that the leaves can be kept green.

Our train passed through Nebraska and across Iowa. As we headed north, it became colder and colder. At around noon, we reached the southern part of Minnesota. We passed through dense forests of oak and white birch. After crossing the upper portion of the Mississippi River, we arrived in Wisconsin. I thought that we would be arriving at our destination sometime within the day. After a while, a light snow began to fall.

At three-thirty on March 9, 1942, we arrived at Camp McCoy in Sparta, Wisconsin. As our train entered the local line, I saw to our right barracks in the snow. They were surrounded by barbed wire fences. I could see several people who looked like they had arrived earlier—they looked like our countrymen.

FOUR HAIKU DEPICTING THE VIEWS FROM THE TRAIN:

Through the forest
Houses come into sight
A silo in the northern country
Stands in the twilight
森あると家ありて北国サイロが夕陽のなか

Needles of ice grow
On the surface
Of an ice-covered brook
氷はりつめし小川の氷の上にも霜

Snow falls gently
On streams and steel bridges
Of this foreign land
河や鉄橋やしらぬ土地の雪がちらつく

Red sunlight reflects off a tombstone
Its marble casts a cold light
赤い陽が墓地へ大理石のつめたい光り

We had endured a painful journey of four days and three nights. We got off the train, carrying our duffel bags on our shoulders. We then lined up and walked to the camp. It was quite a strange sight—men, young and old, marching through the snow in second-hand military overcoats and straw hats.

The camp, once occupied by National Park Service workers,[2] was comprised of fifteen or sixteen barracks, each capable of housing forty to fifty people. Forty internees, including myself, were assigned to Barracks 2.[3] First, we were sent to another empty barracks to retrieve our beds. I felt very sorry that I could not help the elderly carry their iron army cots through the snow, but I was carrying my own at the time. There were two stoves in our empty barracks, but we internees from Hawai'i had no idea how to light the coals to get warm. After shivering and bickering and making several attempts, we were relieved when the coals finally lit. We arranged our army cots in the barracks, and each of us was given three brand-new military blankets, two sheets, and a pillowcase. I felt alive again when I laid myself between the white sheets and put my head on the covered pillow.

| 8 |
Camp McCoy

Autonomy Allowed

Having come such a long way from my home, I thought I would not be able to sleep well that first night. On the contrary, I slept very well, for I was dead-tired. The next morning, I washed my face and then took a look around the snow-covered camp. The unusual scenery made me temporarily forget that I had been interned. The place looked so much like my hometown in Japan. Pine trees grew here and there among the oaks. I imagined that the tracks of rabbits could be seen in the snow.

At this camp we were allowed to have paper and pencil. However, we were unable to mail letters to our families, because we did not have the money to buy the five-cent stamps. I sent a prepaid postcard—which I had gotten from a friend while at Angel Island—to my Caucasian friend in San Francisco, asking him to send me a small amount of cash. But I was doubtful that he would dare to oblige a person who had been interned as a citizen of a hostile nation at a time when people were saying, "Remember Pearl Harbor."

We had been very interested in Ensign Kazuo Sakamaki, the first Japanese POW. He happened to be confined with some internees in Barracks 1, and so we paid him a visit out of curiosity and to console him. Although we expressed words of support, he merely said, "Thank you." He appeared unwilling to talk to us, so we did not dare to ask any questions. The next day, he was transferred to a cabin in Block B to be by himself.

The position of "spokesman," unofficially called "battalion commander," was changed to "coordinator," which sounded more democratic. Dr. Akio Kimura was appointed to the post, and Totaro Matsui and Heigo Fuchino were named secretary and chief of the Post Office, respectively. "Group leader" was renamed "barracks captain." The coordinator appointed a barracks captain for each barracks, namely Mr. Takahashi from Sumitomo Bank in Seattle for Barracks 1, Katsuichi Kawamoto for Barracks 2, myself for Barracks 3, Shujiro Takakuwa for Barracks 4, and Kenji Kimura of Nippon Yūsen for Barracks 5.

The coordinator also appointed Masao Sakamoto chief of the mess hall. Tokuji Baba, Shoho Fujiie, Hiroshi Honda, Tomoichi Hayashi, Tanehiro Isobe,[1] Tamotsu Ihara, Shozaemon Masaki, Shunichi Odo, Aisuke Shigekuni, Goki Tatsuguchi, Yasuo Toda, and Sokan Ueoka became the mess hall staff.

The duty of the service group, which was mainly to bring coal to the barracks, was carried out by such young men as Hiroshi Motoshige, Suijo Kabashima, Tatsuo Motoshige, Noriaki Atsuumi, Shigezo Maekawa, Isaku Orita, and Shinzaburo Sumida.

Soichi Obata, Tomoaki Nakamura, and Kakujiro Nishiki were assigned to clean the shower room and latrines. And Joei Oi, Masaichi Hirashima, and others were given boiler-watch duty. Dr. Kazuo Miyamoto and Seiha Asami, editor-in-chief of the *Nippu Jiji*, took the broadcast department assignment. Tetsusaburo Uyeda, a former baseball player at Keiō University, who had been interned from St. Louis, was selected baseball chief. And finally, George Otani volunteered for chimney cleaning.

What with all these assignments, our self-government should have worked out smoothly. But in reality, some of the younger internees—primarily the mess hall group—caused constant trouble with their arrogant behavior.

Since Dr. Kimura, our coordinator, was a good friend of mine and my "home doctor" as well, I told him everything that our barracks residents complained about. I disliked doing it, but I thought it was my duty as a barracks captain. Unfortunately, somehow the people working in the mess hall found out, and I became the victim of harsh retaliation.

A Welcome Ration of Cash

Our camp commander was a man named Horace I. Rogers. Although he was a lieutenant colonel, he was also a Rotarian and did not look like a military man. He clearly understood our situation, supporting us as far as regulations allowed and treating us with compassion. I cannot fully express how much our aching hearts were healed because of him.

At the camp, there were five internees who had arrived ahead of us. Interned from Seattle, they were Jiro Nishimura of Yamashita Steamship, Mr. Takahashi and Mr. Senzai of Sumitomo Bank, Mr. Arai of Specie Bank, and a railroad worker named Mr. Matsumoto. Soon afterward, Rev. Hisanori Kano, a Christian minister, joined us from Nebraska, and Tetsusaburo Uyeda came from St. Louis. Also, there was Hisashi Tominaga who had joined us at Angel Island and traveled with us. All the other internees in the camp had come from Hawai'i.

The top priority of the Hawai'i group was to obtain postage stamps so that we could mail letters to our families. As I mentioned earlier, all the money that our families had sent us through the army had been frozen, and so none of us had any money. As the saying goes, "Where there's a will, there's a way." Rev. Masayuki Kodama of the Konko Mission happened to have a money order with him, and he turned it in to the internee officers to use as they saw fit. In addition, Mr. Tominaga, who had been interned from Samoa and lived in our barracks, offered twenty dollars to help us, his barracks mates. Instead of taking the money as a gift, I asked him to lend it to us for a while.

Somehow news of the twenty-dollar loan reached the internee officers, and Secretary Matsui asked to borrow that money. Mr. Tominaga insisted it was only for the use of our barracks mates, and so we had no alternative but to decline Mr. Matsui's request. Instead, I offered Mr. Matsui all the money that my Caucasian friend in San Francisco had sent me. One thing led to another, and we finally collected enough money for everyone to buy airmail postage stamps. One dollar was distributed to each and every internee, and we were so happy to finally be able to send letters to our families. I spent my dollar on the following items:

Airmail postage stamps: 20 cents
Tin cup: 6 cents
Tooth powder: 10 cents
Laundry detergent: 13 cents
Matches: 1 cent
Cough drops: 5 cents
Candies: 5 cents
Total: 65 cents

I was able to get all of the daily necessities that I wanted. I have never appreciated money as much as I did then.

A Mess of a Mess Hall

Earlier I mentioned that I had suffered mistreatment at the hands of some young mess hall workers. Let me tell you about one of these incidents, just to give you an example. At mealtime, all of us barracks mates were expected to go to the mess hall as a group and to get our food on trays from the kitchen workers, who stood behind the counters. Some of the workers would dump the food onto the trays of the men they did not like. On cold mornings, when the strong north wind blew and the line moved slowly, we sometimes sheltered ourselves by hiding under the cover of the mess hall building. If the pace of the line was ever broken even for a moment, the workers yelled at us, complaining that we were not keeping up the speed.

One morning, when I was suffering from a cold and diarrhea, I planned to go last in our group, so as to avoid being exposed for a long time to the cold wind. I asked Manzuchi Hashimoto to ask Nihei Miyamoto, who was on KP duty from our barracks, to warm up some milk for me. The milk was not warmed, however, for one of the kitchen workers refused my request, claiming that I had been very nasty. This was my reward for trying to help my barracks mates.

During the internment, we were paid seventy cents a day for our work, although in the early days we were not paid at all. Accordingly, it was only natural that young workers felt they were supporting those of us who did nothing but eat. Besides, no one had money or clothes with us, and we were all frustrated in those days. I could understand their wanting to be hard on us. However, other internees, including myself, had never wanted to be idle, so to be treated as a burden was quite unbearable.

Probably because we, Hawai'i internees, had moved to a cold place, we had unusually big appetites. We were downhearted that the food served there was so little and tasted so bad. It was often the talk of the camp that the kitchen workers were manipulating the food supply so that they could get an unfair share.

There is an old saying that the samurai may be hungry, but he behaves as if fully fed. Behind the barbed wire, maintaining our health by eating became our top priority, while maintaining our dignity was only secondary. One day for lunch, we were given only one piece of potato and two slices of bread without butter. That night we had two slices of bread and a bowl of dumpling soup. The dumpling soup was supposed to be served with a piece of meat stewed in the broth, but the workers often scooped two or three pieces into the bowls of their friends and none into the bowls of the ones they did not like. When some protested that the workers needed to be fair to everyone, they started putting the meat in the bowl first and then pouring in the soup. It seems very childish now, but we were serious then. Although we were limited to only two slices of bread, we did have the chance to get extra slices of crust with each meal. But because everyone wanted an extra slice, it always caused problems. It was then up to the workers: whom to favor with two pieces or whom to give none at all.

A Talk of Food

One day, during a period when we were suffering a shortage of food supplies, an ironic coincidence had me sitting opposite Kenji Kimura, the captain of Barracks 5. The reason I say "ironic" is that I was the captain of Barracks 3, whom mess hall workers disliked, while Mr. Kimura was captain of a barracks where there lived the internee officers, who were always being treated favorably by the mess workers. I noticed Mr. Kimura had an enormous amount of food on his plate. I, on the other hand, had only a small amount on mine. I have to admit that I was feeling nasty at the time. I was very embarrassed to see the difference in the amount of food.

"A barracks captain who does not speak out is certainly treated differently," I said. I immediately regretted my words. After all, Mr. Kimura had not intentionally curried favor from the mess workers. The aftertaste was so bad that I wanted to avoid him whenever possible.

When you train animals, you do it with food. We had a canteen, but we could not afford to buy anything. At the time, I had the irresistible urge to buy certain kinds of food, although I normally would have been indifferent to them. Before long, George Otani had a chance to complain about the food situation to the commander, who had come to our barracks for roll call. The next morning, three officers came to the kitchen to investigate. Then one day, Mrs. Kano, the wife of Reverend Kano, made a visit to our camp and brought homemade cookies. Reverend Kano kindly distributed them to every internee. We were as happy as children.

Although Commander Rogers was attentive to daily operations and a kind gentleman, he left kitchen matters to the mess officers, since he was busy. The situation improved immediately following Commander Rogers's investigation. Yet, we rarely had good-tasting meals, although we were fairly satisfied with the quantity of the food. Everyone behaved obediently, like children, and the number of complaints to the coordinator was considerably reduced. Some even praised the coordinator for a job well done. Looking back, I feel this experience shows that, unless one is a saint, food can seriously affect one's psychological state.

The Empty Can Incident

There were no buckets or washbasins in the shower room and laundry, so we used empty ten-gallon cans instead. Some inconsiderate internees soaked their laundry in soapy water and brought the cans back to their barracks. A notice was sent to every barracks calling for the return of all cans. I reminded my barracks mates to turn the cans in at once. Most of the internees complied, however there were some cheeky guys who refused.

"Supplies for the shower room and the laundry should be provided by the army," they insisted. The coordinator then called on each barracks to check and complained to the barracks captain when cans were found.

Unfortunately, in my barracks, two cans were found under Charlie Hasebe's bed. The coordinator barked at me, "You guys complain a lot, but you don't cooperate at all." There was nothing I could say or do, but take the cans Mr. Hasebe had been using as bedpans back to the shower room.

Mr. Hasebe had not been there at the time. But when he returned to the barracks, I scolded him, "You can't go around doing things as you like!"

"Hell no!" Mr. Hasebe responded in a particularly loud voice. "They were not brought from our shower! I got them from the German barracks. You have no grounds to be complaining to me!"

I regretted my mistake and told him apologetically that I would get the cans back. But Mr. Hasebe was still offended.

"Although you crawl to the *haole*,[2] you always stand on your dignity when you talk to us," he retorted. "I'll talk to the coordinator myself." I had a hard time convincing him not to.

The title "barracks captain" sounds nice. But in reality, it was a difficult job, and I did not like it, for I had to listen to all the complaints that my barracks mates brought to me. Those who lived in a far corner of the barracks wanted the stove to be kept at a higher temperature, while those closer did not. Some wanted the windows to be kept open, while others did not. Someone complained that he had been annoyed by the snoring and teeth-grinding of his neighbor. Others grumbled that the barracks was smoky because we had not tended to the stove correctly. You name it, we had it.

All in all, however, there were many gentle residents in our barracks. Besides, our barracks secretary, Kazuma Araki, looked after us very well. I believe our barracks had less trouble than any of the others.

Let me put down the names of our barracks residents, even though I may miss someone. They were Kazuma Araki, Tamaki Arita, Seiichi Fujii, Kenkichi Fujimoto, Hideo Fujisawa, Teiichiro Fukuda, Manzuchi Hashimoto, Ichitaro Hasebe,[3] Shigenari Hattori, Masaichi Hirashima, Yoshio Hino, Toshio Iinuma, Taketo Iwahara, Teikichi Kojima, Shozo Kawakami, Motoichi Matsuda, Nihei Miyamoto, Ryujun Mutobe, Shigemaru Miyao, Kakujiro Nishiki, Hakuai Oda, Yoshiro Ogawa, Suekichi Oka, Tokuichi Niimi, Kazuhiko Ogata, Ryoshin Okano, Shinri Sarashina, Tadao Sasaki, Yoshinobu Sasaki, Taichi Sato, Kinzo Sayegusa, Hideyuki Serizawa, Hisashi Tominaga, Tokuye Takahashi, Heitaro Tarasawa, Hatsutaro Toyofuku, Katsuichi Tanaka, Takinosuke Toyama, Giichi Sasaki, and myself, for a total of forty-one.[4]

Commander Rogers' Thoughtfulness

Like soldiers, we internees did not like roll call. The sergeant who had this daily duty was a little slow, and we could never finish without having to repeat the process a few times—like at all the other camps where we had been held. It was especially annoying to have to stand for a long time in the clearing with the north winds blowing constantly.

Commander Rogers abolished this troublesome procedure, and he personally came to every barracks for bed inspection after lights-out at nine. We all appreciated this favor. When families sent money, we could cash the money orders at the post office in the nearby town. But when they sent cashier's checks, those could only be handled in Chicago, and the commander himself would go there to cash them for us.

One night, when the rare Northern Lights were visible, he kindly told us about it and let us enjoy the view from outside the barracks, although it was after lights-out. When Kensaku Tsunoda started conducting English classes, he even allowed Ensign Sakamaki to attend with a guard.

Later, when we were to be transferred from this camp, he thoughtfully advised us of our departure in advance. Up until then, we had never been told anything and had simply moved like sheep following orders. The feeling of helplessness had been overwhelming. The commander hinted that we were heading for a place about eight hundred miles away to the south. Naturally, we had no idea where the military camps and internment facilities were located, but his information gave us some kind of relief, for at least we knew in which direction we would be heading.

As we were leaving the camp, the commander shook hands with each and every one of us.

"You'll be passing through the famous stockyards of Chicago," he said. "If you look carefully through the window, you can see what's going on. When the train stops in Chicago, you'd better pull down the window shades. It's pretty dangerous around that area. Some people may throw stones at you." It was very kind of him to have warned us about where we were going.

On April 8, when we celebrated the birthday of the Buddha, he came to attend the ceremony, gave a warm-hearted speech, and donated a lot of cake and fruit. We appreciated his gesture very much. Some Americans do discriminate against people of other races, but there also are kind men like Commander Rogers who are worthy of respect.

Camp McCoy was later converted into a POW camp that held a few thousand Japanese prisoners until the war ended. I firmly believe that only Commander Rogers was capable of serving as its chief, allowing the POWs to live humanely in the camp until they were able to go home safely.[5]

My Impressions of Non-Hawai'i Internees

In our barracks, the problems seemed endless. Although I tried to negotiate with the internee officers, resolving the problems was very difficult, and I occasionally became quite irritated. When this would happen, I would take a break and visit Barracks 1, where Tomoaki Nakamura and Soichi Obata lived.

Jiro Nishimura, of the Yamashita Steamship Company in Seattle, also lived in the same barracks. He liked shōgi and owned a good game set. I enjoyed playing against him, and for a while I forgot about the troubles that had been annoying me. I have kept in touch with him to this day. After the war, when Japan was suffering from a shortage of consumer goods, I sent him some packages to express my gratitude for what he had done for me during those days in camp. He now serves as president of Pacific Steamship Company. I heard that he welcomed Mr. Obata, when the latter visited Japan. Mr. Nishimura, like the other internees from Seattle, had enough money with him, and he often treated me kindly, offering me tea, sweets, and coffee. I felt a little guilty about visiting him so often.

Mr. Takahashi of Sumitomo Bank was also gentle and friendly. No doubt that was why he had been appointed barracks captain. There was, however, a man named Arai of Specie Bank, who was like a bank employee of the olden days, snobbish and conceited. Whenever he went out for a walk, he would wear his fancy hat and jacket with rabbit fur on the collar. He even strutted along. His silent stare and looks of scorn at us, dressed in second-hand military overcoats and oversized shoes, angered everyone.

Rev. Hisanori Kano, who had been interned from Nebraska, was famous for his snoring. He was a cheerful and lively Christian minister, who knew how to lift our spirits. Tetsusaburo Uyeda from St. Louis was, as I mentioned earlier, a former Keiō University baseball player. He was gentle and took good care of us, arranging softball games and always volunteering to be the umpire. Having been a manager at a country club for Caucasians in St. Louis, he also was a good cook. When we were transferred to the Tennessee camp, he would entertain us by cooking his special recipes. He was married to a Caucasian lady and had a beautiful daughter, and when they came to see him in Camp Livingston, they became the talk of the camp.

In the Seattle group was a good-looking young man named Senzai.

He was pure of heart and gentle. Despite our short association of a little more than two months, he came to see me before leaving the Tennessee camp to board the exchange ship. He tearfully thanked me for what I had done for him and wished me good health. Feeling like a father bidding his son farewell, I was overcome with emotion and moved to tears.

Hisashi Tominaga, the only internee from Pago Pago, Samoa, had married an attractive Samoan lady, who was the daughter of a chief. She was also quite skillful. He carried with him from Samoa such items as tablecloths dyed with the astringent juice from the banana tree, beautifully embroidered pillowcases, and other pieces that had been handmade by his wife. Later, in the Tennessee camp, we shared a hut, and he gave me a tablecloth and pillowcase that his wife had made. I still keep these items to remember him by.

News Broadcasts and the Internees' Lament

Since we had nothing else to do but eat, listening to the news broadcast every evening became our sole source of entertainment. These were not radio broadcasts exactly, since radios were not allowed in camp. But newspapers and magazines were permitted, so our News Department wrote scripts based on articles from these sources and read them aloud to the internees who gathered.

I was particularly interested in the articles of the military commentators Hansen Baldwin and Walter Lippman, which were translated and commented on by Dr. Miyamoto.

"Raiding every island in the Pacific is like spreading butter on each small slice of bread," he read one day. "We should change our strategy to be more efficient." I remember it well for the way he said it, gesturing like a professional storyteller.

Seiha Asami specialized in Hawai'i-related news, writing articles based on the letters internees had received from their families. There was hardly anything noteworthy in them, as the names of people and places, figures, and war progress reports were always censored. Still, we enjoyed the news very much.

After every program, we all sang together under the baton of Shoho Fujiie. We sang "The Pacific March," "The March of the Flag of the Rising Sun," and so on. Although we sang lively marching songs like these, deep in our hearts, we felt melancholy. One day we sang "The Song of the Yalu River," with the lyrics rewritten by Seiha Asami. It was quite moving, and some of us began to weep. The song goes like this:[6]

Two hundred countrymen detained in this camp
Mounting hardship burdens us,
But for emperor and country,
I gladly make the sacrifice.

The snowy Sierra Nevada
Stretches endlessly to the right of my train.
Though I know not where we are bound,
This wandering journey continues.

A cold wind blows across the American and Canadian border
And the moon shines on Camp McCoy.
The moonlight never changes,
Though we are forced from camp to camp.

Every time I watch the moon,
I recall my wife and children.
My soul is torn apart,
And I shed tears in spite of myself.

果てしなきシェラネバタの雪景色
右に眺めてアラ行く汽車のヨイショ
行方も知らぬヨ旅の空ヨ
続くマタ流転の道遠しチョイチョイ

アメリカとカナダ境の風寒し
マコイ・キャンプにアラ照る月のヨイショ
月の光はヨ変らねどヨ
変るマタ配所の憂き思いチョイチョイ

月見れば後に残せし妻や子の
面影そぞろにアラ偲ばれてヨイショ
うたた断腸のヨ思いありヨ
男マタ不覚の一としずくチョイチョイ

Reading the lyrics now, you may feel them too emotional, and you may find it difficult to understand their meaning. But at the time, they were the cries from our hearts.

The Buddha's Festival and Softball Games

Now that the windy season was over, the warm sun began to shine even on Camp McCoy. With the coming of spring, our mood brightened also. Our meals improved, and gradually money from our families started to reach us. During this time, the very sensitive topic of repatriation arose, and it gave us hope. Of course, fewer people complained to me about the camp coordinator as our situation improved.

The Buddha's birthday was on April 8, and a festival was planned with all the Buddhist priests officiating at this religious event. Skillful Aisuke Shigekuni led a group in making an altar using bread wrapping paper and can labels. Artificial cherry blossoms made with beet-dyed toilet paper were used to create a festive atmosphere. Commander Rogers and a major, who was chief of the medical group, came to participate in the festival. They enjoyed our decorations, and with a smile on his face, the commander delivered a speech. Coordinator Akio Kimura thanked him for his speech, and then we all chatted and enjoyed the cakes and oranges that the commander had given us.

In May, an announcement was posted that workers would get a stipend of twenty-one dollars a month and non-workers ten cents per day. This made the non-workers feel happier, for they now no longer needed to feel indebted to the workers.

As spring arrived and the ground became dry, every barracks formed a softball team to battle each other. Each team had an average of four to five experienced players, while the rest had not played at all. Even though they were younger, men like Tomoichi Hayashi, Noriaki Atsuumi, Hiroshi Motoshige, Suijo Kabashima, Masao Ishimoto, Jikyo Masaki, Sokan Ueoka, Norizane Tsuha, and Hiroshi Honda had no playing experience. They often stubbed their fingers with the balls, dropped the balls, and were less reliable than the older, experienced players. Nevertheless, we enjoyed their unorthodox playing. To compensate for their teammates' poor fielding abilities, the young, vigorous shortstops, like Shinzaburo Sumida, Akizaki, and Isobe, had to cover second and third base, and sometimes even the outfield, all while wearing their oversized shoes.

Since the games were inter-barracks matches, many barracks mates came out to root for their teams. Among the experienced men who played frequently were Toraichi Uyeda, Ryuichi Kashima, Kazuma Araki, Tokuichi Niimi, Shujiro Takakuwa, Shigeo Oshima, Tamejiro Nakano, Yoshinobu Sasaki, Giichi Sasaki, Soichi Obata, Masao Sogawa, Tamaki Arita, Akio Kimura, Isaku Orita, Goki Tatsuguchi, Seiha Asami, Kinzo Sayegusa, Osuke Shigemoto, Takeo Kagawa, Manabu Tashiro, and yours truly. Daizo

Sumida, Manzuchi Hashimoto, Taichi Sato, and others played only once in a while, when the teams needed someone to fill a position. It was quite apparent that the atmosphere had become much more pleasant because of these games.

The saying goes, "For a man without virtue, idleness leads to mischief." Even if you are not a man without virtue, you tend to feel the gloom and strain of idleness. I believe *kami*[7] created man to work. If you do nothing, you are acting against the will of the kami. Even though the kami may not punish you, there is no good at all in not working. That's how I feel.

Relaxing in the Spring Wind

More than forty people lived together in the same barracks. In the beginning, we felt awkward, for we did not know each other well and were on edge, and sometimes this caused friction among us. However, as our life gradually improved, the atmosphere of the camp became pleasant and friendly.

At the time, there was no barber in the camp, and no one could get his hair cut. So we came up with the idea of asking some talented internees to become makeshift barbers. We had no barber's scissors, but someone said that Reverend Kano was carrying a pair with him. When we asked him to loan it to us, we discovered that it was made for using on school children, such as you would find at a dime store like Kress. Since we had no choice, we decided to use it. Tamaki Arita, Kenkichi Fujimoto, and Hatsutaro Toyofuku generously volunteered for the job. Thanks to these gentlemen, we were able to get our hair cut, which left us feeling like new men.

We sometimes held "hidden-talent" shows. Dr. Takahashi surprised us with his version of an *Umakata-bushi*, as did Reverend Okano with his *Izumo-bushi*. Both of them sang unexpectedly well. In his typical, native Tōhoku style, Reverend Fujisawa did a fine job on his version of an *Obako-bushi*.[8]

Giichi Sasaki, principal of a Japanese language school in Kahalu'u, was skilled at judo and an expert in Japanese-style massage. He gave massages to us when we suffered from colds.

Heitaro Tarasawa, a very straightforward, elderly man, originally from the Tōhoku area, was a postal worker for the Japanese on the 'Ewa plantation.[9] Since he also had been assigned as a *toritsuginin*, he was one of the unfortunates who was interned. In our barracks, Mr. Tarasawa was assigned the duty of taking care of the stoves. When someone in the barracks exaggeratedly complained that it was smoky, he begged with tears in his eyes for me to reassign him. In time, Mr. Tarasawa became very good at lighting up the stoves. All of us also appreciated his voluntary cleaning of our barracks.

Reverand Miyao, a Shinto priest, was famous for talking in his sleep.

One night, someone insisted that he heard Reverend Miyao saying, "Hello, Yuki dear, Yuki dear." The barracks mates made up a raunchy story and teased him with it, livening up the barracks.

Roadways in the camp were paved with gravel from a nearby river. Internees found some black circular stones among the gravel and converted them into *go* pieces. We played games using boards made from cardboard. Messrs. Serizawa, Ogata, Miyao, Sato, Mutobe, Takahashi, Okano, Hino, Hattori, and I played frequently.

In this way, not only did the atmosphere of our barracks change, but the attitude of the mess workers toward us improved greatly. The winds of spring eased the pent-up frustration within me. I learned that time can sometimes resolve problems, be they major international disputes or minor barracks discord.

Our Suitcases Arrive at Last

With all these troubles resolved, spring came to our discordant camp and with it a succession of positive happenings. Mr. Takahashi of Sumitomo Bank received a telegram from Japan through the International Red Cross. The news itself was not so significant, but it raised our morale to learn that we could communicate with those in Japan. In time, letters from Hawai'i written in Japanese reached us, and we were allowed to write letters in Japanese as well. We were not fluent in English so we could barely express ourselves in writing. It felt very awkward to write a letter in English, as if "scratching an itch through our shoes." That's why we were so happy to finally be able to communicate in Japanese.[10]

The suitcases from home that we had been waiting for arrived at last, after more than two months. Even those men who had been so angry about the delay were all smiles. We wanted to see what was in our suitcases as quickly as possible, but they had to go through inspection. I sorted the ones for our barracks according to alphabetical order of the last names and took care of their delivery. I wanted to open my suitcase at once, but I had to finish delivering the others to my barracks mates first.

It was around four o'clock before I finally got my suitcase. I opened it immediately and found a sports jacket, an *aloha* shirt,[11] an overcoat, a muffler, a bathrobe, wool socks, and knitted underwear. I noticed that my eldest son had labeled each item with my name. I could tell that my whole family had worked in a rush to put everything together. By looking at the winter clothing my family had put in my suitcase, I also imagined that Emergency Service Committee members must have given hints to our families that we had been interned to a cold place.

Whether they were rich or poor, our families had packed the suitcases with loving care. It made me keenly aware that love is priceless, and it warmed my hardened heart. That evening, we had a good dinner—five pieces of deep-fried pond smelts from the Great Lakes, a bowl of rice, and even dessert. Everyone was in good humor, and the conversation at the table was pleasant and lively.

Rain Falls and the Earth Settles[12]

At one point, many internees were not happy with our coordinator, and the situation became so critical that all the officers turned in their resignations, requiring an election of new officers. A rumor spread that Dr. Miyamoto, a strong candidate for the next coordinator, was too mild-mannered, and it interrupted the momentum of his supporters. During this time, our situation had changed considerably, as daily life had improved, our suitcases had arrived, and our money had reached us. So the election was put off for a while, and when it was finally conducted, Dr. Kimura was re-elected by a wide margin. Some people who did not like Dr. Kimura still complained that I, as barracks captain, had been brainwashed and that fair voting had not been conducted. I was not against the coordinator himself, and as long as our situation improved, I was satisfied with him.

Now that the pending election was over, our camp problems and anxieties soon vanished like the spring mist. Many events were held in the camp. Although the most popular entertainment was softball, lecture meetings were also held almost every evening in an unoccupied barracks. Some of the lectures in which I was particularly interested were "My Eye-Witness Account of the Pearl Harbor Attack" by Rev. Norizane Tsuha, "My Experience as a POW" by Rev. Ninryo Nago, and "My Experience as an Airman in Northern China" by Hiroshi Honda. Tsuha's story was based on his experience of watching the attack from the ʻEwa Plantation. It was a vivid account, presented in his own animated style. Back in the INS office, I had taught him how to play *go* using round pieces of orange peel. As he was a very talented man, he soon surpassed me, and he is now president of the Aloha Go Club.

Hiroshi Honda was a Nisei, but had been drafted by the Japanese army while studying in Japan. He had belonged to an air division and fought in northern China during the Sino-Japanese War. He spoke with much humor, and we enjoyed his lecture. He had returned to Hawaiʻi after being discharged, and a local newspaper had written about his brilliant achievements in China. Had there been no news article, the FBI might not have known of him. He was arrested immediately after the war broke out, only because the FBI had blacklisted him.

Old Reverend Nago had been a Japanese Third Division trooper during the Russo-Japanese War. While reconnoitering in the Mukden area, he was injured and lost consciousness. When he came to, he found himself a prisoner of the Russians. Until the end of the war, he was held near St. Petersburg, then the Russian capital. After the war, he boarded a prisoner exchange ship in Hamburg, took a long trip through the Mediterranean and the Suez Canal, past Ceylon and Singapore, before landing in Kobe. At the time, what he felt could not be easily described—a mixture of happiness, sadness, and shame. When he and the others landed at the pier in Kobe and marched to the station, spectators along the street stared with curiosity and contempt. But as the spectators saw men with amputated arms or legs and some who were blind, their scorn turned to sympathy, and they thanked the men, wiping tears with their handkerchiefs. Reverend Nago was relieved to see the reaction to the former POWs. As we listened to his story, we thought of Ensign Sakamaki and felt a kind of relief, too.

The Northern Lights (The Aurora Borealis)

It was already the middle of April, but in Wisconsin, it was about the time when trees start to grow new leaves. In Camp McCoy, lights-out was at nine o'clock. When the clock turned to nine one night, Reverend Hino, who was in charge, yelled in his high-pitched voice, "Lights out, everyone!" and immediately turned off the switch. The barracks became pitch-black.

"I'm still getting my bed ready," complained fussy Charlie Hasebe. "What're you so afraid of? You guys have no guts."

After we had all turned in, Commander Rogers himself came by to inspect us. Being barracks captain, I sat up immediately.

"Attention!" I called out in a nasally voice like a serviceman.

The commander switched on the lights and conducted his inspection. Afterwards, he came toward me. I thought he was going to scold me, and I stood upright like a soldier.

"Good evening," he said, to my relief. "How do you do? You've never seen the Northern Lights before, have you?"

I did not fully understand what he meant and thought he was referring to the North Star.

"Yes, I saw it every night at Sand Island in Hawai'i," I said. The commander laughed and said that was impossible.

"Come on out with your overcoats and take a look," he said. We all happily followed him.

The northwestern sky was covered with black clouds. From what appeared to be the horizon, bands of light shone in midair through the clouds, as if millions of searchlights were lighting up the sky. Half of the sky was filled with glowing lights that looked like the tail of Halley's Comet. The sky was so bright that no star could be seen. The lights moved and changed colors. It is difficult to describe, but it was very beautiful and quite spectacular. Two hundred of us, who had lived in Hawai'i for so many years, now stood thousands of miles away in the northern Mainland, a line of black figures under the glow of the white Northern Lights—I felt strange, as if I were on another planet.

I remember the old popular tune, "Katyusha's Song" from the play "Resurrection," in which Shimamura Hōgetsu cast Matsui Sumako in the part of Katyusha. There is a part of the lyrics that goes, "I wonder if I should go forward, or back under the Northern Lights; Russia stretches endlessly to the north."[13] We had thought that something like the Aurora would have nothing at all to do with us. And yet, here we were, interned to America's northernmost reaches, with the Aurora right before our eyes. Fate certainly moves in mysterious ways.

Later, we would be moved from place to place throughout the south for about a year and a half. When we spent a year at Fort Missoula in Montana, I expected to see the Northern Lights again. I later learned that the Aurora appears only under particular weather conditions. Missoula is at 46.8 degrees north latitude and is located 3 degrees north of Camp McCoy, yet we never saw the Aurora again, for we would be transferred south to Santa Fe.

We will never forget Lieutenant Colonel Rogers who treated us with compassion and understanding.

Repatriation

An agreement for the exchange of internees was reached between Japan and the United States, and those who wanted to return to Japan were expected to apply to the proper authorities. Around that time, I heard that an organization called The Group that Supports the 100-Year War had been formed in Japan. Moreover, it was said that another influential group called The Group that Supports the Twenty-Five-Year War,[14] headed by the former Minister of Foreign Affairs Arita Hachirō, had also been organized. I did not believe that the war could last for one hundred years; instead I thought twenty-five years was more realistic. Besides, with as noted a man as former minister Arita acting as chairman, I thought the organization was trustworthy.

No one could deny that the elderly would be fated to die behind barbed wire if the war were to last for twenty-five years, which is why most of the internees applied for repatriation. Some of us even petitioned the Spanish Embassy and the Ministry of Foreign Affairs in Japan.[15]

We were not quite sure what the outcome was going be when five Hawai'i internees, Motoichi Matsuda, Shigenari Hattori, Norikazu Nakano, Genji Otani, and Kichitaro Sekiya, received notice that they were to be repatriated to Japan. The exchange ship, the *Gripsholm*, sailed out of New York harbor on June 18, 1942.[16] She made a call at Rio de Janeiro to pick up 380 of our fellow countrymen living in South America. After crossing the southern part of the Atlantic Ocean and sailing around Cape Town, the *Gripsholm* arrived at Lourenço Marques on the east coast of South Africa. There, the repatriates were transferred to the *Asama Maru*, which had brought American internees from Japan. And then, finally they were returned to Japan.

There, in Lourenço Marques, American Ambassador Joseph Grew arrived from Japan, and Japanese ambassadors Kurusu Saburō and Nomura Kichisaburō arrived from New York. Ambassador Nomura had hoped for a meeting with Ambassador Grew during the stay, but Grew declined Nomura's request, and a potentially historic meeting was never realized.

The second exchange ship sailed out of New York a year and two months later, on September 1, 1943. She carried seventy-one Hawai'i internees and their families, who had come to the Mainland to join their husbands and fathers. The ship returned to Japan, taking a route similar to that of the first trip. Those internees who remained behind envied them at the time, but, as the proverb goes, "No one can tell what will happen in the future." With the exception of bankers and others originally from Japan, few Hawai'i repatriates were happy to have returned to Japan. I think those who were left behind in the States were happier.

My good friend Shoichi Asami was particularly unlucky. A correspondent for the Dōmei News Agency, he disembarked in Singapore with his family when the ship called there. He had been assigned as chief of Dōmei's Singapore bureau. As the war turned against Japan, he decided to return with his family to his homeland. In late March 1945, he and his youngest son were aboard the hospital ship the *Awa Maru*, when it was mistakenly struck and sunk by a torpedo from an American submarine. Mr. Asami was lost in the South China Sea along with his beloved son. His wife and their other children were returning on another ship and made it home to Japan safely. Because he loved his children very much, Mr. Asami took his youngest son, ten-year-old Ryozo, with him. As I thought of him gasping with his beloved son in his arms, I could only bow my head in deep respect.[17]

An Incomprehensible Selection of Repatriates

Nothing was more incomprehensible to us than the list of repatriates. It contained more than ten names that we had never heard before, while men who had left their families behind in Japan, such as Rev. Gikyo Kuchiba and Rev. Shinri Sarashina, both of the Hongwanji Mission, were not among them. The reverends were forced to stay in the United States until after the war. Although some Japanese families in Hawai'i had already moved to the Mainland in the hopes of returning to Japan, they were not allowed to board the second ship and had to stay at the Family Camp until the end of the war.[18]

Later, I had a chance to personally ask Mr. Arita about the Group that Supports the Twenty-Five-Year War, which had so influenced our decision to repatriate. When Mrs. Sei Soga, my wife, and I visited Japan some years after the war, we attended a welcome reception hosted by the Japan-Hawai'i Society. I happened to be seated next to Mr. Arita, so I dared to ask him about the organization. He said it was the first time he had heard of such a thing, and he denied having been its chairman, telling me he had, in fact, never accepted the position. He thought the organizers had simply been seeking publicity when they approached him, and as a result the news had spread to the American media. He apologized for causing such a misunderstanding for us internees. When I learned that the organization that had so influenced us had not been authentic, I was angry. Several other situations similar to this incident occurred during the war.

My friends and acquaintances who repatriated on the second exchange ship were: Horyu Asaeda, Seiha Asami and his family of six, Eishu Asato, Tokuji Baba, Sutematsu Endo, Utanosuke Fujishiro, Kyoichi Hamamura, Shinichi Hashibe, Teruzo Hirama, Minetaro Hori, Misao Isobe, Shigemi Isobe, Taketo Iwahara and family, Tsutomu Imamura, Shozo Kawakami, Kazoe Kawasaki and family, Eiichi Kishida, Kenji Kimura, Motoichi Kobayashi, Taiichi Komatsu, Masayuki Kodama, Kyokujo Kubokawa, Ishichi Matsuda, Eimu Miake, Yoshiye Mikami, Seigo Miwa, Shushin Matsubayashi, Jikyo Masaki, Tamotsu Matsumura, Shuun Matsuura, Nihei Miyamoto, Hiroshi Motoshige, Tatsuo Motoshige, Tamejiro Nakano and family, Shunichi Nekomoto, Dengo Nakayama, Seiichi Ohata, Torataro Onoda, Kazuhiko Ogata, Ryoshin Okano, Yoshiro Ogawa, Shigeo Oshima and family, Koten Suyetomi, Koshiro Tofukuji, Takinosuke Toyama, Genshin Tatsutani, Sokan Ueoka, Toraichi Uyeda, Takashi Wada and family, Heiichi Yamanaka, Goichi Yamane, Konosuke Iwakami, and Tokuye Takahashi and family.

To the best of my knowledge, this list is complete, but there may be other families who returned to Japan in addition to the internees listed above. Out of this group, only twelve or thirteen people returned to Hawai'i after the war.

Farewell to Camp McCoy

Once our camp problems disappeared, life became more comfortable, and we gradually recovered our composure. But then it again became time for us to be moved elsewhere. If you live in a place for a while, you grow attached to it. We were so reluctant to leave Camp McCoy that we held a meeting to console each other. We assembled in a barracks, where we used to gather during our leisure time, and we held a hidden-talent party. We also sang some military marches together. Mr. Asami presented a new song that he titled "Wandering Internees."[19] Naturally, because of our circumstances, we found the lyrics to be very sentimental.

> A cold night in Camp McCoy
> We are like birds in a cage
> Moonlight shines on barbed wire.
>
> The moon is clear, but my heart is cloudy
> Guards watch us with guns and bayonets
> We have no place to live, always on the road.
>
> I miss the good old days of the Hawaiian paradise
> Robbed of fathers, separated from husbands
> Wives and children in tears.
>
> Wandering for months on thorny roads
> Though we know nothing of our destination
> We hope to return to beloved Japan someday.

インタニー道中

夜が冷たいマッコイ館府
籠の鳥かよ囚われの身は
バッブワイアに月を見る

月は冴ゆれど心は曇る
ガード銃剣命をかけて
渡る流転の旅の空

ハワイ楽園昔のことよ
父を奪われ夫と別れ
泣いて月見る妻や子は

流転幾月いばらの路を
越えて行方の知れない旅も
末は愛するわが日本

Besides this, Shozaemon Masaki sang his version of a *sumō* song, which he performed well. We enjoyed his singing.[20]

I was reluctant to leave this camp, because the setting looked very much like my hometown in Japan. I strolled to a hill behind the barracks and came upon a grove of oak trees. They were covered with light brown flowers that gave off an overwhelmingly strong scent. I also found that the ground was covered with weeds. Looking carefully, I discovered many shoots sprouting from among the weeds. I was surprised to see the new growth so soon, for the ground had been covered with snow until quite recently. I had never seen such a phenomenon in Japan. I was impressed by the power of nature and stood there for a while.

WEEDS

A field covered with snow awakens
Under warm rays of the sun.
Spring bursts forth
After a long sleep.

Where weeds begin to grow
I stare at new shoots.
How busy and alive

Weeds work steadily to complete their task
Before the short summer ends.
With the help of abundant sunlight
Soon they will be rewarded.

雪におほわれた野辺も
暖かい陽が照り出すと
地は永い眠りからさめて
春がそこから
ふくらむでくる

と、そこには
しこ草が青むでいる
よく見ると―
もう穂を出している
その営みのあわただしさ

かれらはかれらの本分を
短い夏のうちに果すべく
黙々とつとめているのか
恵まれた陽光をうけて
実を結ぼうとしている

HAIKU FROM CAMP MCCOY

People already interned here, it seems
In this camp
Where snow covers everything
先着が居るらしい雪にうづもれたキャンプ

Through the falling snow
We carry our beds
雪のなか自分の寝るベッドをかつぐ

We were sent faraway
And within the fence
I gather pebbles
遠く送られて柵の中で小石を拾っている

Under your light, Mr. New Moon,
I go to mail my letter at the post
三日月さまへポストへ手紙を出します

THE AURORA EMERGES

The whole sky fills with bright lights
On the ground
Our tiny figures stand
大空白く輝くまえ小さいわたしたち立つ

As trees sprout
And birds sing
Times goes by
木が芽をひらく小鳥が鳴く時は過ぎ行く

A wind that carries the scent of flowers
Brings the hint of another transfer
花の香おくりくる風のどこかへ移動とか

To birds nesting outside the window
I bid farewell
窓へ巣をかけた小鳥よさようならです

Moving South

A day before our departure, we cleaned our entire area—the barracks inside and out and burned our trash—as a way of expressing our appreciation for Commander Rogers' kindness. Cleaning up was also intended to express our traditional values, as in the Japanese proverb, "A bird does not foul the nest when it is about to leave." Commander Rogers was deeply impressed by our gesture and praised us, saying that we had proven what he had heard before, that the Japanese like to keep things neat and clean.

The morning of our departure had come. When we had first arrived here at McCoy, the whole camp had been covered in snow, but now, a little over two months later, it was already early summer with fresh, green leaves shining under the sun and birds singing joyfully. Commander Rogers came to see us off at the train, giving us helpful information and shaking hands with each and every one of us.

When we got on the train, we were surprised to see how very old it was. Oil lamps hung from the ceiling of the cars. The train that had carried us to Camp McCoy had been equipped with dining cars and waiters had served us delicious meals. This time we had to cook for ourselves, as it seemed that the army was now in charge of feeding us.

I had thought the train would head south after departing Sparta. On the contrary, we found ourselves heading in the opposite direction, and as we passed many lakes and marshes, I began to wonder why we were heading north. After a while, the train began to travel eastward, and we crossed the plains of Wisconsin, passing through green fields and farmland. Eventually, we arrived at a city where many tall buildings stood.

I thought it was Chicago, but the city turned out to be Milwaukee, famous for its beer brewing. We then journeyed south, passing through Kenosha, a town that had grown into a large city when the Simmons Corporation, the largest bed manufacturer in America, built its headquarters and factory here.

Under a reddish twilight, the train entered the country's second largest city, Chicago. Here were many factories and businesses, each with its own track line, making it seem as though we were in a gigantic railroad yard. The train passed by the famous Chicago stockyards and pulled into the railway station. We followed Commander Rogers' suggestion and lowered our window shades. When I peeked through them, I saw a great many workers and students hurrying to the platforms, looking as if they were heading home.

We left Chicago at around six in the evening, and the train entered Lafayette, Indiana, by way of Ford City. We had a Japanese dinner on the train, which included *nigiri-meshi*, *yakiniku*, and *nishime*.[21] We felt as if we were on a picnic, for such dishes are often served on such an occasion. When it became dark, we went to sleep.

Entering Tennessee

We must have passed through Indiana during the night, for the train was entering Kentucky when I woke up. Familiar names and places often draw a sentimental reaction from people. Every time I hear the word, "Kentucky," I am reminded of Abraham Lincoln's home state and the song, "My Old Kentucky Home." But the scenery I saw outside the train did not impress me in such a romantic way. Along the way, we saw nothing but green fields and ranches. Wild, yellow chrysanthemum-like flowers, as we had often seen in Hawai'i, were in bloom everywhere.

When we stopped in Bowling Green, a vendor came down to the platform to sell cigarettes. I asked for a pack of Camels, and I handed him a quarter, thinking I would get at least a dime in change, but he only gave me back five cents. A close look at the package label made me realize that a two-cent tax had been imposed. At nine that night, we arrived in Nashville, the capital of Tennessee. A group of lady Red Cross volunteers was fundraising, carrying baskets of loose cigarettes that they sold by the piece. As our train was departing from the station, one of the attractive ladies in the group waved her hand toward me. When I waved back, the internees teased me. The whole car was filled with gay laughter.

The surrounding area looked quite tropical and was very different from Wisconsin. At ten-thirty, our train stopped in Fosterville. There it changed to a branch line that headed toward the mountains. Houses were scattered here and there, reminding me of the Kona area of Hawai'i. Along the railroad track were farms where Negro and French American farmers worked. I did not see any Anglo-Saxons. Few towns had English names; instead there was Louisville, Nashville, Hopkinsville, and the like.

I was surprised to see so many Caucasian people living in pig-pen-like shacks down in the valley. I understand that they came from southern Europe in the early days of immigration to America. They have very little contact with the outside world and do not pay taxes, much like the Sanka in Japan.[22] Moreover, they do not send their children to school, and I hear that they have become quite a problem for the government. They are called "hillbillies," and approximately 150,000 of them are living in the south alone.

Finally, our train stopped at the town of Tullahoma, located on a plateau and the site of Camp Forrest. It was slightly past noon on May 27, 1942. The camp looked a little like Hawai'i's Schofield Barracks.[23] Many people watched us with curiosity as we pulled into the station. I believe this was the first time they had ever seen Japanese people. We rode buses to the camp, which had just recently been built in a nearby forest. It occurred to me that we might be staying here for a very long time.

| 9 |

Camp Forrest
Tullahoma, Tennessee

Things Good and Bad

This camp was newly built in the middle of a forest on a plateau, and here we lived in small huts, not barracks. Each hut was built to house five internees. The huts were made using rough, uncured lumber that was full of knots. Because the huts had been put up in a hurry, they were poorly constructed, with many gaps in the walls. Fortunately, we did not start living there until after winter was over. However, I imagined we would be in for a hard time if we were to spend the coming winter there.

The roads were covered with limestone gravel, but the surface had not yet been leveled with rollers, so it was difficult to walk on the road. The mess hall was an old structure that was located in the upper portion of the camp, far from our huts. It was irritating to have to walk up and down the graveled slope for every meal.

We had expected that the second group from Hawai'i would be there when we arrived, but we found only five internees from Miami, Florida. We slept on army cots, using the mattresses, pillows, and blankets that had been previously used by members of the CCC. No sheets or pillowcases were provided, and the filth and the smell were overwhelming.

On the positive side, the food was good. There were always bowls of sugar on the table, and we could take as much as we wanted. I especially liked this, for I prefer sweets to liquor, and so I could use as much sugar as I wanted.

As I mentioned earlier, our chef was Mr. Uyeda from St. Louis. He displayed his culinary skills and we enjoyed his dishes. Lights-out was at eleven and we got up at seven. Players of *go*, *shōgi*, and cards were happy with this schedule. Mr. Tsunoda and Mr. Tatsutani, who lived in a hut at the far end of the lower section, played *go* every night, using wooden pieces that the Red Cross had donated.

We again organized our internee administration. Internees who had held posts at Camp McCoy were re-elected, with a few exceptions. Dr. Akio Kimura was elected coordinator, and Dr. Kazuo Miyamoto was chosen vice coordinator. As I recall, the rest of the officers were Heigo Fuchino, labor department chief; Kazoe Kawasaki, treasurer; Tetsusaburo Uyeda, chef; and Totaro Matsui and Takeo Kagawa, secretaries. I was designated barracks captain. This time, I was to take care of two huts, but with ten internees only, so I felt I could comfortably perform this duty.

A new type of letter-writing paper was distributed to everyone. At Camp McCoy, we had been able to use any type of writing paper we wanted. This new letter paper was similar to an aerogram. Each sheet was printed with twenty-six lines, and the paper had been chemically processed, so that if I pressed the surface with my moist fingers, it immediately turned a bluish color. I later learned that this letter paper had been made specifically for use by POWs and internees. Finding it a curiosity, we quickly used it to write to our families to tell them that we had arrived here.

A Man's Angry Outburst

The U.S. government had interned many Germans during World War I.[1] Apparently, many of them suffered nervous breakdowns when they were forced to stay in one place for a long time. I am not sure whether the authorities had been trying to avoid the recurrence of a similar problem, but they moved us several times during our four-year internment. The transfer from a stable life at Camp McCoy to Camp Forrest seemed to trigger a new round of irritation among us.

One of my acquaintances, a well-educated and intelligent man, complained bitterly that he had been interned because a certain group of people had conspired against him. I was somewhat surprised by his allegation.

In another incident, one day as we were climbing the gravel slope to the mess hall, a man behind me suddenly yelled out, "That stupid Sato said we'd never be interned, even if war broke out. But look at what's happened to us!" He said it in a loud voice, so that Mr. Sato, who was walking right in front of me, could hear it. Certainly, Mr. Sato had heard the remark, but he pretended not to hear anything.

Since July 1941, the United Japanese Society of Hawai'i had been hosting lectures on the current situation. Mr. Sato, then president of the society, had given lectures on several occasions.[2] As vice president, I, too, was responsible for his presentations. I felt badly for Mr. Sato, because he had become the lone target of criticism, and I also felt uncomfortable about being accused indirectly. Although the man had accused Mr. Sato in such a rude manner, he was only partially correct. However, I dared not explain this to him in detail, for I thought it would have taken too much time for him to understand. So I just ignored his remarks.

A Different Sort of Man

A man named Gunjiro Maruyama, an internee from Miami, came to visit me three days after we arrived. He was originally from Nakamaki village in the county of Higashi Yamanashi in Yamanashi Prefecture, and he somehow knew that I was from Yamanashi as well. Maruyama appeared to be middle-aged, and he told me that he was a professional photographer and an amateur pilot. He also said that his wife ran a restaurant and that she was the daughter of Chiba Taneaki, a high-ranking official of the Imperial Household Agency. Her elder sister was married to Major Akiyama of the Army Intelligence Bureau.

"That's why the authorities had good reason to detain me," he told me with a smile. He was a small-aircraft flight instructor, and he had suffered an accident that had left him crippled. He once made an interesting remark. "Small aircraft is much safer than automobiles," he said. "Even if a light plane falls to the ground, you won't be killed as long as you maneuver it carefully." I heard this for the first time from him and thought that he just might be right.

Two Ministers and Their Sermons

On the fifth day in camp, Sunday service was held in the mess hall. Reverend Kano gave a sermon on "What Prayer Is Accepted by God?" He said, "The existence of God cannot be recognized unless you are very religious, but prayers are something that exist above God." His approach was direct and enthusiastic, so that even those who were not very religious could comprehend it. His was a good example of how to preach to those who were not very religious, and I was very much impressed.

The following Sunday, Reverend Ikezawa preached about "War and Peace." I thought it would have been more appropriate to have called it a "speech" rather than a "sermon." He supported Japan's position in the current war, saying it was necessary for the happiness of humankind. I thought it was quite unusual for a Christian minister to justify war, and I was surprised by his courage to speak out in spite of his age. Or, one might say, only an old man would dare to make such a statement. After the war, Reverend Ikezawa visited Japan. But the lack of self-discipline among the Japanese youth was such a disappointment to him that he returned to Hawai'i, having become quite neurotic.

Reverend Kuchiba Has Surgery

Thus far, the two hundred internees who had been brought on the first ship from Hawai'i were all well, and none suffered from any serious illness. But now, Reverend Kuchiba of the Hongwanji Mission had to have his appendix removed at the camp hospital. We worried about him, for we had no idea what kind of care he would receive. Fortunately, the hospital was well equipped, and he was released after ten days.

Feeling pain in two of my rear molars, I, too, went to the hospital to be checked. There were no dentists among the internees, so an army surgeon examined me. All he said was that he would pull out the teeth. Even though I asked him to somehow treat me without pulling my teeth out, he flatly refused, saying that to do so would not improve the situation, so I reluctantly agreed and had both teeth extracted.

Hasebe Shakes Hands with a Major General

About five days after we arrived, a major general, who appeared to be the chief commander of the army camp, came to inspect us. He was accompanied by a captain. The general was speaking to coordinator Kimura, when, as we watched from afar, Charlie Hasebe walked up to him and greeted him like a friend.

"Hello, General. How are you?" Hasebe seemed to be saying as he shook the general's hand.

Even Dr. Kimura seemed to have been taken by surprise. I later learned that Hasebe had once run a restaurant at Castner.[3] Some officers, who were now generals and colonels, had been stationed at Schofield Barracks in their younger days, and Hasebe had known many of them well. Hasebe was rumored to have been killed at Camp Castner on the day of the Pearl Harbor attack. Despite his bragging, he was actually a nice, timid guy.

Heavy Showers

Our huts had been built hurriedly and poorly. Although winter was not yet near, we already were having problems in the summer when it rained. No sooner would black clouds appear in the distance, then rain would start pouring down like a waterfall. Showers rained on us not only from above, but from all sides as well, as the rain was blown in by gusts of wind. Windows had been simply cut from the walls, with the cut-out pieces hinged on the top edge to act as shutters. When we wanted to keep the windows open, we propped open the hinged covers. As soon as we noticed a shower approaching, someone would immediately go outside to remove the props. In just that short time, we would get drenched. Rain would also enter the hut through the gaps in the walls, soaking the entire floor. With five people living in the small hut, space was limited, so we would pile up our suitcases and duffel bags on the cots. It was pandemonium. I understand that sudden downpours are common in the central states, from Tennessee to Oklahoma.

Outdoor Movies

After a rain shower, it would become very humid. The guards told us they were going to show a movie in the forest behind our huts, so we happily gathered there. I strolled around the area before the movie started. In the dusk, I saw fireflies flying here and there. For a moment, I forgot that I was interned and enjoyed the relaxing summer evening. A sixteen-millimeter Paramount movie about a Hawai'i-related story was shown. It had not actually been filmed in Hawai'i, so some parts of it seemed ridiculous. But it was nostalgic and, all in all, we enjoyed the movie.

Blackouts

We had not experienced any blackouts since coming to the Mainland, but once we did have a statewide blackout drill. All the lights surrounding our camp were turned off, and we were ordered to stay in the forest while the guards patrolled to prevent anyone from escaping. Since we had no such intention, we simply enjoyed the thirty-minute break, watching the fireflies and listening to the chirping of the insects. Italian internees living in the next block were noisy, singing songs and chatting loudly. Some of us worried that the Italians might creep into our huts and steal something, for we feared that some of them were light-fingered.

The Rehabilitation of Ensign Sakamaki

We finally felt settled, having built shelves in our huts for our belongings. Kensaku Tsunoda and Kazoe Kawasaki began giving us English lessons, and I, having little to do, as the saying goes, "Began studying at age sixty." The textbook that had been written for newly arrived immigrants was relatively easy to understand, and I enjoyed reading it, as the system of American self-government was explained in detail.

Among the twenty or thirty of us attending the class was Ensign Sakamaki, the first Japanese POW. At Camp McCoy he had been isolated in a separate area at, but here he lived in a hut in our area. As I briefly mentioned earlier, he was in low spirits, which was natural, since he was a POW. Not only that, I heard that the mini-submarine operations he had participated in on December 7 had most likely ended in failure, without even sinking a ship, while the naval pilots had been successful in their mission. Five mini-submarines had been dispatched, and all of them had reached the outskirts of Pearl Harbor as scheduled. However, the gyro-compass in Ensign Sakamaki's I-24 mini-submarine was faulty from the beginning, and he could hardly maneuver his craft. On top of that, it had been exposed to severe gunfire from American surveillance boats at the narrow entrance to Pearl Harbor.

The mission of the mini-subs was to torpedo only battleships and aircraft carriers or to ram directly into them, so crews on mini-subs could not attack surveillance boats, for that was against orders. Ensign Sakamaki and Petty Officer 2nd Class Inagaki, his only crew member, struggled desperately with the malfunctioning craft from the early morning of December 7 and all throughout the day. Blindly navigating under the water, they scraped against the rocks, damaging the torpedo-launcher and causing fumes to leak out, which made breathing difficult. Exhausted, they tried desperately to reach the pick-up point off of Lānaʻi Island, but while navigating around Diamond Head, they fell asleep. The sea was calm at dawn on December 8, and as they passed through what they thought was the Molokaʻi Channel, they again struck a reef. When they looked outside, the two men discovered that they were near the Kāneʻohe Air Station in Windward Oʻahu. They decided to abandon their craft, and after planting explosives in the mini-sub, they jumped into the water. Ensign Sakamaki lost consciousness and was captured by American soldiers at the water's edge. Petty Officer Inagaki was never found.[4]

Sakamaki found it unbearable to think that he had accomplished nothing and had become the mission's lone survivor and prisoner, while his subordinate's fate was unknown. He especially regretted his single-mindedness in targeting only the largest vessels—battleships and aircraft carriers—thereby missing the opportunity to strike at the surveillance boats and destroyers. Because of this, he seemed distracted while at Camp McCoy. An army surgeon and Dr. Miyamoto examined him, but he did not respond to any of the questions they asked, and so it appeared that he had suffered a nervous breakdown.

After he started attending our camp classes and studying hard like a schoolboy, he began to relax. He started to come alive and exchanged daily greetings with us. He told us that he could feel the change in the weather. The English class served its purpose of providing not only knowledge, but also relaxation.

Squirrels and Fossils

All of the previous camps in which we had been held were built in large clearings adjacent to military barracks and were quite unattractive. However, here at Camp Forrest, the military barracks were located far away, and our huts were in a forest full of many big trees. We felt more relaxed living in this camp. I often went into the forest during my leisure time to dispel my gloom, to listen to the birds sing, and to play with the squirrels. The squirrels were never afraid of us, and they were very cute.

The forest also contained rare fossils. Plant fossils can be found in any forest, but the fossils found in this area seemed to be mainly of animals. They were hollow cylinders, light gray in color with spiral lines, about an inch long and one-eighth to one-quarter of an inch in diameter. Using a boring tool, openings could be drilled out at the ends. Surely they could not be the fossils of worms, I thought. I knew I had to show them to a scholar to find out exactly what they were. At any rate, it was fun to gather the fossils.

I had collected seashells and pieces of coral at Sand Island and pebbles at Angel Island. At Camp McCoy, I had tried hard to find small stones to use as *go* pieces. It had since become a habit to always look for stones, something I continued doing, even later on at Camp Livingston and at Santa Fe. More than half of all the internees, myself included, enjoyed polishing the stones we had collected. Even after I had been released and was heading home, I could not bring myself to throw them away. I brought back a few hundred stones that I had collected from several places. I still keep them as something to remember my internment by.

It was in Livingston, Louisiana, where I found various types of stones. Because of the camp's geographical location, most stones seemed to have been washed down from the central states, rather than having been of local origin. The region's native stone, commonly known as a "living stone," is brownish in color and looks like a lump of clay and pebbles. It is certainly not very pretty. It is hollow with small pebbles inside that make a rattling sound when shaken. It is said that the name Livingston is derived from this stone.

Agonizing over Repatriation

Although many people applied for repatriation to Japan while at Camp McCoy, the only ones who received permission to return to Japan were five Seattle bankers and six Hawai'i men. The six were Motoichi Matsuda of Specie Bank, Torataro Onoda and Shigenari Hattori of Sumitomo Bank, Kenji Kimura of Nippon Yūsen Steamship, Norikazu Nakano of Bon Temps Store, and Genji Otani of Home Insurance. On June 14, a telegram from Washington, D.C., reached Kichitaro Sekiya of Wahiawā, notifying him that he had been added to the list. Mr. Sekiya was lucky, for the first exchange ship was scheduled to sail out of New York on June 18, giving him just enough time to get ready to board the *Gripsholm*.

We felt a little empty after seeing these men off and comforted one another with the wishful thinking that all of us would repatriate aboard the second ship, which was scheduled to depart in August, according to the information we had received. We learned that Mr. Sekiya had sent a copy of his petition to the Swedish Embassy in April just to make sure. We assumed it had worked. Everyone was quite envious of him and his good fortune, and many internees followed suit, sending petitions to the Swedish Embassy.

Since we believed that we would get on the second ship, which was scheduled to depart in August, Kinzo Sayegusa and I jointly sent a telegram to our families asking them to send us money and summer clothing. The reply, written in English, read, "Sending $200; Are you repatriating; Is it necessary, we prefer you stay in United States; answer."

Earlier, I had sent my family a letter, consulting with them about repatriation. Although there had not been any agreement about it, they told me that they would leave it up to me. Now with the arrival of this telegram, I was put in a difficult position. It would have been unbearable for me to remain behind barbed wire in a faraway place on the Mainland for ten or fifteen years, after most of the internees had returned to Japan. I could not deny the possibility that I might die of illness during my internment. However, were I allowed to repatriate, I might have a chance of returning to Hawai'i if Japanese forces seized the islands. I wanted to send a message explaining all this, but I could not write this, for I knew it would be censored.

At any rate, we had to notify our families that we had received the money, so Sayegusa and I sent a telegram in English to Kenichi Sayegusa, saying, "Remittance received, Furuya and Sayegusa may repatriate August; Send clothing."

Soon another telegram came with the response, "Mother and I prefer that you do not repatriate; Details by letter." Learning that my wife and children were against my repatriation, I agonized over this matter for days. I did not want to be selfish and return against their wishes. I finally decided to postpone my repatriation and to try to persuade my family. There were quite a few similar cases among us internees.

Our Third Departure

Here in southern Tennessee, the end of June brought hot, mid-summer-like weather. Cicadas chirped loudly in the forest. I thought the embroidered pillowcase that Mr. Tominaga of Samoa had given me would feel nice under my head, but I decided not to use it, because the pillow was heavily stained. One day when it was sunny, I washed my down pillow. I was happy when it dried and became fluffy before nightfall. I covered it with the pillowcase and showed it to Mr. Tominaga with a word of thanks.

Here, it never cooled down, even after darkness fell. The cicadas continued their noisy chorus. I had not known that cicadas also chirped at night. The Japanese saying, "Different places, different ways," is quite true.

We had spent only a month here when we were ordered to move again. This time, we were given neither advance notice nor hints as to where we were being sent next. All of us were utterly surprised by this news. We were quite disappointed that we were to be transferred, for we had just installed shelves in our huts and had placed our belongings upon them. We had to pack up again, just like traveling entertainers. We had no idea what the authorities were trying to do to us. As the expression goes, we were "in the middle of a five-*ri* fog" about our future.[5] It is a pity that we, ordinary beings, cannot be as easily enlightened as Issa. One of his poems expresses his feelings upon accepting his fate:

> Trusting the Buddha, good and bad,
> I bid farewell
> To the departing year.[6]

On June 29, 1942, our train left Tullahoma Station and took the same route back to Nashville. We crossed the Tennessee River into Memphis, the largest city in the state of Tennessee. From the train, I could see huge swarms of fireflies. It was such a beautiful sight. Our train turned south as it crossed the Mississippi River and entered Arkansas. As we crossed the Arkansas River, we noticed that the water under the bridge was reddish and muddy, like that of the Yellow River in northern China. I was afraid to look at the old bridge as our train crossed over it. It became extremely muggy as we passed through the swamplands. Then the train turned left-ward, toward a hilly area where many pine trees grew. I guessed that oil drilling took place here, for I saw many derricks. The train made its way up a hill for a while, and then came upon some watchtowers. I gathered that this was our destination, and I was relieved that we had finally reached it.

SIX HAIKU WRITTEN IN TENNESSEE

At night
Imprisoned in a faraway place
I hear the cicadas sing
遠く囚われている夜鳴く蝉を聞く

The light of a few fireflies
In front of my hut at twilight
蛍二つ三つまだ暮れきらぬキャビンのまえ

Leave it to a squirrel
To befriend a Japanese
栗鼠なら日本人の我等にも馴れる

Fireflies slip smoothly by
As our outdoor movie begins
蛍スーイスーイ野天で映画はじまる

Summer clouds
Is it time for another move
To an unknown place?
夏雲行方のわからない旅立か

Over rows of yellow flowers
Yellow butterflies flutter by
黄色い花がいちめんとんでいるのが黄色い蝶々

| 10 |

Camp Livingston
Livingston,[1] Louisiana

Our Reunion with Group Two

Here we were in the southern portion of the Mainland, and although it was at a latitude only slightly north of Hawaiʻi's, it was much warmer. The camp was on a hill in the midst of a forest of Georgia pines.

We got off the train and found our baggage, but we had no idea where to go, for there was no camp in sight. We thought that perhaps we would be taken to there aboard military trucks, but we saw none. We were wondering what to do, when four or five guards appeared and ordered us to pick up our suitcases and start walking. And so we marched, with a rope slung over one shoulder, our suitcase and duffel tied at either end, one in front and the other in back. There were no trees along the road, and walking under the burning sun, we soon began to perspire. Although we walked for quite a while, we saw nothing but mountains covered in white summer clouds. Exhausted, some of the older men sat down on the roadside to rest. The guards did not object, so once in a while we would take a break from the walking.

We had gone about a mile, when we came upon some barracks in the middle of a pine forest. Cheered by the sight, we started walking, our spirits high. As we approached the camp entrance, we saw a banner that read, "Welcome," and many men waiting for us. I looked at them closely and found most of them to be Hawaiʻi people. I recognized high-spirited Sawajiro Ozaki first, and then Sadasuke Hamamoto, Kyoichi Miyata, Miyuki Sokabe, Mankichi Goto, Masayuki Chikuma, Kametaro Maeda, Buntetsu Miyamoto, Masahiro Himeno, Suekuma Takaki, and Iwaki Watanabe. I shared the joy of reunion with the Honolulu men after a four-month separation, for they had been kept behind at Sand Island when our group left there.

This camp was made up of four barracks, namely J-1, J-2, K-1, and K-2. A fence separated the J and K blocks. Earlier arrivals had been divided into their own areas. The Hawai'i group was assigned to Barracks J-2 and the Panama group to Barracks J-1. The Mainlanders were in Block K.

The Hawai'i group had been sent on the second ship and had arrived here via Fort Sill in Oklahoma.[2] Twenty-one men were from O'ahu, eighty-five were from the Big Island, thirty-five from Kaua'i, twenty-four from Maui, and one from Moloka'i, for a total of 165. Although 166 men had left Hawai'i, Kanesaburo Oshima of Kona had been shot to death by a camp guard at Fort Sill when he attempted to climb over the barbed wire fence. He became the sole victim in the Hawai'i group.[3]

I was assigned to Barracks J-1 where I lived together with the Panama group. The men from Panama had been living in the Panama Canal area and had been forced to leave rather than be interned. The leader of the group was a middle-aged man named Otsubo, who could speak a little English. An elderly man, a Mr. Komatsu, was the advisor of the Panama group. Takaichi Saiki[4] was the group leader of Barracks J-2.

I was asked to be chief of the athletic department, and I willingly accepted the post. The corporal in charge of the internees' recreational activities was a frank and cooperative young man who had been drafted when he had been a sophomore. I asked him to provide us with various sporting equipment and with it we formed softball, sumō, volleyball, and table tennis clubs. Later a golf club was started. However, we were not allowed to practice *kendō*.[5]

Assigned to the Panama Group

Our barracks were new, small structures that could house fifteen people.

Together with Toshio Iinuma of Waialua and Kusuro Ishida, Shozo Kawakami, and Tsutomu Imamura of Honolulu, I was assigned to a barracks already occupied by ten Panama internees. That's why we were called the Panama group.

All the occupants of the adjoining Barracks J-2 were from Hawai'i. Although we used separate mess halls, we could move freely between the two areas since there was no fence between them. Takaichi Saiki of the Big Island was the J-2 leader, and friends like Seiha Asami, Rev. Ninryo Nago, and Totaro Matsui of Honolulu, and Rev. Jukaku Shirasu and Masato Kiyosaki of Hilo lived there. I often visited them. I enjoyed chatting with Asami, but there was another good reason to visit their barracks. Reverend Shirasu worked at the hospital as a cook, and he sometimes brought back food that he had taken from the kitchen. Also, Iwaki Watanabe, who was another cook from Barracks J-2, sometimes brought food to Reverend Shirasu in appreciation for his teaching him how to play *go*. In this way, I benefitted, using their burdock for the meal at my Buddhist service.[6]

Small Perks

About ten days after we had settled in, a corporal in charge of recreational activities took Mr. Segawa, who also worked in the athletic department, and me by truck to the clubhouse to get some sporting equipment. No guard escorted us beyond the gates, so we were able to enjoy the scenery from an elevated point outside the camp, and we were even treated to a highball. Before heading back, we loaded into the truck the sporting goods and some desks and flowering plants that the corporal allowed us to take. We returned to the camp in high spirits. Everyone envied us.

Scraping Meat off the Bone during KP Duty

This heading may give you the impression that KP duty was hard work, but this wasn't so in my case. Instead of having to work myself to the bone, I had to scrape meat off from some pork ribs.[7]

The cooks in our block were all from the Panama group. They had rarely cooked western dishes before and could barely prepare Japanese food.

One day spare ribs were provided for dinner. After cleaning up the dishes, pots, and pans, and just as we were about to return to our barracks, the chief cook told us to scrape the meat off of the spare ribs. He was angry because he thought the meat was meant to be removed from the ribs. I wanted to tell him otherwise, but cooks tend to be headstrong and his pride might have been hurt, so I said nothing. We followed his orders and cleanly scraped all the meat from the ribs, working an additional hour at the task. In the evening, however, before the others got their share, we enjoyed pork *sukiyaki*[8] until we were full.

A Variety of Classes Are Offered

Many internees enrolled in the various classes that were started in the camp. We called this "Internee University." Included were classes in English, carving, *shakuhachi*,[9] and Spanish, which were attended by not only younger people, but a seventy-year-old man as well. The English class was conducted by Reverend Kano and Reverend Himeno, and carving was taught by Mr. Takatsuka, a young man from Panama. For the shakuhachi class, the instruments were water pipes with holes drilled in them, and Shuji Mikami, a Hawai'i internee, was the instructor. Michio Ito, a famous dancer, was interned in Block K, and it was rumored that he would be starting a dancing class, but unfortunately it never materialized.[10]

A Concert without Musical Instruments

With so many talented people from Panama, they decided to conduct a concert. The men obtained permission to make supports by cutting down some pine trees that surrounded our camp. They built a stage using the boards that had been left outside the camp after the barracks construction was finished. The men practiced for about two weeks, and then the day came for them to demonstrate their talents. Everyone in camp was curious, and so many people showed up that there was no room left to stand.

Their first number was the "The Warship March."[11] Their musical instruments were unusual. Empty barrels became drums, much like the ones used for performances of *Yagi-bushi*.[12] In addition to barrels, large and small pots, frying pans, and live whistling were used to make a very loud noise, like that of a rural marching band. The audience applauded wildly.

Itsuo Hamada of Maui joined the actors in a *Naniwa-bushi*[13] production and surprised the Panama people with his spectacular performance. There also were soap-opera-style skits, magic acts, and the like. The program was more than adequate. During the intermission, members of the audience jumped up on the stage and performed songs and Naniwa-bushi. Koichi Iida, who liked to sing, represented the Hawai'i group, displaying his talent by singing a *ha-uta* entitled, "Spring Rain." He was unexpectedly good. He had announced that he would sing a *naga-uta*, so when he actually sang a *ha-uta*, the audience roared with laughter.[14]

The concert was a big success, and the audience tipped them with ten-cent and fifteen-cent coupons. The Panama internees were very happy to receive the extra money, for they had nothing beyond the three dollars that the camp administration allotted to each person once a month. Encouraged by their success, the Panama internees decided to hold more concerts in the future and left the stage as it was.

But then a middle-aged priest from Hawai'i dismantled the floorboards and took them to his J-2 barracks, probably because he wanted to install some shelves. It caused loud complaining from the Panama group.

"How could a priest steal public property?" I was embarrassed to hear them exclaim. "Do all priests in Hawai'i do such things?"

Unfortunately, the stage was right next to my barracks. Members of the entertainment group demanded that the boards be returned at once, or they would take them back by force. Although I also was very angry about this incident, I did not want the priest to be publicly humiliated. So, I asked them to leave the matter to me, as I intended to tell him to return the boards secretly at night. In this way, the matter was resolved.

The priest was from a neighbor island, and I had never spoken to him before. I was so embarrassed that a fellow internee would do such a thing, and I felt as if I personally had committed the act. Besides this priest, there were quite a few priests and principals of Japanese language schools whose behavior was intolerable. Those of us who had always held such people in high esteem were given a rude awakening indeed.

Digging Holes under the Floor

Although the camp was located on top of a small hill, because the whole area was swampland, it was always extremely muggy. It was very hot in the barracks and in the pine forest, as well. Someone dug a hole in the ground[15] and found it was more comfortable to be in there, lying down and reading books. I visited the hole and found it to be much cooler indeed.

The soil at Camp Livingston was made up of mud and sand carried by the waters of the Mississippi River. Like in Waiʻanae, the ground was sandy and easy to dig, and so one after another we started digging holes. These holes were very comfortable—cool in the summer and warm in the winter. Perhaps this is how the gods taught primitive man to protect himself from heat and cold.

There was no problem staying in the hole during the daytime. In the evening, however, it was still so hot that I could not touch my bedstead, even at nine o'clock. With no lights and mosquitoes buzzing about, I could not escape the heat even in my hole. I had no choice but to keep cool by fanning myself with a newspaper.

Craftwork Becomes Popular

Because of the heat, the making of folding fans came into fashion first. I, too, tried to make one, but having been born clumsy, I was not very good at it. Although I could complete one, and the shape resembled a fan, the top portion would not fold in completely. It looked like it was made of iron.[16] I tried many times to fix it, but my efforts were in vain.

With the guidance of Tsuruzo Hasegawa of Kauaʻi, who was known to be a good fan-maker, I finally completed one. Although I was not entirely satisfied with the piece, I was happy that I had completed my first craft project. I thought that I should reward Mr. Hasegawa somehow. Instead, I was embarrassed when he gave me a beautiful fan that he had made. I asked Reverend Kubokawa of the Jodo Mission to write something appropriate on it. I still have this fan today.

For some reason, craftwork became popular from this time. Some of us dug tree roots from the ground, worked them into various shapes, and polished them to create art objects. Others made walking sticks from the *sankirai*, a rattan-like plant. Some internees were skillful enough to weave bags and hats out of Georgia pine needles. Mr. Iinuma, of my barracks, worked very hard whenever he was free, and the results were impressive. At a glance, those Georgia pine needles look like the Japanese pine *goyomatsu*, but Georgia pines only have three six-inch needles on each cluster. In Japan, regular pines have clusters of two needles, and goyomatsu have five.

A Formal Funeral by the Internees

During the early stage of our internment, none of us suffered serious illness, probably because our defenses were up in reaction to the crisis. As time went by after our move to the Mainland, some of us became sick.

The first to succumb was Gosaku Masuda of Lāhainā, an influential figure on Maui. The camp hospital had fairly good facilities and several doctors. They tried their best to cure him, but he eventually died. Mr. Masuda's death was the first in our Hawai'i group since we had moved to the Mainland and the first camp tragedy of its kind. It was a great shock to us.

We decided that all internees would pay their last respects at a formal funeral. The funeral site was set for Block K, and approximately four hundred internees from Barracks J-1 and J-2 were expected to attend. Rev. Gijo Ozawa of Kaua'i was appointed to lead the proceedings. Having been a Japanese military reserve officer, he gave commands in typical military style. All of us solemnly paraded to the funeral site. Among us were fifty-eight Buddhist priests, twenty-two Shinto priests, and seven Christian ministers, who all offered prayers according to their respective rituals, with some internees delivering eulogies. While we attended the funeral in our regular military-issued clothing, Reverend Ban, a Christian minister from Los Angeles, stood out in his college cap-and-gown. The voices of dozens of Buddhist priests reciting sutras blended in harmonic rhythm with the sound of the wind blowing through the pine forest, creating a strange atmosphere of both solemnity and splendor.

Mr. Masuda had been a Japanese pioneer in Hawai'i. He had lived a full life, but to have died behind the barbed wire fence, far from home with no loved ones present at the funeral, must have been bitterly disappointing for him and his family. On the other hand, none of us in our normal life would have been given a funeral with more than eighty priests and ministers in attendance. So, one could say that Mr. Masuda's soul found some peace, after all.

The first casualty after our arrests on December 7, 1941 was Hisahiko Kokubo from Kaua'i, who died of a heart attack on March 9, 1942, at Sand Island. The second came on July 27, 1942, when forty-eight-year-old Yoichi Kagimoto died suddenly. The third casualty was Kanesaburo Oshima, who was shot and killed by a guard at Fort Sill, Oklahoma. Mr. Masuda was the fourth Hawai'i casualty of our internment.[17]

Ensign Sakamaki's View of Japanese Internees

Ensign Sakamaki had been with us from the time we were at Sand Island. In Livingston, he lived in a cabin next to the hospital in Block K. He was allowed to move freely within the camp during the daytime, so he attended English and religion classes every day. In the middle of the Block J pine forest, Rev. Nisshu Kobayashi gave lectures on little known episodes of Saint Nichiren's life.[18] Ensign Sakamaki and Miyuki Sokabe listened intently.

One day I had a chance to speak with Ensign Sakamaki. We sat on the roots of a pine tree and talked. He said that our way of thinking and lifestyle as immigrants had been influenced by American culture. I had never before thought about us as having been Americanized, but the many years away from Japan must have had a subconscious effect.

"Your unique philosophy and lifestyle show in the attitudes you have acquired through daily life among Americans over many years," he said. "I find a new sense of humanity being expressed in your internment life, as I see you polishing stones and making carvings from tree roots, while you wait for the day when you will be freed. In socializing with all of you, I have been forced to question Japan's ideology and militarism. Your outlook on life has convinced me that being a POW is not the end of the world and that I should adopt a positive will to 'live.' I have learned from your diligence that I should devote myself to further study, whether or not I am facing adversity." I thought that he spoke from his heart.

Although I felt that there were many internees who were very stubborn and too Japanized, in the eyes of a traditional navy man like Ensign Sakamaki, we must have appeared to be quite democratic. Above all, most of us had American children, who had graduated from high schools and colleges in this country. Subconsciously, we would have been influenced by their thinking. Unlike the observations made by Japanese politicians and the crews of training ships, Ensign Sakamaki's comments were accurate and a little embarrassing, as he was in a situation similar to ours.

A Reunion after a Long Time

I went to see Yoshihiko Kasai at his office in Block K, since I had heard he also was being interned in this camp. We had been friends when we were young, and I had not seen him since he had left Japan for the United States. He had accompanied his father in their move to the Mainland some thirty-seven or thirty-eight years ago while we were still in elementary school. Later I learned he had graduated from a high school in California and had married a Caucasian girl. He told me he had been a successful insurance agent in Salt Lake City. We reminisced about our elementary school and the village shrine, and we forgot about our current situation for a while.

Among the second group of internees from the Big Island, Maui, and Kaua'i were many friends and acquaintances. I was very happy to see them. From the literary field, there was Otokichi (Muin) Ozaki, Minoru (Koran) Murakami, Hisashi (Getsugaku) Fukuhara, Shigezo (Kasetsu) Shigekane, and Haruto (Fuyo) Saito. My businessman friends were Kiyoshi Ichikawa, Shizuma Tagawa, Gunichi Kuwahara, Takaichi Saiki, Masato Kiyosaki, Atsuo Sakimizuru, Masaichiro Shinoda, Kyuhachi Tanaka, Torao Iseri, Setsugo Togioka, Kosuke Hirose, Yoshio Kobayashi, Motoichi Kobayashi, Itsuo Hamada, and Katsuichi Miho. Tasuke Kajiwara, Gempei Miura, Kanryu Mochizuki, and Kichisuke Yoda were friends from my home prefecture. Other friends were Kunisuke Sakai, Ryugen Matsuda, Hiseki Miyazaki, Saichiro Kubota, and Hozui Nakayama. For a while I was kept busy visiting these friends or hosting their visits at my place. Our conversations seemed endless, talking about what had happened since we had been interned.

I also made quite a few friends during my internment. They were: Kazuma Araki, barracks secretary at Camp McCoy; the former Waimea postmaster Tokuichi Niimi;[19] Rev. Umeo Wada, who gave me massages; principal Giichi Sasaki; Dr. Kazuo Miyamoto; Rev. Masahiro Himeno, a Christian minister who taught English class; and Shunichi Odo, a cigarette lover. As incarcerated men, however, it was our destiny to be separated again with a single order to move on.

Nisei Return to Hawai'i

Hawai'i's German Americans, who had been interned at Camp McCoy, complained to the authorities that it was unreasonable to incarcerate them on the Mainland, although they reluctantly understood that the government needed to intern them during wartime. As a result, they were allowed to move back home, and I wondered why they did not similarly return Nisei to Hawai'i.[20] But then in August, nineteen Nisei were allowed to return. They were: Takeo Akizaki, Kazuma Araki, Noriaki Atsuumi, Kenkichi Fujimoto, Shigeo Fujino, Hiroshi Honda, Tamotsu Ihara, Masao Ishimoto, Takeo Kagawa, Kazuo Miyamoto, Tokuichi Niimi, Shunichi Odo, Seiichi Sugimoto, Masao Sakamoto, Sanji Sakamoto, Shinzaburo Sumida, Manabu Tashiro, Norizane Tsuha, and Toraji Kawahara of Lordsburg.[21]

There is a scene from the movie *Sanga Ari*, in which a Nisei boy is interned in Japan. He becomes ill while in the camp and is allowed to live with his mother, who is staying at her parents' house.[22]

"I just want to go home to Hawai'i," he says wistfully. Those simple words aroused sympathy in those of us who had experienced internment life on the Mainland. During our internment, we had always felt, "I just want to go home to Hawai'i."

We wished we could be those Nisei, who were not necessarily being freed, but were at least going back to Hawai'i.

Cloth-Dying Becomes Fashionable

Our G.I. shirts and pants had been previously worn by soldiers and then re-dyed blue. They looked pretty nice for a while, but soon the color faded to its original light brown—especially on the shoulders and back—probably because of the cheap dye that was used. There was no need to show off while we were in camp, but still, our clothes did not look good at all.

This must have been the general feeling within the camp, because someone bought some dye and started re-dying his clothes using empty cans. The dye cost only twenty-five cents a packet, so it was not expensive, and we had time on our hands. Soon we all started dying our clothes and to do so became fashionable.

Men, who may have ridiculed women for following fashion trends, or who were otherwise totally ignorant of such things, followed along once something became the fashion in camp. It seems that copying is instinctive. In our normal life, most of us had considered it shameful to copy others as monkeys do. Now, behind the barbed wire, we tended to be childish. We copied one another and kept an eagle eye on food. Camp life had made us abandon our pride as men.

A Strange-Looking Procession at Mealtime

In Camp McCoy, we wore our heavy coats to the mess hall. In this camp, the weather was extremely hot, so we lived in short pants and handmade *geta*.[23] The government-issued mugs were of poor quality, and if the KPs washed them roughly, the handles would break off. So, everyone took his own mug to the mess, cleaned it, and brought it back to his barracks. It was a strange sight: men walking in short pants and *geta*, and carrying mugs.

In the afternoon, when the temperature rose, we stayed in our holes. There we spent the whole afternoon, reading books and taking naps. The entire camp became so quiet that it was as if no one were there.

The sun shone brightly over our heads, and the only sound was that of cicadas chirping noisily in the pine trees. It gave me a strange feeling, as if this world were nearing its end. The weather in this region was very bad. In the evenings, a north wind would start to blow, and it would immediately become freezing cold. Hardly anyone caught a cold, however. We had no idea why.

The Oiwake School

Interned in this camp were more than one thousand people from the Mainland and Hawai‘i who had been detained for about six months following the outbreak of the war. All kinds of classes were offered. English was the most popular. On the lighter side, there were classes on such topics as Noh songs, shakuhachi, and carving.

Later, an Oiwake class opened unexpectedly.[24] The Oiwake instructor was a man named Sato from Panama. He was originally from Niigata, and he had a beautiful voice. Among the first group of students were Seiha Asami, Totaro Matsui, Dr. Tokuye Takahashi, and Muin Ozaki. Having ample time to practice and being very eager to learn, they made remarkable progress in a short period. In time, so many people wanted to join the class that Mr. Sato became unable to teach it by himself. So, Messrs. Asami and Matsui volunteered as teaching assistants, and the class became the Oiwake School. Some students were already very good at singing Oiwake, but the instructors had a difficult time correcting their unorthodox style, for they had learned to sing by themselves.

Mr. Asami had been interested in Oiwake prior to his internment, having received instruction from Chumu Mita and Seiho Tamaki. Under Mr. Sato's guidance, Mr. Asami now became a top-notch singer. Mr. Matsui had been the general manager of Pacific Bank and had always looked grim at his work place, so I could not imagine him singing Oiwake. But, contrary to my expectations, he sang beautifully in his baritone voice. I was impressed by his singing and thought he was well qualified to be an assistant.

A Class in Farming

Reverend Kano, whom I had known since Camp McCoy, was a doctor of agricultural science and had been operating a farm in Nebraska before his internment. He began a class in farming. Not many people were interested in attending, because we felt it was too late for us to learn to farm. But Reverend Kano was a very wise man, and he announced that he was going to take students outside the fence to do research on the soil of the area. Many people rushed to join the class, and with several dozen students it soon became full. The class was too large to take out in one group, so Reverend Kano decided to split it into two and take each group out once a week.

In the streams and valleys outside the camp, we found many things that were unfamiliar to us. We competed to be the first to find rattan-like trees, similar to the *sankirai*, which would make good walking sticks.

In a creek, we saw eels with fins that looked like feet. The fins seemed to have evolved in response to the narrowness and shallowness of the creek, for they made it easier to crawl around in the grass and between the stones. They probably worked like salamander feet. You might get the impression that these eels were tiny creatures living in narrow creeks, but the one we caught was quite fat and more than two feet long. They were creepy.

I had heard that in this region there lived many loathsome animals like the armadillo, the black widow spider, and the sidewinder. On this outing, I managed to find a big piece of *sankirai* and a stone that rattles called a "living stone." I brought them back to the camp.

Golfing Behind the Barbed Wire

Since there was a large clearing between the barracks and the fences, we built a nine-hole golf course. The men built another nine holes in the adjoining Block K area, and so between the two we were able to play eighteen holes.

We played with only No. 3, 4, 7, and 9 irons and putters—no wood clubs.

The course was rather flat, but because it skirted the barracks, it was hard to hit the balls around the corners. Most of the golfers were beginners, but as they got better they began to complain that the course was too easy. So, we built a mound and made an elevated green like a *dohyō*.[25] If we hit the balls too softly, they would roll back, and if we hit them too hard, they went over the mound. Some golfers took as many as twelve or thirteen strokes on that one hole. I also eventually improved my skill and once won a Block J tournament by scoring 125 on twenty-seven holes. However, I must confess, that course was much shorter than a regular golf course.

A Quarrel with Barracks Leader Otsubo

One morning after having finished our KP duty, we were playing golf when barracks leader Otsubo came and told us not to play until all the kitchen workers had finished their jobs.

Now, those people working in the kitchen were paid twenty-one dollars a month. Although the amount may have been very small, we KP workers undertook most of the harder jobs. I felt that we should not have been asked to hold ourselves back, and I told Mr. Otsubo that I did not agree, but he did not seem convinced. Unable to accept his order, I again complained to him the following day. But this time, as chief of the athletic department, I tried to reason with him.

"We didn't volunteer to come to this camp," I said. "We were detained by the military authorities, even though we didn't do anything wrong. We could be playing golf anytime we want, if we were living a normal life. You should think of us as you do the kitchen workers. I don't think the majority of us should have to stand around, just waiting for four or five men to finish their jobs. Of course, you are aware that the authorities encourage us to participate in athletic activities in order to maintain our mental and physical health."

Ever stubborn, Otsubo reluctantly accepted my argument. After that, we were able to play without any problems. Actually, I doubt that he understood what I was saying. Rather, I think he gave up trying to convince us because of my close relationship with the young corporal in charge of recreational activities.

A Man with a Personality Problem

Having lived in Honolulu for thirty years before my internment, I knew several hundred people from various communities. I had not met many whose personality was out of the ordinary. However, I was surprised to discover that in camp there were a fairly large number of people who had personality problems.

A weird man named K lived in my barracks. I had not met him prior to this, although he used to work as a manager of a retail store in Honolulu. He worked at the Block J canteen and almost every day brought back things like beer, candy, and canned food to give to those from Panama who could not afford to buy them.

In the beginning, I was impressed by his generosity. But he gradually began to behave arrogantly. He looked down on the Panama people and addressed them without using polite titles. Yet, elderly men flattered him, for he frequently gave them things. On the other hand, younger men such as Morita and Tashiro began to turn down K's treats and would walk out whenever he started bragging. We Hawaiʻi internees grew tired of hearing his stories. He bragged almost every day about being a renowned Honolulu entrepreneur, and we apparently revealed our disdain of him. He then started speaking badly about Sumida, Inc. and Fujii Store, which were quite successful in Honolulu.[26]

One of his barracks mates, Toshio Iinuma, a former principal of the Waialua Japanese Language School, did not know much about business in Honolulu. But Tsutomu Imamura and Kusuro Ishida were businessmen and were, therefore, quite knowledgeable.

"Sumida, Inc. and Fujii Store looked nice from the outside, but they were in the red," K told both gentlemen. We were very disgusted to hear him ridicule them. I don't believe that this man had any hostile feelings toward the Sumidas or the Fujiis, but he may have wanted to make himself look like a successful merchant, or perhaps he was just venting his frustration over his internment life.

K's uncalled-for accusation prompted either Mr. Imamura or Mr. Ishida—I don't remember which—to tell him flat out, "I don't know about their finances, but the difference between your firm and theirs is like night and day." This made K shift his focus to the personal backgrounds of the Sumida and Fujii families, but by then no one was listening.

Kakuro Shigenaga of Maui, who apparently was from the same prefecture as K, would visit him occasionally and ask, "Hey, how are you doing?" K seemed to have lost his dignity as a millionaire merchant.

Not long after this, Mr. Ishida, who was K's barracks mate, had a stroke and was hospitalized. Then K became ill and entered the hospital. With the two barracks mates hospitalized, we became quite lonesome. We visited them frequently to cheer them up. Even though K had bragged too much, his act of giving was rewarded. The internees from Panama often visited and comforted him.

All in all, there were fifteen or sixteen internees who seemed to have personality problems, although the types of problems were varied. Perhaps their personalities had been altered by the separation from their families and the life behind the barbed wire.

Broadcasting the News

Broadcasting the news was by far the most popular program in the camp.

Within the Panama group, Mr. Komatsu, the group advisor, broadcast news that was picked up from local English newspapers and translated into Japanese by a Mainland internee, Shonan Kimura, who lived in Block K.[27] Among the Hawai'i group from Barracks J-2, Seiha Asami and Koran Murakami of Hilo broadcast news from Hawai'i.[28] A Mainlander, Mr. Iseda, broadcast the news in Block K. He was well known among the internees, for he often pronounced Japanese words incorrectly. Many people from Block J went to hear his broadcasts just to hear his mispronounced Japanese.

One day, I was urged to go and listen to him. It was true: he made a lot of mistakes. For example, he pronounced *shuryūdan* as "*teryūdan*," *shōsai* as "*yōsai*," *oboegaki* as "*kakusho*," *kakudai* as "*kōdai*," *zenpukuteki* as "*zenhabateki*," *tachiba* as "*tateba*," and *sūjikukoku* as "*sashakoku*," just to name a few.[29] Our reporter in Barracks J-1 also made mistakes, but he did a much better job. But then, I may have been biased.

Shonan Kimura wrote scripts using the classical Chinese style of writing, and the reporter, Mr. Komatsu, read them in a stiff, formal tone that made me feel as if I were going back in time.

"Our Imperial Army, advancing over a thousand miles of rough seas to faraway New Guinea, has extended its reach to Australia," he droned. Because he often used the expression "to extend its reach," we became accustomed to his use of the saying.[30] He also became famous for pronouncing Secretary of War Stimson's name as "Stevenson." Nicknamed "Jan," Mr. Komatsu became a target of hecklers, who used his name as a pun in the phrase, "*Mainichi janjan yaru ne.*"[31]

On the other hand, the J-2 team of Asami and Murakami were professional reporters. When they did not have any news to report, they picked up interesting topics from various sources and retold them with a touch of humor. Mr. Toguchi would come all the way from Block K every day to hear their program.

One story dealt with a school principal whose wife was very attractive. She became the victim of the unfounded rumor that she was of loose morals. Some people even envied the principal. One day she wrote her husband a letter describing her loneliness and deep affection for him. Unable to suppress his joy, he showed the letter to his barracks mates, one of whom secretly passed it on to the broadcast team so they could make fun of him. The sentimental letter, read word-for-word as a special news scoop, lit a spark of sensuality among the listeners weary of their dull camp life and released a flood of laughter.

Sometimes the broadcasts told the sad news of Nikkei soldiers killed in action. Sergeant Takata of Waialua, who was well known as an excellent baseball pitcher, died soon after deployment in a battle in the Italian theater. The news that he was the first Nikkei soldier killed in action came as a big shock to us.[32]

A Dispute over Labor

Large piles of pine logs lay on a hill behind the camp. The authorities ordered us to cut them to a specific length and then to chop them. We protested that the order went against the Geneva Convention, since the job was to be done outside the camp grounds. The authorities insisted that the area was still within the military complex and that the logs were to be used by the internees to keep themselves warm. We reluctantly obeyed and got the job done in a week or so.

Soon another order came for us to help soldiers load pine logs that had been cut down in the forest about two miles east of the camp. Since we had grudgingly obeyed the first order, this time we strongly resisted. We demanded that the order be rescinded, because the ground was being cleared for a military airfield, and we would be working for the enemy if we helped.

The army refused to back down, and they told us we would be treated accordingly if we did not cooperate. They locked the gate to the adjoining area and prohibited us from going to the softball field or walking outside the camp, which had been allowed once a week. At the gate two armed guards stood by, and the machine guns in the watchtowers were pointed at us. The atmosphere of the camp became tense. Those internees who in the beginning had been strongly opposed to the order started to give in, and we finally conceded.

The job turned out not to be as hard as we had expected. We rode to the site on trucks driven by soldiers, and in teams of two we slowly loaded the logs one by one. The logs were of a size that required only one man to carry them.

The experience was more enjoyable than staying in camp. I was surprised to find a five-foot-deep gully winding through an area that used to be a pine forest. The gully wound right and left and then towards the mountains. It must have taken many years for rainwater to carve the soft soil of the area so deeply. The source of the famous Snake River is the Yellowstone National Park in Wyoming, which is located to the east of the Rockies. As the Snake River flows into Idaho, it turns south, then west at American Falls. It twists and turns until it reaches the Oregon border. From there it flows north, then turns west, and pours into Lake Wallula in Washington to merge with the Columbia River. The total length of the river is more than 240 miles. I imagine that beginning hundreds of thousands of years ago, the Snake River has probably grown from many small gullies like that in the pine forest. Although not immediately apparent, the power of time is quite enormous.

Makeshift Cooks

I referred to our makeshift cooks earlier when I wrote about golfing in camp. It was my understanding that all workers in the kitchen and other areas were being paid twenty-one dollars a month, as had been announced in Camp McCoy on May 15. However, according to a letter I received after the war from Mr. Kiyoshi Ichikawa, who used to be a senior cook in Barracks J-2, only three of them were paid.

Three cooks could not possibly prepare meals for two hundred internees, so they recruited volunteers. From the Big Island: Jitsuji Wakayama of Waimea, Motoi Shiotani of Volcano, Tokio Itsuno of Pāhoa, Tasuke Kajiwara of ʻŌlaʻa, Kakuo Shiba of Pāpaʻaloa, Kiyoshi Ichikawa and Myoshu Sasai of Hilo, and Kakusho Asano of Kohala; from Maui: Yoshio Kobayashi of Kahului and Kyodo Fujihana of Puʻunēnē; from Molokaʻi: Kozan Nishizawa; and from Kauaʻi: Kyojo Naito of Kōloa. They were priests, school principals, storeowners—all of them used to working in managerial positions. Since Masayuki Chikuma, Kiyoshi Ichikawa, and Yoshio Kobayashi were knowledgeable about cooking, they managed the volunteers and divided them into two groups. The volunteers took turns every other day in the kitchen. None of them had any experience working in a professional kitchen, and food supplies were far from adequate, so the J-2 Hawaiʻi group very much appreciated their hard work.

Mr. Ichikawa wrote in his letter that some of the former volunteer cooks would feel uneasy reading what I wrote. I understand how Mr. Ichikawa feels, but I think he is wrong. I don't think anyone in our group, who was not capable of working in the kitchen or the administrative office, took for granted those who worked, even though they were being paid for their labor. After all, while back in Camp McCoy, we resolved to compensate in some way all internee workers, and Sumida, Fuchino, and I had been appointed to come up with a suitable solution.

We always appreciated what the kitchen workers were doing, but I did not think it was necessary for us to stand around waiting for them like mourners before beginning our physical activities. I don't know what the situation was at J-2, but workers in our Barracks J-1 received benefits in addition to the monthly allowance. They were excused from other duties in the camp and in the barracks. They could order KP men to do minor tasks, and they could make special dishes for themselves. I personally had the chance to enjoy some of their food while I was on KP duty. In the heat of summer, however, while we cooled off in our holes, the kitchen workers had to stand before the hot stoves, so it was not a job one would volunteer for unless he felt he was helping people.

Hand Grenades

A reader called the other day, after I had written an article about hand grenades, to tell me that the pronunciation *"teryūdan"* is correct.[33] The Japanese army had begun using hand grenades during the Russo-Japanese War. The army called them *"shuryūdan,"* and this can be verified in *Daijiten*, published by Heibonsha. However, the reading must have been changed in recent years to *"teryūdan,"* as it appears in *Jikai*, a dictionary edited by Dr. Kindaichi Kyōsuke. Many things changed after World War II, and I believe this is one example.[34]

Experiencing My First Autumn in Thirty-Five Years

As we entered October, the heat of the burning sun weakened, but the wind from the Gulf of Mexico remained warm and humid. When evening came and the wind shifted from the north, it became cold immediately.

One morning I happened to look upon a gum tree growing in the valley near the camp. I was surprised to see that its leaves had turned yellow over night. We had been unaware of it, but autumn was just around the corner. Acts of nature occur in spite of environmental conditions. The *aburazemi*[35] had finished their noisy chirping. Now they were replaced by the *kanakana*,[36] whose cheeping reminded us of the coolness of evening. In this distant internment camp, I experienced autumn for the first time in many years.

When I looked up at the sky after the broadcast was over, I saw flocks of wild geese flying in a beautiful pattern. I had learned many things about wild geese through books, but this was the first time I was actually seeing them. Their beautiful and orderly flying formation was something beyond human ability. They appeared static, yet dynamic at the same time. Even skillful painters would not have been able to depict the scene as beautifully as it actually was.

Some Look Skyward, Others Check the Ground

During this season, there were two gentlemen who stood at the edge of the camp and looked at the western sky every day. Both men had beautiful young wives. They may have been waiting for the wild geese to come and fly over them in the beautiful evening sky. But some people believed differently and speculated that they were thinking about their wives. The Japanese have a habit of speculating about private matters and then talking about them publicly. Even during our camp life, some enjoyed peeping into the private lives of others.

In this region, there were pinkish stones that could be used for white *go* stones, and I hoped to find some to go with the black ones that I had collected at Camp McCoy. Because I always tended to walk with my head down, people often asked me if I had lost something. It may have been rumored that I was mentally abnormal.

Some people looked up when they walked, as in the recently popular phrase, *"Ue o muite arukō,"* while others walked looking at the ground.[37] Digging up tree roots, polishing stones, playing mahjongg from morning until night, these were the things some of us internees did every day.

The Missoula Group Joins Us

It became cooler in the mornings and the evenings, for autumn weather had arrived, and softball games were now held frequently. At about this time, twenty or thirty internees were moved to this camp from Missoula in Montana. As a result, our only softball field at Block H could not accommodate all the planned games. We were allowed to build another field on a hill across the valley, and I was among those who went every day to help. I could find autumn flowers blooming there, like in Japan, and it made me recall my home country. Working very hard to complete the job as quickly as possible, we built the field in about ten days. We all shared the joy of having our first game there the following week.

Many good baseball players were in the Missoula group. They formed a softball club called Mizora and challenged the J-1 and J-2 clubs.[38] Many became very enthusiastic about playing, and they used the new field nearly every day. The Missoula people were not only good players, but they also brought with them some beautifully polished fossils. They were flat and circular in shape and were blue, brown, black, or yellow in color. I was impressed with those beautiful fossils.

The internees from Missoula were a refreshing addition to our dull internment life. According to them, those who had been detained right after the war had broken out were sent directly to Fort Missoula in Montana. At the time when we were in the INS office and were told of our transfer to the Mainland, we had talked about where we were to be sent. Some people said we were being sent to either Missoula or Santa Fe. It seems that confidential information had been leaked somehow.

Some internees who were attracted to rare fossils eagerly wanted to acquire them. Shoroku Ono, owner of Goshado Store in San Francisco, had the clever idea of organizing a bazaar. I wanted to buy a fossil, but the prices were too high, ranging from three to five dollars each. While I hesitated, all of them were soon bought by others.

At first, we polished stones and tree roots as a way to forget our hardship, but as time went by, it became a hobby. To see men go so far as to buy these fossils was a sign that a year into our internment we had begun to relax. For me, the bazaar was like the market during a Japanese festival, and it made me feel lighthearted.

POWs from the Battle of Midway Join Us

The United States had already deciphered the Japanese secret codes before the Battle of Midway. Unaware of this, the Japanese navy attacked as planned, but the U.S. Navy was ready with its counterattack. The Japanese navy was severely beaten, its warships sunk by U.S. aircraft. I learned about this from the newspaper, but to see the Japanese POWs joining us in camp confirmed for me the Japanese navy's defeat. Commander Nakamune, chief engineer of the aircraft carrier *Hiryū*, along with his thirty-five crewmen and about fifty navy men, including those assigned as lookouts at Wake Island, were brought to our camp.

When the new POWs arrived, Ensign Sakamaki was put in their group. Former commanding officer Ensign Kanda took command of the rank and file, while Commander Nakamune, Lt. Commander Kajimoto, and Ensign Sakamaki were treated courteously because of their rank as POW officers. If they had remained peaceful and obeyed orders, life could have been easier. However, as time passed, along with the easing of their tensions over having to commit suicide, many became nihilistic. They seemed to have given themselves up to despair. In such a situation, it was very difficult to organize the POW group.

At the time, it happened that Commander Nakamune's group of sixteen was ordered to move to another camp. Some rank-and-file POWs feared that they were to be sent to a place where they would be treated cruelly or even killed. They surrounded Commander Nakamune, demanding that he resist until death the order by the U.S. authorities. Embarrassed by this ridiculous demand, Commander Nakamune was at a complete loss. The men held a meeting and resolved to not obey the transfer order. Consequently, two hundred American soldiers marched into the camp, ready to crush the rebellious POWs. Ensign Sakamaki and the other officers desperately tried to dissuade the POWs, yelling, "Don't fight them! Just obey the order!"

In the end, thirty-six POWs, including Ensign Sakamaki, were moved to another area of the camp, and Commander Nakamune's group of sixteen was transferred to Fort McDowell in San Francisco, as originally planned.[39] Ensign Sakamaki took command of the group of thirty-six who remained in camp, and although some of them initially took a defiant attitude toward him, they eventually calmed down. They became friendly, playing softball with us internees. In time, even Ensign Sakamaki seemed to be relieved.

About two months after this dispute, Commander Nakamune's group of sixteen, which had been sent to San Francisco, returned to our camp. Another group of ten men lead by Commander Matsumoto, who had been captured in the Solomon Islands, was also sent here at about this time. With the addition of these twenty-six men, a total of sixty-two POWs were now being held in Livingston. Commander Matsumoto was appointed commanding officer of the POW group and Ensign Sakamaki his assistant. Commander Matsumoto had begun his career as a non-commissioned officer and had a gentle demeanor. He had often visited Honolulu while assigned to training ship duty.

When the idea of playing softball with us internees was first brought up, some of the POWs objected, saying it was disgraceful. I heard that Ensign Sakamaki wholeheartedly explained our attitude and feelings, and so the POWs were finally convinced. At any rate, we began playing games together. In consideration of their situation, we avoided using the term "POW." Instead, we called them, "the brave men of the Japanese imperial army and navy." I think they appreciated our gesture and came to enjoy playing softball with us.

The most unfortunate POW was Commander Nakamune, who had a nervous breakdown and attempted suicide while in San Francisco. He still had the fresh three-inch scar on his neck. I heard that he had felt excessively responsible for the conduct of his men and had worried too much. The cause of his neurosis was not the U.S. Army, but hot-blooded, thoughtless men. Among the POWs, there were quite a few who were mentally sick from battle fatigue, but none of them went insane in the camp.

A New, Understanding Camp Commander

The commander of our camp, Lieutenant Colonel Dunn (later promoted to colonel), was a good man, but about half-a-year later he was replaced by Colonel Weaver. Colonel Weaver was well groomed and sociable, like a diplomat. Immediately after taking command, he issued the following statement:

My brother was a Navy lieutenant and died at the battle off of Savo Island.
He was an officer aboard the USS *Astoria*, which once carried the remains of
the late Ambassador Saito, representative to the United States, back to Japan.
At the time, he was welcomed by the Japanese government and many of its
citizens. He frequently talked about his experience and spoke highly of Japan.
He was killed when the USS *Astoria* was sunk by the Japanese navy. For me,
Japan is the cursed enemy country that killed my brother. However, I know
how my brother felt about Japan, so I will try to understand the sentiments of
the Japanese and carry out my duties as commander of this camp.

He backed up his words with deeds. Koichi Iida received a telegram
that his wife was critically ill, and he immediately petitioned the commander to be allowed to visit her. We thought it would be very difficult
for him to gain approval, because a guard would need to accompany him
to Hawai'i. But, contrary to our expectations, permission was granted.
He began preparing for the trip happily. Unfortunately, he was unable to
get on the airplane in time, and he was informed of her death before he
departed.

Mr. Iida, his close friend Toka Ida,[40] and I were very appreciative of
the commander's humane gesture. Twenty to thirty people gathered once
they heard of Mrs. Iida's demise. Rev. Yoshio Hino recited a sutra, and I
spoke about the details of her passing on behalf of Mr. Iida. Everyone shed
tears in sympathy of him.

Organized by friends, Mrs. Iida's memorial service was held ten days
after her death. Those in charge were Kyoichi Miyata, Daizo Sumida, Taichi Sato, Manzuchi Hashimoto, Katsuichi Kawamoto, Osuke Shigemoto,
Toka Ida, and me. We had decided that the *kōden*[41] should be one dollar or
less, and that no tokens of acknowledgement from the Iida family would
be sent. More than 150 people, including twenty-nine priests, attended the
service, with Toka Ida presiding. Daizo Sumida offered the eulogy, shedding tears as he made an impassioned speech. At the end of the service, I
expressed to the congregation some words of appreciation on Mr. Iida's
behalf, but I felt his sorrow so deeply that I could not hold back my emotions and stood speechless for a while.

I Decline Repatriation

Soon after we had arrived at Livingston, a rumor spread that the second
exchange ship would depart from New York City in the middle of August.
The news soon reached us, confirming the truth of the rumor. It was
reported that some 137 family members of repatriates had moved from

Hawai'i to the Mainland, accompanied by Dr. and Mrs. Isao Murai, and that they were staying at the Grove Park Inn in North Carolina.[42]

The actual departure, however, came into doubt, as the year 1942 ended and a new year began. Then on January 7, the passenger list was announced by barracks leader Otsubo. All the Panama internees as well as Misao Isobe, Shozo Kawakami, Taketo Iwahara, and I from Barracks J-1 were on the list. Since I had already decided to stay in the United States for the sake of my family, I submitted to the authorities a note with my signature that said, "Do not desire repatriate." When I realized that I had finally made the decision to stay permanently in America, I was overwhelmed by a sense of loneliness. In time the feeling subsided, and I resigned myself to my fate.

"Lord Takeda's Twenty-Four Generals" in Captivity

As the expected departure of the exchange ship neared, those of us from Yamanashi gathered to bid each other farewell. Ten men attended from the Hawai'i group. They were Kinzo Sayegusa, Tomoaki Nakamura, Rev. Kyokujo Kubokawa, and I, all of Honolulu; Rev. Gijo Ozawa and principal Kichisuke Yoda of Kaua'i; and Rev. Kanryu Mochizuki, principal Gempei Miura, principal Haruto Saito, and Tasuke Kajiwara of the Big Island. Fourteen internees from the Mainland also joined the gathering: *Rafu Shimpo* president Toyosaku Komai,[43] Makoto Toguri, and Yoshinori Nozawa of Los Angeles; Shoroku Ono, Shingo Watanabe, Inokichi Amino, and Magotaro Hirose of San Francisco; Yoshihiko Kasai of Salt Lake City; Itaro Takano of Panama; Gunjiro Maruyama of Miami; Yoshitaka Watanabe and Hanpei Ueno of Seattle; and Hachiro Asakawa and Kinsuke Matsudo of San Diego. It was a grand total of twenty-four.

We jokingly referred to ourselves as "Lord Takeda's Twenty-Four Generals."[44] Since we were behind barbed wire, however, the contrast to historical fact was too real, and we never quite felt uplifted. Incidentally, we wondered why a large number of Hawai'i and Mainland people from Yamanashi had been interned, although compared to the total number of immigrants we were few, like being but one hair from nine bulls. Someone said it was because many Yamanashi men were assertive and honest to a fault. I could see his point.

Airing Out Folded Bedding

As I mentioned before, Commander Weaver was a scrupulous British-type gentleman who stressed neatness and cleanliness, and the sergeant assigned to enforce this policy in our barracks was a very nervous fellow.

One beautiful day, the sergeant ordered us to air out our bedding, so we took them to the clearing. We placed the mattresses on the cots and hung the blankets on the ropes. At adjoining J-2, however, the cots were lined up in a row, with each mattress rolled up and placed in the middle of a cot. A pillow was laid at the head of the cot and a blanket folded into a square was at the opposite end. It looked more like a display than an airing out. The sergeant, noticing the difference, arrived in a fluster and told us to do what the J-2 group had done.

We insisted that we were airing our bedding in a more reasonable fashion, not just displaying them. He said that he understood why we had done this, but he asked us to change to the J-2 style anyway, because the commander liked things to look neat and clean. We reluctantly obeyed him. There are many things in the military that do not make sense, and this was one of them.

Everyone liked this sergeant, who walked with a limp and was a good-natured man. One day, he ordered some elderly men to take away some pine logs that had been left in the camp. I went to see him.

"Why don't you let the young men do it?" I asked. "Please consider that the Hawai'i internees here are men of religion, school teachers, and businessmen who haven't engaged in physical labor. The Hawai'i group is different from the Panama group—there the entire Japanese community was interned."

"Thanks for your advice. I'll be more careful," he answered. I was happy that he had readily agreed.

Generally speaking, American servicemen are rough and simple-minded. They do not use their heads and say whatever comes to mind. At both the Sand Island camp and the INS office, guards gave orders to us directly without going through our spokesman. That is how elderly Mr. Soga was called out from his hearing and ended up being made to clean the cell of the German prisoner Otto Kuehn, the only Japanese spy in the Pacific area during World War II.

Sometimes Commander Weaver's penchant for enforcing appearance worked in our favor. There were many internees who had let their hair and beards grow, and they looked unkempt. After first cautioning them, the commander later ordered them cut their hair and shave their beards. We felt more comfortable after this, as there was always the chance of seeing them and being in close contact with them, especially during softball games.

A Young Man's Blood Saves an Old Man

One day, principals Hideyuki Serizawa and Toraki Kimura of Block K came to our barracks. They said that principal Kazuhiko Ogata had been hospitalized for a stomach ulcer and needed a blood transfusion because he was passing bloody stool. There was no supply of blood at the hospital, and most of the Hawai'i internees were elderly and reluctant to donate their blood. Mr. Ogata needed the transfusion urgently. No one knew what to do—then the Panama group came to mind. Because the majority of them were young, chances were good that some Panama internees would be willing to give their blood. Thus, the two principals had come to see Tsutomu Imamura and me, who were living with the Panama group.

Although Mr. Ogata had no close connection with anyone from Panama, we decided to speak with their barracks leader, Mr. Otsubo, for it was a matter of a man's life. We were overjoyed when, like typical active, young men, five or six quickly volunteered to donate their blood. Thanks to them, Mr. Ogata recovered his health in no time. This experience made me keenly aware that in a situation like this old men are no match for young ones.

Meeting with a Representative of the International YMCA

Dr. Fisher, who represented the International YMCA, once came for a visit and asked us what we needed. As chief of the athletic and entertainment departments, I boldly asked him to supply us with sporting equipment, and to my delight, he readily gave his consent.[45]

In my normal life back in Hawai'i, I was not very interested in such organizations as the Red Cross and the Young Men's Christian Association, although I had a rough idea that they were undertaking significant community works. Once I experienced internment—a life I would have never imagined—I became deeply appreciative of their support.

I knew the Red Cross and the YMCA were busy supporting the war-wounded and war-sick and their families, so I never expected that they would help us internees. However, during the early days of the internment, the U.S. Red Cross once supplied us not only with sets of American playing cards, but also handmade *go* stones, and *hanafuda* cards. The *go* "stones" were not actually stones, but wood that looked like the halves of abacus balls. They sat well but were difficult to stack when placed in containers after the game.

We did not know how the *hanafuda* cards had been made, but we were struck by the quality of the paper and printing. The gloss of the colors was not the best, if I am allowed to say so, but at any rate, the cards impressed us. With the many services the Red Cross had to provide, the fact that they had thought of us and made these cards and then distributed them within such a short time showed the big-heartedness of the organization. I was humbled by the thought. It made me realize that a man can boast about his knowledge and credentials, but without first-hand experience, he remains ignorant.

Correspondence Misery

After I decided that I was not going to repatriate on the exchange ship, corresponding with my family became my biggest concern. Letters came very slowly sometimes, and quickly at other times. The letters made me happy—and sad.

As I now write *Haisho Tenten*, I sometimes refer to my diary, but because at the time I had no intention of writing a formal account, I did not record much about our everyday situation other than about the letters I wrote or received. I was shocked to discover this.

I single-mindedly hoped my letters would reach my family as soon as possible and that their letters would arrive just as quickly. I was disappointed most of the time. I found that the mail service was not very dependable.

Someone suggested that registered mail would get to the addressee faster than regular mail, so we began sending our letters registered, paying twenty-five cents for air mail, plus ten cents for registered mail, for a total of thirty-five cents an envelope. This was not a small amount for us internees.

We were allowed to send one letter per week, to be written on a sheet of paper provided by the U.S. government. If it was for business purposes, two sheets were allowed. My business correspondence mailed to New York on November 26 was returned fifty days later with a notification that registered mail would not be accepted from internees. Since there was no other way but to send it again through regular airmail, I did so. Then, the camp post office sent it back, saying they would not regard my letter as business-related. I was so angry that they now refused to send a letter that had once been allowed. I knew, however, that I was in no position to complain, so I had no choice but to suffer in silence. Because I had wanted the letter to travel faster, I had paid extra for registered mail, but in the end, it had taken twice as long to reach its destination. It was absurd, but I could do nothing but, with indignation, accept the facts.

In addition to this story, I heard about how an official letter from the Spanish Consul in New Orleans to Takaichi Saiki, the Hawai'i barracks leader at J-2, had taken as many as forty-two days to travel less than one hundred miles. I don't know what caused the delay, but I assume that it was due to some confusion over censorship. On the other hand, there were times when mail delivery was prompt. A letter my family sent on January 3 reached me just nineteen days later, on January 22.

My earlier experience with the registered business letter had me suspecting the authorities of intentionally delaying the processing of our mail, but that was not necessarily the case. Sometimes the military did things that were simply beyond our comprehension.

Spring Rain

Spring came the previous year not long after we had moved to the Mainland. As we moved south from cold Camp McCoy, we missed the chance to experience a spring rain. We probably were in no mood to enjoy it anyway. Here in this camp, for the first time in many years, I enjoyed watching the spring rain drizzling on the Georgia pine trees. Under the pines, white flowers like camellias were in bloom, and pearl-like raindrops fell from the flower petals to the ground. I felt as though I might at any minute hear the call of a nightingale. I recalled the hometown scenery of my youth, and it healed my aching heart and made me forget where I was.

It stopped raining the following day, and the sky became very clear. Trees shone with bright green leaves, and birds flew about cheerfully. Tomato vines growing by the wall of our barracks were thick and in bloom. It seemed that the whole world was singing a song of springtime joy.

Haiku from Camp Livingston

ARRIVAL

Baggage hanging over our shoulders
We trudge toward summer clouds
荷物をさげて徒歩で行く手の夏雲

My friends greet me with smiles
What a warm welcome
同胞が居て笑顔で迎えてくださるので

In this camp among the pine trees
We finally settle down
松林の中がキャンプでここにおちつく

Machine guns atop the guard tower
Sounds from a radio drift down
機銃を据えた見張櫓でラジオが歌っている

Young prisoners make music
Without musical instruments
囚われの若人らが奏でる楽器のない楽隊

In the pine forest, fireflies everywhere
An evening sky in a foreign land
松林に蛍とぶなど異国の夕空

Free for a day
I choose to go rock hunting
今日は石拾いにでられたので石を拾います

Under the blazing sun
The camp sleeps
炎天、キャンプがねむっている

MR. MASUDA'S FUNERAL

Sound of the wind through the pines
Accompanies voices chanting a sutra
I join the other mourners
読経松風の声会衆の一人として

Kanakana begin their song
As watchtower beams light the evening clouds
カナカナ鳴きだすと哨燈のともる夕雲

A sign of autumn in the pine forest
The sound of American *kanakana*
秋のけはいはここ松林アメリカのカナカナ

From this faraway land
We view Orion's Belt in the sky
はるばる送られて異郷の空の三つ星

Wild geese fly high above
Today's news is all good
空高く雁渡る今日のニュースはよろしい

I gaze at the sky from my bed
And find the same stars out tonight
ベッドから眺める空の今夜も見えるあの星

December rain reminds me
A year has passed like a dream
過ぎてみれば一年は夢です師走のあめふり

Is that the crackle of pine needles freezing?
The moon is like a scythe
松の葉いてつく音か月が鎌のような

The dew on the pine heavy
The fog thick
On this, the second day of the New Year
松の雫や霧の深い正月二日

Rumors of impending peace go nowhere
Only pine shoots grow and mature
平和が近いという話も松の芽のびるばかり

Weed blossoms and spring
Both arrive
Even behind barbed wire
しこ草の花が、春が鉄柵の中へも来た

Gentle spring rains fall
Tear drops from white blossoms
春雨らしい春の雨で白い花しずくしている

NEWS OF MRS. IIDA'S DEMISE

An evening stroll through the pine forest
Fond memories of her shared by friends
ありし日を語る友と松林の夕日のなか

Navy men we welcomed in the past
We now see as prisoners
歓迎せし海軍を今ここに捕虜として見る

TRANSFER ORDERS

Flowering summer grasses
Perhaps they will send us north this time
ここは夏草の花の今度は北の方へやられるとか

We leave tomorrow
I water the grasses and flowers
On this last evening
あすは出立の草花へ水をやる夕べ

Ordered to Move for the Fourth Time

Camp Livingston was a new camp built for POWs and internees. It could hold up to five thousand people in its eleven blocks, A through K. Since May 1942, internees had been transferred to this camp from various places, such as Panama in Central America, Fort Sill in Oklahoma, Camp McCoy in Wisconsin, Camp Forrest in Tennessee, Camp Missoula in Montana, and Camp Bismarck in South Dakota.[46] The population in the camp increased to more than 1,200. We expected that all internees would move into this camp eventually, since there were still many unoccupied barracks. Eleven months after we had settled here, and just as we were feeling that nice weather would prevail for a while, we were again ordered to move. One hundred-and-fourteen internees, almost half of the internee population, were to be moved to Missoula, with the remaining ninety-five internees going to Santa Fe and the POWs to Camp McCoy. The camp became very noisy as everyone prepared to move out.

Our Missoula group departed ahead of the others on the early morning of June 2, 1943.[47] We rode on trucks to Alexandria and then headed north by train. Coming to Livingston last year, our train ran south along the eastern bank of the Mississippi. This time, we proceeded in a northwesterly direction along the west bank of the river. We arrived at two in the afternoon in Shreveport, the biggest city in the area, located along the Red River. As the train crossed the Red River and entered Arkansas, we passed over the plains. We saw nothing but small hills, which was typical of southern scenery and quite dull.

Darkness fell at a place called Camden. We were tired, so no one talked, and we all got to sleep early. The train must have turned in an easterly direction during the night, because I saw the Mississippi to our right when I woke up the next morning. At around nine o'clock, we reached a very big city. It was the famous St. Louis. I could see many tall buildings on a hill. I found it interesting that a part of this big city could look like the rocky hills of Shōsenkyō in Yamanashi prefecture.[48]

The train headed northwest through Missouri and reached Montgomery City after crossing the Missouri River. It reminded me of the north, where I had seen hexagon-shaped houses and silos standing like chimneys. We passed through Iowa during the night and entered Minnesota in the early morning. I was curious to see the twin cities of Minneapolis and St. Paul. It became colder as the train headed north. The buds on the trees were starting to open, snow still covered the upper reaches of the mountains, and the sky was clear.

As we moved from South Dakota to North Dakota, nothing but the wide prairie came into sight. The train crossed the upper branch of the Missouri River and entered Montana, travelling west along the Wyoming border. After climbing a deep valley, we arrived at Helena, the state capital. You might think it would be a big city, since it is the state capital, but Helena was a small country town with a population of only twenty thousand. In the United States, cities located in the central part of the states are designated as state capitals, regardless of their size.

The train crossed many small streams, passed through many short tunnels, and climbed many hills. After passing through a tunnel in a watershed area, from which rivers flowed all the way to the Pacific Ocean, we arrived at Missoula Station at ten at night. After transferring to waiting cars, we reached the camp at about eleven.

This time, our trip took us three days and two nights, but it was less painful than the trip to Camp McCoy.

| 11 |

Fort Missoula
Missoula, Montana

Shangri-La in America

Our group of 114 arrived at Fort Missoula on June 5, 1943. The name Fort Missoula might give you the impression that it was a military site, but instead it had been converted into a detention station under the Department of Justice.

A long time ago, Indians prevailed in this area. The U.S. government built a military post in order to control them, and so there existed such buildings as a mess hall, hospital, theater, and laundry. Now the entire facility had been converted into an internment camp. A tall mountain called Lolo soars in the southwest near the Idaho border, and ranges of high and low mountains surround the area. It is like a mini Kōshū Basin.[1] Located to the east of the camp, in the narrows, is an old Indian battlefield that reminded me of Okehazama, where troops loyal to Oda Nobunaga defeated Imagawa Yoshimoto.[2] Many had died in the battle against the American Indians, turning the river red with blood. The name of this narrows, Hell Gate, is derived from this battle. A wide river running beside the camp is a tributary of the Columbia River and contains good fishing spots for trout, sucker, white fish, and squawfish.

The sky was very clear, and snow still lay on the gentle slopes of the mountains when we arrived. Dandelions bloomed all around, like a large, golden carpet. In the camp, bright purple irises, planted by those internees who had come before us, were in full bloom. In the tropics, like Hawai'i and the south, red and yellow flowers tend to be bold and rich in color, while purple and pink ones are not, but the irises in this camp bloomed big and bright. They were refreshing to my eyes. The early summer sun cast a soft light, and everything was quiet. I felt as though I were in another world. Unlike in other parts of the Mainland, our view of the sky was restricted because we were surrounded by the mountains. It felt as if we had a beautiful giant mirror over our heads, and many of us intentionally read "Missoula" as "*Mizora*."[3]

I had assumed this camp was unoccupied, but when we arrived, we found 103 Mainland people already living here. To my surprise, I found Mr. Kimura of Nippon Yūsen and Mr. Onoda of Sumitomo Bank among them, people I thought had returned to Japan on the first exchange ship. I was later told that they had been unable to get to New York in time for the ship's departure.

In the barracks adjoining our area were about five hundred Italians, Germans, and Czechs. A Nicaraguan army lieutenant general stood out prominently among them. He was short and wore a long beard. These people were soon moved elsewhere, but another group of more than one hundred internees arrived from Peru, making the camp quite lively.[4]

Hawai'i Men Take the Reins of the Internee Self-Government

A man named B. H. Fraser was the commander of Missoula camp.[5] He was nice to us and had a good understanding of us Japanese. In this camp, the spokesman, called "mayor," was Iwao Matsushita, but he soon resigned, and new officers were chosen as follows:

Mayor	Takaichi Saiki
Chief Secretary	Totaro Matsui
Assistant Secretary	Yoshinobu Sasaki
Treasurer	Katsuji Onishi (Mainland)
Auditor	Yasujiro Shiio (Mainland)
Clerk	Ryuichi Kashima, Isamu Kurotobi (Peru), Takeshi Morita (Mainland)
Canteen Manager	Kinzo Sayegusa
Assistant Manager	Setsugo Togioka
Clerk	Kumaji Furuya, Saichiro Okada (Mainland), Yukio Nakamura (Peru)
Mail Clerk	Ichiro Konno
Liaison Officer	Sawajiro Ozaki
Supply Officer	Akira Tsujita (Mainland), Kichisuke Yoda

Emergency Doctor	Akio Kimura, Yukihide Kohatsu
Chief Cook	Sekitaro Nagai (Mainland)
Steward	Masato Kiyosaki
Liaison	Masaichiro Shinoda
Tailor	Santaro Sonoda

Most of the officers were from Hawai'i, so we, the Hawai'i group, lived comfortably.

Up to this point, before coming to this camp, my internee serial number, "ISN-HJ-188-CI," had to be written on all my correspondence. But I soon was notified that from now on I only needed to write, "Kumaji Furuya, P.O. Box 1539, Missoula, Montana." It may not appear to have been a significant change, but we felt as happy as if we had been released from the camp.

When internees were under the jurisdiction of the Department of the Army, our mailing address was first "Sand Island Detention Camp," then "Camp McCoy, Sparta, Wisconsin." Later the address changed to "Look Box 7600-A, Chicago Post Office." When we were in Tennessee, our address was "A.E.I.C. Co. 3, Camp Forrest, Tennessee," and "Box 20, General Post Office, New York" while we were in Livingston. It was later revised to "3rd Internment Co., Camp Livingston, Louisiana."

In the beginning, we were instructed to write our internee serial number on every piece of correspondence. This was possibly because the authorities did not want anyone to know where we were. As the war progressed in favor of the United States, they seemed to become less nervous about the conspicuousness of our whereabouts.

Here in Missoula, living quarters were not called barracks, but dormitories, and I was assigned to Dormitory 21. With me were: Masayuki Chikuma, Josen Deme, Ichitaro Hasebe,[6] Kaneki Honda, Tomiji Kimura, Eiichi Kishida, Masayuki Kodama, Taichi Komatsu, Gikyo Kuchiba, Totaro Matsui, Konin Matano, Shushin Matsubayashi, Yoshifusa Nishida, Hakuai Oda, Joei Oi, Kazuhiko Ogata, Gendo Okawa, Yoshiro Ogawa, Isaku Orita, Sawajiro Ozaki, Shinri Sarashina, Yoshinobu Sasaki, Giichi Sasaki, Kinzo Sayegusa, Taichi Sato, Yazo Sato, Hideyuki Serizawa, Osuke Shigemoto, Aisuke Shigekuni, Santaro Sonoda, Masao Sogawa, Daizo Sumida, Tetsuo Toyama, Setsuzo Toyota, and Tokuya Uyehara.[7] Thirty-six in all. Reverend Deme was appointed the leader and Reverend Okawa his assistant.

With ten dormitories assigned to Japanese internees, I would say there were approximately 360 people living here. Duty assignments were few, only KP, dormitory cleaning, and boiler maintenance. We enjoyed our life, as if we were on vacation, playing softball, golfing, and fishing all day long.

The Hawaiʻi Club Wins the Softball Championship

Finances varied with each internee, and some had only a small amount of spending money. The government had frozen the assets of bankers, company employees, and some men of religion, who had already sent their families back to Japan, as well as those who had expressed their intention to repatriate. Since they were unable to ask their families to send them money, they had to live on their monthly three-dollar allowance. I felt sorry for them, for they did not have much money, and their repatriation was still uncertain. No Japanese internees worked to earn money, other than carrying out assigned duties. Some Italian internees also did not have enough, but they earned money by shoveling coal and cleaning the camp. There was so little for us to do that it was almost boring.

There were two softball fields in the camp, and so teams were quickly organized. At first, dormitory teams played against each other, but later leagues were formed, made up of All-Mainland, All-South-America and All-Hawaiʻi clubs. The Peru group had young players, but they were not very skilled. The All-Mainland and All-Hawaiʻi players were relatively older, but they were experienced. All the clubs were evenly matched, and the games were always close.

Tamaki Arita and I pitched for the All-Hawaiʻi team. The fastballs Arita pitched and my slow balls mixed well during the games, and we won the series by a small margin. Since we were allowed to take photographs in this camp, we took commemorative pictures and had a party to celebrate our victory. We celebrated with glasses of beer, instead of champagne. For the first time since our internment, we forgot ourselves and engaged in boastful talk.

Having heard this news, the American guards of the border patrol club challenged us to a game and, of course, we accepted. Their six-foot-tall pitcher did well, winding up his arm to throw very fast balls. He struck us out three times in a row. They put us to shame—after all, we had won the championship. But we felt it was a comical rather than embarrassing ending.

Fishing Is Allowed

Hearing that various kinds of fish were living in a nearby river, many internees began fishing as soon as it was allowed. The number of fishermen reached sixty or seventy. We expected that fishing would become popular and prepared an abundant supply of fishing tackles at the canteen. We were very busy, as many customers rushed to buy their supplies, and I did not even have time to buy a fishing tackle of my own. It was difficult to get fishing rods, although hooks, sinkers, and lines were available at the canteen. So, we made our own rods by cutting the slender trees that grew along the banks of the river. But we had a difficult time casting the lines into the deeper parts of the water because the rods were not long enough.

A Funny Fishing Story

It happened when I went fishing for the first time. The water level was very high because of the melting snow, and I could not find a good place to fish. I reluctantly cast my line in a spot that was not promising. I was getting no bites at all and was feeling quite bored, when suddenly I felt a tug. I pulled up the line with a jerk, but it caught on something behind me. When I looked back, there was no sign of a fish. Instead I had caught principal Yoshinobu Sasaki, who had been sitting on the side and watching with his mouth open. I was very upset by the embarrassing incident and apologized deeply to him. When I caught a trout on another day, I gave it to him before anyone else as a gesture of apology.

When the water level dropped, someone found a good fishing spot where rocks jutted out into a pool in the river. Here were schools of big fish called suckers, which looked like carp in shape and color, but with soft suckers for mouths. They looked like steamed Chinese pork dumplings. Besides being repulsive, they were slow moving and stupid. In America, the slang for someone who is gullible is "sucker." I've heard that this comes from this fish.

I rarely fished at this spot, however, because too many people crammed into the tiny space, making it dangerous. But my neighbors in the adjoining dormitory always fished there, from early in the morning, sometimes proudly returning with suckers that measured more than two feet in length. One day, Torao Iseri, Kaua'i bureau chief of the *Nippu Jiji*, caught what seemed to be a huge one. He finally landed it after a long fight, only to find that the hook had caught on the dorsal fin of the fish. Of course, that had made the fish seem like a big catch. The crowd roared with laughter.

Fishing for Brook Trout

I usually enjoyed fishing for small, guppy-like fish in a shallow pool on the edge of the stream. Suckers, although large, did not have much flavor. On the other hand, the small fish tasted very good. Hilo's Mr. Ichikawa always invited me to enjoy the marinated fish that went so nicely with beer.

One clear day, I was fishing at the usual spot, sitting and smoking and waiting for a bite. Suddenly, I felt a strong tug. I pulled the rod up too hard, unfortunately, and cut the line. I was very excited and tried to catch this mysterious fish using a thicker line. I waited, concentrating for a long time. But there were no more tugs. Soon it was time to go back to camp. I started to put my tackle back, when I felt a big tug. I excitedly pulled the rod up and caught the fish. Although I had changed to a thicker line, I had been quite anxious, for the tug was so strong.

The fish was not very big and looked like a type of trout. I was curious to know what it was, and so after I got back to camp, I went to see Toyo Hirai, who was knowledgeable about fish. He took one look at it and immediately told me the fish was a mountain trout. Knowing that trout is the king of river fish, I bragged to my neighbors, who were always hooking suckers, "It's small, but I caught a trout."

One of the Mainlanders said he had never seen such a trout, and so I felt I needed to prove that the fish was indeed what I claimed it was. Fortunately, I found a man who had a book titled, *The Book of Fishes*, and I borrowed it. The book covered all fish species in detail with 443 colored illustrations. It was published by the National Geographic Society in Washington, D.C. To my surprise, the originals of these watercolor illustrations had been done by a painter named Hajime Murayama.[8] According to the book, the fish I had caught was an Eastern Brook Mountain Trout. This species was first found in the high mountain ravines of Georgia. Because they can only survive in cold water, an aquarium in New York City chills its tank water during the summer to keep the captive fish from dying.

When they were first found, some of the brook trout reportedly weighed about ten pounds, however, the ones living in various streams these days weigh only about a pound. They are small but full of spirit, allowing fishermen to enjoy a good fight, as well as an unusually tasty meal. Because of this, these fish were released in the mountain streams of the Rockies and the Sierra Nevadas.

Discovering that my catch had been a brook trout made me very proud of myself. I became keen on catching them, preparing new thinner, but stronger, one-pound test lines and smaller sinkers. I also tried various kinds of bait in order to find the most suitable one. Soon, I was catching two or three trout every time I went fishing.

Whenever I had a good haul, I shared it with my dormitory mates. Everyone enjoyed the brook trout. Mr. Toyama remembers it even now, calling, "Hello, Trout Boss," every time he sees me. With so many people living in my dormitory, a few trout were not enough for everyone. So, I made a small pond to keep them alive until I had enough. As a result, people would come to see how many fish I had caught each time I got back to camp. When I caught many, I entered the dormitory triumphantly from the front entrance, but when I did not, I sneaked in through the back door.

Poisonous Mites and River Fish

All fishermen were immunized at the hospital, for there were poisonous mites in the river area. The river is a tributary of the Columbia River and is called the St. Regis. It flows through Idaho toward Washington, merging with the Spokane River and eventually joining the Columbia River. The main species of fish living in this river are salmon, trout, suckers, squawfish, and white fish. Of course, there are other small and unknown fish of the type that I used to catch in the early days. The best fishing season depends on the species—trout in the early autumn, whitefish in mid-autumn, squawfish in winter, and stupid suckers all the time. The best places to catch whitefish were difficult to get to without a boat. Borrowing a boat from the Mainland group, Dr. Kimura and Reverend Himeno were proud whenever they caught a lot of fish.

When it became colder and ice formed on the river surface, I found a good fishing spot where I caught a lot of squawfish. Everyone was very curious about how I did it. The surface of the river was frozen in most places, but a section along the riverbank was not, perhaps because water from the nearby mountain was continually gurgling. It was so cold that the line I pulled from the water turned as stiff as wire. Catching a squawfish—and a large one at that—was a quite a surprise. It was a rare and inspiring moment, indeed, bringing up such a big fish amid the gently falling snowflakes.

Uncommon Names

Because we had just one mess hall in the camp, I soon became acquainted with the Mainland internees who had come here before us. Besides that, I worked at the canteen and made friends with many internees that way. Among them were several people with uncommon names. They were: Imakiire, Mena, Omaru, Abiko, Chuman, Hora, Koba, and Sanematsu. You probably have no idea how to write them in *kanji*.[9] But if you write them in kanji, they are not so strange: 今給黎 [Imakiire], 目七 [Mena], 小丸 [Omaru], 安孫子 [Abiko], 中馬 [Chuman], 洞 [Hora], 木場 [Koba], and 実 松 [Sanematsu].

This is not to say that all people from Hawaiʻi have common names. The name of Hanapepe's Rincho Onaga 翁長林長 looks like a Chinese name.[10] He was somehow sent alone from Camp Livingston to Camp Kenedy.[11] Other unusual names were Mende, Deki, Deme, Kanja, Kokuzo, and Akegarasu. Also, in the Peru group were Kurotobi, Ganyoko, and Doita.[12] Their names were as uncommon as those of the Mainlanders. The mind works in strange ways. Uncommon names of those from Hawaiʻi are not considered unusual, because we hear them often enough. Yet, such names of non-Hawaiʻi internees draw reactions of amused surprise.

Speaking of names, Mr. Chikuma's looks somewhat unusual when written in *kana*.[13] I have no idea what advice he would have received from a specialist in *seimeigaku*,[14] however the fact that he took his wife's family name upon marriage resulted in his incarceration. He had come from Japan as a professional entertainer and would otherwise never have been interned in his position as manager of the Toyo Theater, whose owner at the outbreak of the war had been Caucasian.[15] When he married, the family of his beloved wife adopted him, and his original name, Yoshiro Sakaya, was changed to Masayuki Chikuma. He became the son-in-law of the priest of the Inari Shrine on Sheridan Street.[16] He was mistaken for a Shinto priest and considered to be a suspicious alien by the military authorities. His father-in-law, Rev. Takiji Chikuma, who was actually the priest, may have been exempted because of his age. Young Mr. Chikuma was interned instead. Masayuki Chikuma was an easygoing man, who never complained about being interned and was always cheerful. Not only did he serve as a cook until he was released, but he entertained us with his *kōdan* and *rakugo* performances.[17]

Pants from the Stable

Alongside the camp, there was an old stable. Junk had been piled up on the second floor, and we were ordered to clean it up. Mr. Ozaki, who was the Clean-up Boss,[18] sought volunteers and many agreed to help since they had no other work to do. Among the rubbish to be burned, we found many pairs of old woolen pants. It seemed too wasteful to burn them, so each of us took a few pairs. We asked Mr. Sonoda, our tailor, to mend the tears, and we wore the pants proudly. As people heard the story, many rushed to the stable and soon everyone was wearing them. The pants all looked alike—it was as if we were all wearing government-issued trousers. If people saw someone wearing woolen pants that had been sent from home, they jokingly asked if it was from the stable. For a while, the word "stable" was very popular.

This stable remains in our memories as a source of many jokes. Recently, Kiyoshi Ichikawa of Hilo took a trip to the Mainland. He sent me a picture of the former Missoula camp. "The barracks have been torn down and no longer exist," he wrote. "But, the stable is still there and can be seen in the background." Masayuki Chikuma and Setsuzo Toyota, of our dormitory, were busy working in the kitchen and had no time to go to the stable and get some pants, so we gave them some extra pairs.

Speaking of Mr. Toyota, he, too, was an innocent victim of the war, like Mr. Chikuma. He was not a man of religion or a teacher, but a house-keeper for a Caucasian family in Hau'ula. The *toritsuginin* of that area was Naoyoshi Ohara, an influential man, who was about to move to Honolulu. He needed an honest young man to take his place and wanted Mr. Toyota to become his successor. Because of his new title, "Japanese Consulate Agent,"[19] Mr. Toyota was interned behind the barbed wire, leaving behind his young wife and children for four long years. Some influential men who escaped internment made a fortune during the war and were later commended by the Japanese Ministry of Foreign Affairs. I feel very sorry for Mr. Toyota, who was never recognized for his work.

Both Toyota and Chikuma worked diligently and kept the kitchen spotlessly clean. In appreciation, the Caucasian chief steward gave them expensive baseball gloves, with which they enjoyed playing catch. When our dormitory organized a softball club, they could only list themselves as substitute players because they were busy working in the kitchen. Although they did not have a chance to demonstrate their skill with their expensive gloves, they were featured in the commemorative photographs of the Eagles, the Dormitory 21 softball club.

The Passenger List for the Second Exchange Ship Is Announced

The camp came to life as rumors spread that the long-expected second exchange ship would depart soon.

One day a pleasant-looking gentleman dressed in civilian clothing showed up at camp. We thought he was a representative from the Spanish Embassy, but he turned out to be a merchant who came to take orders for tailor-made suits. Concerned about our welfare, our families had been sending the maximum allowable amount of cash on a regular basis, even if they had to go into debt, so we had enough money to buy suits. Many internees placed orders and the merchant was very happy. Having heard of the good business opportunity, a department store opened a branch in the camp and apparently did well.

While all this was happening, the list of repatriates for the second exchange ship was announced. Only those internees from Hawai'i are listed here because there were so many repatriates. On the other hand, not everyone from Hawai'i was on the list. It included the names of twenty-three Missoula internees from Hawai'i, if my memory serves me correctly. They were: Eishu Asato, Tokuji Baba, Taketo Iwahara, Shozo Kawakami, Eiichi Kishida, Kenji Kimura, Taiichi Komatsu, Masayuki Kodama, Kyokujo Kubokawa, Shushin Matsubayashi, Nihei Miyamoto, Shintaro Miyagawa, Hiroshi Motoshige, Tatsuo Motoshige, Tamejiro Nakano, Toratoro Onoda, Kazuhiko Ogata, Yoshiro Ogawa, Iwataro Shimonishi, Sokan Ueoka,[20] Toraichi Uyeda, Heiichi Yamanaka, and Kuromitsu Banba.

Hawai'i internees who repatriated on the SS *Gripsholm*, the second exchange ship, totaled seventy-one. Most of them were from Santa Fe. A few others were from Crystal City, and they boarded with their family members. They were Shoichi Asami, Kazoe Kawasaki, Tokuye Takahashi, and Ryoshin Okano.

We could not figure out the basis for the authorities' choice of passengers for the second exchange ship. We argued quite seriously amongst ourselves about this matter. Among the Buddhist priests of the Jodo Shinshu Mission, young Shunshin Matsubayashi, who had not been living in Hawai'i for very long, was on the list, while Bishop Kuchiba and Reverend Sarashina, whose families were living in Japan, as well as Reverend Deme, Reverend Oda, Reverend Fujiie, and Reverend Kabashima were not. Among those who had applied for repatriation, prominent men like Sumida, Iida, Matsui, Kurokawa, Sayegusa, Tokairin,[21] and Shigemoto were not approved, while Iwataro Shitanishi, a laborer from Kekaha, Kaua'i, and the relatively unknown Kuromitsu Banba, a waiter at the Moana Hotel, were included. Everyone was puzzled by the selection.

This Kuromitsu Banba was a mysterious man. His name did not appear in the directory published by the *Nippu Jiji*.[22] In kanji his name could be written as 番場玄光; it could also be written as 伴馬黒松. He had been sent to the Mainland on the third ship that departed Sand Island on May 23, 1942 and arrived in Houston, Texas, on June 8. I was able to trace him up to when he arrived at the Lordsburg camp on June 18. After that, I do not know how he ended up in Missoula, while the rest of his group was sent to Santa Fe. Similarly, no one knew when he came to Hawai'i and why he had been arrested by the FBI.

Golfing in the Snow

As the enthusiasm for softball grew, golfers who had been active at the Livingston camp did not remain idle. With Mayor Saiki's help, we approached the authorities with a request for a golf course. We figured our chances were slim, as there was no space to build a golf course within the fenced area. But in fact it turned out to be easier done than deliberated. Permission was immediately granted.

The designated site was an open field just outside the camp. The golfers were very happy and, using hoes, shovels, and rakes, worked hard to build tee boxes and greens for a nine-hole golf course. None of us would have ever dreamed of playing golf on such spacious links surrounded by the mountains. While we were there, guards on horseback could be seen in the far distance. It seemed as though we were receiving preferential treatment.

We did a good job building the tee boxes and greens, but could not spare the time to tend to the rest of the clearing. Players sometimes hit slices and lost precious balls in the bush, even after a thirty-minute search. Because of errant balls, there were times when games had to be stopped before the nine holes were finished. Novice golf buffs even played in the snow, brushing the snow from the tee boxes. When we could barely find the balls that we hit into the snow, some clever player decided to dye his golf balls red. Everyone copied this unique idea. So, as golfers hit their balls through the green, many red spots marked the white snowy surface. Such a scene is probably unimaginable even by a novelist.

Compatriots Laid to Rest in the Back Country

Not many Japanese lived in Montana, so when I heard that there were dozens of Japanese graves in the Missoula Cemetery, I thought it strange. I was told that they had helped build the Great Northern Railway line a long time ago and had fallen victim to the extreme working conditions during the nine-year period between 1900 and 1909.[23]

Hearing this story, twenty-four Buddhist priests in the camp visited the graves, where they held a memorial service and offered flowers they had picked from the field. According to Rev. Joei Oi, the individual gravestones were made of marble, and the area was kept clean. He copied down the names, ages, and dates of death, which are listed below. Not all of the records are complete. I wondered why the people of Missoula would have taken such good care of the graves of these Japanese laborers. It could have been that they appreciated the efforts of the laborers, or perhaps it was simply that they were religious. At any rate, the story warmed my heart.

Name	Age	From	Date of Death
Miyata Jusaku	22	Kumamoto	09/03/1900
Yamada Moemon	18	Wakayama	06/15/1900
Oishi Kumakichi	30	Kochi	06/18/1900
Omura Matsuzo		Yamanashi	01/26/1901
Moriyasu Manjiro		Okayama	12/10/1904
Furukawa Hanshiro	39	Kumamoto	02/08/1904
Ogawa Kazuji	27	Okayama	02/03/1904
Kawahara Etsujiro	32	Okayama	06/18/1904
Inoue Kyuemon	37	Okayama	06/08/1904
Omija Kansho	34	Okinawa	03/25/1905
Kawamoto Tanehachi	28	Hiroshima	06/03/1906
Kunimoto Shinroku	21	Hiroshima	08/27/1906
Kumagai Kazujiro	42	Kochi	05/31/1906
Tsuru Ichitaro	20	Kumamoto	10/12/1907
Onishi Yakichi	25	Hiroshima	07/12/1907
Matsumoto Yoshiyasu	29	Tottori	08/03/1907
Momose Washio		Nagano	11/25/1908
Yonemoto Tomekichi	40	Hokkaido	12/15/1909
Miyakita Santaro		Niigata	02/15/1909
Okada Toyozo	42	Ehime	01/27/1909
Watanabe Ikuta		Fukuoka	05/30/1910
Takahashi Rinji	49	Fukushima	07/12/1911
Watanabe Tashizo	41	Fukushima	10/13/1913
Takemoto Shosuke	63	Yamaguchi	11/29/1915
Takenaka Kumakichi	59	Hiroshima	07/25/1917
Matsumoto Hirokazu	42	Hiroshima	11/17/1919
Fujita Fusano	30	Hiroshima	08/08/1920
Kamimura Kenkichi		Kumamoto	
Ota Rinzo	30	Okayama	
Nakatogawa Hanjiro	31	Kanagawa	
Ishikawa Shuji	23	Hiroshima	
Sakamoto Yoshitaro	30	Wakayama	

Name	Age	From	Date of Death
Okimasu Gunichi	19	Hiroshima	
Watari Toyotaro	19	Hiroshima	

Miyata Tokuzo, Hattori H., Hamamoto I., Ishizaka R.

H. Maekawa, T. Torusuge, T. Okase, I. Osumi, S. Yokata, S. Ikawa, T. Hasono, K. Nakayama, Yamada, U. Kujiki, Yagura, Maeshita.[24]

These are the names inscribed on the gravestones, according to Reverend Oi's notes. The names were beautifully written in kanji.

Commemorative Photographs of the Hawai'i Group

Oddly enough, since coming to Missoula, things were turning out just fine. We were allowed many types of recreational activities, such as softball, golfing, fishing, and movies. Besides, outside merchants were permitted to open stores in the camp, and we could even have our photographs taken. Professional photographers sometimes came to the camp to take our pictures.

Since more than twenty internees from Hawai'i were going back to Japan on the second exchange ship, we decided to have a commemorative picture taken. Unfortunately, fifteen or sixteen men could not join the picture taking because of a scheduling problem. Even without them, there were as many as sixty-eight internees in the picture. It turned out pretty well.

The ancestors of Americans were immigrants from all over the world. Depending on the part of the country, social attitudes and customs differ. In the northern region, comprised of Wisconsin, North Dakota, South Dakota, and Montana, there are many German Americans, and they are trustworthy in every respect. The photographs taken in Missoula were inexpensive, but they are still in good condition. On the other hand, the pictures taken at the Santa Fe camp were expensive, but they have already turned yellow.

Crows, Sparrows, and Cats

Although the Missoula internment camp was near the city of Missoula, it was located in a secluded basin, which gave it an otherworldly atmosphere. Various types of birds inhabited the area, and they were not afraid of humans. It occurred to me that Shangri-La of the old Chinese story might have been a similar kind of place.

One day I was catching cicadas in the field, when a crow suddenly flew from a branch of a tree and, much to my surprise, perched on my shoulder. It might have been going after the cicadas I was catching. When the mess hall opened at mealtime, sparrows would fly in with us and fearlessly hop around on the tables. Interestingly, there were also many cats, although there were not a lot of houses in the area. Elderly Mankichi Goto always collected our leftover food, which he would leave on the sewer cover in the garden, where the cats waited in an orderly fashion for him. Animals here had no fear of man and lived a life of ease. Likewise, we became more peaceful.

It is immeasurably significant that we spent ten months in the Missoula camp, from June 1943 until April 1944. Our time there gave us comfort and helped us tremendously to maintain our mental and physical health. At first, no one could understand why the authorities kept moving us from camp to camp. Someone said that German and Italian POWs and internees had been kept in one place for a long time during World War I and that many of them had become mentally ill. Learning from this experience, they apparently kept us moving from one place to another.

Each time we were moved, we had the distressing experience of riding for days in the most dilapidated trains, but this was soon forgotten, as we came across all the different scenery and were settled in our new barracks. Our spirits lifted as we installed shelves and put our belongings in order. As I mentioned earlier, everything turned out quite well here, so our move to Missoula was an absolute blessing, for which we were very grateful.

President Sogawa of *Hawaii Shimpō* Passes Away

Like many of us, Masao Sogawa had left Japan alone as a young man to seek his fortune abroad. He was a self-made man, who worked his way up the career ladder from workman at the newspaper to company president.[25] He had a well-rounded personality, was energetic and cheerful, and especially enjoyed sports and entertainment.

In Missoula, we were assigned beds next to each other. It was the morning of August 30. Mr. Sogawa had washed his face, then sat down on his bed and suddenly said, "Oh! Oh!" He appeared puzzled as he looked at his left arm.

"What happened?" I asked. He did not respond and instead lay down.

Dr. Kohatsu, who was three beds away, examined him and diagnosed a cerebral hemorrhage. He gave Mr. Sogawa first aid and then immediately sent him to the hospital. Mr. Sogawa must have suffered a serious stroke. He passed away at eight-sixteen in the evening on September 5, having been in a coma all the while. We telegraphed his wife to tell her of his demise, and she responded that she would leave all the arrangements to us. We decided to hold his funeral service on September 8.

He was the first casualty among the group that had come on the first ship to the Mainland. Rev. Gikyo Kuchiba presided at the service, and all the Buddhist priests recited sutras. The atmosphere was solemn. Totaro Matsui offered the eulogy on behalf of all the internees.

"When this unfortunate war broke out, you impressed us with your mature comments in your newspaper," he read with deep emotion. "You were regarded as an influential man among us Japanese in Hawai'i, and so you were arrested by the FBI along with us. For the next year and a half, we lived together, first in the crowded detainment room in the INS building, then in the tents at Sand Island, in the hold of a military ship, in snowy Wisconsin, amid thunderstorms at the hilltop camp in Tennessee, and in the blazing heat of Louisiana. You were always cheerful and encouraged those of us who tended to be dispirited. Now that you are gone, we feel such deep sorrow." No one uttered a word, and a silence came over us. Some wept, feeling so deeply for him.

The main cause of a cerebral hemorrhage is said to be drinking. Mr. Sogawa used to be a heavy drinker when he was young, but in recent years, he had not drunk as much. Of course, no alcoholic drink was allowed during the early days of the internment. Even after beer became available, he drank only a small amount. He had done nothing detrimental to his health, and yet he had suffered a stroke. Although he had received the best possible care at the hospital, he died within five days. Whenever I think of Mr. Sogawa, I must admit that it is but the fate of man that life comes to an end.

Reverend Oi Becomes a Poultry Farmer

Unlike most government officials, Mr. Fraser, the director of our camp, was a sensible man, who did an excellent job of managing our camp operations. With the dual objective of making use of unused space outside the camp and starting a poultry farm to provide an inexpensive but tasty food source for us internees, Mr. Fraser set out to find a suitable leader to take on the job. During the process of selecting candidates, Assistant Secretary Yoshinobu Sasaki and Rev. Masahiro Himeno recommended Rev. Joei Oi.

Reverend Oi was a Nichiren Mission priest and a close friend of mine, who had been teaching at the Kalihi Japanese Language School when I was the school board's member in charge of educational administration. He was arrested at his Kalihi Valley home on December 7 and hauled away in the same car that I was in. He once said he had raised fifty or sixty chickens, and so because of this experience, he was put in charge of the project. Although skilled in composing *tanka*[26] and in writing, he did not look or act like a priest. He had been living in Dormitory 21 with me, but he soon moved out into a cottage on the farm and led a life that was quite free. If this had happened in some other camp, everyone would have envied him. But since we all led a semi-free life here in Missoula, we were not terribly jealous.

A man named Momiyama, who used to run a restaurant in New York City, was the cook on the farm. Reverend Oi was able to have food cooked just as he liked it, and so it was the most suitable job for a gourmet like him. On my way to go fishing, I often visited him to have a cup of tea. On one occasion, he invited me, along with a few of my dormitory mates, to have some handmade *udon*[27] together. My time for fishing was now limited, and I did not have enough time to look for a good fishing spot. But I had asked Reverend Oi in advance where to go to find a good spot, so I was able to get there straight away and begin fishing immediately.

In the river area, the famous Missoula fossils can be found, but since I was more eager to fish, I did not have the time to look for them. I could not kill two birds with one stone, so I had to give up fossil hunting. Reverend Oi had many nice fossils, for he had a lot of time on his hands, and he kindly gave me one from his collection when I asked for it. You can see why I was quite indebted to him.

Ladies Join Us in Camp!

Just as the camp was buzzing over the repatriation issue, a group of Nikkei ladies came to live outside our area of the camp. Like a sudden shower in the midst of a drought, they drenched our otherwise parched lives. Transferred from a relocation center, the thirty to forty women were all we talked about at the time.

Reverend Oi and his group of farmers, who were living outside the camp, were now envied by all of us behind the fence. There was a theater outside the camp, and movies were shown twice a week. The theater was now suddenly packed with people. With the ladies going to the movies, even those internees who normally would stay in their dormitory and read books rather than watch old movies were coming out.

The women lived next to the poultry farm cottage, and some of the more sociable ones visited the farm to observe its operations, which made the men there very happy. While visiting the farm, the women discovered a *furo*[28] in the bathroom. They asked to use it, and the poultry farmers instantly agreed without asking for Reverend Oi's consent. Every night after that, a group of seven or eight ladies took turns using the *furo*. They were even nicely treated to cups of tea after their baths.

According to a weekly magazine published recently in Japan, Japanese office ladies, called "BGs," are shy when alone, but become bold when in a group.[29] Their aggressiveness sometimes surprises men, but these Nikkei ladies were middle-aged housewives and much bolder than their Japanese counterparts. They took no account of us internees.

In the beginning, the farmers were curious and wanted to indulge in a little seduction, but they later became fed up with the ladies' conduct. Since the bathroom was located in the poultry farm, the ladies had to get undressed and dressed in the cottage. Every time the women went in and out of the bathroom, they intentionally exposed some of their bodies to the farmers. Even spiritually enlightened Reverend Oi finally sighed, "Women and children are difficult to deal with."

The ladies emptied the *goemon* bathtub[30] after each use, so while their water warmed up and they waited their turn, they talked to the farmers. They did not mind staying up until late at night. It was no problem for them, but not so for the farmers, who had to be up early in the morning to feed the chickens. It was an embarrassing situation, but no one had the courage to deny the ladies their luxury. Eventually, three weeks passed. And then, these demanding and seductive women were ordered to move again, gone with the wind to New York City.

Not only the farm but the whole camp once more became a lonely place.

Shopping in Town

Summer in the north was quite wonderful, what with the vivid colors of the leaves and flowers. However, we could enjoy them for only a short while before autumn would arrive. One day, I went out to town in a car driven by a guard to buy some merchandise requested by my fellow internees. As we headed east toward the town of Missoula, the trees on both sides of the road were a golden color, and even the road was covered in golden leaves. The shape of the leaves looked like those of the *kukui*,[31] and they were about the size of a man's palm. The richness of autumn was here.

As we drove through the tunnel of golden branches, I could see a large "M" on the hillside behind the University of Missoula campus.[32] This road reminded me of the approach to Daimonjiyama. Nyoigatake, commonly known as Daimonjiyama, is located at the northern end of the thirty-six hills of the Higashiyama mountain range in Kyoto. Every year on the night of August 16, a ritual fire is lit in the shape of a large 大. The big "M" in

Missoula has nothing to do with such a romantic custom. It simply serves as a necessary landmark for aircraft to identify the city. At any rate, it is not so bad to have the sign of an "M" in the background of the town. It looks like a city crest. You could call it a fine sight, from the American point of view.[33]

Missoula is beautiful, with several bridges spanning the St. Regis River that runs through the city. I was interested in and impressed by the large overhanging white birch tree at the entrance to the city. The Missoula Mercantile Company, a large department store in the middle of town, was unlike other stores for it carried a wide variety of goods, including fabric, clothes, cosmetics, art work, medicine, groceries, farming equipment, and sporting goods. I was particularly interested in the heads of bear, buffalo, deer, wolf, wild boar, and sable that had been stuffed and hung on the walls and columns of the sporting goods department, along with plaques engraved with the names of hunters who had caught them. With dresses, hats, and other accessories beautifully displayed in the women's department and many ladies strolling the aisles, this store seemed to be more successful than any other.

With us interned, it was our wives who were having the hardest time financially, as well as mentally and physically. We could comfort them only by writing letters. When I found some nice material for a lady's dress, I bought three-and-a-half yards without even asking the price and had it sent directly to my wife. As I watched the sales clerk wrap the fabric, I imagined my wife happily opening my package. I was so pleased with what I had done that I became a little emotional. Because there were hardly any appropriate birthday gifts for my children in the canteen, I never sent them any from camp. But now I bought a few other items, which I found suitable to be mailed home at a later date. As I could from then on mail them to my home, I became very happy, as if a dense fog had suddenly been lifted.

The Sun Shines on All Corners of our Dormitory

Having not been to any foreign lands since coming to Hawai'i from Japan, I had not encountered any strange natural phenomena, and so I was surprised to see the beautiful Northern Lights at Camp McCoy in Wisconsin. Here in this camp, there was no opportunity to see the lights. At approximately forty-eight degrees north, Missoula lies on the same latitude as the former Japan-Russian border of Sakhalin. I have heard that for more than two months during the summer, it never gets dark in northern Siberia and the north Alaskan area of Point Barrow. This phenomenon is generally known as the nights under the midnight sun. Although we did not experience this phenomenon here, the days were still very long, while the nights were quite short.

We did experience the unusual sight of the sun shining on all outside corners of our dormitory. Our south-facing dormitory was one hundred and ten feet long and eighteen feet wide. In the morning, the sun shone on the north side of the building and again on the same side in the evening, before setting behind the mountains. We all know that the earth is round, but until now, we could not grasp it as a reality, since no one could actually see the earth as round. Watching this phenomenon now, we could not help but acknowledge this fact.

In the winter, on the other hand, dawn came at around nine o'clock, and the sun shone at ten. Since the sun set at five o'clock, we had darkness for as much as sixteen hours and daylight for just eight. Laundry would not dry within a day's time, even though we hung it in the sun at the south side of the building. We did not experience extremely cold weather, owing to the topography. Yet temperatures did go down to as low as minus seven degrees, although the average was about ten degrees, with a high of twenty-five. Because there was almost no wind, it did not feel very cold. So fishermen never missed a day of fishing even during the winter.

When I look back on those days, I wonder how we could have done such a thing in that adverse weather. Perhaps it was because all of us were healthy, as well as in a heightened state, having been forced to adjust to such a situation.

Wild Ducks Come with Leeks on their Backs

It was late one foggy night. For about thirty minutes, thousands of wild ducks came flying very low over the camp. I had never before heard such a loud flapping of wings and squawking of duck calls.

The following morning, some ducks lay dead on the ground, and those people who were lucky enough to find them were very happy. When experiencing some unexpected good fortune, one might use the Japanese proverb, "The wild duck came with leeks on his back."[34] Although the ducks did not unexpectedly bring leeks with them this time, it was still a pleasant occurrence to have them fall in our yard.

Elderly Rev. Kametaro Maeda, who lived in the next dormitory, usually rose earlier than others, and he was the first to find a duck. When we told him that he had been lucky, he said, with a serious face, "God had mercy on us. This is a gift from Heaven." We all laughed at his joke.[35]

With so many ducks flying very fast through the fog, some had been killed when they flew into electric cables and bathroom chimneys.

The Exquisite Flavor of Yakima Apples

The best thing I tasted in Missoula was a Yakima apple. I like trout, but fruit lovers like me enjoy apples even more. I still remember the sweet taste of the Yakima apples.

Dozens of years ago, crunchy, red apples that tasted slightly tart were imported from New Zealand, but for some reason they are not brought over any more. Deep red Yakima apples are a little longer than common apples. They are similar to the New Zealand variety, except that they are much larger, sweeter, crunchier, and juicier. But they spoil easily. If you find a dark spot on an apple, it will begin to rot within a few days. That is why the apples, transported to Missoula on freight trains, are packed in boxes without covers.

It is a pity that only the local residents can enjoy these delicious ripened apples. Researchers seem to be working to improve their hardiness, but I am always disappointed with the taste of the Yakima-like apples that are sold now in Honolulu markets. They are not crunchy, and the sweetness and juiciness are lacking.

Every year when apple season arrives, I buy some in spite of myself, for they are beautifully displayed in the showcase. I am always disappointed, because they are not even half as good as I expect. I guess the delicate taste created by sunlight and the natural environment cannot yet be duplicated by man.

News Broadcasts and Japanese Language Class

As we regained our presence of mind, not only life-related but hobby-related, classes opened in our community. First, a news broadcasting department was formed under the direction of Kazuo Arai, a Japanese student from Nagoya, and Minoru Murakami from Hilo. Secretly borrowing a short-wave radio from an Italian internee who had arrived before us, they listened to the Japanese news and kept us informed. They gathered the news that even the local papers never reported, so everyone in the camp came and listened eagerly.

At Camp McCoy, we used to sing all together before and after each broadcast. At Livingston, there was none of that. Here, in Missoula, Mr. Fujiie and Mr. Sarashina took the lead in reviving the singing. At Camp McCoy, we sang "The Pacific March," which made us feel highly spirited, for we still believed in a Japanese victory.

Such passion gradually faded away after the battles of Midway and the Coral Sea, when we followed the dictates of reason, understanding that the chance of a Japanese victory was now very slim. Although we pretended not to be in such a somber mood, I think it was reflected in the choice of songs we sang at the news broadcasts. We loudly sang "The Pacific March," but it sounded rather empty. We had lost our passion. With this sentiment prevailing among us, we chose to sing "Earth and Soldiers" and "The March of My Beloved Horse." We continued to sing "The Patriots' March," however, because it reflected our love for our motherland and the melody was too pretty to abandon.[36]

The education department was organized next. Similar departments at the previous camps had taught English grammar, conversation, and simple forms of writing. But here we started a Japanese class, which was a unique step. Saichiro Kubota headed the department, and Hideyuki Serizawa was in charge of the class. Unexpectedly, twenty to thirty people attended and studied hard. Among them was Rev. Nisshu Kobayashi, who was also a scholar of Buddhism.

During the lecture one day, Instructor Serizawa and Reverend Kobayashi began arguing about the proper way to write the Chinese character for halberd, 戈, *hoko*. Even though they argued for a long time, there was no way to prove who was right, for no comprehensive character dictionary, like the *Kanwa daijiten*, was available in camp.[37] Many students became curious about who was correct, and they began arguing amongst themselves, checking their dictionaries after going back to their dormitories. The argument even continued into the following day's class. Both seriously discussed the subject, while for others it was simply an amusing pastime.

The Light and Dark Sides of Winter in the North

In the north, although summer was comfortable, winter was quite gloomy. A thick fog often descended on the whole area, and we became depressed as it became dark. We could see nothing but the dark fog around us, followed by waves of even darker fog. The moment the fog touched the trees it turned to frost. The snow and frost were beautiful in the sun the following morning. But when the snow fell and the fog rolled in, it was dark and depressing, and I felt as if I were in a world of death.

My hometown gets a lot of snowfall, for it is located in mountain country. But I was never gloomy there, because it never became dark when it snowed. I was a child at the time, and so I enjoyed the snow. In our region, where the elevation was not very high, the fog did not turn to frost. Instead, frost formed at the higher elevations during the night and created a very beautiful sight in the morning. It made the trees look like flowers, which is why in Japan we use the expression "tree flowers" 木花. The next morning, after the snowfall, when the sun came up, it would be bright and warm. We children happily threw snowballs and made snowmen.

Even in this northern region of Missoula, located at forty-eight degrees latitude, it was warm and bright the morning after a snowfall, and there would be a complete change in attitude to go along with the silvery world. Perhaps this is all part of the laws of nature. It was humorous to see adult men, like children, cheerfully rolling balls of snow and making snowmen. One would never have guessed they were prisoners behind barbed wire.

Fishermen in long rubber boots hurried to secure good fishing positions, dashing through the fields instead of taking the usual path to get to their favorite spots. To see them running in the field was not something to boast about, that's for sure. At the end of the day, the fishermen returned empty-handed, trudging back like crippled, old ducks, yet they never gave up and, with the usual spirit, continued to go out into the snow.

There are lyrics to an *Awa ondō* that go "Dancers are crazy, and spectators are crazy, too. If you're crazy anyway, why not dance?"[38] The same can be said about fishermen and spectators. But since there were no spectators to those who were fishing in the snow, I think I can safely say that the fishermen were the champions of all the crazy people.

Mistaken for Being Mexican

As it got colder, many more internees needed hats and gloves, and so I often went out to the Missoula Mercantile Company. One day I had the chance to chat with an attractive Caucasian saleslady, who I had come to know. To my surprise, she asked whether I was Mexican. I had heard that Mexicans and Japanese look alike, but since I had never seen a Mexican before, I was not offended. But, at the same time, I did not feel that I had been flattered either. When I said that I was Japanese, she looked surprised and gazed at me curiously.

Even people in Missoula had known about the Pearl Harbor attack, but they were not aware of the presence of Japanese in their town. Since the start of the war, hundreds of Japanese had been relocated in and out of town, but because the newspapers had not reported this, no one knew we were there.

When I asked the lady why she thought I was Mexican, she said she could not imagine Japanese being in Missoula, and so, therefore, she figured I was Mexican. When I asked if any Mexicans were living in Missoula, she said, "No, but they come every year to take seasonal jobs."

After I returned to the camp, I asked Hatsutaro Kasajima, who had been interned from Mexico, about Mexicans. He said, "Most Mexicans are uneducated and lazy, with characteristics similar to American Indians." Though blessed with natural resources, the country did not prosper because of the people, he added.

It was quite natural that this beautiful saleslady at the Missoula Mercantile Company was surprised to learn that a man she had thought was Mexican turned out to be of the same ethnic group that had attacked Pearl Harbor and killed thousands of American sailors. I explained that I was not a soldier and that I had been arrested at four o'clock on the day of the attack and sent to the Mainland, leaving my wife and five American children behind.

Instead of looking at me with hostility, she said, "I'm sorry to hear that, but this is what war is about." I thought she reacted like a typical American girl. From then on, we became friends. She took good care of me and even took me to other department stores. Going to the Missoula Mercantile became a pleasure.

A New York Hon'imbō and His Group

One day as I was playing *go* with Isaku Orita, Miyuki Sokabe came by and suggested that I challenge a man from his dormitory who was known as "the New York Hon'imbō."[39] I asked him how good he was. Sokabe said he thought the man was very good, but as Sokabe himself was a beginner, he felt he was in no position to judge. Sokabe also mentioned that this man was the best *go* player among the five or six players in his dormitory and that the man himself had admitted that he was "the New York Hon'imbō." Sokabe urged me to challenge him, and so I visited his dormitory.

I put down the first stone in the first game. As I was a player of the seventh *kyū*, I thought I would never win the succeeding games, but I went ahead anyway and played the game with the black stones.[40] Contrary to his reputation, he was not a strong player, and he gave up the game before it reached the end. For the next game, I took the white stones. He again surrendered before the end. Nonetheless, he was still confident in himself, and he challenged me to another game, which I won. He continued to challenge me again and again.

In New York City, there must have been many good players, like company employees from Japan. From what I knew, Professor Ryusaku Tsunoda of Columbia University had skill of the *shodan* level, and I was sure there must have been other highly ranked players.[41]

This man was a cook, and he must have been the Hon'imbō of his group, which consisted mainly of cooks and waiters, who probably for many years had not had much contact with people from Japan. Naturally, their lifestyle would have been quite different from ours. They did not seem like gangsters, however, they were vagabonds, who went anywhere they pleased.

The rumor was that they were interned because they had been suspected of espionage. I think some readers will recall the painter Naoji Yoshida,[42] who aired a radio series of interesting and detailed stories of the lives of such groups. There were seventeen or eighteen men of this kind who had been interned from New York, Boston, and Alaska. Interestingly, all of them had something in common—they were single men in their mid-fifties. About half of them did not have passports when they arrived in the United States. I heard that they had jumped ship in New York, Philadelphia, and Boston. No one knows what happened to them at the end of the war, but they were a group that shared a strange fate.

Hospitalized with the Flu, Fed Up with Medicine

It was right in the middle of winter, and we were snowed in, with the thermometer pointing below zero every day. Fishermen, as well as golfers, had no choice but to stay in their dormitories. *Go* players were never bored, but other people spent most of their time polishing stones.

Influenza became epidemic at this time. Because we stayed inside all day long, we were susceptible to getting sick. Six or seven men in our dormitory immediately caught the flu. I had been proud of myself for having not caught the flu from the time I was interned, but now at last I became sick. Mr. Toyama and Mr. Chikuma were the first to be hospitalized. Others who became ill were Messrs. Shigemoto, Deme, Okawa, Ozaki, and Tomiji Kimura. On the advice of Mr. Matsui and Dr. Kohatsu, I was confined to a hospital bed for the first time in my life.

It was December 21, and even though there was a nicely decorated tree in the hospital, it did not make me feel that Christmas was coming soon. The room temperature was comfortable, and the nurses took good care of me, but the anti-pneumonia medication that I had to take every three hours was a nuisance. Thanks to the good care at the hospital, I was discharged on Christmas Eve. I did not feel at home back in the dormitory, but still I was happy to see my dormitory mates welcoming me back. There were others who were hospitalized after me, and another seven internees were treated in their dormitory when the hospital ran out of beds.

No activities were held on Christmas Eve due to the epidemic. But everyone was happy with the turkey dinner served at the mess hall and with the ration of candies and nuts. Some dormitory mates kindly suggested that I stay in the dormitory to avoid being exposed to the cold wind, and they offered to bring back my meal. Not wanting to impose on them, I declined their kind offer and went to the mess hall, which turned out to be a bad choice. My condition worsened, and I was hospitalized again on December 29.

This time I suffered from a high fever all day long. I had never experienced such a fever before, and I agonized over the possibility that I might have been suffering from some other illness. The next day, however, my temperature dropped to 102 degrees, and I felt better. When I saw an Italian priest set up an altar and begin to pray, I was puzzled until I learned it was already January 1.

I had not realized how quickly the days had passed since I had been readmitted to the hospital. In the afternoon, an orderly named Mr. Kotaka unexpectedly brought me, with the doctor's permission, *zōni*, *nishime*, and *gomoku-meshi*.[43] My temperature was down, and the welcome surprise made the food all the more delicious.

Although the fever was gone, I was still not back to my usual self. An orderly told me it was because of an excessive amount of medicine. I agreed with his assessment and stopped taking the medicine, although I acted like I still was. Within two days, I felt better, and my appetite increased. When I looked at myself in the mirror, I noticed that my eyes were still bloodshot and looked terrible. Nonetheless, I left the hospital on the eleventh day with the approval of the doctor.

A Recovery Celebration in the Dormitory

The sky was clear on the day that I got out of the hospital, and the sunlight reflecting on the snow's surface was so dazzling that I could hardly open my eyes. I felt so good and returned to my dormitory in high spirits.

Everyone welcomed me back, but even so, I felt uneasy with the others and did not feel as comfortable as I would have if I had been at home. Having learned my lesson the last time, I did not go to the mess hall for my meals, but gratefully accepted Rev. Shinri Sarashina's kind offer. His bed was next to mine, so he brought food to me on his way back from the mess hall. He was very obliging, so his other close friends began to depend on him, too. I felt sorry for him, having to carry all that food through the cold, and I appreciate his kind gesture even now.

Kinzo Sayegusa, my canteen supervisor and my senior and close friend from the same hometown, was happy to see me back. He bought chicken for sukiyaki and invited all the dormitory mates. It was an enjoyable evening. The following week, I invited all of them to a party to express my appreciation. Although there was no special food but chicken and beer, Sawajiro Ozaki took good care of us and made sure we enjoyed a wonderful party.

A New Year's Reception

I regretted not having been able to attend the New Year's reception because I had come down with the flu. According to a news article written by Mr. Matsui and Mr. Obata, it had been a large reception. *Kadomatsu*,[44] made with tall pine trees cut down in the mountains, decorated the entrance of the reception hall, as well as that of the mess hall. The decorations created a festive atmosphere to welcome the New Year. The camp director and his staff were aware of our hardship as internees, and they were very generous to us. We carried on as though we were back in *shaba*, pounding mochi and preparing food, like sushi and nishime on New Year's Eve. We distributed what we had made to all the dormitories and the mess hall was closed for two days.

A big banner reading "The Whole World under One Roof" was hung in the center of the entrance to the reception hall. The Shinto altar was decorated with red and white striped ornaments, and it created a solemn atmosphere. Master of ceremonies Minoru Murakami began the proceedings by asking all in attendance to join in singing the national anthem of Japan, "*Kimigayo*."[45] A celebratory speech by Mayor Saiki, the reading of the message that was to be sent to Japan by Chief Secretary Matsui, and *banzai* cheers[46] led by Kiyoshi Ichikawa followed. More than twenty representatives of the German and Italian internees from the neighboring areas, including their mayors, attended the ceremony in matching black shirts. We were very glad and welcomed their timely visit.

Wonderful Gifts

On Christmas Eve 1943, wonderful gifts were delivered to our camp. They were from the Red Cross of Japan—or so we thought. After the war ended, however, we learned that the Relief Association for Overseas Japanese had sent them. We also learned after the war that this organization had been headed by then-senator and former foreign minister Arita Hachirō, with Maruyama Tsurukichi, former chief of the Tokyo Metropolitan Police Department, serving as secretary.

We were surprised by the unexpectedly large amount of books, high-quality tea, Kikkoman shōyu, miso from Sendai, and medicines. We had no idea how the items had reached this camp, but we thought it was not a coincidence that they arrived on Christmas Eve. It was a wonderful surprise, and we appreciated the chance to taste fragrant Japanese tea and Kikkoman shōyu in this remote internment camp in the northernmost region of the Mainland.

In 1955, Maruyama Tsurukichi, who had been instrumental in collecting and sending these gifts, fell ill and was hospitalized in Tokyo. He passed away on February 20, 1956 at the age of seventy-two. At a time of critical shortages in Japan, Mr. Maruyama had arranged to send us through the Red Cross one hundred million yen worth of gifts in the form of fifty thousand pounds of tea, sixty thousand pounds of miso, eight thousand six hundred barrels of shōyu, and five hundred tons of books and entertainment items. When this became known, an organization called the Committee to Recognize and Commend the Honorable Mr. Maruyama was formed by a group of Tokyo residents with ties to Hawai'i and America under the leadership of Tahara Haruji, Azumi Suimei, Ozawa Takeo, Yamashita Soen, Murayama Tamotsu, and Sakakibara Kamenosuke. They notified us that they were going to praise the virtue of Mr. Maruyama's deeds and send *kōden* to his family as a condolence offering. In Hawai'i, Katsuichi Kawamoto, Sawajiro Ozaki, Shinzaburo Sumida, Hideo Tanaka, Seiichi Shimamoto, Yasuro Kurita, and I started our own collection. Money donated by 262 people was later sent to the organization.

In the camp, we divided the tea amongst us, while the shōyu and the miso were used in the kitchen. When we were ready to move to Santa Fe in April of the following year, there was a considerable amount of the gifts still unused. We distributed the shōyu equally to all the dormitories. Books were taken with us to Santa Fe and donated to the library in the camp. I heard, after I had arrived at Santa Fe, that similar gifts had also been sent to that camp.

New Officers in an Enlarged Internee Self-Government

With the turn of the New Year, Mayor Takaichi Saiki turned in his resignation. Thus, Totaro Matsui was appointed the new mayor. Accordingly, there were changes in the officers.

Mayor	Totaro Matsui
Chief Secretary	Takaichi Saiki
Assistant Secretary	Yoshinobu Sasaki
Staff	Ryuichi Kashima, Takeshi Morita (Mainland), Isamu Kurotobi (Peru)

Accounting	Katsuji Onishi (Mainland)
Auditor	Taijiro Tochio (Peru)
Canteen	
Canteen Manager	Kinzo Sayegusa
Purchase Clerk	Setsugo Togioka
Clerk	Kumaji Furuya, Saichiro Okada (Mainland), Yukio Nakamura (Peru), Kaichi Tokutake (Peru), Kiyoshi Ichikawa
Mail Superintendent	Ichiro Konno
Clerk	Hiroshi Yamamoto (Peru), Masaichi Hirashima
Supply Manager	Masato Kiyosaki
Clerk	Mitsutaka Horiuchi, Kenzo Watanabe (Peru)
First Aid	Akio Kimura, Yukihide Kohatsu, Yojo Taira
Orderly	Rien Takahashi, Katsuo Hamamoto (Peru)
Labor Manager	Sawajiro Ozaki
Assistant Manager	Masaichiro Shinoda
Clerk	Ichiro Wada
News Broadcasting	Kazuo Arai (Mainland), Minoru Murakami, Tadao Watanabe
Poultry Farm Manager	Joei Oi
Barber	Kazuo Tomita
Chief Cook	Sekitaro Nagai (Mainland)
Assistant Cook	Masayuki Chikuma
Steward	Kichisuke Yoda
Fire Department	Tamaki Arita
Tailor	Santaro Sonoda
Plumbing	Osuke Shigemoto
Recreation	
Softball Manager	Soichi Obata
Judo Manager	Suijo Kabashima
Tennis Manager	Tsuneyoshi Kiba (Mainland)
Golf Manager	Atsuo Sakimizuru

Kendō Manager	Shuji Mikami
Movie Manager	Muneo Kimura
Education Manager	Saichiro Kubota
English Education	Masahiro Himeno, Itsuei Hisatake
Commerce Education	Miyuki Sokabe
Painting	Masao Ikeno
Shakuhachi	Shuji Mikami
Religion Department	
Christian Religion	Kametaro Maeda
Buddhist Religion	Shinri Sarashina
Library	Itsuei Hisatake

As you can see, Hawai'i internees were assigned to most of the important positions in all departments. It gave the impression that it was a Hawai'i organization.

Harmful Mites

It is said that mid-January is the coldest time of the year in Japan. Strangely enough, it was not very cold in Missoula, Montana, which is located farther north than Hokkaidō. On January 17, temperatures were a low of thirty-two degrees and a high of forty-two. We thought spring had finally come. However, at the end of the month, it went down to a low of seven degrees, with a high of twenty-two, and this type of weather continued for several days. Then again, from January 15, the temperature rose to a low of twenty degrees and a high of thirty-three degrees. This lasted until January 30.

When I went fishing after a long absence, I noticed that tree branches that had been bitten down by beavers were now growing new shoots. It was becoming spring, which would be favorable for sports and fishing. The weather made those of us who had been inactive during the winter feel vigorous once more. At the same time, poisonous mites became active, as well. Thus, the secretary's office instructed us to get our immunizations.

The mites lived only on the other side of the river, but all fishermen and poultry farm workers had to be inoculated just to be on the safe side. I had thought mites are harmful only to dogs, not to humans. But I learned that they are harmful not only to dogs and cats, but to birds and reptiles also. Their shapes and sizes vary: round, square, hexagonal, large, and small. They are all considered noxious insects, but there are some species that eat harmful plant lice. Some live on their host animal as larvae and never leave the host for their entire lives. Others live on their host while in the microscopic stage and leave when they are fully grown. The mites in this area were very dangerous and were found only in a few other places in the United States. Their bite may not trigger any pain or itching, but if not treated in time, it can be deadly. Anyone who had occasion to go to the river was given a shot. Even a nervous man who had never been outside the camp received a shot.

At about this time, an internee—I've forgotten who—landed a big sucker while fishing on the frozen river. When the big sucker pulled on his line, the internee braced himself, and the ice beneath him cracked. The portion he was standing on began to flow toward deep water, so he quickly jumped toward the riverbank. He was soaked to his chest when he got back. It was comical, but I couldn't laugh in a situation like that, so I had to struggle to control myself.

Fish Never Die, Even if the Water Freezes

When I held my recovery celebration party, I went to my fish preserve, where I had been keeping the trout I had caught. I discovered that the water in the preserve was frozen, and the trout could be seen in the middle of the ice, like in a framed picture. I tried to crack the ice, but I could not because it was very thick. Later, when I went to check on them after the ice had melted, I was surprised to find the trout swimming in the water. I realized then that the power of life is very strong.

Frozen tofu never reverts to its original form after it is thawed. Being inanimate, it becomes *kōya tōfu*.[47] Creatures in cold areas, however, do not freeze to death, but become even more vigorous when freed from their icy environment.

The Peru Group Is Transferred

In February, the Peru group of 111 internees left for Camp Kenedy, located at the southern tip of Texas. After all this time together, we were sorry to be parted from this group of young people we had gotten to know. Several days later, I received a letter from Hiroshi Yamamoto, a young man from my hometown, informing me that the Peru group had arrived safely at its destination. He wrote that the place was hot and dreary and that the treatment they were getting was vastly different from what it had been in Missoula. He did not say outright whether Camp Kenedy was better or worse than Missoula, because he feared he would be censored. I interpreted this to mean that his situation was incomparably worse, since we had been treated well in Missoula.

Soon after this letter arrived, twenty to thirty Peru internees visited our camp. I heard they had volunteered for road construction jobs and were on their way to Kooskia, Idaho.[48] I remembered that they had earlier tried to recruit volunteers for Kooskia from this camp. At the time, few internees volunteered because someone claimed that the job was to build a military road running from Idaho through Canada to Alaska and that this would benefit our enemies. Only Rev. Hozen Seki of New York, Rev. Yoshio Hino, Rev. Sokan Ueoka, Aisuke Shigekuni, Ittetsu Watanabe,[49] and Kuromitsu Banba volunteered at that time.

Actually, the purpose was not to build a military road, but one leading to hunting and fishing grounds in the interior of Idaho. Being unable to allocate an appropriate budget for the construction project, the clever governor of Idaho planned to recruit internees from various camps, who could be hired at cheaper rates. I understand he was unable to recruit many internees, and the project failed to accomplish much. Some internees in Santa Fe, namely Hitoshi Hanamoto, Koichi Kurisu, Giichi Nomura, Saburo Uyehara, Seizaburo Yogi, and Kokichi Nakamura, volunteered and stayed in Kooskia for two years. Monthly salaries ranged from forty dollars for regular workers to fifty dollars for those with special skills. These salaries were more than twice what was being paid internees working in the camps.

About two hundred internees applied for the job in Kooskia. According to the internees who returned from the job, they were housed in a former state prison, where inmates had been used as construction laborers. With the arrival of the internee workers, several wardens who had been working in the prison became temporary guards. Since the site was located deep in the mountains, there were inconveniences, but the internees also had many interesting experiences in that remote place. During the day they enjoyed much success at fishing, but at night the surrounding silence made them feel very lonely.

A Meeting with the Spanish Consul

Spanish Consul A. R. Martin came to our camp to interview us internees. We had been notified earlier of his visit, so we were prepared with questions and matters of concern, which we hoped to present to the Japanese and U.S. governments. Attending the meeting were the following: Takaichi Saiki and Totaro Matsui from the mayor's office, Iwao Matsushita and Katsuji Onishi from the Mainland group, Tetsuji Kurokawa and Minoru Murakami from the Hawai'i group, and Taijiro Tochio and Masao Mochizuki from the Peru group.

Absent from the meeting were the two State Department officials and the immigration officer who had come with the consul, as well as Camp Commander Fraser. Thus, they discussed matters frankly, as if they were speaking with a representative of the Japanese government.[50]

Outline of the Questions and Answers

Consul:	How is the food? Is tofu served?
Answer:	We have no complaints, in general. We wish more Japanese ingredients could be provided.
Consul:	Has anything improved since my last visit?
Answer:	Yes, but nothing of significance.
Consul:	I believe conditions are better here compared to other internment camps and relocations centers. I think you are fortunate.[51]

Repatriation

Question:	We would like to know why Agena and Kakiuchi were repatriated against their will.[52]
Consul:	According to Commander Fraser, he received a reply from Immigration Headquarters that their repatriations were by order of the State Department.[53]
Question:	Why were some repatriates denied boarding at the port of departure?
Consul:	It was simply because there was no room on the ship.
Question:	Was the selection of repatriates based on the instructions of the Japanese government?
Consul:	Yes.
Question:	Will there be a third exchange ship? When will it depart?
Consul:	I think it is a possibility. The result of the present survey will probably form the basis for further consideration, so please send me a list of interested parties right away.
Question:	How will the passengers be selected? Will it be based on the old list or a new one?
Consul:	The selection is made solely at the discretion of the Japanese government, so we must send them a new list.[54]
Question:	In the case of repatriates who have family left in Hawai'i,

	will these families be brought to the Mainland before the ship's departure?
Consul:	Give me in written form the names of those concerned and the details about their families. I will do my best to address each case.
Question:	Do sick and elderly people have priority over others?
Consul:	I have no idea, but I will ask for clarification.[55]
Request:	Internees whose families live in relocation centers or the Family Internment Camp[56] should be released upon reinvestigation and should be able to join their families. Keeping innocent men apart from their families for more than two years runs contrary to the doctrine of human rights, which the United States has always advocated. We would like you to emphasize this point to the authorities. We understand that rehearings were held at the Santa Fe camp and that more than ten internees were released as a result.[57]
Consul:	Send me the list of internees who want to live with their families. We have consistently tried to help, but because of insufficient building materials, there has been little progress in increasing the number of family camps. I will work with Mrs. Halsey, the welfare representative, to pursue this matter.
Request:	We would like an adequate supply of Japanese cooking ingredients.
Consul:	The camp administration has just informed me of the scheduled delivery within a few days of 150 gallons of shōyu and ingredients for tofu.[58]
Request:	At the Hawai'i branch of Specie Bank only citizens are allowed to withdraw money from their accounts. The accounts of internees are frozen, which leaves them suffering from a shortage of money. We ask for adequate relief.[59]
Consul:	We will check into it.
Request:	We would like to know if we can recover personal belongings that are missing or were confiscated in the internment camps.
Consul:	Have a detailed list mailed to us. We will make efforts to take appropriate action.
Question:	What is the truth about the Tule Lake incident? [60]
Answer:	I have no knowledge of the details of this incident, since I have not gone there, but the newspaper reports were

probably exaggerated. I do know that some people were
taken into custody, but there were no casualties. Tule
Lake Relocation Center is now under the control of the
military.

Request: Personal belongings left by the late Gosaku Masuda,
who died last year at Camp Livingston, have not been
returned to his family. We ask you to investigate this.

Answer: We will take immediate action.

Question: Some of the internees wish to move to Tule Lake. How
should they proceed?

Answer: They should negotiate with the immigration authorities.
However, I understand that Tule Lake is only for those
who have indicated their intention to repatriate.

This meeting extended from morning until afternoon and lasted for
two and a half hours. We discussed many other topics that are not included
above. Minutes of the entire proceeding were officially recorded, and four
copies were made. We asked the Spanish consul to send a copy to the Japanese government and also requested prompt action in negotiating with the
United States government regarding the concerns that were mentioned.

Fishing for Forbidden Trout

With the coming of March, even the cold north became spring-like. As
melted snow raised the water level of the river, fish began to swim upstream
seeking food. The temperatures rose day by day, signaling the arrival of the
fishing season. However, it turned out to be egg-laying time for the trout,
and trout fishing was, therefore, prohibited.

On an unusually rainy day, I saw fish jumping over the rapids. Taking
a chance, I threw in a line without a sinker and felt a good tug a moment
later. I was very excited and pulled up on the rod. A two-pound trout leapt
out of the water. I knew that trout season was closed, but I was quite reluctant to release it. I decided to put the trout into my creel. I looked around
to make sure I was alone. But oh, no! There on horseback was a guard
watching right behind me.

"Good job! You've landed a trout," he said with a smile. I was shocked
to hear his words.

But because he spoke in a gentle manner, I dared to say, "It looks like
a squaw fish."

"You're a lucky man," he said and left.

It was then that my usual hatred of the guards turned into gratitude, and I nearly jumped for joy. I assumed that he had not cited me because he was not a fishing warden, but later Reverend Oi told me that this guard happened to like fishing very much.

A Fishing Joke

There are a lot of fishing jokes in Montana, where many rivers run. Here is one:

> A man was fishing in the river, when another man came along.
> Man: Have you caught anything?
> Fisherman: No, but I landed forty whitefish here yesterday.
> Man: Is that right? Do you know who I am?
> Fisherman: No, I'm afraid not.
> Man: I'm the local big shot, and I own this whole area.
> Fisherman: Is that so? By the way, do you know who I am?
> Man: No.
> Fisherman: I'm the No. 1 braggart in all of Montana.

Long-Awaited Parole Begins

Either owing to our efforts in presenting a well-planned agenda before the Spanish consul or because the war was nearing an end, the authorities conducted investigations on us again. As a result—although I am not absolutely sure whether it was because of this—Sueji Iwasa, Ichiro Konno, Shozaemon Masaki, Taichi Sato, and Tadao Watanabe were paroled and left the camp for relocation centers or free zones.

It might have caused a sensation and people would have envied them if it had happened a year earlier. After more than two years of incarceration, however, and particularly under the comfortable circumstances of the present, the significance was somewhat lost. Nevertheless, it gave the rest of us hope that we might be paroled someday.

Moving for the Fifth Time

The snow had melted, and it had become even warmer. Since Mr. Matsui had become mayor, the treatment toward us continually improved because he dealt with the camp administration frankly and openly in the American way. Such a situation did not last long. We were told on March 2 that we were to be moved to the Santa Fe Internment Camp in New Mexico on about March 13.

We were very disappointed. Having endured the cold winter, we had been expecting a beautiful summer to come. After having packed most of our personal belongings, we were notified that our departure was being postponed to March 23. On March 22, we were again told that our departure would be delayed ten to fourteen days. We did not want to move from Missoula, for we thought it was the best of all the internment camps in which we had lived. Once the decision had been made, however, we wanted to move to Santa Fe as soon as possible so that we could see many of our old acquaintances, from whom we had been apart for so long. The delays were irritating.

A month after the first notice, at six-thirty in the evening on April 3, we left the camp where we had lived comfortably for ten months and headed south.

Haiku Written in Missoula

Snow covered mountains beyond
A domed hill carpeted with buds
雪山まえのまるい丘いちめん芽ぐみ

A field of dandelions before me
In the distance
Snow capped mountains
いちめんたんぽぽほうけて遠い雪山

The sun sets in the north
For internees living in the northern country
囚はれて夕日が北からさす北国

Mail arrives this morning
The scent of lilac fills the air
郵便が来たリラの花かほる朝です

Today a crescent moon
Outlines sharply a mountain ridge
くっきりと山の線けふは三日月

The city's neon lights
Beckon the evening breeze
町がはるかにネオンがまねく風が夜となる

In the coolness
A pleasant surprise
A sparrow alights on my shoulder
涼しさはすずめわたしの肩へとまりて

Just about to feed a bird
Suddenly a crow appears
鳥にやろうとつかまえるや烏ひょいと来る[61]

Life has become routine
Men spend their time polishing stones
このくらしにも慣れて石を磨いている

At the edge of town
An over-hanging white birch
Grows lush in the rain
町はずれのしだれ白樺しぐれている

At peace with myself
As clear as an autumn day
何もかも心も澄んだので秋晴

Fine autumn weather
Good fishing spots
Fishermen try their luck
秋晴、よい釣場があって釣っている

Leaves large
Bright yellow
A profusion of fallen leaves
大きな葉のまっ黄なゆたかなる落葉

A truck loading fallen leaves
Its hood covered with falling leaves
落葉する落葉を積む車の幌にも落葉

Night deepens under the shining moon
Snow capped mountains sleep
月夜更けて雪山ねむっている

In blinding sunlight
Reflected by the snow
I leave the hospital
雪に照る陽のまばゆく退院する

Released from the hospital
Back to the same
Rows of barracks and beds
退院してもバラック、ベッドが並んでいる

Morning sun tints the mountain snow
Reminding me of home
朝日雪の山頂を染め思い出はふるさと

A trout is hooked
Amidst swirling peony snowflakes
ツラウト釣り上げた牡丹雪うずまく中

Young shoots appear on a beaver-felled log
Spring is coming
ビーバーが倒した木も芽がふくらむので春

A letter arrives after circling the war-torn world
Words from my sensei
動乱の世界を廻って師の手紙が来た
　　　　　(The letter is from my haiku teacher, Seisensui Sensei.)[62]

Slowly melting
Mountain snow
Spring is near
だんだん無くなる山の雪春が山から来る

Bound for Santa Fe

The train headed east after leaving Missoula, the city that had provided us an oasis during our dreary internment experience. As we watched the city lights from the train, we passed the old battlefield, Hell Gate. It became dark when we reached the Rocky Mountains, and we proceeded in total darkness. The train passed through the Montana state capital, Helena, at about eleven-thirty, and exhausted from the day's stress, we fell sound asleep.

We stopped in Laurel the next morning and changed to a southern line. No farmland came into view, and there was nothing but wasteland as far as the eye could see. It was already eleven o'clock, and we had had no breakfast. Hungry, we began to complain. Finally, at eleven-thirty, we were told to proceed to the diner. It had been a long time since we had eaten a meal in a dining car. Negro waiters served us. Although we had been complaining a moment before, we were now very happy as we drank our hot coffee.

We traveled through the northern part of Wyoming. Yellowstone National Park was located to the west, and we could see the snow-capped Bighorn Mountains to the east. In between was a plateau of wasteland that looked like a desert without any vegetation. As we moved further south, oil pumping stations, sheep farms, and houses could be seen scattered about.

We passed through Denver the next day. The last time we had passed through, we had been traveling from west to east. This time, we crossed the city while we went from north to south. As we proceeded south from Denver, prairies seemed to stretch endlessly. There were no houses, and the only living creatures we saw once in a while were antelope that looked like the Japanese *kamoshika*.[63]

We were simply amazed at the vastness of the American continent. We noticed the construction of military barracks underway in the middle of the wasteland. We wondered why they were being built in such a remote place. Later we learned that the atomic bomb test site had been built in northern New Mexico.

In the early morning of April 6, we arrived, by way of Albuquerque, at the Santa Fe camp. Located halfway up the hill overlooking the old city of Santa Fe, the camp had held German internees during World War I. It looked like a village of old barracks.

Military police at the Honolulu Immigration Station fingerprint Hōryū Asaeda, a Buddhist priest from Honolulu, for his FBI arrest record, February 1942. *Japanese Internment and Relocation Files, University of Hawaiʻi Archives*

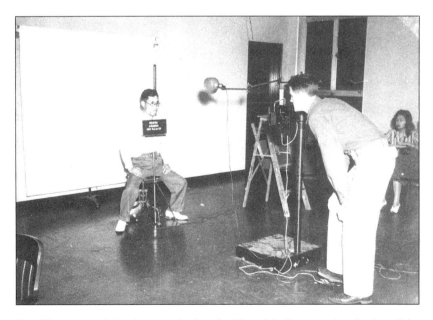

Rev. Hōryū Asaeda is photographed at the Honolulu Immigration Station, February 1942. *Japanese Internment and Relocation Files, University of Hawaii Archives*

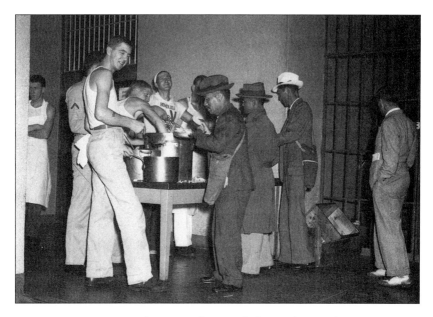

Internees carrying gas masks receive their meals from military police at the Hono-lulu Immigration Station, February 1942. *Japanese Internment and Relocation Files, University of Hawai'i Archives*

Charles Ichitarō Hasebe, a storekeeper from Leilehua, O'ahu, being interviewed by Lieutenant Robert I. Freund and interpreter Forrest Garnett at the Honolulu Immigration Station, February 1942. *Japanese Internment and Relocation Files, University of Hawai'i Archives*

Sand Island Internment Camp, January 1942. *Japanese Internment and Relocation Files, University of Hawai'i Archives*

Double rows of barbed wire fence, Sand Island Internment Camp, January 1942. *Japanese Internment and Relocation Files, University of Hawai'i Archives*

Internees putting up tents, Sand Island Internment Camp, February 1942. *Japanese Internment and Relocation Files, University of Hawai'i Archives*

Internee tents and barracks near completion, Sand Island Internment Camp, February 1942. *Japanese Internment and Relocation Files, University of Hawai'i Archives*

The Army-run INS station on Angel Island, where the Hawai'i internees were processed before being transferred to camps in the interior. Today it is the U.S. Immigration Station Barracks Museum on the grounds of the Angel Island State Park. *Japanese Cultural Center of Hawai'i*

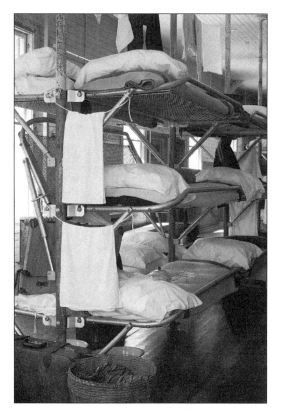

A re-creation of the bunk beds on the second floor of the Angel Island INS station, where Furuya and the rest of the first group of Hawai'i internees would have been held in March 1942. U.S. Immigration Station Barracks Museum. *Japanese Cultural Center of Hawai'i*

東走亞兮西走歐
南來北美苟禁愁
任君入到囚困此
若不流涕也低頭

Carved into the wooden walls of the Angel Island detention barracks are several hundred poems that were written by Chinese immigrants at the turn of the twentieth century. This is the poem, "I went east to Asia," discussed by Furuya in Chapter 6. U.S. Immigration Station Barracks Museum. *Japanese Cultural Center of Hawai'i*

In September 1943, Furuya, *fifth from right*, attended the funeral for Masao Sogawa, a Japanese newspaper publisher from Honolulu who died of a cerebral hemorrhage at the Fort Missoula Internment Camp. Rev. Gikyo Kuchiba, *center*, bishop of the Honolulu Hongwanji Buddhist temple, conducted the funeral. *Courtesy of the Historical Museum at Fort Missoula*

Internees at Fort Missoula made themselves a nine-hole golf course, which they played with a shared set of golf clubs. *Courtesy of the Historical Museum at Fort Missoula*

The tournament-winning Hawai'i internee softball team, Missoula, c. 1943. *Front row, left to right:* Tomoichi Hayashi, Ryuichi Kashima, Kazumi Matsumoto, Shujiro Takakuwa; *middle row, left to right:* Masayuki Iwata, Kumaji Furuya (author), Goki Tatsuguchi, Yoshinobu Sasaki, Masahiro Himeno; *back row, left to right:* Soichi Obata, Akio Kimura, Isaku Orita, Tamaki Arita, Masato Kiyosaki, Suijo Kabashima. *Soichi Obata Collection, Japanese Cultural Center of Hawai'i*

Artist unknown. Untitled. Reproduction with pastel application, 14 x 11 in. Santa Fe Internment Camp. This work is likely by Koshi Tatsuhara, a Japanese language school principal from Kauaʻi, who led the Japanese Painting Club at the Santa Fe camp. Several versions of this painting exist. It is believed that Tatsuhara used reproductions of his artwork to teach internees the application of paints. *Yoshio and Haruko Takahata Collection, Internment Artifacts Collection, Japanese Cultural Center of Hawaiʻi*

The Santa Fe camp internee News Broadcasting Department with Takegoro Kusao, head of its newspaper section, holding a sign identifying the group. Furuya is in the middle row, far right. *Patsy Saiki Archival Collection, Japanese Cultural Center of Hawaiʻi*

Santa Fe Liaison Department head Julian P. Langston, *holding white hat,* and Officer-in-Charge Lloyd H. Jensen attend an exhibit of internee art. Next to Jensen is Masao Ikeno, head of the internee Western Painting Club and a Japanese language school principal from Oahu. August 1944. *Joan Oya Collection, Japanese Cultural Center of Hawai'i*

Internees sometimes got together in the mess hall to celebrate special events, such as the Meiji emperor's birthday. Furuya can be seen in the back at right in this photograph likely taken at Santa Fe. *Riuichi Ipponsugi Archival Collection, Japanese Cultural Center of Hawai'i*

Bannosuke Yoshida. Untitled. Watercolor (original). 16.5 x 11.5 in. Santa Fe Internment Camp, 1944. Yoshida was a farmer from Heʻeia, Oʻahu. *Yoshida Family Collection, Internment Artifacts Collection, Japanese Cultural Center of Hawaiʻi*

Hawai'i internees in the Santa Fe Internment Camp, January 1945. *Front row, left to right:* Furuya, Shujiro Takakuwa, Mankichi Goto, Chosuke Kayahara, Suekichi Oka, Nisshu Kobayashi, Shuji Mikami, Sadasuke Hamamoto, Konin Matano, Isaku Orita, Makitaro Tamura, Minosuke Hanabusa, Giichi Sasaki, Ryosen Yonahara, Tomiji Kimura, Ninryo Nago, Shin Yoshida. *Second row, left to right:* Katsuichi Tanaka, Yasuemon Miki, Ryoichi Tanaka, Hatsutaro Toyofuku, Toshio Iinuma, Masaichi Hirashima, Tamaichi Tanaka, Uemon Ida, Kinai Ikuma, Hanzo Shimoda, Yoshizo Ishikawa, Taira Ida, Katsuichi Kawamoto, Daizo Sumida, Aisuke Shigekuni, Sadato Morifuji. *Third row, left to right:* Takegoro Kusao, Setsuzo Toyota, Jinshichi Tokairin, Hidekichi Nakamoto, Gendo Okawa, Joei Oi, Yasutaro Soga, Zensuke Kurosawa, Tsunetaro Harada, Tamaki Arita, Heigo Fuchino, Kogan Yoshizumi, Osuke Shigemoto, Hakuai Oda, Shinri Sarashina, Yoshinobu Sasaki, unknown, Seiichi Fujii, Tokikichi, Sugimoto, Shuntaro Ikezawa, Goki Tatsuguchi, Suekuma Takaki. *Back row, left to right:* unknown, Suijo Kabashima, Koichi Iida, Sawajiro Ozaki, Shoho Fujiie, unknown, Shigeki Mizumoto, Soichi Obata, Muneo Kimura, Yukihide Kohatsu, Tomoichi Hayashi, Kakujiro Nishiki, Takeo Miyagi, Josen Deme, Gikyo Kuchiba, Eita Sato, Ryuichi Kashima, Hideyuki Serizawa, Kinzo Saegusa. *Joan Oya Collection, Japanese Cultural Center of Hawai'i*

The Santa Fe camp cast and crew of "Hiroshima miyage to Tamazo" (Hiroshima souvenir and Tamazo), which was performed in March 1945. The script for this drama was likely written by an internee. *Patsy Saiki Archival Collection, Japanese Cultural Center of Hawai'i*

配所転々

古屋翠溪著

This cover illustration for the original *Haisho Tenten* was painted by Furuya's poetry friend, Akira Bunshiro Furukawa. It depicts the Santa Fe internees waiting for a meal by the mess hall, their coffee mugs hanging to dry in the branches of nearby trees. *Courtesy of the Furukawa family*

Furuya returned to Honolulu on November 13, 1945, after an absence of four years. *Left to right:* Hanzo, Seizo, Albert Tomochi, Robert Keiichi, Furuya, Florence Yoko, and Jun. *Courtesy of the Furuya family*

Relatives and friends gather at Honolulu Harbor on December 10, 1945, to greet Hawai'i internees being brought back to the islands aboard a military transport vessel. *Hawaii War Records Depository, University of Hawai'i Archives*

Koichi Iida, a businessman and former president of the Honolulu Japanese Chamber of Commerce, disembarks at Honolulu Harbor, November 13, 1945. *Hawaii War Records Depository, University of Hawai'i Archives*

Akio Robert Kimura, a Honolulu physician and surgeon, upon his return to Honolulu, December 10, 1945. He was sent alone from Santa Fe to Crystal City to fill the shortage of doctors at the family camp. *Hawaii War Records Depository, University of Hawai'i Archives*

The Furuya family several years after the war. *Front row, left to right:* Kumaji, Jun, Florence Yoko; *back row, left to right:* Seizo, Robert Keiichi, Albert Tomochi, Hanzo. *Patsy Saiki Archival Collection, Japanese Cultural Center of Hawai'i*

Kumaji Suikei Furuya, 1964.
Japanese Cultural Center of Hawai'i

| 12 |

Santa Fe Internment Camp
Santa Fe, New Mexico

Surprised to See Tomizo Tanigawa, the Famous Man of Kalihi

Of our Missoula group of 223 internees, most were assigned to newly built barracks. Amongst ourselves, we called the area *"shitamachi."*[1] As close friends from Dormitory 21 in Missoula, we wanted to be assigned to the same barracks and flocked together while waiting for our assignments. Unfortunately, this tactic did not work. Nonetheless, we were lucky that Sumida, Iida, Shigemoto, Sayegusa, Chikuma, Toyota, and I were assigned to Barracks 61 together.

Our barracks leader was Seigo Takai, a man from Sacramento. Nine Hawaiʻi internees had already been assigned to our barracks. They were: Tomizo Tanigawa, Ryosen Yonahara, Choshu Kuniyoshi, and Shuhei Oyama of Honolulu; Shosaburo Seki and Tetsunosuke Sone of Maui; Kashin Isa of Hilo; Kamasuke Higa of ʻEwa; and Shigeto Takashima of Molokaʻi. I had not met most of them before. I was very surprised to find among them the famous Kalihi resident Tomizo Tanigawa, who was wearing a gold watch, a gold chain with a magnet, and a gold ring with jewels.

Beginning in September 1941, as Japanese and American relations deteriorated and the assets of Japanese in Hawaiʻi were frozen, Mr. Tanigawa often visited his friends in the Kalihi area, suggesting that they prepare to repatriate, as war seemed unavoidable. He urged them to keep their belongings packed in large *shingen-bukuro* duffel bags like soldiers, so that they would be ready to board the Japanese warships that would come to pick them up should war break out. The FBI came to know of his doings and sent him a warning through the United Japanese Society. He might as well have been interned in the first place, but he somehow managed to

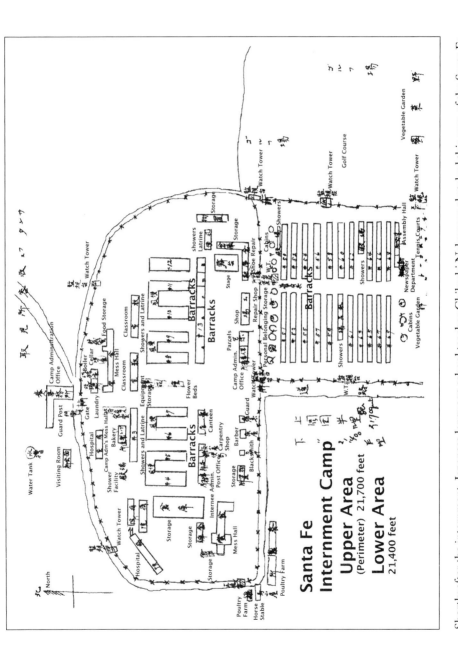

Shortly after the internment, Japanese language school teacher Chikashi Nakayama sketched this map of the Santa Fe Camp. It represents the only known map by an internee of the Santa Fe Camp and is published here for the first time. *Courtesy of the Nakayama Family*

avoid arrest for two years, before being sent to the Mainland with the tenth group.[2]

He made his fortune when the used automobile tires he had stocked piled for the purpose of making *zōri* gained value during the war. It was said that he had bought precious metals and wore them in camp, because he knew he would not be allowed to carry cash when he returned to Japan.

Incidentally, about four hundred years ago during the Warring States Period, Lord Takeda Shingen invented the *shingen-bukuro* for use by his samurai. It was interesting to see American servicemen using this same type of bag. I am not praising Lord Shingen just because he was born in the same region that I was. What is important is that this story shows what an extraordinary general he was. He might have conquered the whole country if he had lived another five years.

Coming back to the original subject, Mr. Tanigawa packed a lot of things in the large, government-issued duffel bags that he had urged his friends to buy. Then, after the war ended, he returned to Japan with his expenses paid by the U.S. government.

A Summary of Santa Fe

Santa Fe is the capital of New Mexico and the oldest city in the United States.[3] Santa means "saint," and Fe means "faith" in Spanish. Four hundred and twenty-five years ago, four crewmen from a wrecked Spanish ship landed on the coast of Texas. The leader of the four was a man named Cabeza Vaca. Cabeza means "head" in Spanish, and Vaca means "stupid" in Japanese.[4] So it is interesting that his name can be translated as "stupid head," if the Spanish and Japanese languages were mixed together. Mr. Lewis, a radio announcer in Honolulu, calls himself "*Aku*-head *Pupule*." I think "stupid head" is better than "crazy bonito head."[5]

Cabeza Vaca was an ambitious man and made his way from Texas to Santa Fe. But, pursued by Indians, he was forced to retreat to the Mexican capital. Not stupid at all, but very ambitious, he made plans to return to Santa Fe with an expedition. He spread a rumor that an El Dorado existed in the northern country, where seven villages were decorated with gold.

Perhaps motivated by this rumor, General Francisco Coronado and this army of three hundred men undertook an expedition to Santa Fe in the summer of 1540. There, Coronado established his headquarters, routed the Indians, and extended his domain. A true hero, he ventured east and west, eventually occupying the entire territory from California in the west to Kansas in the east.

In 1846, General Stephen Kearney, encountering no resistance, entered Santa Fe and hoisted the Stars and Stripes for the first time. During the previous three hundred years, bloody warfare had continuously raged. The area was now officially integrated into the United States and became the state of New Mexico in 1912. Since then, Santa Fe has become famous for its sanatoriums for tuberculosis patients because of its mild temperatures and abundant sunshine. Many tourists and patients visit this old city, which is located on a plateau seven thousand feet above sea level.

To the east of the city, the Sangre de Cristo mountain range rises. To the west, the Rio Grande River and its tributaries run through the wastelands. Mission San Miguel, built in 1620, has been designated a historic site. The Museum of Navajo Ceremonial Art is known for its collection of Spanish weaponry and armor and Indian stone implements and earthenware. At the Las Cass Monument, built on a hill northeast of the city, there is an epitaph that describes a tragic scene in which a large group of pioneers were attacked and killed by Indians during the days of the covered wagons.

Scenery in the Dust

The contrast between picturesque Missoula and the landscape surrounding this Santa Fe camp was shocking. I had heard there was a golf course east of our camp, so I went to take a look and found only sagebrush, a cactus-like plant of the desert, growing scattered in the red clay soil. I could see no green trees at all.

On the way back from the golf course, I reached an area above our camp, when there came a sudden gust of wind, carrying dust and sand. I could not open my eyes and mouth. I had to stand still for a while, hiding against a barracks wall, like a leaf blown by the wind. I had thought that the Chinese expression "ten thousand feet of yellow dust" was an exaggeration, but this gust seemed even worse, and I could only stand there, stunned. Not only the surrounding hills and fields, but also the camp right before me, vanished in the dust. Dust and sand pelted my face, and I could hardly bear it. When I returned to my barracks, I was surprised to see my bed covered with brown dust and sand.

Not everything here was bad, however. I heard that an inexhaustible amount of rare fossils could be found in the surrounding hills. I also learned that gold, silver, copper, and platinum ore could be found in the sand, so I looked forward to the one time a week when we would be allowed to go outside the camp. There were not only wood fossils, but animal and seashell fossils, as well. Being that seashell fossils could be found here at an elevation of seven thousand feet meant that in prehistoric times, this area had been at the bottom of the sea. I also saw trees several thousands of years old that had fallen by some means and fossilized. After a long time, these fossils had broken into small pieces.

When I think about these long cycles in nature, our three to five years of internment was but "one hair from nine cattle." For us mere humans, however, a four-year break during the most productive period of our lives was a severe blow. Nevertheless, those four years in the camps were not a complete waste. Those of us who were already middle aged learned many things and came to appreciate our wives. We observed people of all classes as they really were. We learned that some people who had been respected in their communities were, contrary to expectation, just *tempura*[6] and that other people, thought to be petty, had some strong points.

A Reunion with Our Sand Island Compatriots

Although the weather and scenery here were not as pleasant as in Missoula, this place did have many things that were exotic to me. Before coming here, I had never seen the lizard called the Gila monster or the horned toad, locally known as a "good boy." Good boys look grotesque, but they are in fact gentle and harmless to humans. Although they remain motionless while being held in the palm of your hand, they move very fast when catching ants.

There were also a lot of hummingbirds living here. They are smaller than *mejiro* birds, and they have long, sharp beaks that are like the thorns of the *karatachi* shrub. Instead of perching on tree branches, they hover in the air with their wings flapping rapidly, as they draw nectar from the flowers with their beaks. Their strong wings carry them like bullets through the air. Probably because the land was so dry, there were no sidewinders, other snakes, or centipedes to be seen.

The good part about coming to this camp was that nearly all of the internees from Hawai'i were here, so we were able to learn about what had happened after we had been sent to the Mainland. I shook hands with Yasutaro Soga, Ryoichi Tanaka, and Sadato Morifuji, from whom I had been separated some two years and two months before while at Sand Island. I had presumed that I would find Mr. Soga and Mr. Tanaka in poor health for they were elderly. But on the contrary, I was surprised and delighted to see them healthy.

Before the war, Mr. Morifuji and I had been good shōgi opponents. We were often in the same photos taken by the FBI, when we went to the pier to welcome Japanese warships.

"We can enjoy playing shōgi together on Moloka'i, if war breaks out and we are both interned," we had joked. Just before the war, the rumor among us was that all Japanese in Hawai'i were to be detained on Moloka'i if there was war. Fate works in strange ways, for Mr. Morifuji and I were arrested on the day of the Pearl Harbor attack and eventually interned in the same New Mexico camp, where we did get to play shōgi together. The fate of man is certainly unforeseeable.

Sharing the same barracks with Mr. Morifuji was Kaichi Miyamasa of Waipahu. He also liked shōgi and played fairly well. I played him once in a while and found him to be slightly less skillful than Mr. Morifuji. These two lived in the barracks we named "Shikishima" on the hill in *uemachi*.[7] Most of the residents of Shikishima were internees from the Mainland.

Officers Increase as the Camp Grows

Our camp became very lively as almost all eight hundred of us Hawai'i internees were gathered here from the various camps on the Mainland. I was surprised to learn how many officers and staff members there were in our self-government. Twelve people were assigned as administration chief, assistant chief, secretaries, treasurer, and auditors. Fifty-eight people were designated barracks leaders and assistants.

We had many departments with three to ten staff members each. These departments were: Canteen, Security and Fire, Medical, Public Health, Mail, and Labor. The Labor Department was divided into Carpentry, Labor Force, Painting, Iron Works, Electrical, Plumbing, Transportation, Repair, Masonry, and Tools. Other departments included: Supply, Broadcast, Newspaper, Food, Upper Area Mess Hall, Lower Area Mess Hall, Farming, Laundry, Barber, Tailor, Shoe Repair, Hospital, Hospital Mess Hall, Liaison, and Poultry Farm.

In all, there were thirty departments with a chief, assistants, and supervisors assigned to them. Now that the Missoula group had joined the camp, a new election was held and the following men became officers and staff members:

Chief of Administration	Katsuma Mukaeda
Assistant Chief & Secretary	Takaichi Saiki
Secretary	Kazuto Taketa, Hideo Tanaka, Toyokichi Sakurada
Treasurer	Isamu Kurotobi
Auditor	Toyosaku Komai, Matsuo Marutani

The following Hawai'i internees were designated barracks leaders and assistants:

> Kaichi Miyamasa, Wataru Takamoto, Hideo Tanaka, Kiyoshi Ichikawa, Heigo Fuchino, Tetsuji Kurokawa, Muneo Kimura, Ninryo Nago, Munetaka Sakamoto,[8] Matsuo Marutani, Kazuto Yokota, Minoru Murakami, Josen Deme, Toshio Iinuma, Shimpuku Gima, Torao Iseri, Toraichi Kurakake, Shigeki Yamada, Sawajiro Ozaki, Heiji Yamagata, Shukichi Nagasawa, Hisato Isemoto, Goki Tatsuguchi, Masaichiro Shinoda, Haruto Saito, Rien Takahashi, Masayuki Iwata, Masaichi Kobayashi, and I.

Newspaper Manager	Takegoro Kusao
Canteen Manager	Wataru Takamoto
Broadcast Manager	Gempachi Tsushima
Post Office Chief	Tetsuji Kurokawa
Security and Fire Chief	Yasutaro Miyazawa
Farming Chief	Jitsuma Murata
Medical Department	Masayoshi Tanaka, Sadakazu Furukochi, Yokichi Uyehara, Jiro Yoshizawa, Tokujiro Yanagi, Yukihide Kohatsu, Akio Kimura
Dentist	Ryuichi Ipponsugi
Pharmacist	Mannosuke Komu
Hospital Chief	Usaburo Katamoto
Supervisors	Teisuke Takahashi, Eijiro Suzuki, Ryuichi Murata, Ryuichi Moribe, Koemon Yamamoto, Suguru Hidaka, Chiei Ikeda, Masahiro Himeno
Staff	Tetsunosuke Sone, Riichi Togawa, Ichiji Kinoshita, Kenju Otomo, Teizen Imamura, Katsuichi Miho

Education, Religion, Hobbies, Athletic, and Entertainment Departments

Besides the basic governing departments listed above, there were special divisions in education, religion, arts, and entertainment.

Education Director	Yoshinobu Sasaki
Recreation Director	Hatsuichi Toishigawa
Hiking Manager	Shigeo Shigenaga
Baseball Manager	Sawajiro Ozaki
Tennis Manager	Ichiji Adachi
Golf Manager	Sadamu Nakamura
Lecturers:	
English Language	Ikugoro Nagamatsu, Itsuei Hisatake, Kikujiro Kondo, Keiichi Watanabe, Yoshinobu Sasaki, Masahiro Himeno
Japanese Cultural History	Michikazu Ochi
U.S.-Japan Diplomatic History	Daiichi Takeoka
America	Osamu Fujii
Bookkeeping	Miyuki Sokabe
Poultry Farming	Yoshio Koike
Mineralogy	Toyo Hirai
Japanese Penmanship	Kogan Yoshizumi
Western Painting	Masao Ikeno
Japanese Painting	Koshi Tatsuhara
Tanka	Matsujuro Nishiyama
Kendō	Shuji Mikami
Shakuhachi	Shuji Mikami
Gidayū[9]	Kazusaburo Uranaka
Biwa[10]	Kazuto Taketa
Shigin[11]	Isamu Kamijo
Oiwake	Eita Sato
Calligraphy	Yoshio Koike
Chōwa-hō[12]	Koichi Iida
Tanka	Tokiji Takei
Haiku (Santa Fe Club)	Kazue Miyata
Haiku (Pueblo Club)	Minoru Murakami
Senryū[13]	Shigekichi Kajiwara

Karate	Shobun Maehokama
Symposium	Masamichi Sekiguchi
Buddhist Council	Gikyo Kuchiba, Nisshu Kobayashi, Hozui Nakayama, Josen Deme, Teizen Imamura, Horyu Tanaka, Nanshin Okamoto, Tenran Mori
Christian Council	Ikugoro Nagamatsu, Tamasaku Watanabe, Daiichi Takeoka, Eijiro Suzuki, Teiichiro Maehara, Shohachi Nishizaki, Isuke Horikawa, Naogoro Hirano
Shinto Council	Kinai Ikuma
Entertainment Director	Ichiro Deki
Assistant Director	Soichi Obata
Manager	Kunizo Koyanagi
Stage Director	Masayuki Chikuma
Stage Manager	Shigeki Tani
Stage Setting	Yuichi Nakaichi
Costume	Kiyoshi Yonemura
Music	Hajime Nishimoto
Scriptwriters	Gempachi Tsushima, Shoho Fujiie, Kazuo Arai, Muneo Kimura, Itsuo Hamada
Advisor	Tsuneichi Yamamoto
Staff	Choichi Ito, Minosuke Hanabusa, Otoshiro Hamada, Wataru Takeshita, Yoshihisa Tamura, Isamu Ueoka, Takichi Kinoshita, Shigeo Shigenaga, Kazumi Matsumoto
Treasurer	Katsuichi Kawamoto
Secretary	Masaichi Kobayashi

Nine Peruvian and Mainland internees joined the entertainment division. The troupe grew to be bigger than the groups of traveling entertainers from the good, old days in Hawai'i. They performed pretty well. Besides, their costumes and wigs were all handmade. After all, they had enough time to make them look authentic.

Newspapers and Broadcasting

Up to now, our only source of information about the outside world was the internee news broadcasts. But here in Santa Fe, we also had a daily two-page mimeographed newspaper called the *Santa Fe Times*.[14] Being able to first hear the broadcast in the evening and then read the newspaper at night was useful.

The chief of the Newspaper Department was Iwao Koyama, a man from my home prefecture. Takegoro Kusao, who had been the Haleʻiwa branch manager of the *Nippu Jiji*, assumed the post of assistant chief. I used to visit their office when I had free time. Besides translating the English and editing articles, writing on stencil sheets using steel pens was time-consuming work. Three men from Hawaiʻi, Hosho Kurohira, Wataru Takeshita, and Kiyoto Izumi, undertook this job. Later, Katsu-toshi Hirai and Hatsutaro Toyofuku of Hawaiʻi and Takahisa Furuya, Toyoaki Okuyama, and Shuhei Suguro of the Peru group joined the workforce.

Although we had a camp newspaper, broadcasting the news remained very popular, and the audience always filled the hall. The Broadcast Department chief was Genpachi Tsushima, who also translated the scripts into Japanese. Toshio Sakaguchi was the announcer. News coverage expanded substantially when Minoru Murakami and Kazuo Arai arrived from Missoula, bringing with them their short-wave radio. Mr. Sakaguchi reported the news with his crisp Tokyo accent, making him very pop-ular among the listeners, who felt as if they were listening to an NHK broadcast.[15] Besides, the Japanese reading ability of the announcers had improved. Arai was originally from Nagoya and had been arrested in Los Angeles while studying there. He read the news scripts with an unfamiliar Nagoya accent.

After the news reports, readings of popular serial novels were pre-sented by Tsushima. He had a unique talent for introducing the erotic novel, *Battles in Bed at Dan-no-ura*, to his *aikāne*,[16] who also enjoyed his seductive paintings of beautiful ladies.

Murakami's main role was to introduce Hawaiʻi's local news, collected from the letters of internees' families. Although his voice was not suitable for broadcasting, he reported the news with a sense of humor. He was also good at assigning nicknames and did so to many people. I especially liked the nickname Shozaemon "Lord So-Exhausted" Masaki. He even gave himself a nickname—"Buddha" Murakami—arguing, "Everyone in Hilo calls me 'Buddha' Murakami." But I had never heard that name before, so I think he must have simply invented it after having been interned.

We Learn What Happened after We Left Hawai'i

After arriving in Santa Fe, we were finally able to hear the news of Hawai'i that we had not been able to get until now. Those of us who had been in the first group of detainees had no idea what had happened to our friends in Hawai'i, despite the correspondence from our families, for they had been strictly prohibited from mentioning names or providing any information about new detainees. At Santa Fe, we heard the stories of the internees who were detained after we had left Hawai'i, and we learned that they had suffered psychological hardship beyond our imagination.

Most of them had been summoned by the FBI several times and had suffered severe interrogations over several months. They became very nervous and were always afraid when cars stopped in front of their homes. They would startle whenever the telephone rang. If they saw a man, whom they knew to be an FBI informer, coming toward them, they would slip in between the houses to avoid him, for if the informer noticed them and put down their names in his memo book, within a few days they would certainly be summoned by the FBI.

That is why even those who seemed most likely to be detained, but who had somehow escaped, were eventually caught. Only a few people whom I thought would have been detained managed to escape detention throughout the war.

On the other hand, I was surprised by the number of unlikely captives among the internees. One of them was a spirited barber, nicknamed "Taikō,"[17] who declared in his shop one day, "Japan will win the war. Those lazy American soldiers are no match for Japanese troops." He said this because there were only Japanese customers in his shop at the time. Within a few days, he had been detained and was forcibly made an internee.

When the U.S.-Japan relationship had reached its worst stage and the assets of Japanese were being frozen, Tsuneichi Yamamoto, known as "the brains of the citizens," was smart enough to escape detention for more than a year after the war began. He was finally detained and sent to the Mainland with the eighth group.

Friends and acquaintances whom I had not expected to be interned were: Iju Sueoka,[18] Riichi Togawa, Hiroemon Yamamoto, Hatsuichi Toishigawa, Yoshio Tagashira, Yojiro Osaki, Takasuke Isomura, Masayoshi Uyehara, Kanji Tanaka, Kiyoshi Yonemura, Ichiro Nakamura, Kikujiro Kondo, Giichi Nomura, Yoshihisa Tamura, Mamoru Suga, Eijiro Suzuki, Toyosuke Yamamoto, Sakazuchi Okimoto, Ichiro Deki, Yonematsu Sugiura, Shimpuku Gima, Katsuichi Kida, Kazuaki Tanaka, Shinzo Iwasa, Ryuichi Moribe, Koichi Kurisu, Aisuke Kuniyuki, Yuichi Nakaichi, and Yoshinobu Kato.

They were all from O'ahu.

A Difficult Situation for Elderly Hawai'i Nisei

Rumors and observations within the camp were apt to be based on emotion. If a man, who should have been interned, was not detained, people whispered that he was perhaps an informer for the FBI. As a matter of fact, I heard there were one or two informers among us. Not a few people were interned owing to the information they provided.

It was very unfortunate that elder Nisei were misunderstood by the internees, although this lasted for just a short while. Elder Nisei, aware of the difficult situation Japanese faced, guided more than one hundred thousand younger Nisei and Sansei[19] to take a stand that was most appropriate for them as Americans and encouraged them to willingly cooperate with the U.S. government. They also made efforts to help the authorities understand the position of the Japanese Americans.

The men of the Emergency Service Committee, especially, spared no trouble for the benefit of the internees. They were Masaji Marumoto, Masatoshi Katagiri, Isao Murai, Katsumi Kometani, Yasuo Goto, and Shigeo Yoshida. A fair number of internees did not like that these men worked for the authorities. However, I think it was only natural that, as American citizens, they cooperated with the U.S. government. Moreover, they considered the welfare of the younger generation and made the best of a distressing situation. I could understand, however, how difficult it was for the internees to be objective, having been forcefully separated from their families. Some angry individuals made inflammatory comments when Chomatsu Tsuki-yama[20] and Masaji Marumoto applied for military service, saying it had been a self-serving gesture, since their ages would disqualify them anyway.

As a result of the everyday values emphasized by their parents, together with prudent guidance from the elder Japanese, younger Nisei and Sansei were able to demonstrate the spirit of the samurai and fulfill their obligations as American citizens. They not only proved their loyalty to the United States, but also achieved brilliant military results, fighting in the 100th Infantry Battalion and the 442nd Regimental Combat Team. It can be said that their efforts opened the door to naturalization for Japanese citizens and contributed to the attainment of statehood, a long-cherished dream of the people of Hawai'i.

Since then, many Nikkei have gone on to succeed in various fields. Among them are Chomatsu Tsukiyama, chief justice of the state Supreme Court; Masaji Marumoto, justice of the state Supreme Court; Shiro Kashiwa, state attorney general;[21] Ken Inouye, U.S. senator;[22] Masayuki Matsunaga, member of the U.S. House of Representatives;[23] Isao Murai, chief of the Honolulu district Customs Office; and Masatoshi Hara, Honolulu district postmaster. Others have become state senators, members of the state House of Representatives, court judges, prosecutors, high-ranking officers of state, city, and county governments, and professors at the University of Hawai'i. No one could have imagined such a situation ten years ago.

I have nothing but the greatest appreciation and respect for those elder leaders who guided the Nisei most calmly and appropriately in the midst of unprecedented turmoil during the war between America and Japan.

The Hawai'i Group Holds a *Go* Tournament

As the *go* player population increased with the addition of the Missoula group, someone suggested that all Hawai'i players compete in a tournament. By this time, most *go* players had their own boards and stones, so all of us agreed at once. Kurokawa, Tatsuguchi, Marutani, and Togioka took the initiative to organize the games. At first they divided us into an East team made up of Honolulu players and a West team made up of players from the other islands. They tried to make a *banzuke*,[24] but without the good players from the other islands, like Shirasu, Tagawa, and Kitajima, who had already moved to the Family Camp, this plan did not seem to be working out, for the top-ranks were now all occupied by Honolulu players. So, it was decided instead to simply divide the players into East and West.

The two teams were formed, below, and everyone enthusiastically fought on the boards.

East (Honolulu)	Tetsuji Kurokawa, Hideyuki Serizawa, Goki Tatsuguchi, Tsuneichi Yamamoto, Buntaro Kan, Daizo Sumida, Mankichi Goto, Toraichi Kurakake, Jikai Yamasato, Ichiro Nakamura, Sawajiro Ozaki, and I
West (all islands)	Isaku Orita, Setsugo Togioka, Takeo Seike, Matsuo Marutani, Kakuho Asaoka, Chikyoku Kikuchi, Gunichi Kuwahara, Takuji Shindo, Atsuo Sakimizuru, Toshio Iinuma, Eizo Nagakura, Yaroku Tanaka

Total: 24

Before I was interned, I used to play *shōgi* often and rarely played *go*. Naturally, I had never competed in a *go* tournament. Because I did not have a rank in *go*, I registered as a player of the seventh *kyū* on the advice of my seniors. Strangely enough, I won first place in my first tournament and received a photo album as a prize. I was very excited, but at the same time, I became quite conceited and thought that during my internment I might obtain the rank of first dan. Seventeen or eighteen years have passed since then, and I am still a third-*kyū* player.

Since only Hawai'i internees participated in this tournament, we were comfortable and felt at ease. I thought it would have been an even better tournament had others been here to play such as: those who had repatriated on the exchange ship like Tokuye Takahashi, Seiichi Ohata, Genshin Tatsutani, and Kazuhiko Ogata; those who had moved to the Family Camp like Kensaku Tsunoda, Shigemaru Miyao, Jukaku Shirasu, Shizuma Tagawa, Masao Kitajima, and Kozan Nishizawa; and those who had been paroled like Genyei Miyagi, Taichi Sato, Jiro Okada, Iju Sueoka, and Koichiro Nakamura.

In all my years behind the barbed wire, there was never a more invigorating time for me than when I threw my heart and soul into the tournament, playing from morning until night. I could replenish my energy during that time.

Internees Who Were Paroled

When we were told that we were to be moved to Santa Fe, one of the things I looked forward to was reuniting with acquaintances who had been detained in Hawai'i and interned later. By the time we got to Santa Fe, however, fifty to sixty people had already been paroled or had moved to the Family Camp.

I was disappointed to hear that Tomoaki Nakamura, not only my hometown friend, but my internment companion all through to Livingston, had left two weeks earlier for Jerome,[25] where his family had been waiting. Yoshihiko Kasai, another hometown friend, whom I had met again for the first time in many years while we were at Livingston, had also been paroled and had returned to his home in Salt Lake City. Other people from my hometown, whom I came to know while in Livingston, such as Toyosaku Komai, president of the *Rafu Shimpo* newspaper in Los Angeles, and Shoroku Ono, of the Goshado store in San Francisco, had not been paroled and were still active in the camp. I heard that Gunjiro Maruyama, a dear, old friend, had been paroled and had returned to his home in Miami. Dr. Motokazu Mori left for Crystal City, the Family Camp in Texas, on August 10, 1943 and joined his family after an eighteen-month separation. Masayoshi Uyehara, the first parolee from the Hawai'i group, was paroled on August 12, 1943 and moved to Salt Lake City. I was unable, therefore, to see these two gentlemen while on the Mainland.

From the beginning of 1944, there was an air of excitement in the camps, as many people were released or paroled. While we were in Missoula, Taichi Sato and four others were the first to be paroled. Here at Santa Fe, we learned that many internees had already been paroled or relocated to the Family Camp. Among them, were the following Hawai'i internees:

March 4   Yasuro Kurita, Kyushichi Hayashi, Hiseki Miyazaki, Tokuji Oikawa, Motoi Shiotani, Tomizo Kanno, Kiyoichi Koide, Tetsuzo Kiyotsuka, Takeo Miura, and Sensho Hida

March 16   Kyojo Naito, Hironori Nishii, Kamekichi Kirita, Shigezo Maekawa, Ryugen Matsuda, Seikaku Takesono, Shigeru Ando, Tessui Hanada, Tsuruzo Hasegawa, Shuzui Hino, Iju Sueoka, Jinji Murakami, Takahiko Chinen, Yoshio Takahata, and Shoten Matsubayashi

March 22   Tokuji Adachi, Takao Ama, Gentaro Arita, Kaetsu Furuya, Unji Hirayama, Tetsuei Katoda, Toraki Kimura, Masao Kitajima, Yoshio Kitajima, Shoichi Koide, Zenkai Kokuzo, Ryudo Kubota, Umesuke Matsuo, Gyokuei Matsuura, Genyei Miyagi, Kanryu Mochizuki, Koetsu Morita, Tomoaki Nakamura, Minoru Nakano, Kozan Nishizawa, Yuko Nonomura, Chiko Odate, Jiro Okada, Yoshimi Okumoto, Otokichi Ozaki, Gijo Ozawa, Myoshu Sasai, Tadao Sasaki, Kakuo Shiba, Jukaku Shirasu, Seiichi Shoda, Yukiyasu Sodetani, Yonezo Sueyasu, Sadaichi Suzuki, Shizuma Tagawa, Kameo Tahara, Torao Taketa, Kyuhachi Tanaka, Tetsuo Tanaka, Shodo Umehara, Masayuki Yoshimasu, and Sosuke Toda

A total of forty-two.

With many people leaving, the remaining Hawai'i internees had been feeling lonely when we Missoula transfers arrived. Everyone was very happy to have new companions.

Peach Flowers

In mid-April, spring reached our dull camp on the plateau. Flowers blossomed on a peach tree that may have been planted by German internees during World War I. I had not seen flowers for more than six months, so their deep red hue left a fresh impression in my mind.

Chief Langston[26] issued an order on April 13 prohibiting us from keeping birds. I wondered why. I later learned that catching and keeping wild birds was a violation of federal hunting laws. No matter where you live, government officials are always inflexible.

As far as athletic activities were concerned, however, the chief was very flexible and even a strong supporter. When softball buffs wanted to have a welcome game for those of us who had come from Missoula, the chief not only gave his permission, but offered to pitch the first ball, even though baseball season had not officially started. Soichi Obata was chosen to form our team. On a Sunday afternoon, a Missoula-Santa Fe all-star game took place, and Missoula won eight to five. Obata was very happy, chuckling in his usual way.

A Celebration of the Emperor's Birthday

April 29 was the birthday of the emperor. The internee administration held a ceremony at ten in the morning. The day was beautiful in the aftermath of a dust storm that had lasted a few days. On the field, where the ceremony was being held, more than a thousand internees gathered. Reverend Yoshizumi presided over the ceremony, and Ichikuro Kondo, the internees' chief administrator, offered a congratulatory message, followed by banzai cheers to the emperor and the imperial armed forces. The cheers were so loud that they could be heard in the city of Santa Fe.

The April 29, 1944 edition of the *New York Times* reported the following from the Dōmei News Agency: "The Emperor is in good health, as he greets his forty-third birthday. We are awe-struck and humbled by His Highness's deep concern over the country's aircraft production. His Highness is expected to attend the military review to be held on his birthday. The department of the army has appointed General Fujiye as commander and Lieutenant General Tatsumi as chief of staff for this review."[27]

Honolulu Blackouts Are Cancelled

On May 4, U.S. Army commander Lieutenant General Richardson issued an order lifting blackout restrictions in Honolulu, which had been in effect since the day of the Pearl Harbor attack. It was welcome news for those of us who had been concerned about our families at home.[28]

Fifteen Hawai'i Internees Are Paroled

One week after we had arrived from Missoula, Tetsuo Toyama and Koichiro Nakamura of Honolulu, and Meijiro Hayashi and Enichi Saiki of Kaua'i were suddenly paroled to Jerome. A month later on May 18, Ryosei Aka left for Minneapolis. Then, Kametaro Maeda, Ginpachi Nakama, Yazo Sato, Mitsuji Kasamoto, and Matagoro Mikuni departed the camp on June 6. A little later, Nekketsu Takei, Yoichi Hata, Manzuchi Hashimoto, Kazuo Tomita, and Ichitaro Hasebe were paroled. A total of fifteen internees were paroled to Denver, Amache, and other locations.[29] All of them left the camp in good cheer.

Stowaways

The camp was divided into two—the upper area and the lower area. The upper area was an older section, where German internees had been held during World War I. The upper area's barracks extended from the foot of the hill up to the middle of the hillside. The barracks were old and shabby, but the mess hall was located in the middle of the camp, and so that was convenient. The lower area was on the flatlands, at the foot of the hill, where the baseball field and the vegetable farms were. The barracks in the lower area had been built recently.

The mess hall was located at the same level as the upper area, so internees living in the lower area had to walk uphill in a straight line at every mealtime. Since this camp was seven thousand feet above sea level, we all became short of breath while walking up the slope.

Several elderly internees, who had been respected as intellectuals in *shaba*, always sat in a clearing in front of the mess hall, where they waited for it to open. When the mess door opened, they would casually sneak into the line. Their excuse was that they had a difficult time keeping up with the younger ones, so they gathered in advance and snuck into the line as we went in. Some internees called them "stowaways" because of their sneaky behavior. No one would have complained if they had followed the last person in line, but they never did. This behavior was not tolerated during times of rationing, however, and these "stowaways" did have to get in line from the beginning, like everyone else. Their conduct drew criticism from some internees, but I thought they were not necessarily to blame. Because some shrewd, young Buddhist priests "stowed away," without much thought, elderly internees began copying their behavior. I thought it childish to have criticized only the conduct of the elderly internees.

In camp, social standing had little or no meaning. Among the internees, there was a wide range of personalities, from the short-tempered and irascible, to the fastidious and nervous, to the calm and easy-going. Some were outspoken and did not mince their words, which gave me some anxious moments. There is a Japanese saying about power changing hands constantly.[30] While living in the outside world, priests, teachers, and storeowners were accustomed to giving orders to the people under them. But, here in camp, it was the ordinary workers who were considered superior to those who could not work. Those incapable people were the ones, when assigned to KP duty, who had to take orders and were sometimes scolded by the mess hall workers.

Field Studies, but Fossil Hunting Is Our Real Intent

In May, when the weather became comfortable, Chin'yei Kinjo was chosen to initiate a field study program. I immediately asked to participate, but because so many others had also applied for this program, the camp administration would not allow us to go out in a single group. So we decided to draw lots and take turns by barracks. The idea of making field studies was reasonable enough, but in fact we wanted to look for fossils. We trotted up and down the hills, and, with our eyes constantly focused on the ground, we made a frantic search for fossils instead of inspecting the fields for research.

There were not many fossils buried in the ground, so I could only find four or five during the half-day tour. Although they were hardly precious, I valued my worthless fossils for sentimental reasons. I even brought them back to Hawai'i, and I still keep them in my home. Toyo Hirai, who was famous for his knowledge of stones, once told me that there was a fossil of an animal's liver in my collection.

There are many kinds of fossils in the world. I have seen only seven or eight different kinds. I once saw, in Wisconsin, a sandy stone two inches thick. I do not know whether you could call it a fossil. In Tennessee, I picked up several white spiral fossils, as I briefly mentioned before. I also found a mud-like hollow fossil in Livingston, Louisiana. It contains a small stone that rings like a bell when shaken. These are called "living stones." On other occasions, I picked up several fossils, possibly of fruits. The famous Missoula stones are round and flat with a beautiful grain. Some are soft and others hard. Even the soft Missoula stones are beautiful when polished.

Fossils in the Santa Fe area are mainly of trees. I have seen the intact fossil of a large tree, which, although rare, was not very pretty. Tree fossils can contain such colors as reddish-brown, gray, or black. They become beautiful when polished, but because they are so hard, a polishing machine is necessary. Also found in the Santa Fe area are the fossils of seashells mixed together with mud.

I understand that many beautiful fossils can be found in Oregon. Among them, tidal stones are very rare. Round and slightly larger in size than the stones used by *kānaka*[31] in battle, they look like dried chunks of mud. When the stones are cut in half using a machine, the results are a hard, glass-like surface with colors of purple, blue, black, and white. When they are polished, the stones become so shiny that you can see your face reflected on the surface.

No Nikkei Soldiers to Fight in Battles against the Japanese, Says the U.S. Army

As the war in the Pacific theater intensified, parents of Nikkei soldiers were placed in a sensitive position. They were already determined to face the possibility of the injury or death of their sons while fighting for their country. And although it was theoretically acceptable that sons might fight their Japanese counterparts, emotionally it remained intolerable. Parents were put in a very confused emotional state.

Then the U.S. Army issued a statement saying that Nikkei servicemen could not participate in combat missions against the Japanese. At the same time, Lieutenant Colonel H. A. Gerhardt sent letters to all War Relocation Authority camps stating, "The decision to exclude Japanese American soldiers from combat [against the Japanese] is not based on racism, but out of concern that [Japanese American soldiers] may increase the possibility of counterattack, create confusion among our servicemen on the battlefront, and allow the enemy to penetrate our lines."[32]

He added that this order applied to Japanese American soldiers only. The parents of those affected breathed a deep sigh of relief.[33]

The Deportation of Japanese Is Proposed in Congress

U.S. Congressman Mott, a Republican from Oregon, introduced a radical bill that called for the deportation of all resident Japanese nationals after the war's end. The bill was intended to authorize Attorney General Biddle[34] to issue deportation orders within thirty days after the end of the war to those Japanese seen as *personae non grata*, which in this case meant Japanese who would not have been immediately released from internment at the war's end. Mott insisted that the measure was absolutely necessary in order to maintain the national security of the United States. He said that he had grave concerns about a Christian ministers' group that was urging that Japanese not be seen as America's enemy once the war was over. Mott said he feared the possibility of the bill being scrapped because of this propaganda.[35]

Had we been interned under a dictatorship, we would have been treated in the way Representative Mott proposed, but in the United States, where democracy prevails, bills must pass both the House and the Senate and be approved by the president. One man, regardless of how much power he has, cannot break this rule, so not many people were worried that the bill would pass Congress.

In the United States, while there are people driven by emotion, like Representative Mott, there are also many who are intellectually mature. According to a survey by the National Opinion Research Center, which was sponsored by the Field Foundation and the University of Denver, among the 2,563 Americans interviewed, fifty-seven percent believed that Japanese in the United States wanted Japan to gain more power by means of war. Thirty percent of all respondents felt that influential leaders could easily sway the Japanese into opting for war, while fifteen percent believed that the Japanese could become good world citizens, if given the same opportunities as people in democratic countries. The center con-cluded that the majority of the American public believed Japan would play an important role in the reconstruction of the post-war world and would, no doubt, become an influential partner in promoting world peace.

Nineteen years have passed since the war ended. When I look at the current world situation and the U.S.-Japan relationship, I am impressed by the accuracy of the views of the American public at that time.

Lightning Strikes Before our Eyes

One sunny afternoon, thunderclouds suddenly emerged, extending south-ward and covering the city of Santa Fe below us. Soon heavy showers began to fall, and thunderbolts—not mere lightning—streaked to the ground. We had rarely seen thunderbolts before coming to Santa Fe. Interestingly, the area where we were stood overlooking the city was not wet at all. It felt as if we were in a different world. You may see this kind of scenery in the movies, but in reality it is almost impossible to experience such a phenom-enon unless you live in a place like this.

The World's Largest Limestone Cavern

Although Santa Fe is the oldest city in the United States, New Mexico itself is geologically newer than many of the other regions in America. The area from New Mexico to Arizona is rocky and wild, and many unique features can be seen there.

Although New Mexico is not a large state, there are seven national parks within it.[36] The limestone cave of Carlsbad Caverns National Park is believed to be the largest in the world. Its exact size is still unknown, and only an area a little more than ten miles into the entrance has been explored. Currently, the cavern is believed to contain three layers—upper, middle, and lower. The diameter of the upper cave is 750 feet and the middle 900 feet. The lower cave is 1,320 feet wide and seven miles deep. Only these areas are presently accessible to the public. The cavern was under the sea until about two hundred million years ago, and numerous fossils of saltwater animals and plants can be seen buried in the limestone rock. An enormous number of bats inhabit the cavern. At dusk on summer nights, the bats leave the cave in such gigantic swarms that they obscure the cave opening.

An inexhaustible amount of minerals and fossils is known to be buried around the area. The amount of coal lying under the ground is estimated at 192 billion tons. Also abundant is mica, estimated at 3,300 tons. Sometimes the mica falls as particles, diluted by the rain, so, if you leave your laundry hanging outside, you may be surprised to find it has turned a glittering white.

At Great White Sands, near the atomic bomb test site, I have heard that the entire plain is white, as are the field mice there. Rain puddles are said to be five-colored like a rainbow, a strange but natural phenomenon.[37]

The Red Cross in Japan Sends Books

We received 950 Japanese books from the Red Cross in Japan. All of them were new publications and included such categories as fiction, religion, philosophy, commentary, essays, tanka and haiku, and calligraphy. There were more novels than any other type of book. The expanded collection made booklovers very happy. Haruo Koike and the others who worked in the library became very busy cataloguing and lending out the books.

Military Results, according to the Japanese Navy

On the occasion of Navy Day, May 27, Japan's Armed Forces Headquarters released the following tally of results achieved by the Japanese navy:

		U.S.	Japan
Battleships	Sunk	18	1
	Seriously Damaged	16	1
Aircraft Carriers	Sunk	28	3
	Seriously Damaged	12	2
Destroyers	Sunk	79	23
Submarines	Sunk	149	11
Other warships	Sunk	180	
Aircraft	Shot down	7913	

The Japanese navy appeared to have won an overwhelming victory against the United States, but for those of us who knew of the Japanese losses at the naval battles of Midway and the Coral Sea, these figures were not convincing at all. The U.S. government issued a statement ridiculing Japan for celebrating an achievement that was based, not on the power of their navy, but on the world's most optimistic adding machines.

Then, on June 5, we learned that Vice Admiral Katagiri Shigeru, commander of the New Guinea campaign, had been killed in a naval battle off New Guinea. Those who had believed in the brilliant results of the Japanese navy, as reported on Navy Day, had been shocked to learn that Admiral Toyoda, who had replaced Admiral Yamamoto Isoroku as commander-in-chief of the naval fleet, had been killed in action like his predecessor. Now with Vice Admiral Katagiri also dead, they became even more depressed.[38]

American Bombers Crash in Kalihi

On June 9, it was reported that two medium-sized U.S. bombers had collided in midair over the Kalihi residential area, destroying four houses and killing five airmen and three residents. Because my house was located in that area, I was shocked and worried that the worst may have happened to my family. I immediately inquired by telegram about their safety and was relieved to learn that my family and home had not been affected by the accident. News of the accident put a lot of stress on me until I received their reply.[39]

A Theatrical Performance by Internees

There were many talented amateur actors among the internees, some of whom had performed in plays at Lordsburg. With the addition of the internees from Hawaiʻi and Missoula, the Entertainment Department now had even more skilled performers. The department decided to stage a drama entitled *A Short Story of a Samurai*,[40] an original play written by our own Tsuneichi Yamamoto. They rehearsed diligently every night and even built a theater in the clearing between the upper and lower areas. The program leaflet listed eighteen actors, together with the director, choreographer, dresser, musicians, and curtain operator. The cast and crew totaled more than thirty people, just like a film-making production. Actors with featured roles were Daisei Obata, Kiyoshi Yonemura, Keigetsu Ito, Kunizo Koyanagi, Takichi Kinoshita, Jukichi Tsushima, Itsuo Hamada, Taikō Yoshimoto, Yuichi Nakaichi, Shigeru Yano, and Otoshiro Hamada.[41]

Since no admission was charged, the play was very popular. Later, an appreciation party was held, paid for by donations from the admiring audience. Encouraged by the success of their initial project, the actors put on other shows, such as period dramas like *Edokko* and *Shirai Gompachi*, the Naniwa-bushi drama *Osakaya Kihachi*, the social drama *Kikai no ichiya*, and the comedy *Hatsukago*. People enjoyed the plays very much.[42]

Parole Continues

Parole remained the focus of most of our interest, and parole notices continued to come through a few at a time. In May, Kazuichi Takanishi of Kauaʻi was paroled to Chicago, and in July Hisashi Tominaga of Samoa went to the Miami home of Gunjiro Maruyama, a friend he had become reacquainted with in camp. On July 25, Matsujiro Otani and Empei Fujita received their parole notices. Rev. Toshio Hirano was paroled to Raleigh, North Carolina, in August and Haruzo Hasegawa of Lānaʻi to Denver on September 4. Also, Rev. Masahiro Himeno and elderly Shin'ichi Miura of Pearl City received their notices on September 20.

Three Resign from the Internee Administration

After the parole of Ichikuro Kondo, who had been our chief administrator for four terms, an election of new officials was supposed to be held by a balloting of all barracks leaders, as was our custom. But no one wanted to be elected, because some of the barracks leaders they would have to deal with were political fanatics—always picky and critical.

At the time, the internee administration made public the following letter:

August 18

To: Internee Administration

I understand that I was nominated as a candidate for Chief Administrator at the nominating committee meeting held yesterday.

Please be informed that I am unable to accept the nomination because of my health. Even if I am elected, I will be unable to serve my term.

Please inform all the internees of my intentions.

Respectfully yours,
Totaro Matsui

In addition, the *Santa Fe Jihō* reported that both assistant administrators, Ichiji Adachi and Kazuto Taketa, had turned in their resignations. As a result of these resignations, Katsuma Mukaeda was appointed chief administrator, and Takaichi Saiki became assistant administrator and secretary.

The Eviction of Japanese Americans from the West Coast Spawns a Backlash

Caught by surprise by the Pearl Harbor attack, American military leaders panicked and overreacted, making emotional decisions lacking in objectivity, which proved unproductive in the long run. In the case of Hawai'i, only influential leaders were interned, while others were allowed to remain in their domiciles, owing to the geographic distance from the Mainland and the enormous number of Japanese among Hawai'i's total population. On the other hand, all Japanese and Japanese Americans living on the West Coast were ordered to relocate to inland regions, where they experienced great hardship.

As a result, many young Japanese Americans, offended by the government's actions, refused the draft call for military service. They did not cooperate with the authorities, but instead held meetings and created disorder at the relocation centers. They were mainly Kibei, who had been educated in Japan. The authorities later moved them to the Tule Lake Relocation Center. Contrary to government expectations, this did not end the chaos, but rather fueled their anger by gathering them all in one place.[43]

Finally, an incident occurred at Tule Lake on May 24, in which James Shoichi Kunimoto[44] and six other young men were shot by MPs. Kunimoto died of his injuries, despite receiving four blood transfusions that were administered by American and Japanese doctors. The incident caused an uproar at the center. A news agency in London reported that the Japanese government, greatly concerned, was investigating the case. America's Interior Secretary Ickes[45] said at a press conference in Washington, D.C., that the guards would be court-martialed since Kunimoto had been unarmed and had not threatened them.

Tried for Draft Resistance

George Takamoto, a young evacuee at Granada Relocation Center in Colorado, was charged with draft evasion. In court he testified before Judge Sims as follows:

> I don't know if I'm an American. The way I've been treated since my forcible removal from the West Coast has made me question my citizenship. I volunteered for military service, only to be repeatedly rejected by the government. I

can no longer see a future for myself as a citizen of this country. Out of respect for and in defense of the Constitution, I have been eager to take up the battle against all enemies. It is not I, but the government itself, which is in violation of the Constitution.

Takamoto was the eighth of fourteen defendants who were prosecuted for failing to appear before the draft board. Unfortunately, I do not know the outcome of this case.[46]

Sumō Tournament

I am not sure if the success of the stage plays provided the incentive, but some sumō fans decided to stage a Hawai'i-Mainland sumō tournament. A committee was formed, with Tetsusaburo Uyeda, chief of the Athletic Department, as its head.

Honorary Chair	Ichikuro Kondo
Chair	Tetsusaburo Uyeda
Vice Chair & Executive Director	Seigo Takai
Accounting	Daizo Sumida
Setting	Shigeo Shigenaga, Jitsuma Murata, Sadamu Nakamura, Shigeru Nagata
Wrestlers	Seigo Takai, Yasutaro Miyazawa, Shobun Maehokama, Takeshige Sado, Goki Tatsuguchi
Advertising	Iwao Koyama, Gempachi Tsushima
Prizes	Koichi Iida, Daizo Sumida, Samonji Taketa
Gyōji [47]	Teisuke Takahashi
Yobidashi[48]	Nekketsu Takei
First Aid	Sadakazu Furukochi, Yokichi Uyehara

With many prominent people becoming committee members, they inspired wrestlers to go into serious training, and so the tournament generated a great deal of interest among the internees. More than five hundred internees donated a total of $301.70.

The tournament was held in official sumō tournament format, arranged by the wrestlers on the committee. The Hawai'i team won by a substantial margin.

Rank[49]	East (Hawaiʻi)		vs	West (Mainland)	
Ōzeki	Wakahibiki[50]	(L)		Satsumanada	(W)
Sekiwake	Wakayanagi	(L)		Tsuyashima	(W)
Komusubi	Kabashima	(W)		Miyazawa	(L)
Maegashira	Tatsuguchi	(W)		Mitamadake	(L)
Maegashira	Nippudake	(W)		Oikawa	(L)
Maegashira	Shigenaga	(W)		Wakaisamu	(L)
Maegashira	Omiya	(L)		Yamauchi	(W)
Maegashira	Asahigawa	(W)		Takai	(L)
Maegashira	Kinoshita	(W)		Oikawa	(L)
Maegashira	Hamada	(W)		Yamauchi	(L)
Maegashira	Kita	(W)		Maeda	(L)
Maegashira	Togawa	(W)		Todoroki	(L)

Before the East-versus-West Tournament, matches of three-wins and five-wins were held, thrilling the audience.[51] There was no five-wins winner because the wrestlers were about equal in strength, so all matches were changed to the three-wins format. The winners were Todoroki, Kita, Oikawa, Tatsuguchi, and Satsumanada.

Our internment life was so monotonous, with only men inside the barbed wire fence, that the sumō tournament was an unexpectedly big success. Flowers of money[52] were thrown into the ring, and there were even additional matches not listed on the program. The huge audience reminded me of Shinto shrine festival events.

They closed the accounting books with proceeds of $301.70, expenses of $176.45, leaving a profit of $125.25. The tournament also was an unexpected financial success. On July 27, a reception was held in the upper area mess hall to recognize the work of the committee members. More than fifty people attended. It was decided that a second tournament would be held at the beginning of September.

A Dispute at Tule Lake

The problems among the Nisei at the Tule Lake center continued, and seventeen of them were sent to our camp on July 1. Two days later, on July 3, a merchant named Tasaku Hitomi from Sacramento suffered serious injuries when he was assaulted by a thug with a hammer who mistook Hitomi for his younger brother. Hitomi's brother was murdered the following day and the authorities were not able to find the killer. The atmosphere in the camp became quite tense and the violence escalated. The authorities finally confined fourteen young men within the double-fenced area. In protest, the men went on a hunger strike, and despite the authorities' attempts to resolve the situation, the young men vowed to continue the strike unless they were released.[53]

The Peru Group Arrives from Camp Kenedy

On August 22, eighteen Mainlanders were paroled from Santa Fe, and on the following day, 216 internees from Peru and Bolivia came over from Camp Kenedy in Texas, as had long been rumored. Initially, with so many parolees leaving the camp, we were a little lonesome, but on the other hand, it was more comfortable with fewer people in the barracks. Then, when 216 people arrived all at once, an average of forty-five men packed into each barracks.

Within the Peru group, I found some of the friends I had made while in Missoula. We shook hands and celebrated our reunion. The closure of Camp Kenedy made it possible for the new arrivals to bring with them 778 books, which they donated to our library. Booklovers were happy with the enriched collection.

With Camp Kenedy closed, Santa Fe became the only internment camp in operation. There were many younger people within the Kenedy group, and they enlivened the atmosphere at Santa Fe.[54]

Territorial Senator Heen Visits the Camp

On his way to attend the National Democratic Party Convention, Hawai'i Territorial Senator William Heen came to see Matsujiro Otani of 'A'ala Market to discuss some business matters. According to the senator, Honolulu was enjoying a booming economy as a result of the war. Liquor stores, restaurants, laundries, all were doing well. We heard that many guests now dined at the famous Chinese restaurant Lau Yee Chai, once rumored to be on the verge of bankruptcy.

Four Means Death

The *Santa Fe Jihō* included in its August 1 news briefs column an article ridiculing Japan. It was written by a reporter named Young of the International News Service.

"In Japanese, the words 'four' 四 and 'death' 死 are both pronounced *shi*," he wrote. "So, Japan will die twice in 1944."

A reporter of the *Santa Fe Jihō* counterattacked, "If that is right, then Roosevelt's acceptance of his fourth term, *shiki* 四期, predicts the time of his death, *shiki* 死期. Will he finish his term safely?"

I was impressed by his bravery. Japan's surrender came a year later, in 1945, but President Roosevelt also died in 1945, six months after he started his fourth term.

Developments in the Camp as the War Winds Down

As 1944 began, internees were more frequently moved around. New internees from other camps moved in to fill the spaces of former residents who had been paroled. It seemed as though the internment camps and relocation centers were being reorganized. While Japan still put on a bold front for her people, the United States seemed to believe that the war had passed the critical point. Parole notices continued to be issued to internees.

The following is a list of Hawai'i internees who received notices after the initial round of paroles: Takazo Arita, Ichiro Deki, Shimpuku Gima, Otoshiro Hamada, Shodo Kawamura, Shu Kato, Masaichi Kobayashi, Yoshihisa Mayeda, Tokiji Takei, Shigeru Murakami, Usaku Morihara, Aisuke Kuniyuki, Takejiro Nakagawa, Hajime Nishimoto, Ryuten Kashiwa, and Kazuyuki Kawano.

These men were granted either partial or full parole and left for the Family Camp or a relocation center a while later. I was happy to see them leave the camp. However, I could not help feeling a tinge of loneliness.

Autumn Twilight on the Plateau

I longed for a quiet life with some privacy, as living in a group for such a long time had begun to wear on my nerves. But in reality, a quiet life did not seem possible.

One day, I happened to find an isolated grassy field on top of a hill between the lower area mess hall and the hospital. It was a tranquil spot that commanded a good view. Every evening, I went there and gazed at the Santa Fe plateau stretching out endlessly in the twilight. I could see the thirteen-thousand-foot-high Sangre de Cristo Mountains in the east and the Rio Grande River flowing in the west. Far to the south, I could make out the city of Albuquerque in the distance. Birds like mynahs left their mountainside nests early in the morning, flying toward the Rio Grande, and came chirping back in flocks of families in the evening. As I watched them fly overhead, I was reminded of my family, and I was overcome with loneliness.

In the evening, people like *Nippu Jiji* president Soga and Dr. Uye-hara[55] customarily took walks along the fence around the camp. But my feet naturally headed for the grassy field. I could not understand why a usually optimistic man like me would now prefer solitude.

Apple Picking Is Said to Serve the Interests of the Enemy

Autumn deepened, and at a place called Tesuque, located deep in the valley east of the camp, the apples turned red and ripe. The farm owner worried that the apples would rot, for laborers were few. Then, he noticed there were a few hundred people doing nothing in the internment camp and asked the camp commander for permission to temporarily hire the intern-ees. Commander Langston agreed to recruit volunteers. Several dozen internees applied. Those who returned from the farm said the job had been rather easy. Moreover, they had gotten a chance to visit a place they had never been before, to enjoy the scenery of the many ripe apples hanging from the trees, and to eat the sweet fruit. Besides all these benefits, they were paid three dollars a day. Hearing this, many people wanted to work there.

Out of curiosity, I applied for the job. Mr. Takai, our barracks leader, took a firm stand against working on the farm. He claimed it would only serve the interests of the enemy, although he acknowledged the right of each individual to make his own decision. Because of his contention, I hes-itated to take the job.

Seigo Takai had a unique personality. He held a third *dan* in kendō and was good at sumō. He was also a Christian and had once been a leader in his church. He was a good barracks leader, who took good care of others and pursued his duties diligently. But his stubbornness was a problem. Sev-eral barracks mates were opposed to him and tried to get Mr. Sumida, Mr. Iida, and even me to become the barracks leader. But none of us were will-ing to take over, and Mr. Takai continued in his position until the last day.

He was older than I, but full of vigor. He once got into a fight, for rea-sons unknown to me, with Yoshiaki Fukuda, the North American bishop of the Konko Mission. They scuffled on the street in broad daylight. His opponent was ten years younger and was a third *dan* black belt in judo. Mr. Takai was thrown to the ground and covered in snowy mud. But old, vigorous Mr. Takai would not give up.

On the evening before Reverend Fukuda was to leave camp to join his family in Crystal City, Mr. Takai challenged him to a rematch. Visit-ing his barracks with two sets of sticks, he handed one set to Fukuda and told him to come outside to fight. Fukuda reluctantly stood up and went outside. And then, like a coward, he surprised Mr. Takai by grabbing the latter's arm and throwing him to the ground, where he beat Mr. Takai about the head with his fists. Bystanders finally managed to separate the two. Hot-tempered Takai could not overcome his age and instead lost a fight that he had intended as revenge. Takai's side of the story, however, was that he had not lost completely, as he had punched Fukuda a few times.

I thought it in bad taste and most disrespectful for a man in a high position of religious leadership to beat up an older internee, not once, but twice. I suppose the depressing camp life affected everyone's nerves. I heard Fukuda was like a different man after joining his wife in the Family Camp.[56]

In Celebration of the Emperor Meiji's Birthday

Emperor Meiji's birthday fell on November 3. Since the majority of us had been born during his reign, we decided to hold a big celebration, hosted by the internee administration. The celebration was held at nine in the morning at the outdoor theater. It was presided over by principal Yoshio Koike and began with the singing of the Japanese national anthem, followed by words of celebration by our chief, Katsuma Mukaeda. We then all bowed to the west, sang "The Patriots' March" together, and ended the ceremony with banzai cheers led by assistant administrator Takaichi Saiki. The ceremony was conducted with solemnity.

In the afternoon, softball games and a popularity contest were held, and a large-scale entertainment program was presented in the evening. The program included *rakugo* by Peru's Kicho Furuya, *kōdan* by Muneo Kimura, and *manzai* by Mukuchi Ueoka[57] and Shuhei Suguro. The finale was a two-act play, enthusiastically staged with the added participation of the Peru group. It featured such actors as Daisei Obata, Kiyoshi Yonemura, Wataru Takeshita, Kicho Furuya, Shuhei Suguro, Shoho Fujiie, Kuniharu Matsukawa, Minosuke Hanabusa, and Yoshihisa Tamura.

A commemorative dinner was held that night in the upper area mess hall. Chief cook Furukawa from Peru did a wonderful job preparing a Japanese menu, and for dessert everyone enjoyed a piece of the cake that was decorated as a Japanese flag.

The Sale of Beer Starts

With the sale of beer now allowed on the premises for the first time, drinkers celebrated the occasion in good cheer, drinking bottle after bottle. Actually, the canteen at Missoula had been selling beer a year earlier, but the word had not reached the authorities at Santa Fe, perhaps because of wartime communication problems.

Most of the internees had become resigned to life without liquor, but those who used to drink every day in Missoula had complained about beer not being sold here. At any rate, it was unlikely that anyone would have tried to make home-brewed sake or beer.

The authorities here would not allow us to sell beer at the canteen, but set up a special liquor store instead. Takuji Shindo was in charge of liquor sales. Some internees seemed to give him a hard time, asking him to sell them more than the allotted number of bottles for each individual.

Karate Lessons Begin

Up until now, Shobun Maehokama had been the only karate instructor for the younger internees. But when six or seven karate experts joined us from among the South American internees from Kenedy, Maehokama organized a club to promote interest in karate. The officials of the karate club were:

Adviser	Shobun Maehokama
Manager & Head Instructor	Kuniharu Matsukawa
Assistant Instructor	Hirotomo Kishimoto, Yukiteru Nakamura, Hiroshi Yamamoto
Director	Jikai Yamasato, Jitsuei Yogi, Kizo Yamamoto
Accountant	Shingo Hayasaka
Secretary	Shuhei Suguro

Classes began immediately, meeting four evenings a week. Many younger internees joined the club and practiced very hard. Having never seen karate before, I was quite surprised to see Hiroshi Yamamoto, who had slender arms, split a brick with his bare hand.

Seeing Off Friends Bound for the Family Camp

The Family Camp in Crystal City held the families of internees who had expressed their intention to repatriate to Japan. When it first opened, the number of residents was small. Later, families separated by the internment, as well as internees and evacuees from various internment camps and relocation centers, moved to Crystal City so that they could be reunited. As a result, the camp's population had increased considerably by the end of 1944.

Dr. Motokazu Mori was the only doctor in the camp, and he had been tending to patients since the camp's opening. With the increase in Crystal City's population, he could no longer care for all of the patients by himself; the camp needed another doctor. A request to transfer a young, competent doctor to the Family Camp was made to our camp commander. The commander thought to move Dr. Akio Kimura there, but those of us who trusted the doctor objected, carrying out a campaign to block the transfer.

Dr. Kimura was skilled and kind, but he was also business-like and blunt. Some of the internees at Camp McCoy disliked him, but people got to like him over the course of time because he was good to patients. I, personally, wanted to stop him from leaving. I worried that, being single, he would be alone among the many internees enjoying their lives with their families. It was not because I did not want to lose one of my close friends.

Transfers to the Family Camp continued, and Kuramatsu Matsumoto of Kaua'i soon received his notice. On November 22, Totaro Matsui, our mayor at Camp Missoula, and Tokiji Sojin Takei, a member of the tanka club,[58] were notified of their transfer to Crystal City. Having learned that their departure would be sometime in the beginning of December, tanka club members held a farewell reception for both gentlemen. "Reception" sounds fancy, but only *udon*, *senbei*,[59] and tea were served.

On November 29, former Missoula residents and friends held a large farewell reception for Totaro Matsui. They charged "as much as" twenty-five cents for admission, and a small bottle of beer was served to each of the more than two hundred internees who attended. The formal ceremony consisted of words of appreciation by Minoru Murakami and Mr. Matsui, an exchange of banzai cheers, and the presentation of a gift of fossils.

Former Japanese Chamber of Commerce members planned an authentic farewell reception for Totaro Matsui, Akio Kimura, and Masaichi Kobayashi, and this was held on December 2. It was a grand party and generously financed. Takasuke "Chicken" Isomura demonstrated his skill with a *kaiseki* menu.[60] Although the dishes were served on the aluminum trays that were used in the mess hall, the menu was superb, especially with the beer that accompanied it. As vice chairman of the organization, I read the farewell message, and Mr. Matsui followed with his words of appreciation. All thirty-one of us attendees knew each other well, so the atmosphere was harmonious and pleasant, although a little subdued.

At this time, a total of thirteen men from Hawai'i and one from the Mainland—the extent of those who had received parole notices up until now—departed for Crystal City. They all looked happy, except for Dr. Kimura, who somehow seemed lost. I felt sorry for him.

Sixty-Seven Japanese Americans from Hawai'i Are Sent to Tule Lake

On November 23, the head of the Western Defense Command announced that sixty-seven Japanese Americans, who had previously been interned at Honouliuli, had arrived in Seattle on November 19, while in transit to Tule Lake. Among them were Shinzaburo Sumida and Masao Sakamoto, who initially had been interned in Hawai'i, sent to the Mainland, and then, because of their U.S. citizenship, allowed to return to Hawai'i, where they were again incarcerated at Honouliuli.[61] In addition, I found other friends on the list: Takuzo Kawamoto, Shigeru Matsuzaka, Tetsuo Shinagawa, Masaru Urata, Kuniaki Nishioka, and Masao Uyehara. They were all Kibei, presumably affected by the rebellions of the Kibei Mainlanders at Tule Lake.

I often wondered what had led the authorities to this decision. I later learned that the men had been formally exiled to the Mainland as a result of reinvestigations. I could not understand why the authorities would exile younger Japanese Americans, while at the same time many Issei internees were being paroled. I could only surmise that the continuous troubles at Tule Lake had made the authorities nervous. Because of some Kibei Nisei on the Mainland, younger Kibei Nisei in Hawai'i had to suffer the consequences.

Sometime later, a second group of sixty-seven Japanese Americans from Hawai'i were exiled to Tule Lake. Uncooperative internees were kept isolated within a double-fenced area. The Hawai'i group was initially put among them, but later was allowed to live with the other internees. When the anti-U.S. group at Tule Lake was later sent to Santa Fe and Bismarck, the Tule Lake center became peaceful again.

The President Admits His Mistake

The International News Service reported that during a press interview, President Roosevelt stated that for the past three years Japanese Americans had proven to be good examples of American citizenship. Roosevelt expressed regret over his decision to remove all Japanese Americans from the West Coast immediately after the Pearl Harbor attack. He said that he would revise as soon as possible the regulations governing relocation.[62] I thought this a great country to admit its mistakes. This would never have taken place in a dictatorship.

My Third Winter

The year 1944 was coming to an end. In December, the number of Nisei in Santa Fe increased considerably with more arrivals from Tule Lake and other centers. These younger people were ideologically pro-Japan rightists, and it came as no surprise when they formed a group called the Shichishō-kai.[63] They held a kick-off ceremony on the evening of December 12 in the eastside classroom. They began the ceremony with a roll call, and then they all stood up and pledged in unison to become the sons of the emperor and to sacrifice themselves for the sake of his country. They were full of patrio-tism and purity of heart, but their grasp of the world situation was limited, and they were inclined to act on impulse driven by youthful ardor.

We were already into the middle of December, with the days becom-ing very cold and morning temperatures dropping below ten degrees. The cold weather was especially hard on the elderly. The venerable Mr. Soga, together with Dr. Uyehara, continued to take his usual walks along the fence, braving the wind and cold. It was admirable.

On the night of December 18, I saw Venus shining brightly beside the new moon. It was very beautiful and quite solemn. Some said it was a sign that there would be peace again. I, on the other hand, felt uneasy about our future.

An Animal Called the Coyote

Animals slightly smaller than wolves and called coyotes inhabited this region. When snow covered the fields, they came in packs down from the hills to the places where people lived, looking for food and running off with chickens and lambs. One night, a pack of coyotes passed by the camp, howl-ing horribly. It made me feel very uneasy, and I did not go out to take a look. I went outside only after they had passed. The air was hazy with dust, and it clouded the moon. I could imagine from this how big the pack had been.

I once saw a coyote caught in a trap set in a cornfield near the camp. It looked fierce enough, but not wild. Clever in their ways, coyotes form packs and can even prey on large animals that are not on their guard, like horses and cattle. One coyote is no match for a running hare, but a pack of coyotes surrounding it can cut off its escape. Any animal unlucky enough to be sighted by a pack of coyotes is doomed.

According to the Wildlife Preservation Department of New Mexico, losses attributed to coyotes amount to several hundred thousand dollars annually.

The War Turns Against Japan, Our Motherland

Three years had passed since December 7, and the war situation seemed by no means favorable to Japan. The Japanese military, although no lon-

ger possessing sufficient power to attack U.S. forces in the Philippines
and Saipan, was intent nevertheless on desperately defending these areas.
Kamikaze attackers inflicted considerable damage on U.S. forces, but not
enough to turn the war to their favor.

According to an announcement on December 12 by the General
Military Headquarters of Japan, thirteen admirals, vice admirals, and rear
admirals had been killed in action, with 168,000 troops killed or injured
in battle. On December 13, Vice Admiral Yano Hideo, chief press officer
of the Yokosuka Naval Command, was reported killed in action. So far
during this war, an army general and six navy admirals—including vice
and rear admirals—also had been killed in battle. From May of this year,
the number of casualties among high-ranking officers steeply increased to
seventy-three admirals and eighteen generals of various ranks, for a total of
ninety-one dead. Among them was Vice Admiral Nagumo Chuichi, commander of the Saipan theatre, who had taken a leading role in the Pearl
Harbor attack.

Tokyo's *Asahi Shinbun* reported that the government was not allowing workers of munitions plants, factories, transportation services, and the
press to evacuate to rural areas, except in special cases. It was also reported
that officials of the air defense agency, doctors, and scientists were prohibited from evacuating without permits. From such news reports, I could
only conclude that Japan's strategy for national defense was mere propaganda and not reliable.[64]

It was at this time that the president of the United States lifted the
eviction order concerning Japanese from the three West Coast states, as
he had previously committed to at his press conference.[65] Thus Japanese
American evacuees in the Manzanar, Rohwer, Tule Lake, Gila River, Poston, Topaz, Jerome, Minidoka, Amache, and Heart Mountain relocation
centers were allowed to return to the West Coast. In the beginning, however, not many took advantage of the opportunity.[66]

A Japanese Balloon Bomb Is Found

Forest fires occasionally occurred in the state of Oregon during the fall of
that year. It was rumored that the fires had been caused by balloon bombs
that had drifted over from Japan. The rumor turned out to be true.

According to the FBI, an unexploded Japanese balloon bomb was
found in a Montana forest on December 18. The balloon, which had
Japanese characters printed on it, was fifty feet long and thirty-three feet
in diameter and carried an incendiary bomb with a fuse. It was believed
to have drifted from the direction of the Pacific Ocean at a speed of two

hundred miles an hour. The authorities, fearing that thousands of similar bombs were drifting over the area, began a thorough investigation with the cooperation of the military.

Although we thought the bombs would not do any serious damage to the United States, the news was good enough to cheer up many internees.[67]

Picturesque Christmas Scenery

On Christmas Eve, a gathering took place in the eastside classroom to celebrate the birth of Christ. Reverend Ikezawa gave an impressive sermon. This year most of the internees attended the celebration. Naturally, many Christians attended, and the total from the ninety-six donations came to $102.75. The ministers and the congregation were satisfied with the results.

The snowfall continued until Christmas, and the entire area was covered in seven inches of snow. The picturesque scenery was so much like Christmas.

The Troublesome Tule Lake Group Arrives

On December 30, just before the end of 1944, a group of seventy came from Tule Lake. Most of them were young Japanese Americans, and I was surprised to see that they all had shaven heads like Japanese soldiers. Accompanied by many soldiers and provisional guards, they underwent extensive interrogations, after which they were separated and assigned to various barracks. Most of them were Kibei Nisei and members of the Tule Lake organization Seinen Hōkōkai.[68] They had been labeled extremists by the authorities and sent to this camp. Those with families had been forced to leave them behind at Tule Lake.

Included in this group were two Hawaiʻi residents, Rev. Norizane Tsuha and a youth named Ichiro Hayashi, who was the son of Rev. Kyushichi Hayashi. There also was an elderly man named Zenshiro Tachibana, who used to be the assistant internee administrator of Santa Fe in the early days. His head was shaved and he wore a beard. Tachibana looked like an army colonel and acted like the boss of the group.[69]

In the early morning hours of New Year's Eve, members of the group surprised us with their shouting and group calisthenics, which they performed out in the cold. Their attempts to maintain a visible presence by using empty office space to hold meetings without permission created tension in the camp.

Tule Lake Center, from the beginning, had held a few thousand Issei and Nisei who wanted to repatriate or who had replied "No" to the questions asking if they would swear loyalty to the United States.[70] I think it was natural that, because of their circumstances and their cultural background, Kibei Nisei did not agree with American wartime policy. Dissatisfaction and antipathy mounted. As a result, Issei formed a group called Sokuji Kikoku Hōshikai, while Nisei organized into a group called Hōkokudan.[71] This caused friction between them and the rest of the people in the center. With the arrival of these people from Tule Lake, our camp became noisy and the atmosphere vulgar.

On January 1, 1945, we celebrated the fourth New Year's Day of our internment. We pounded mochi with the sweet rice that had arrived in time, allowing us to celebrate the occasion. We enjoyed *zōni* and beer in place of *toso*.[72] A ceremony was held in the newly built recreation hall and approximately nine hundred internees attended. Chikashi Nakayama, chief of the Education Department, presided and chief internee administrator Mukaeda spoke words of celebration.[73]

In the middle of the program, a group of Tule Lake youths barged in, pushed their way through the crowd and occupied seats at the front of the hall. I thought their actions were quite rude. Chief Langston, who had watched them march in, informed the leader of the young men that such group actions would not be tolerated thereafter. He ordered the young men to remove the "Hōkoku"[74] badges pinned on their shirts.

The Japanese Military Works Hard on Propaganda

On January 1, 1945, as the war entered its fourth year, Prime Minister Koiso Kuniaki issued a statement to all the countries of Asia: "Presently, we are fighting fierce battles in the Philippines and sinking enemy ships that continue to invade our sphere of influence. We are exacting a toll on the enemy, which dared to embark on this desperate mission, flaunting its extensive supplies. I am confident that 1945 will be the year when Japan decisively routs our enemies from Asia."

A little later, General Military Headquarters issued an announcement about Japan's military victories: "Since January 2, the Special Attack Team, the star of our air force, has continuously and fiercely attacked the enemy's convoy of twenty warships and thirty other vessels, while on its way to Mindoro Island through the Sulu Sea. To date, two cruisers, eighteen transport vessels, and a torpedo boat have been sunk. Nine transport ships, two cruisers, and a destroyer have suffered extensive damage. A total of thirty-three enemy ships have been destroyed or damaged, as we increase our military achievements."

The *Yomiuri-Hōchi Shinbun* newspaper in Tokyo commented in an editorial that the strategy of the Japanese military forces was to turn things around and defeat the enemy once its supply of food and ammunition was completely consumed. It appeared to us to be totally unbelievable that U.S. forces would run out of food and ammunition, for we knew that they had already secured control of the air and sea. I wondered how a newspaper as big as *Yomiuri* could not know of America's superior military situation.[75] For its part, the United States not only rejected the Japanese report of its successes, but even went so far as to insist that the U.S. had never dispatched such a convoy.

On January 6, national attention focused on President Roosevelt as he delivered the State of the Union Address to Congress. He addressed various domestic problems and then said, "The year of 1945 will be the year of decisive battles against Germany and Japan. I am confident that the United States of America will establish a world peace that will long be remembered throughout human history." In closing, he asked for God's blessing in the great endeavor.[76]

The U.S. Air Force, which already had command of the skies, sent several hundred B-29s on bombing raids over Tokyo, Nagoya, Osaka, Kobe, Shimonoseki, Taiwan, Okinawa, and Nanjing, inciting panic among the citizenry. At the same time, preparations were underway for a landing in the Philippines.

On January 10, General Headquarters, commanded by General MacArthur, issued a statement that sixty thousand U.S. troops had landed on Luzon Island, transferred their headquarters to Lingayen Bay, and secured fifteen miles of coastline with eight hundred U.S. transport vessels and three thousand landing craft. According to a broadcast from Tokyo, Prime Minister Koiso called a meeting of the advisory committee and conferred with General Tojo Hideki, along with other high-ranking officials such as Wakatsuki Reijiro and Hirota Koki, in order to address the situation on Luzon Island.

In addition, the AP reported that Admiral Nomura Kichisaburo, former ambassador to the United States, had exhorted the citizens of Japan to stand firm, no matter how fierce the American attack. He went on to say that Japan would fight until the time when the United States recognized that it would be impossible to defeat Japan. Only then would the war end, he added.

Icicles Curve Uniformly Like Bows

January brought even colder weather. It had been milder last year in Missoula, located at forty-eight degrees north, where no wind blew into the basin. We had never before experienced weather as cold as at Santa Fe. When I got up in the morning, I saw that icicles hanging from the roof now reached the ground. Looking like waterfalls, they all curved toward the barracks wall like archery bows.

My hometown is a cold place, so I have seen many long icicles. But I had never before seen any that curved uniformly like these. Why were they curved? This is how it works: Snow piles on the roof and melts from the heat generated by the stoves in the barracks. All through the night, the water drips from the edge of the roof. The strong north wind freezes the drops and causes icicles to form like bows.

The Camp Is Renamed

When the government transferred jurisdiction over the internment camps from the military to the Department of Justice, the internment camps were renamed Alien Detention Camps and rules were relaxed. Then, for some reason, the names were changed again to Alien Internment Camps. Chief Langston announced the name change and instructed us to notify our families to address letters to "Santa Fe Internment Camp."

We thought the renaming was not so important, but we feared how it would affect our status. Some internees blamed the younger men from Tule Lake who were always bucking the authorities for creating the situation. However, the attitude of the authorities toward us did not change at all.

The war situation was changing quickly, and the *New York Times* in its February 6 issue reported that the German government had moved its capital from Berlin and that Ambassador Oshima had left Berlin for the new capital.[77] On February 7, American forces entered Manila, and General MacArthur set up headquarters on the campus of St. Thomas University, turning the city into a battle zone.

Our administrative chief and his assistant, Mukaeda and Taketa, turned in their resignations on February 8, making way for an election to select their successors. When Takaichi Saiki, a former chief, who seemed to be a strong candidate, declined the nomination through the newspaper, the nominating committee was embarrassed. Eventually Takaichi Saiki and Sawajiro Ozaki were elected chief and assistant. A Hawai'i pair was now managing our internee administration.

For the First Time, Internees Receive Notices of Parole to Hawai'i

On January 24, 1945, seventy-three-year-old Shigezo Sumida, who used to be a teacher at Manoa Japanese Language School, as well as a Shinto priest at Kato Shrine, received an official letter from Lieutenant General Richardson notifying him that he had been issued a parole and that he would be sent back to Hawai'i on the first available ship. This was the first notice of its kind to be received by a Hawai'i internee. Hawai'i internees were very happy to hear the news, for they now thought they could see a light in the darkness.

Amid this euphoria—as rare and joyous as the *udonge* blooming in the spring wind[78]—telegrams with a similar message arrived on February 10 for Teiichiro Maehara, Ryozo Izutsu, and Kichitaro Kawauchi.[79] Then, on the following day, twenty-one more internees received cables. They were Tatsuo Ito, Hikohachi Onouye, Hikojuro Otsuka, Tajiro Suzuki, Yonematsu Sugi-ura, Saichiro Kubota, Toichi Takata, Futoshi Ohama, Toraichi Kurakake, Mankichi Miura,[80] Shinjiro Matayoshi, Tadaharu Torii, Hatsutaro Toyo-fuku, Gihei Tanada, Wasaburo Uranaka, Shinjiro Yoshimasu, Ushitaro Yonesaki, Makitaro Tamura, Katsuichi Tanaka,[81] Shigeji Terada, and myself.

Prior to this cable, I had received on January 18 a notice from Major General William R. C. Morrison of the Department of the Army in Hawai'i that read, "The Reinvestigation Committee has reviewed your personal record and relevant documents and has decided to grant you special consideration in light of your son's service in the U.S. military. This is to inform you that the Committee has recommended to the Commander of the Pacific Region that you be paroled to the continental United States, and the Commander has ordered the Military Police Chief to take the necessary action."

I, however, wanted to be paroled to Hawai'i. If I were paroled to the Mainland, I would no longer have the energy to find work nor could I afford to live in a hotel. Even if I were to be transferred to a relocation center, I would still have preferred to live here, at Santa Fe, among many friends in this familiar setting. Nevertheless, I was surprised and appreciative that I was being included with the fathers of servicemen, although my son was not yet on active duty. As it turned out, none of us were able to return to Hawai'i before the end of the war, except for Shigezo Shimoda, Teiichiro Maehara, Kametaro Maeda, Kyoichi Miyata, Ryozo Izutsu, and Kichitaro Kawauchi.

Two days later, on February 13, others received notices of parole, including Zeichi Fukunaga, Jinshichi Tokairin, Kodo Fujitani, Hozui Nakayama, and Kakichi Okamoto, bringing the total to thirty Hawai'i internees.

Hōkokudan Nisei from Tule Lake Continue to Arrive

The atmosphere of the camp had become tense, ever since the arrival of some seventy young men from Tule Lake. In the midst of this troubling situation, another group of 170 men arrived the following month, on January 29. Among them were five Buddhist priests, Unji Hirayama, Seikaku

Takesono, Tetsuo Tanaka, Shingetsu Akahoshi, and Yoshitaka Abiko, as well as a young man named Seiko Imoto. They all had been at Santa Fe before. Another group of 650 internees from Tule Lake—632 Nisei, who had renounced their American citizenship, and eighteen Issei—were transferred to the Fort Lincoln Internment Camp in Bismarck, North Dakota.

On March 7, another 125 people arrived from Tule Lake. Among them were Minoru Hinoki, leader of the Hōkokudan, and Shigeyoshi Kawabata,[82] head of the Sokuji Kikoku Hōshidan. I had heard that as many as 1,016 Tule Lake evacuees had been moved to other camps. With the arrival of the 125 men, Santa Fe camp administrators, who were already having a hard time maintaining order over even a small number of radicals, tightened their control.

On March 8, the Tule Lake group was ordered to hand over to Chief Langston by the following day all clothing bearing the "Hōkoku Seinendan" logo. Some of the group members wore not only medals, but sweatshirts with such ridiculous phrases painted on their backs as "Action Without Words," "Trust in Our Country," and "Crush America."

More Depressing News of the War

In a radio broadcast over two stations, Japan's Imperial General Headquarters issued the following order: "Our military troops stationed on the islands of New Guinea, Bougainville, and New Britain are instructed to engage in self-sufficient battles, even if a serious situation should arise in the land of Imperial Japan." It was probably this order that kept Japanese soldiers in the Philippines and the South Sea Islands from responding to American appeals for surrender after the war.[83]

On March 10, the National Mobilization Act was passed in the Diet, making men twelve to sixty years old and women twelve to forty years old eligible for the draft. Only women working in Japanese war plants were exempt.

On March 19, Iwo Jima finally fell. All of the Japanese soldiers, including their commander, Lt. Gen. Kuribayashi Tadamichi, fought to their deaths. According to the Dōmei News Agency, Commander Kuribayashi sent the following tragic message to the emperor prior to the final attack: "Although I did all I could, I regret to report that I failed to fulfill my duty to defend this island. We have been crushed by enemy fire. I offer my humblest apologies to Your Majesty. With a pledge to 'serve our country for seven lifetimes,' we now embark upon our final attack." Thus the entire company under the command of Lieutenant General Kuribayashi turned in the direction of their motherland, gave their final banzai cheers, and resolutely charged into battle, sacrificing themselves for their country.[84]

A Petition to Move to Hawai'i

As time went by and nothing happened, those who were scheduled to return to Hawai'i became impatient and began to complain. At around that time, Shigeo Shigenaga started a petition to request that all of us, not just parolees, be moved to a camp in Hawai'i. Most of us signed the petition. At a meeting on the evening of February 16, he reported that Officer-in-Charge Williams[85] was of the opinion that not only fathers of servicemen, but all other internees, should request parole as a way to begin our campaign. He recommended that anyone who had not yet sent his application for parole to Commissioner Kelly[86] in Philadelphia should do so. However, the reality was that even parolees could not get space on the ship to Hawai'i, so in the end our efforts failed.

Now and then, internees who had received official notification to return home were summoned by the authorities. Each time they reported to the office with great anticipation, but they always found themselves disappointed, having undergone questioning without being given a specific departure date. Still, it was worth the expectation, like seeing a light at the end of a distant tunnel.

At the barracks leaders meeting held on February 17, it was reported that a total of twenty-two internees had died in this camp since September 1944. The camp population was reported to be 1,409, of which 893 favored repatriation.

Officers and Managers for the Eighth Term

The following officers and managers were elected for the eighth term, with the Hawai'i group taking most of the posts:

Chief of Administration	Takaichi Saiki
Assistant Chief	Sawajiro Ozaki
Chief Secretary	Ryuichi Kashima
Chief of Finance	Isamu Kurotobi
Secretaries	Zenkichi Morita, Masaya Toma, Hiroshi Tamabayashi (concurrently in charge of mail)
Auditors	Katsuichi Kawamoto, Miyuki Sokabe
Canteen Manager	Kinzo Sayegusa
Security & Fire Department Chief	Yasutaro Miyazawa

Food Supply Manager	Ishima Kusano
Bar Service Manager	Takuji Shindo
Education Manager	Chikashi Nakayama
Hospital Manager	Usaburo Katamoto
Barber Shop Manager	Naoichi Seto
Farming Manager	Shiro Kondo
Broadcast Manager	Gempachi Tsushima
Entertainment Manager	Masayuki Chikuma
Athletics Manager	Hatsuichi Toishigawa
Movies Manager	Muneo Kimura
Poultry Farm Manager	Joei Oi
Newspaper Manager	Yugoro Kusao
Chief Editor	Toshio Sakaguchi
Health & Hygiene Manager	Kyohei Miyaji
Laundry Manager	Kaheiji Yokomizo
Tailoring Manager	Noriyoshi Hamada
Shoe Repair Manager	Kiyoyoshi Inamine
Upper Area Mess Hall Manager	Kumao Akino
Lower Area Mess Hall Manager	Akira Tsujita

Since we could not exercise or hike in the winter, various study groups were formed. Those in charge of the primary groups were as follows:

Western Painting	Masao Ikeno
Bookkeeping	Miyuki Sokabe
Spanish	Tatsuo Manabe
The United States	Osamu Fujii
Japanese Painting	Koshi Tatsuhara
English Language	Yoshinobu Sasaki
English Grammar	Itsuei Hisatake
Japanese Penmanship	Kogan Yoshizumi
Yōkyoku[87]	Ichiro Nakamura
Calligraphy	Yoshio Koike
Karate	Shobun Maehokama
Japanese Cultural History	Michikazu Ochi

Incident in the Camp

Those Tule Lake people with their shaved heads became increasingly active as more people joined the camp. They ignored the order of Officer-in-Charge Williams to turn in clothing with the "Hōkoku" logo by the deadline. In the commander's mind, their refusal suggested that the group in fact possessed "Hōkoku" sweatshirts and weapons, such as daggers. And so on March 11, he dispatched dozens of guards on a raid of the barracks. Some oversized pocketknives and documents were confiscated.[88]

The next morning, March 12, two Kibei Nisei, Zenshiro Tachibana and Norizane Tsuha, considered to be the leaders of the Nisei Hōkokudan, were removed from their barracks along with their baggage and taken by mounted guard to the camp administration office in the upper area.

A group of young Tule Lake supporters with tense expressions on their faces followed behind. When the group neared the upper area mess hall, dozens of waiting guards threw tear gas bombs at them, even though these young men had not behaved violently. Unfortunately, the guards were downwind, so they were caught in the dense smoke. It was as if they had thrown the bombs at themselves. The group of young men jeered loudly, prompting the angry guards to attack the group with their clubs. Another group of guards, who had been watching at the entrance to the lower area, clubbed the fleeing men. Having nothing to protect themselves with, four men—Gontaro Ono, Akira Osugi, Isamu Uchida, and Motoo Hirashima[89]—were knocked to the ground. They looked awful, bleeding terribly from injuries to their head and other parts of their bodies. They were dumped onto a truck bed and taken to the hospital. They were not leaders, but only men who happened to be at the wrong place at the wrong time.[90]

Apparently, the authorities had foreseen serious trouble that day. Two Caucasian ladies who worked at the administration office had not shown up for work that morning, and extra guards had been brought in from El Paso. Camp gatherings had been prohibited, and all business was closed except at the mess halls, hospital, and canteen. The entire camp had been eerily quiet.

The camp administration issued orders for all of the more than three hundred internees of the Tule Lake group, who had been scattered among the many barracks, to now be brought together and isolated in one place. Internee administration called an emergency meeting of the barracks leaders. They resolved to demand that the camp administration withdraw the segregation order and begin negotiating with the camp authorities. Mounted guards continued their patrol of the camp after dark. We were instructed to remain in our barracks and not to go outside. Tension filled the camp.

Confined Within the Double-Fenced Area

The next morning, March 13, the camp became very noisy. I thought that there had been another incident. Instead, a few dozen Mexican workers were building a double fence around the seven barracks from Barracks 63, my neighboring barracks, to Barracks 69. The fence was completed within a day, and the following morning more than three hundred Tule Lake people were quickly moved in. The previous occupants of these barracks were transferred to other barracks. With the officials of the camp acting only on emotion, our request based on the resolution of the barracks leaders meeting was not even taken into consideration. The order to move out was a blow to the barracks occupants, who had made their quarters livable with makeshift tables and shelves.

Of great concern to us were the four men who had been injured by the guards, for we had heard that some were in serious condition. Later, we were relieved to learn that their wounds had not been severe. Mr. Osugi, however, sustained an injury to the head that was deep enough to reach the skull and which required four stitches. Fortunately, no one was killed in the dispute. Those who were confined behind the double fence were not allowed to communicate with us, exercise, or take a walk, and their meals were brought to them in the isolated area. The elderly internees, especially, became very anxious about the miserable situation of the Tule Lake people.

After dinner that evening, another problem arose. Kichitaro Orimo, who was in his sixties and the leader of Barracks 4, was detained within the double-fenced area for security reasons. Although not from Tule Lake, he was very sympathetic to them and reportedly encouraged their actions.

On March 15, another emergency meeting of barracks leaders was held. The meeting lasted from morning to evening, what with so many opinionated leaders, as well as those who enjoyed a good argument. Finally, they concluded that ultimate responsibility for the incident lay with the two Tule Lake group leaders, Tachibana and Tsuha.

At around midnight, guards wearing gas masks entered the barracks of Rinzo Wakayama, who was from Kohala on the Big Island and the leader of Barracks 69.[91] They gave him thirty minutes to packs his belongings and then they took him away. He had been the leader of the Tule Lake group that had first arrived at this camp. He had changed his stance for some reason and had been cooperating with the authorities at the time of the incident. It was rumored that the authorities had taken him away somewhere to protect him from possible harm. The injured four were discharged from the hospital on March 21 and housed in a specially fenced space in the visitor center near the offsite administration office. After two days, however, they were taken out of camp with fourteen others.

The fence that had made us feel so uneasy was torn down two weeks later on March 31. We could move about freely in the camp again and all of us were happy. Those young men who remained in the camp acted cheerfully, as if nothing had happened, gathering together at the library, canteen, and the broadcast square in the evening.

Officer-in-Charge Williams Issues a Statement

Officer-in-Charge Williams, who had ignored the resolution of the barracks leaders meeting, issued the following statement in an attempt to get us to understand his position:[92]

Summary of the Memorandum

Concerning the disputes between the administration and the non-cooperative group who recently moved from Tule Lake Relocation Center to this camp, I provide the following information in hopes of gaining your understanding. The activities of those from Tule Lake Relocation Center are as follows:

The 366 people who were transferred to this camp on December 31, 1944 were members of Sokuji Kikoku Hōshidan and Hōkoku Seinendan. I believe you are aware of their backgrounds and their objectives. Even before the arrival of the first group, leaders were warned by Deputy Attorney General John Burling that group activities would be restricted. This directive has been confirmed by the Attorney General himself.

Upon their arrival, these men were told not to engage in military drills, military activities, or any type of group demonstrations that promoted their ideological position. However, the group did not follow these instructions. I refer specifically to those wearing the "Hōkokudan" logo sweatshirts, who incited other internees and acted violently. It was because they behaved in a manner that could not be tolerated that the administration prohibited the wearing of this logo. If their goal was to demonstrate loyalty to Japan, they undermined their purpose. The U.S. government had already allowed them to renounce their American citizenship, thereby clearly admitting that they were loyal citizens of Japan.

It should be emphasized that the government in no way forced this decision upon them. Actually, as American citizens, they could have been charged with treason. I dare say that the conduct of these people belongs in the aforementioned category of superficial patriotism. This administration pays due respect to the rest of the camp residents, who have exhibited true loyalty to their mother country. It is believed that the men who insisted on wearing "Hōkoku" logo shirts were deliberately attempting to create unrest within the camp. They not only disobeyed the order to turn in their logo sweatshirts, but some of them came to our office in protest, making the inflated claim that everyone in the Tule Lake group was against the order.

The result of our investigation has revealed that, as was expected, Zenshiro Tachibana was responsible for inciting the group. Under his instructions, they disobeyed our orders and attempted to create chaos within the camp. Therefore, we moved him to another location in order to avoid the recurrence of a similar incident. Immediately after we moved Mr. Tachibana, a group of about 250 people rushed to the entrance of the administration office and threw stones at the building. Despite orders to disperse, they did not obey. At this point, we had no choice but to force them to disperse. This led to the decision to isolate the Tule Lake group, which had caused the disruption, in the designated block located in the lower area.

I plan to take appropriate action against those who incited the group and disobeyed orders. It is my greatest regret that such an unpleasant incident has taken place in this camp. However, I remain firm in my commitment to adopt a policy of cooperation with camp residents and to exert my efforts to minimize the burdens of the residents in their daily lives.

While I am pleased that the relationship between the administration and the internees has been a positive one, I am at the same time saddened that this incident has occurred. There seems to be a small group of individuals who have not recovered their normal mental state and continue to promote disorder. They are hysterical about the incident that took place because of their own foolish conduct. A few are guided by selfish motives, while others are naively focused on a single resolution to their problems. I intend to take punitive action against those whom I have mentioned, as well as against the fanatics who call themselves the Suicide Corps and send out threatening letters. This office has every intention of taking appropriate action against these perpetrators.

Let me make it clear that there is no need to fear the Suicide Corps. I want to make myself clear: These men will be transferred out within a short time. I believe that the vast majority of those from Tule Lake are good citizens, regardless of their national background. Now is an important time for you to think about your present and future security. The administration has no intention of keeping the isolation section in the lower area open forever. Use this opportunity to weigh the issues affecting your well-being. Not only will it be to your benefit, but it will contribute to the general welfare of your fellow residents.

I trust that you will exercise common sense in order to resolve this unpleasant situation as quickly as possible.

> Ivan Williams
> Officer-in-Charge
> Santa Fe Alien Internment Camp
> March 16, 1945

Spring Comes to the Plateau

The cold winter passed with little notice, and there were signs of spring
on the Santa Fe plateau. Although the snow continued to fall and collect
in clumps on the young pine trees behind our camp, it melted as soon at
it touched the ground. Even though the temperature on the ground was
relatively warm, the air was much colder. But as the weather became more
spring-like, the snow that beautifully covered the branches like flowers
soon vanished.

Troubles caused by the youthful group from Tule Lake, once at its
worst, were somehow resolved, and the spring softball season began. A
league was formed consisting of teams from the Mainland, South America, Hawai'i, and young men from Tule Lake. These teams were called
Shikishima, Kongō, Sankō, and Kyōjin. Middle-aged internees formed
another league comprised of teams called Yashima, Nankai, Taiyō, Tōwa,
Asahi, Donkō, Sanga, Santa Fe and others.[93] Both leagues held games twice
a week. Many camp residents, most of them having no job to do every day,
came to noisily root for their teams. It was as though a spring breeze had
blown away the dark days of the past.

I volunteered to be an umpire for the middle-aged league games. I
enjoyed the concentration required of this job, as I tried to make fair and
correct calls. The general opinion was that I made pretty good decisions,
however, it was rumored that I favored the pitchers, since I had been one
myself.

Once during an especially tight game, Kuwasaburo Sakaguchi of
Honolulu, who had just learned to pitch while in camp, came close to hit-
ting me in the face. Sour-faced Sakaguchi was desperately throwing fastballs to the outside corner. His pitches not only missed the corner but were
too high. I couldn't call them strikes, so he ended up walking two players
in a row.

It was then that a sour Sakaguchi picked up a bat and came up to me at
home plate, fiercely protesting my decision. I was overcome by his terrify-
ing manner. I knew that in a one-on-one fight I would be no match against
his youth and strength, but there were others nearby, among them Hiroshi

Yamamoto, a karate assistant instructor from Peru, who was also from my hometown and a very close friend of mine. Feeling somewhat encouraged, I calmly said, "I may be easy on pitchers, but those balls you threw could never be considered strikes."

Sakaguchi eventually relented and went back to the pitcher's mound, ending some very tense moments for everyone. Strangely enough, Sakaguchi and I became *aikāne* after this incident, playing together in softball games. We often exchanged greetings, and I would jokingly ask, "How's the great pitcher?"

Elderly President Soga Is Overcome with Emotion

Takegoro Kusao, who had been editing and managing the operations of the *Lordsburg Jihō* and *Santa Fe Jihō* newspapers since 1943, and Rev. Shunjo Shiratori, a member of his editorial staff, departed for the Family Camp in Crystal City on March 28. We worried about the possible demise of the *Santa Fe Jihō*. But soon Toshio Sakaguchi agreed to serve as editor-in-chief, Peru's Kicho Furuya became the marketing manager and an editorial staff member, Wataru Takeshita became an editorial writer, and Shuhei Suguro joined the mimeographing crew. They worked quickly to resume the newspaper's operations.

Besides Kusao and Shiratori, nine other internees left for the Family Camp. They were Yaichiro Akata, Nizo Arita, Teizen Imamura, Konin Matano, Toshio Morishita, Junji Oda, and Kazuaki Tanaka. On April 12, Shujiro Takakuwa, who had received a parole notice some time earlier, was finally allowed to leave the camp and departed for Denver, Colorado. He later moved to his brother's place in California and returned to Hawai'i after the war ended.

On March 19, *Nippu Jiji* president Soga received permission to return to Hawai'i in a letter from Major General Morrison of the Hawaii Military Department. I immediately went to his barracks to congratulate him.

"Finally, I am confident that I will be able to go back to Hawai'i before too long," he said happily with tears in his eyes. I felt a tug of emotion, too.

Koiso's Cabinet Is Dissolved and Suzuki Forms a New One

On April 5, 1945, Prime Minister Koiso turned in his resignation, and General Suzuki Kantaro was ordered by the emperor to form a new cabinet. He immediately appointed the following members, who were officially acknowledged by the emperor:

Prime Minister	Suzuki Kantaro
Minister of Foreign Affairs and Minister of Greater East Asia	Togo Shigenori
Minister of the Army	Anami Korechika
Minister of the Navy	Yonai Mitsumasa
Minister of Finance	Hirose Toyosaku
Minister of Justice	Matsuzaka Hiromasa
Minister of War Industries	Toyoda Teijiro
Minister of Communications and Railways	Hikoyama Naoto
Minister of Education	Ota Kozo
Minister of the Interior	Abe Motoki
Minister of Agriculture and Commerce	Ishiguro Takeshige
Minister of Health and Welfare	Okada Tadahiko
Minister-at-Large and Director of the Cabinet Intelligence Bureau	Shimomura Hiroshi
Cabinet Secretary	Sakomizu Hisatsune
Minister-at-Large	Sakonji Seizo
Minister-at-Large	Sakurai Heigoro
Minister-at-Large	Lt. Gen. Yasui Fujiharu

General Anami, newly appointed minister of the army, drastically restructured the armed forces, reassigning two field marshals, four generals, and five lieutenant generals. These changes were meant to shore up defenses on the home front, however the staggering military losses, shortage of resources, and low morale at home signaled ultimate defeat for Japan. General Anami, under pressure from both the government and the military, committed suicide at the end of the war. It was most unfortunate.

Sooty Sparrows Bathe in the Spring Rain

As winter receded and the seven-thousand-foot plateau became warmer, trees sprouted buds, and birds began to sing. Spring showers left a shimmering dew over everything. Sparrows that had nested under the roofs of the barracks and mess halls through the winter now took quick baths in the puddles, oblivious of the falling rain. It was as if they wanted to wash their sooty bodies. I was reminded of the famous monologue by Tsukigata Hanpeita, an imperial loyalist at the end of the Edo period, who said, "Let's take a walk and get wet in the spring rain."[94] Whether in Japan or America, the atmosphere created by the spring rain was similar, and even the birds enjoyed bathing in the rain.

When the showers had passed, making way for spring in its full glory, a very pleasant, although unusual, sight greeted us. White coffee cups hung from the branches of the trees along the road to the mess hall, looking like strange, yet tranquil, flowers in bloom. It may sound strange, but the only time that we, as internees, had ever used ceramic plates was in the dining cars of the overnight trains. In camp, all we ever ate from were military mess trays made of aluminum. The cups, however, were genuine ceramic.

Dishwashing after the meal was the job of the men assigned to KP duty. With much clattering, trays, knives, and forks were roughly cleaned in the hot running water from the tap. Only the cups could not be treated in this manner. Someone had the good idea that we should each wash our own cup, carry it back to our barracks, and then bring it with us to the mess hall for our next meal. But it was not a presentable sight to be walking back and forth carrying a cup, and on top of that, it had become quite a nuisance.

Some clever people quietly began to hook their cups onto trimmed tree branches. At first, some laughed at the hanging cups, but the number of followers gradually increased, and soon the trees in front of the mess hall were covered with coffee cup flowers. Since they presented no danger to anyone, the administration chose to overlook the situation. But we were expected to pay for any lost cups, which inspired the shrewd ones to start putting their name tag on their cup. Some others officiously worried that they would not be able to enjoy their morning coffee with a name tag hanging off their cup. Even a great writer could not have thought this up. It was a masterpiece of humor created by interned Japanese.

The Sudden Death of a President and the Feelings of the Internees

President Roosevelt, who had been resting at the Little White House in Warm Springs before attending the San Francisco Conference, died suddenly at 4:35 in the afternoon on April 12. His doctor, Navy Commander Bruenn, said that the president had been chatting with his staff in front of the fireplace when he suffered a massive brain hemorrhage.[95]

At nine o'clock the next morning, his body left Warm Springs and was transported to Washington, D.C. A solemn funeral service was held on April 14 in the East Room of the White House, and he was buried on April 15 at a cemetery in Hyde Park, the city of his private residence.

At the news of Roosevelt's death, Japan, being a country that observes propriety, offered its condolences in its report of the president's demise. In contrast, Germany critically remarked that, "President Roosevelt will go down in history as the central figure who led the world into World War II."

With the exception of a small number of people, we in camp expressed our condolences quietly, cancelling all events. The flag on the hill, where the camp administration office was located, hung at half-mast, motionless in the still air.

Many people were optimistic that peace talks would take place as a result of the president's death. Wishful thinking may be a human short-coming, but it is quite common for ordinary people to indulge in it.

Just before the war, Ambassador Kurusu (Hien) Saburo[96] stopped over in Honolulu while on a Clipper flight to Washington, D.C., to assist Ambassador Nomura Kichisaburo. At the dinner held at the Japanese consul general's residence, I looked forward to hearing the ambassador's viewpoint. With my wishful thinking, I had hoped that with his assignment to Washington, Japan-U.S. talks would now proceed smoothly. I feared that he would not answer me frankly if I asked him straightforwardly for his opinion, so instead I wrote a haiku and showed it to him.

Flying swallow soars high
Perhaps spring will come
To the Pacific
飛燕高し太平洋春来るかも

We had enjoyed writing haiku together during the time when he had worked at the Consulate General in Honolulu. He now answered that he had not been writing many haiku recently. Instead, he wrote me a tanka:

Light-hearted
I soar in the sky
On silver wings
Devoting myself
To the Emperor
天翔る銀翼に乗せ身は軽し我大君に捧げつくして

I felt my question had been skillfully dodged. Our wishful thinking that both ambassadors, Nomura and Kurusu, would succeed in restoring peace was but a dream.

Vice-president Truman succeeded Roosevelt and immediately made his policies public:

1. He would follow the policies of the late president;
2. He would ask that the San Francisco Conference be held on April 25, as scheduled;
3. He would ask all secretaries to remain at their posts; and
4. He would carry out plans for a peacekeeping organization that the late president had outlined.

The announcement led us to believe that a solution for peace would not come soon. Thus, our high hopes and wishful thinking were crushed miserably, and all of us were deeply disappointed.

Japan Is Surrounded by Enemy Forces

In camp we were peacefully enveloped by the warm spring weather, yet all the while the war intensified, with U.S. troops finally landing in Okinawa. It was depressing to learn that on the Kerama Islands, two hundred residents including children had killed themselves rather than surrender to the enemy. The men committed *hara-kiri* and the women ripped apart their clothing and used it to hang themselves. There were many in the camp, however, who did not believe such information.

In Japan, the Taisei Yokusankai was dissolved, and a political party named Dainihon Seijikai was formed. It was led by the former governor of Korea, General Minami Jiro. According to a news announcement, the party also was known as the Hissho-tō.[97] I felt that Japan was struggling helplessly in the last stages of this war. But then, there were others who were encouraged by the news.

At about this time, the Spanish government notified the Japanese government that it would no longer serve as Japan's representative. We, internees, worried greatly that this would bring about changes in our situation. Officer-in-Charge Williams assured us that the United States government would continue to treat the internees fairly and in the same manner as it had before. He encouraged us to bring up any issues so that he could take appropriate action and report them to headquarters. His statement lessened our anxiety somewhat.

It was under these circumstances that we greeted the emperor's birthday. The majority of us still believed that Japan would win the war, so we wanted a large celebration to commemorate the occasion. We prepared a congratulatory program as follows:

1. Formal ceremony in the recreation hall, with a ration of one mandarin orange per person to be given out after the ceremony.

2. Softball games
3. Variety show and stage play
4. Sumō matches
5. Movie showing

The Death of Hitler

At a press conference on May 3, President Truman officially announced the deaths of both Hitler and Premier Mussolini. He said he welcomed the news. London's *Daily Express* speculated that since Hitler's body had not been found, it was possible that he had escaped to Japan in a submarine. According to a broadcast from Tokyo, an editorial in the *Asahi Shinbun* advised Japanese citizens to pay attention to how the demise of Hitler would affect the situation in Europe.

On May 6, 1945, Germany finally offered its surrender to the United States. Up until then, we had maintained a faint hope about the war's outcome. Now, however, we had to acknowledge that the war had passed a critical point.

Two Priests Are Sent to Bismarck

The number of younger Nisei who had been transferred from Tule Lake to the Bismarck internment camp in North Dakota totaled 650. The only Issei to be transferred with them were two Shin-Jodo priests and a few doctors and dentists. One day, the Bismarck camp administration requested a transfer from Santa Fe of two Buddhist priests in order to provide stability and help calm the wild emotions of the youth at Bismarck. There was one condition to this request however—that the priests could be from any sect but Shin-Jodo. Bismarck claimed that the Shin-Jodo priests in their camp tended to sympathize with and incite the radical youth there.

Rev. Rien Takahashi of the Soto Mission and Rev. Hosho Kurohira of the Shingon Mission were selected, and they left our camp for Bismarck on May 3. I heard that it was difficult for them to move from comfortable Santa Fe to a strange new camp, where the weather and food were bad and the internees wild.

A Young Spokesman Is Elected

As I said before, being the spokesman was very stressful, so no one wanted to be elected to this position. At the election of officers for the new term, Heigo Fuchino was nominated as spokesman, and Ichiji Adachi and Ryuichi Kashima were chosen as his assistants, but all three declined the nominations in a public announcement printed in the *Santa Fe Jihō*. We all worried about what would become of our internee administration. Fortunately, young Dr. Tsuneyoshi Kiba stepped forth and volunteered for the job.[98] He was, of course, elected and young officers were appointed.

Spokesman	Tsuneyoshi Kiba
Assistant Spokesman	Fumitaka Kuwatsuki
Treasurer	Wataru Takamoto
Chief Secretary	Kazuo Takesaki
Secretary	Zenkichi Morita, Suehiro Uchida
Post Master	Hiroshi Tamabayashi
Auditor	Katsuichi Kawamoto, Miyuki Sokabe

Koba's administration appointed the largest number of officers, department chiefs, and staff members during the camp's existence. The appointment of nine officers and thirty-three barracks leaders was as usual, but department chiefs, staff members, and committee members numbered as many as the following:

Liaison Staff	14
Department Chiefs	29
Education Department Instructors	37
Athletic Department	26
Entertainment Department	40
Sumō Department	74
Hospital Department	47
Newspaper Department	15
Broadcast Department	5
Total	329 (including officers and barracks leaders)

With so many Santa Fe internees being of the younger generation and coming from Peru and Tule Lake, it seemed appropriate to have a young spokesman like Mr. Koba. His promotion of athletic activities in the camp lifted the spirits of the young group from Tule Lake, and the camp returned to its former stability.

Heavy Bombing of Japan by American Forces

The U.S. Army Air Forces had been conducting air raids on many Japanese cities since the American seizure of Saipan, but now with the completion of an air base on Iwo Jima, an all out aerial bombardment of Japan was begun.

On May 25, more than 450 bombers descended on Tokyo, causing damage to a part of the Imperial Palace, as well as completely destroying the palace of the emperor's mother; the residences of Prince Higashikuni, Prince Fushimi, and Prince Kitashirakawa; the Russian Embassy; the Italian Embassy; the Swedish Legation; the Imperial University of Humanities and Sciences; and the official residence of the minister of the navy, Yonai Mitsumasa. Moreover, Viscount Ishii Kikujiro, Executive Vice President Taniguchi Tsunejiro of the Bank of Japan, and Dr. Susumu Oda were killed in the bombings.

Subsequently, the cities of Yokohama, Nagoya, Kobe, Akashi, Naruo, Osaki, and Kōfu also were targeted. Five of the largest cities in Japan suffered serious damage as a result of these bombings.

Houses burned:	Tokyo	3,100,000
	Yokohama	680,000
	Osaka	510,000
	Nagoya	380,000
	Kobe	260,000
Houses damaged:		Approximately 600,000

Matsudaira Tsuneo, minister of the Imperial Household Agency, submitted his resignation to take responsibility for the partial destruction of the Imperial Palace.

At the same time, several Japanese balloon bombs fell over parts of Oregon and Canada, surprising the residents of these areas. In Lakeview, Oregon, one of the bombs killed five local residents. It was a minor incident compared to the American bombing of Japan. Nevertheless, the Allied War Crimes Investigative Committee determined that the Japanese bombing of Mainland America constituted a war crime. The entire discussion seemed like nothing more than a children's quarrel.

By coincidence, a new moon dimly emerged during the day, appearing northwest of Santa Fe. At the time, Venus could be clearly seen, shining near the moon. Some citizens spread the rumor that it was a Japanese balloon bomb. Many Santa Fe residents were so surprised and curious that they went outside to take a look. Public squares and the streets of

Santa Fe were filled with spectators, and even traffic was suspended for a while.

On June 18, Buntaro Nakahara of Waiʻanae committed suicide by ingesting poison. He left no note, so we did not know what had led him to take his life, but the incident made us depressed. His funeral was conducted in the recreation hall, with Rev. Gikyo Kuchiba of the Hongwanji officiating.

On June 21, Shigezo Shimoda of Honolulu, Ryozo Izutsu of Kauaʻi, Teiichiro Maehara of Maui, and Kichitaro Kawauchi of the Big Island—one man from each island—departed for Hawaiʻi, the first group of internees designated to return to the islands. They left the camp being both congratulated and envied by the rest of the internees. With their departure, our return could not be far behind, and a few internees began preparing for that day. I felt sorry about Mr. Nakahara—had this news reached him one week earlier, he might not have killed himself.

Tragic Last Battles for Okinawa

The fighting in Okinawa intensified, and Japanese forces were in serious trouble. American troops that seized Oroku Peninsula announced that Rear Admiral Ōta Minoru, commander of the Oroku underground fortress, and his staff had been found dead from ritual suicide.

In turn, on the afternoon of June 18, American forces suffered the loss of Lt. Gen. Simon B. Buckner, commander of Okinawa landing operations. A Japanese artillery shell exploded as he was observing an attack by Marine Corps troops on a Japanese stronghold. Major General R.S. Geiger was immediately appointed as his successor.

Japanese forces, attempting one final attack, dispatched a few hundred kamikaze bombers, and although they inflicted tremendous damage on U.S. forces, they failed to turn the situation around. On June 19, Lt. Gen. Ushijima Mitsuru, general commander of the Japanese forces in Okinawa, sent a farewell message to General Headquarters: "I offer my humble apologies to the emperor. We have been overcome by enemy forces." On June 20, commanding all troops with Rear Admiral Ōta Minoru, General Ushijima ordered a final attack and perished.[99]

On June 26, the U.S. Army announced that American forces inspecting the seized area reported finding the makeshift graves of both Commander Ushijima and Chief of Staff Cho Isamu. They appeared to have killed themselves in a dignified manner, wearing their medals on their chests. It was said that Lieutenant General Cho had written, "I die with no regrets," on a piece of silk cloth that covered his body.

The cook who had served Commander Ushijima later said that they had held a last banquet on the evening of June 21. At three-thirty the following morning, both Ushijima and Cho solemnly performed *hara-kiri*, sitting on a white cloth placed on the beach. Dressed in formal attire, they faced the Imperial Palace and, with dignity, killed themselves.

At the Shimajiri district, Governor Shimada Akira had been supporting the Japanese military forces together with the citizens of Okinawa since the start of the battles there. They lost all contact with Japanese forces on June 22.

America's Leaders of Religion and Education Submit a Petition

Prominent Americans in religion and education submitted a petition to the U.S. government containing the following declarations:

1. Any military operations to destroy the Japanese mainland will not only cost the lives of our beloved sons and daughters, but also will go against God's love for all mankind.
2. The targeting of innocent women and children in Japanese urban areas is not only ineffective, but also senseless from the standpoint of strategy. It also violates our national doctrine of justice and humanity for all.
3. It is impossible to kill the entire Japanese population of seventy-five million, as claimed in America's threatening propaganda, in order to win the war and expedite Japan's unconditional surrender.
4. It is against the will of God to foster hatred among Americans by claiming that the Japanese people are inhuman.
5. Not all Japanese people are evil. We must not overlook the fact that there are many pacifists among them. We believe many of them would contribute to world peace in the future.
6. Hating our enemies and attempting to destroy them will only increase the risk of loss of American lives. Demanding unconditional surrender and emphasizing enemy atrocities do not constitute justifiable reasons for continuing the war against Japan. They by no means contribute to mutual understanding among the people of the world.

We expected that an agenda of reconciliation would be discussed, because this appeared to be the logical solution. However, this never occurred, and instead the horrible bombings of Hiroshima and Nagasaki took place. There is nothing more dreadful than war.

Flower Gardens behind Barbed Wire

It was depressing to hear the news of the war every day. But whenever I turned my eyes to the natural world around me, it soothed my aching heart. Trees and grasses grew greener, as the plateau eased into early summer. All was as it should be, according to the laws of nature.

Although we were interned behind barbed wire, we had not lost our appreciation of beauty. Many internees began to grow flowering plants, and when it became mid-summer, many small flower gardens sprung up around the barracks.

I may be *moloā*,[100] but I appreciate flowers. So, I started a small flower garden on the east side of my barracks, planting some cosmos, cornflowers, sweet peas, California poppies, and red poppies. The sweet peas did not blossom, perhaps because the soil was poor, but the California poppies did very well, as did the red and violet ones. I had never seen poppy flowers before, and so I watched them with fascination. I heard that the poppy flowers open suddenly with a pop. One morning I stood in the garden for twenty minutes watching the poppies bloom. The buds quickly opened in the morning sun, and although they did not pop, I felt as if I had heard a sound. My hearing is not good, but someone else might have been able to hear it.

The cosmos bloomed beautifully because the soil was suitable for them. I have a boyhood memory of some cosmos: My father liked flowers and used to grow chrysanthemums, peonies, irises, and roses. He also raised western flowers, which were uncommon in those days, buying seeds from vendors in town. He would put a name tag on each plant. One of them had the name *Cosmos bipinnatus*. Being a young boy, I thought that the name was long and incomprehensible. Although the plants grew very tall and reached the eaves of the barn, I could not find any buds. After a while, only a few flowers bloomed at the top of the tall stalks. They did not look very pretty to me. I later learned that this had been caused by giving the plants too much manure and by seeding them too early, as my father had done with the chrysanthemums.

Since my garden was as tiny as a cat's forehead, I grew only a few types of flowers. There were some internees who had been flower growers in California. The flowers they planted were everywhere in the camp, making it look like a flowering paradise. One could find hollyhocks, irises, marigolds, zinnias, nasturtiums, phloxes, larkspurs, dahlias, cornflowers, red poppies, sunflowers, and some wild flowers that looked like wisteria.

In Japan, it is said that flowers and plants are better grown in ground lit by the morning sun. In Santa Fe, I learned that the afternoon sun was better because it is weaker at the high elevation. The proverb, "Different places, different ways," certainly is correct.

The old city of Santa Fe that spread out beneath us had been very dry during the winter, but now the silver tower of City Hall could be seen rising above the lush greenery. It provided a striking contrast of natural and man-made beauty.

Distressing News of the War

Three-and-a-half years had passed since the Japanese attack on Pearl Harbor on December 7, 1941. Shortages of goods affected not only Japan, but also the United States, and this was reflected in the rationing of supplies. Coincidentally or not, the United States stepped up its military offensive. In July, as the Allies met at Potsdam, American forces bombed many Japanese cities, including Muroran, Kamaishi, Chiba, Numazu, Hiratsuka, Shimotsu, Shimonoseki, Himeji, Tokushima, Takamatsu, Kochi, Omuta, Tokuyama, and Kure. Warships bombarded Kushimoto, Shionomisaki, Yokosuka, Nojimamisaki, Takahagi, and Sukegawa in the Hitachi area.[101] News of this kind suggested that landing operations on Japan's mainland would start soon. I was rather despairing, as I could easily imagine a tragic end, if such operations took place. At such times, I took walks on a hill behind the camp or gazed at the flowers, because I did not want to talk to anyone.

On July 13, a note to President Roosevelt from Rear Admiral Ichimaru Rinosuke, written before he and his troops perished at the fall of Iwo Jima, was released by the censorship agency and published in the *Denver Post*. The following is a summary of Ichimaru's message:[102]

Mr. President,

Though you are taking advantage of our Pearl Harbor attack to justify the war against Japan, the people of the world fully know that it was your political maneuver of pressuring Japan to protect your own interests that led Japan to fight against your country.

Deliberating over your policy, I am aware that the white races, especially you Anglo-Saxons, are aiming to control the world's natural resources at the sacrifice of the yellow races. You intend to deprive the yellow races of any strength by playing shrewd tricks in order to achieve your goal.

Japan rose against your imperialism-oriented policy to release Asians from your shackles. Thus, a once-friendly nation has become your obstacle. Is it your country that is masterminding to clip off the buds of freedom in Asia? The Greater East Asian Co-prosperity Sphere is the core of the plan to achieve everlasting world peace, and it is, by no means, intended to put your country in danger. His Imperial Majesty's true aim is no other than achieving everlasting world peace.

It is beyond my comprehension that the United States, opponent of Hitler's Nazism, would cooperate with Soviet Russia, the leader of communism. As long as cruel acts are repeated as a way to dominate the world, the world will never know peace or attain the everlasting welfare of mankind.

I earnestly hope, Mr. President, that with your ambition for dictatorial position, you deliberate on President Wilson's military and political strategy, which failed despite his concerted efforts.

The note is self-serving in some parts, attempting to justify Japan's military strategy, as in the Japanese saying, "Drawing water to one's own paddy." However, it is also true that the criticism of the alliance with communist Russia touches on a sensitive spot for the United States.

The Potsdam Declaration Is Announced

As expected, the United States, Great Britain, and China issued a joint statement on July 26, 1945. In essence, it promised the complete destruction of the Japanese mainland, if Japan were to continue to pursue the war. The declaration called for Japan's unconditional surrender and detailed seven additional demands.

In his response, General Minami,[103] chairman of Dainihon Seijikai, said that Japan would never stop fighting and that the declaration ran contrary to Japan's hopes for world peace. He concluded that there was no choice but to continue the sacred war.

Atomic Bombs Are Dropped on Hiroshima and Nagasaki

President Truman announced on August 6 that an air raid by the U.S. Army Air Corps over the city of Hiroshima had involved the use of a new and powerful atomic bomb. It weighed less than ten pounds, but was said to have performed with such astonishing power that it had turned everything within a two-and-a-half mile radius to ash. The Japanese government, after an emergency cabinet meeting, confirmed that it had indeed been an atomic bomb.

At noon on August 9, the U.S. Army Air Corps dropped another atomic bomb, this time on Nagasaki. It devastated the city, nearly reducing Nagasaki to ash. In a radio broadcast, the Japanese government accused America of committing atrocities against civilians. Japan claimed that it had already developed the atomic bomb, but had never considered using it for the sake of mankind. Now that the United States had taken the first step in killing many innocent civilians, Japan declared that it would retaliate by dropping its atomic bombs, annihilating American warships and its military. This broadcast gave many Japanese Americans in our community the incentive to join the so-called pro-Japan group.[104]

Russia, whose decision was greatly anticipated by the other Allied members, finally declared war against Japan. At midnight on August 9, the Russian government delivered to Japanese Ambassador Saito Naotake a communiqué containing five points. Premier Stalin had once flattered the sentimental Matsuoka Yosuke, then minister of foreign affairs, by saying that Russians and Japanese were fellow Asians. In making an anti-war pact with Japan, Stalin eliminated the threat of an attack from the back door and enabled Russia to win the war against Germany. Stalin had not made clear the Russian position during the talks at Potsdam. He saw that Russia had gained an advantageous position and recognized Japan's inevitable defeat resulting from the damage sustained by the American atomic bombs. He then declared war on Japan. What Stalin had done was dishonest and intolerable to us, Japanese. We learned that the Japanese government, honest to a fault, had trusted Russia and had asked her to intervene in a truce with the Allies. Russia flatly turned down this request after obtaining much valuable information from Japan.

It could be said that Matsuoka's clumsy diplomacy, which had been influenced by Stalin and Hitler, led to the suffering of extreme hardship by Japan's people and the country's total defeat, something it had never experienced before. Although Japan was not the only country to have been betrayed by Russia, the dishonesty was nevertheless intolerable.

Japan Finally Accepts the Potsdam Declaration

On August 10, we received shocking news from the Dōmei News Agency: "The government of Japan is prepared to accept the terms of the Potsdam Declaration. However, should the Allied powers refuse to allow us to form a new government under our Imperial Majesty, Japan will end all further discussions. The government of Japan requests an immediate response from the Allied powers."[105]

This response to the Potsdam Declaration was delivered to the United States, Great Britain, and China through the governments of Sweden and Switzerland. Foreign Affairs Minister Togo Shigenori also delivered a similar message to the Russian ambassador in Japan. Most of us in camp did not believe the news report.

As if unconcerned by this significant piece of news, the INS ordered the parole of Kiyoji Hotta, Shinroku Kanamori, Hikojuro Takemoto, and Sannojo Tanabe to places on the Mainland. Eizo Nagakura, who had been granted parole earlier, left the camp for Chicago.

On August 22, Japanese General Headquarters announced that an Allied air fleet would arrive at Atsugi Air Field on August 26, followed by General MacArthur, Supreme Commander of the Allied Powers, who was scheduled to enter Tokyo on August 28. Furthermore, the Instrument of Surrender was to be signed on August 31 in Tokyo Bay aboard the super battleship USS *Missouri* commanded by Admiral Nimitz.[106]

Vice Admiral Onishi Takijiro, deputy chief of the military headquarters, formerly chief of Philippine regional navy air command and the founder of the kamikaze special attack unit, committed hara-kiri at his official residence. The note he left behind was tragically touching.

> I dedicate this message to you, the fallen heroes of the kamikaze special attack unit. I express my deepest appreciation for your all-out effort. I was confident that your brave acts of self-sacrifice would bring ultimate victory to our nation. Having failed to achieve victory, I offer my life in apology to you and your families.
>
> To all young men: It is my hope that my death will serve as a lesson in the difficulties you face in rebuilding our country and in the tragic consequences of imprudent actions. Nothing would please me more than to have you serve our country in accordance with His Majesty's wishes. The Japanese ethos will never be lost, as long as you practice forbearance. Our youth are the treasure of our nation. I pray that you will fully embrace the spirit of the kamikaze special attack unit and exert your utmost effort to restore the dignity of our race and to establish world peace.

Gen. Anami Korechika, army minister in Prime Minister Suzuki's cabinet, who had consistently argued in favor of continued fighting, killed himself, finally, like a true Japanese soldier. Lt. Gen. Okamoto Suemasa, military attaché at the Japanese Embassy in Sweden also was reported to have committed hara-kiri in Zurich.

The whole camp became depressed but noisy. It was indescribably ominous. Our internee administration, as well as the camp authorities, apparently aware of this situation, ordered a temporary closure of the beer hall.

Respected Yesterday, Reviled Today

There was a gentleman by the name of Hirotatsu Shonan Kimura, who was in his seventies and had formerly been engaged in a law-related business in Los Angeles. Not only was he fluent in English, but he also had much knowledge of the Chinese classics and was a patriot. At Camp Livingston, he wrote the news scripts that were broadcast to the Panama group. He frequently used classical Chinese expressions, which Mr. Komatsu, the reporter, had a hard time reading.

Here, in this camp, elderly Shonan Kimura was a news commentator for the group of internees interested in Japan's victory. He believed in Japan's ultimate victory, even though Saipan and the Philippines had been seized by the United States. He believed the Japanese military propaganda that, after luring American warships to the Japanese mainland, thousands of kamikaze planes would annihilate the fleet in one sweep. His comments were not intended to encourage the internees, but rather stemmed from his own beliefs.

On August 10, Old-Man Kimura was nearly in tears, when he said to an unusually large audience, "All is lost. A shortage of matériel has resulted in the surrender of our valiant military forces." Overwhelmed with emotion, he could not continue.

Many Tule Lake youth, there to listen to Mr. Kimura's commentary, became furious and walked out immediately. Feeling betrayed, and having no other outlet to vent their anger, they berated Mr. Kimura, calling him the "All's-Lost Man" and "Senile Grandpa." Poor Mr. Kimura did not step out of his barracks for days, feeling so reviled by the very people who had respected him so much.

Kazuo Arai of Broadcast Department stammered as usual as he read the news of Japan's proposed surrender: "The government of Japan, through the Swiss government, has proposed to accept the Potsdam Declaration, if the Allied Forces are willing to recognize the existence of the emperor." Internees were stunned, as if they had been struck on the head with a sledgehammer.

In the midst of this turmoil, Officer-in-Charge Williams called an emergency meeting of the barracks leaders. He told them in a roundabout way that Japan had proposed peace and called for prudent behavior on the part of all internees. The *Santa Fe Jihō* did not publish its usual evening news, and the camp was wrapped in a heavy silence. But here and there, people gathered outside their barracks and on the roadside and whispered to each other. They were, of course, talking about the war, but most of them did not seem to be able to accept the fact that Japan had proposed peace. The weather the following day was clear and beautiful, but I felt very gloomy and was in no mood to join my friends in their conversations.

On August 13, a strange rumor spread throughout the camp. No one knew where it had come from, but the rumor told of Japan's victory. It claimed that ten thousand kamikaze planes loaded with atomic bombs had demolished Admiral Halsey's Pacific Fleet[107] and that thousands of similar planes, heading east and west, had bombed not only five major cities on the West Coast, but also New York and Moscow. It was said that the U.S. government had ordered a nationwide blackout. This was far beyond imagination.

Seen as a Traitor

The surrender of Japan did not occur all of a sudden. Anyone who read the daily news objectively could have foreseen this well in advance. Nevertheless, it was an unbearably bitter reality for a Japanese, especially those of us who were confined within the enemy country.

I could not understand why so many people remained unwilling to believe the news reports. Perhaps they did not realize what was happening, or they just thought everything was fine. To me, it was inconceivable that men of religion, such as high-ranking Buddhist priests and senior Christian ministers, would not accept the facts. Everyone indulges in wishful thinking. It is one of our shortcomings as human beings. I clearly saw that even intelligent people like them could not overcome this. These intelligent people who would not accept the Japanese surrender were mainly those who had sent their families back to Japan, transferred their savings there, or had sent their children there to study. It could be said that these factors played an important role in their attitude.

Besides them, there was a group of people, who for purely emotional reasons, did not want to believe Japan had lost. There were surprisingly many people in this group in addition to the Tule Lake youth. I was surprised to see that those elder men of religion, who should have been in a position to guide the young people, not only sympathized with them, but also incited them by spreading rumors. One of the rumors claimed that as a result of Japan's overwhelming victory, every internee who immediately returned to Japan would receive a compensation of fifty thousand dollars from the U.S. government, while those who returned later would not qualify. It was unfortunate that hundreds of internees actually believed this rumor and gave up their American citizenship and returned to Japan.

The group of internees who spread the groundless rumors was headquartered in an upper area barracks near the hospital. Every morning, representatives from each barracks gathered there and then brought back new false news to spread among their barracks mates. Since I could not possibly believe in this nonsense, I did not join the group to listen. Sometimes, while I was lying on my bed reading a magazine, someone would say in a voice loud enough for me to hear, "Look at that unpatriotic person from Hawai'i. He pretends to be so dignified."

After a few more incidents like this, I made it a practice to go outside to look at the flowers in the garden when they started talking, in order to avoid the unpleasantness. These were people who had been friendly to me when I, as a baseball fan, had made cash donations and volunteered to help with the games. Now that even my barracks leader was on their side and it was as though the whole world was against me, it was very unpleasant not to be able to say anything.

Impassively Watching the Fireworks

A fresh rumor spread throughout the camp on August 15, creating excitement among the victory believers. The rumor was that the United States had agreed to the thirteen conditions Japan had proposed. Moreover, it was said that the western half of Hawai'i would become a Japanese territory, for both governments had agreed that Japan would occupy all land north of 20 degrees north latitude and west of 150 degrees east longitude. The reference to specific coordinates made this weird rumor sound trustworthy and especially pleased the Hawai'i internees.

Ironically enough, President Truman, in a national radio broadcast, said that Japan had agreed to accept unconditionally the Potsdam Declaration. He also announced that General MacArthur had been appointed Supreme Commander for the Allied Powers and that V-J Day would be determined after the Japanese government had signed the instrument of surrender.

From early morning, we could hear the city of Santa Fe below us celebrating, as church bells tolled and factory whistles sounded. Throughout the night, fireworks lit up the sky, but I felt detached from all the excitement. To me, it was just another display of fireworks.

On August 16, it was reported that Prime Minister Suzuki's cabinet had resigned, that Prince Higashikuni had been ordered by the emperor to form a new cabinet,[108] and that the emperor himself had spoken over the radio, informing his nation of Japan's surrender. Since we learned that the emperor's radio message could be heard over short-wave radio, we all gathered in our barracks at the specified time in front of a radio, hoping to hear his broadcast. Unfortunately, there was so much static that we could hardly hear anything. Later, we had a chance to read the emperor's address as it had been translated into English. I could not read it without shedding tears.

The *Santa Fe Jihō* and the broadcast departments resumed their daily operations, only to suspend them again because of the angry reaction from many victory believers who objected to the reports of Japan's defeat. Without the newspaper or news broadcasts, internees had no access to news of the outside world, so barracks leaders held a meeting and decided to resume operations once more. However, they felt so intimidated by the victory believers that they did not report the truth and dealt only with topics that were not controversial.

The Tule Lake organizations Hōkokudan and Shichishōkai were secretly dissolved by their youthful members, who must have had some sense of reality, even though they talked big. I heard from a young man in my barracks that the groups' leaders had ordered the burning of all documents, including oaths signed by their members. They seemed to realize that Japan had not won the war, although they also could not believe that she had lost.

The Instrument of Surrender Is Signed

The AP News Service reported on September 2 that the ceremony of surrender had taken place aboard the USS *Missouri* anchored in Tokyo Bay: "Escorted by eleven uniformed attendants, Shigemitsu Mamoru, minister of foreign affairs, and General Umezu Yoshijiro, chief of staff, took seats on the deck. The instrument of surrender was signed first by the Japanese envoys and then by General MacArthur, Lieutenant General Wainwright, and Admiral Nimitz.[109] Then, General MacArthur, his voice ringing, concluded the ceremony by declaring, 'Let us pray that peace be now restored to the world.' It was 8:20 in the morning."[110]

Hiroshi Tahara, the principal of the Pāpa'ikou Japanese Language School on the Big Island, who had been ill for a long time, passed away on August 31. He was sixty-five years old. A grand funeral was held on September 4 in the recreation hall. After relating Tahara's personal history, a Honolulu school principal said, "The deceased must have been happy to learn before passing on that Japan had achieved its goal of winning the holy war." I was very surprised by his comment, however, upon thinking about it, I found it to be rather innocent, compared to the following comment.

What was more shocking was the one made by Rev. Enryo Shigefuji of the Fresno Honganji Temple. In a speech at a memorial ceremony for the war dead, the minister said that U.S. forces in the Far East—whose inhumane air strikes had caused the Japanese to retaliate ferociously—had been wiped out by Japanese atomic bombs during a three-day attack. He added that the United States had been forced to sign an instrument of surrender as a result of these attacks. I was thoroughly appalled by the intensity with which he spoke. All the Kibei Nisei in our camp returned to Japan after the war. It was unfortunate that these sorts of words and deeds led so many young Nisei to make the wrong decision.

On September 3, the city of Santa Fe cheerfully celebrated the restoration of peace with fireworks displays and the ringing of church bells. For us, however, the bells were ringing in remembrance of Army Minister Anami, Lieutenant General Onishi, and Lieutenant General Okamoto and also the dozens of other men who had committed hara-kiri in the Imperial Palace Square.

SCAP announced that American POWs and internees who had been held in seven POW camps in Japan would leave for home on August 24 under the supervision of the International Red Cross.

Secretary Stimson announced the closing of all relocation centers—Granada, Jerome, Amache,[111] Minidoka, Topaz, Heart Mountain, Gila, Manzanar, Poston, and Rohwer—which by the order of the commander of the Western Defense Command had held more than fifty thousand of our fellow countrymen since the beginning of the war.[112]

Now that our return to Hawai'i was just a matter of time, the camp came to life again.

Autumn on the Plateau

As we complained about the heat, it suddenly became cooler, especially in the mornings and at night. One morning, as I gazed at the towering Sangre de Cristo mountains in the east, I noticed the trees were turning yellow on the hillside known as "Saint's Horse," so named for its shape. I learned that spring spreads out from the foot of the hills, while autumn begins at the top.

Plants that flower-lovers had planted were in full bloom, and the clear sky spread out above us. It felt like the first time in decades since I had experienced such beautiful autumn weather.

The homes of Indians are called adobe, and their walls are brown and made of mud. They look just like storehouses in the rural areas of Japan. I noticed red peppers hanging on the walls. During autumn, throughout the Japanese countryside, festivals are held. Pueblo Indians living in the Santa Fe region have similar festivals. When the moon is full, people from nearby reservations gather to beat drums, play flutes, and dance to the music in celebration of life. You might think that in the movies the drums from the Blood Offering Festivals sound barbaric and discordant, but under the light of the full moon, casting a shadow on the mountains, they are restful and melodious. Grasses and flowers grow well in this area. The entire camp was like a large flower garden, covered with the blossoms of cosmos, sunflowers, and hollyhocks.

Hummingbirds

To our delight, as flowers began to bloom, many hummingbirds could now be seen hovering here and there. We had not seen them since Angel Island, but here we were able to see them every day. Hummingbirds are unusual. They are very small, with a length of about three inches from beak to tail. Their wings can generate tremendous lift. Like origami cranes hanging in the air, they hover, flapping their wings so rapidly that you cannot see them, as they suck nectar with their long beaks. They fly freely in all directions—up and down, left or right. When frightened, they can fly for forty or fifty feet at seemingly close to the speed of sound.

In Japan, small birds called *misosazai* can be seen living near streams. I once heard an interesting story about how they fly into the ears of bears and torment them with their pecking. If their fledglings are attacked in their nests, *misosazai* will fearlessly confront even falcons or hawks. Speed and razor-sharp beaks enable them to quickly attack their enemies. When escaping, they fly very quickly in a zigzag pattern, so that even falcons cannot catch them. Once while at a hospital recovering from an illness, I sat on a bench, sunning myself, and watched these hummingbirds. They were fascinating.

Priests and Ministers Lead Victory Believers Groups

As I mentioned before, a surprisingly large number of people believed that Japan had won the war. This was due to the influence of some men of religion, primarily from the Mainland, who held sway among the internees and had become victory believers. The group was led by Ōzeki Ikugoro Nagamatsu, a Christian minister from Kumamoto prefecture.[113] Rev. Enryo Shigefuji of the Fresno Honganji was a *sekiwake*, and Rev. Gisei Maeda, also from Fresno, was a *komusubi*. Reverend Maeda was a strange man. He appeared to be about thirty-five or thirty-six years old and sported a beard like Shōki.[114] He visited the hospital every day, telling all the patients that Japan had won.

Toyosaku Komai, former president of the *Rafu Shimpo* newspaper, and I were from the same hometown and close friends. One day I teased him about the fact that many Mainland ministers lacked understanding about the current situation. He retorted, "Don't you know there are victory believers in Hawai'i as well? Don't brag, after all, an ardent victory believer like Masao Mochizuki is from our home prefecture."

Educators and men of religion tend to be less aware of daily happenings, even though they have much spiritual knowledge. I became aware of this trend as a result of my internment experience, particularly during the last phase of it, the serious period of Japan's defeat.

In the early morning hours of September 10, more than 120 internees suddenly arrived at our camp. I later learned that they were from the Poston Relocation Center, which was scheduled to be closed.[115] I also learned that these young men had renounced their American citizenship.[116]

Groundless, Provocative Rumors Originate from Hawai'i

I am tired of writing about rumors, but let me tell you about one or two more. The first came in the form of a message sent from Honolulu to Suekuma Takaki. It said that the Japanese language schools would soon be reopening in Hawai'i and that teachers were being recruited from Japan. Some people cheered the news, claiming that this was proof that Japan had won the war.

Another rumor, mentioned in a letter to someone in camp, said that warships with Japanese flags had been anchored in Pearl Harbor. This may have been an optical illusion, seen from far away. Nevertheless, I was appalled to hear that the Japanese flag had been raised atop Hawai'i's territorial government building. I could not imagine what the rumormongers had in mind when they circulated such preposterous stories.

Our Earnest Prayers Are Answered

On September 11, 1945, the Provost Marshal General in Washington, D.C., ordered Officer-in-Charge Williams to clarify the postwar intentions of the 420 Hawai'i internees at Santa Fe: Would we go back to Hawai'i, stay on the Mainland, or return to Japan? Questionnaires circulated by the internee administration office found that fifty internees wanted to return to Japan, while the other 370 intended to go back to Hawai'i.

It took three days, beginning on September 17, for the authorities to inspect the Hawai'i-bound baggage. All personal belongings, except for daily necessities, were inspected and placed in temporary storage. We were appreciative that both Yoshio Kiino and Minoru Uyematsu[117] of our internee administration office performed this duty in a way that was sympathetic toward us. I was especially grateful to Mr. Uyematsu of Kaua'i, who was my close friend, for he did not empty the cardboard boxes that contained my personal belongings. Every year since my return to Hawai'i, he has sent us a New Year's card with pictures of his family. It was owing to the internment that I became friends with him.

Beginning on October 11, the final questioning of Hawai'i and South American internees took place. All the interviews took almost a week to complete with the assistance of volunteer typists and translators. Some of the most vocal victory believers, squirming under intense questioning, feared they would be deported to Japan.

The list of internees who would be returning to Hawai'i within the next five weeks was announced on October 17. Of course, it included the names of those who had been paroled since July 17. It seemed that our long-awaited dream was about to become reality.

However, on the afternoon of that very day, Daizo Sumida, Katsuichi Kawamoto, Tsuneichi Yamamoto, Hatsuichi Toishigawa, Haruo Koike, Hideo Tanaka, Tetsuo Tanaka, Hiroshi Tamabayashi, Jikai Yamasato, Ichiro Nakamura, and others totaling forty-one internees received new instructions from Washington, D.C., that they were to remain in camp. They did not know why they had been singled out nor did they have any idea whether they would eventually be allowed to return. I deeply sympathized with them, for I saw that they were very worried.

The following day, Ichiro Nakamura's name was removed, and instead Riichi Togawa of the *Nippu Jiji* was added to the list.

And then, on the next day, all forty-one men were notified that they were to return to Hawai'i after all. Naturally, the news made them very happy.

But their happiness was premature. On October 22, in another flip-flop, Assistant Officer-in-Charge Schreiber[118] announced that these forty-one internees, plus Chosuke Kayahara who had been in the hospital, were to remain in camp.

At the time, we could not understand why the orders changed so often, like the pupils of a cat. Later, we learned the cause, when we received the passenger list just before boarding in Seattle. The military ship could carry no more than 370 passengers. The authorities could not decide whether to include on the ship forty-two internees who had already been paroled to various places on the Mainland. This matter put the forty-one internees in a situation that made them either happy or sad, depending on how the situation went.

The authorities did not explain why those particular forty-one people had been chosen to remain in camp. But we later discovered that Mr. Nakamura was switched for Mr. Togawa, because they had mistakenly picked Mr. Nakamura.

A Gathering of Kōshū Native Sons from North and South America, Hawai'i, and Alaska

We Kōshū[119] men from North and South America, Hawai'i, and Alaska, who had been brought together in the camps by chance, decided to have

commemorative photographs taken since we soon would be going our separate ways. In Livingston, those of us from Kōshū numbered ten from
Hawai'i, ten from California, and one each from Panama, Florida, Salt
Lake City, and Seattle, for a total of twenty-four. We fearlessly called ourselves "Lord Takeda's Twenty-Four Generals." Rev. Kyokujo Kubokawa,
elderly Itaro Takano from Panama, and young Shingo Watanabe were the
three among us who returned to Japan aboard the exchange ship.

In Santa Fe, although there were fifty-three of us Kōshū men from
different places, thirty were paroled to various locations on the Mainland or to the Family Camp. In 1944, twenty Kōshū men joined us from
Peru; others came from places like Alaska and Portland. With the addition
of these newcomers, membership in the Kōshū club rose to sixty-three.
Young members were twenty-four-year-old Fumiya Yoneyama, twenty-
six-year-old Hiroshi Yamamoto, and twenty-seven-year-old Kicho Furuya.
The elderly group included Rev. Tsunetaro Kanzawa of the San Francisco Tenrikyo Mission, who was seventy-two years old; Toyosaku Komai,
president of the *Rafu Shimpo*, who was sixty-three years old; and Kinzo
Sayegusa, president of the company Cherry Shokai, the eldest among the
Hawai'i group at age fifty-nine. Most of us in the Hawai'i group were over
fifty years old. Only two, Tomoaki Nakamura and Rev. Gijo Ozawa, were
under fifty.

All of us spoke standard Japanese in public, but when Kōshū men
would gather, we unconsciously used our long-forgotten native dialect.
Incidentally, there was an elderly man who always spoke in the Kōshū dialect and embarrassed his friends who were not from our region. His name
was Kohei Mochizuki. This skillful man was a farmer from California, who
had been assigned as a barber in Santa Fe. He liked dramas and worked as a
performance director in our Entertainment Department. Although usually
healthy, one day he suddenly fell ill and died in the hospital. Rev. Gendo
Okawa, who was from his barracks, offered the reading of the sutra at his
funeral, which was attended by many internees from the Kōshū group and
the Entertainment Department. His ashes were to be carried back to his
hometown by Toyoaki Okuyama, a well-liked Peru internee who was nicknamed Thomas. The young Thomas was very cheerful and always had a
smile on his round face. He took good care of other people and worked in
the printing department of the *Santa Fe Jihō*. Thomas cheerfully undertook many assignments, whereas most Kōshū people are generally more
reserved. Naturally, he became popular among the internees.

Another young man, Kicho Furuya, was good at writing and worked
in the mimeograph department of the *Santa Fe Jihō*. He also did a lot of
writing and acting for the Entertainment Department. Most of the Peru

group returned to Japan after the war, but Furuya persevered in the United States. They had not been sent back home to Peru because the government refused to readmit them, claiming that the U.S. had accepted them unconditionally. American authorities had no choice but to give them permanent residency in the United States. I last heard that Furuya was very active on the Mainland. Not being sent back had been a godsend for him.

A Sightseeing Trip to Santa Fe for a Lucky Patient

When I was in Camp Missoula, I frequently visited the city itself on business. But after arriving at Santa Fe, I did nothing every day and had no opportunity to visit this city, which lay spread out below our camp. Here at an elevation of seven thousand feet, the summers were very short, and the cold weather moved in quickly. The hospital was always busy around that time, for many internees caught colds with the change of seasons. I was not an exception. Saying that I had a temperature of 100.4 degrees, Dr. Kohatsu hospitalized me at once. I was assigned to Bed 13 in the C Ward. I am not superstitious, but having been assigned to Bed 13 did not make me feel good. I had a high fever and felt very sick, so I had a hard time conversing with the nine people who came to visit me, such as Mr. Iida and barracks leader Takai.

My temperature would be normal in the morning but would rise in the afternoon. Doctors feared that I might have tuberculosis, and so Dr. Masayoshi Tanaka took me to the hospital in Santa Fe to have my lungs x-rayed. Called St. Ivan Hospital, it was run by a Catholic organization and so had religious paintings displayed in the lobby and office and in the x-ray room, too. The paintings created a peaceful atmosphere, and I felt as if my heart had been purified.

I was unexpectedly lucky, when on the way back to camp, the guard agreed to drive slowly so that I could take a good look at the city. The La Fonda Hotel and other old buildings added charm to this old city. Along the narrow streets, Mexican merchants had put up stalls from which they sold souvenirs such as Indian dolls and woven goods. It reminded me of the scenes at Japanese tourist resorts.

The United States of America is a country that was built by immigrants. Races from all over the world live in specific regions of this country. Germans are predominant in the north, Negroes and French in the south, British and Italians in the east. From what I observed, the states of Tennessee and Louisiana are inhabited, for the most part, by the French and in the case of Wisconsin and Montana by Germans. To us Japanese, all Europeans look very similar, but in the city of Santa Fe I saw many Mexican Americans. Spanish was spoken here, and many place names were also in Spanish. I felt as if I were in South America. I cannot help but think that the United States is a huge country of many ethnic cultures.

Since I was no longer coughing up phlegm and my x-ray showed nothing serious, it was agreed that I would be discharged from the hospital. My stay, however, was extended when kind and prudent Dr. Teiichi Furukochi insisted that he would need a few more days to give me injections to make sure I was completely recovered. Even if I were to be discharged, I would not be going home to where my family waited, but back to the barracks where dozens of guys lived together. I really preferred to stay in the hospital, where the food was better and I did not have to go back and forth to the mess hall. Dr. Furukochi's injections made me happy, as if killing two birds with one stone.

Our Long-Awaited Return to Hawai'i Draws Near

With our long-awaited return to Hawai'i approaching, the inspection of our baggage began, and it was my misfortune to have hurt my back at this time.

Everyone in the Hawai'i group was too busy packing his personal belongings to help me with mine. Several young Tule Lake men, who were scheduled to return to Japan, were housed in my barracks. In the past, they often had done things for me without my asking, because I had helped them out with baseball games. Now that I did not believe in Japan's victory as they did, I was sure they would not help me even if I asked. A few young internees from Peru were also in my barracks, but I did not expect them to help me, for they also were among the victory believers. However, a young man named Hiroshi Yamamoto from my hometown unexpectedly offered to pack my bags, and I gratefully accepted. It was such a relief, much like meeting a Buddha in hell.

The Santa Fe Internment Camp was the last place where we lived. We had experienced much in this camp during the one-and-a-half years from April 1944 to November 1945, and we were overcome by deep emotions when we realized that we were about to leave. During our four-year internment, there were some men of religion who had been denounced by the internees. Yet, there were many others who devoted themselves to helping us in various ways.

Men Who Devoted Themselves to Helping Others

I would like to express my sincere gratitude to some of the many dedicated gentlemen who played a memorable part in my internment experience.

Dr. Akio Kimura: From December 1941 until we were sent to the Mainland in February 1942, the doctor served as our spokesman and worked in a tiny room at the Honolulu INS Office, caring for those who had suffered mental collapse. He continued to serve as doctor and spokesman for our group aboard the ship that transported us to the Mainland and then at Camp McCoy in Wisconsin and Camp Forrest in Tennessee.

Dr. Kazuo Miyamoto: During our early internment days on the Mainland, Dr. Miyamoto helped to calm our nerves by giving talks every evening, taking up interesting topics based on the military commentaries of Hanson Baldwin and Walter Lippman.

Rev. Hisanori Kano: Reverend Kano had owned a farm in Nebraska and had been involved in private evangelical work before the war. He was cheerful and energetic and did not look like a missionary at all. He once conducted an agriculture class and took us on a field study outside the camp, ostensibly to observe the plants and animals in the area. In reality, he simply wanted to provide us with a diversion, a chance to take our minds off our troubles. We appreciated his thoughtfulness.

Dr. Masayoshi Tanaka: Stern and blunt, Dr. Tanaka was not popular among the internees. However, besides being skilled as a doctor, he had a deep sense of responsibility. He was conscientious in caring for his patients.

Dr. Teiichi Furukochi: As a doctor, this man was of perfect virtue. He was mild in manner, unlike many other men from the Kantō region. Kind to all, he was well liked and respected. I understand that when he practiced in El Paso, he would tell those who were too poor to pay their bills to do so when they could afford to, which made him very much appreciated by his Mexican patients. Although gentle in his ways, he had a strong sense of justice. When two internees, Toshiro Kobata and Hirotaro Isomura, were shot to death at the Lordsburg camp, he refused to complete their death certificates in the way the authorities demanded.[120]

Dr. Yukihide Kohatsu: From Sand Island until our return to Hawaiʻi, gentle and kind Dr. Kohatsu cared for us as if he were our family doctor. His sincere attention to our medical concerns made us feel very secure.

Takaichi Saiki and Totaro Matsui: When administrative control of the Missoula camp was transferred from the military to the

Department of Justice, Mr. Saiki became our first spokesman. He energetically negotiated with the camp director to reduce our labor assignments. When we were transferred to Santa Fe, he was asked to be our assistant spokesman and secretary, and he was later promoted to spokesman. He tactfully handled many difficult issues that arose among the internees.

Mr. Matsui had come from Japan and became a banker in Hawai'i. He was active mainly in the Japanese community, but he knew the ways of Americans. He was reasonable, yet assertive, in his dealings with the administration. Because he always fulfilled his obligations, he earned the trust of the administration, and as a result, we enjoyed some unexpected benefits. To name a few, we were allowed to go fishing outside the camp twice a week, play golf outside the camp, buy beer at the canteen, and have staff members procure special items for us from Missoula stores. Because of these benefits, over time we started to feel as if we were not interned.

Ichikuro Kondo: Mr. Kondo, who was more than sixty years old, had run a farm in Salinas, California. Good natured and sincere, he worked as our spokesman in Santa Fe for four terms, an unmatched accomplishment.

Takashi Koyama and Takegoro Kusao: Mr. Koyama and Mr. Kusao were instrumental in publishing our internee directories and newspapers, beginning in our Lordsburg days. They not only provided us with the daily news, they also recorded our history, which is now considered precious. I was able to write the Santa Fe chapter of this book with more accuracy, thanks to the camp directories and the *Santa Fe Jihō*.

Heightened Emotions as Our Departure Draws Near

Our four years as internees, when I think of it, were truly a long nightmare. From the time of my sudden arrest at about four o'clock on the afternoon of December 7, 1941, I became like a domesticated animal, with no free will, not knowing my destination, having no purpose—simply moving my feet according to orders. At long last, it had come time to say good-bye to this kind of life.

A man's emotions change with his circumstances. Where previously I had thought of nothing else but the desire to return to Hawai'i, now that I was sure that I was going home, I began to feel anxious about trivial matters. I looked forward to seeing our youngest daughter, who had been four years old when I left. At the same time, I worried that she had forgotten me and that I would scare her. I had once read an article in the *Santa Fe Jihō* about a parolee returning home, who had been disappointed when his daughter, very young at the time of their separation, would not approach him and kept her distance.

I also was somewhat uneasy about how well I would be accepted by the Hawai'i community when I returned to the islands, my second home. Nevertheless, I considered myself very fortunate to be able to return home safely. I felt deeply about those who had died and for whom funeral services had been held while in the camps. They were Kanesaburo Oshima of Kona, Itsuo Inasaki of Spreckelsville,[121] Gosaku Masuda of Lahaina, Masao Sogawa of Honolulu, Nizo Nishizaki of Pepe'ekeo, Kinzaemon Odachi of Hilo,[122] Buntaro Nakahara of Wai'anae, and Hiroshi Tahara of Pāpa'ikou.

Throughout our long internment, I often gazed at the moon[123] and the mountains, thinking of my homeland and my beloved family in Hawai'i. Eventually, the experiences of the monotonous life behind barbed wire would become an unforgettable memory. Perhaps man is by nature good. Four years of internment made me realize that we tend to forget bitter and painful episodes, but long remember the joyful and happy times.

Being a good-natured man, I think it's all right.

Good-Bye, Santa Fe

On October 25, 1945, frost covered the roofs of the barracks, and the snow on the Sangre de Cristo Mountains shone brightly, creating a beautiful scene. Up until now, we had never been fully informed of plans, but this day was an exception. For the first time, we were told in advance through our spokesman's office that the Hawai'i group would leave camp on October 30 for Seattle, where we would board a ship bound for Honolulu. We were also told that each of us could withdraw up to thirty dollars from our savings, if we wanted money while in camp. The remainder of our money, according to the internee administration, would be disbursed in Seattle. There were 327 in our Hawai'i group, with 170 of us returning to O'ahu, 81 to the Big Island, 43 to Maui, and 33 to Kaua'i.

On the evening of October 26, our group held a meeting in the lower area mess hall to resolve some important matters. Kango Kawasaki was appointed spokesman, with Sawajiro Ozaki and Takeo Miyagi representing the O'ahu group, Kazuto Taketa the Kaua'i group, Kosuke Hirose the Maui group, and Masaichiro Shinoda the Big Island group. Minoru Murakami was chosen secretary. Each internee was to receive nine dollars in profit from canteen sales. We also resolved to collect one dollar from each internee for contributions to various departments and for the miscellaneous expenses we would incur during our trip. Lastly, we agreed to solicit additional money in case there was a shortage. Everyone was relieved that all of these items were resolved quickly.

There was a great deal of activity on the following day, October 27, with many people bidding farewell to friends, asking for autographs, or celebrating in the beer hall their approaching return home. The camp was in a festive mood. Those not leaving with us looked dejected, and I could not find the adequate words to comfort them. Yet, it was just a matter of time before they, too, would be going home. Those to be most pitied were the internees who had died behind the barbed wire.

The day finally came when we were to depart. We were held in the recreation hall where our personal belongs were checked. At two o'clock in the afternoon, we boarded our buses and left the camp. Everyone appeared very relieved, as we looked from outside at the camp that held so many memories.

Our group of 327 boarded a train at the Santa Fe station and headed north for our 1,500-mile journey. Unlike in the past, we were in high spirits, for we were going home. As we passed through Las Vegas, we ate our dinner of sandwiches that we had brought from camp. And then we soon fell asleep. Our train arrived in Denver early in the morning of October 31. We had passed through there twice before, first on our way to Camp McCoy and then when we went from Missoula to Santa Fe. Denver was one of the busiest cities and the largest distribution center west of the Mississippi. In the station yard, many overpasses crisscrossed the railroad tracks, and the traffic was smoothly controlled, as was typical of large stations. Here our train was switched to the northbound line and coupled with a dining car. We then headed north into Wyoming. We reached a plateau after ascending a desert-like plain. The whole area was still covered in snow.

| **13** |

On Our Way Back to Hawai'i

Northwest through Kamikōchi[1] in Autumn

Although the air was cold, the constant jostling of the train made us hungry. Today, we enjoyed a delicious lunch served by Negro waiters in white uniforms. Instead of the usual margarine, we were given butter, and what with the coffee and ice cream being top grade, we all went on an eating spree. Every other time we had been on the train, going from one place to another, it had been difficult to sit for the entire three or four days of travel. However, we had always enjoyed delicious meals, like those served at hotels. Comparing the pros and cons, the traveling was not so bad.

Our train traveled westward across the Green River. In the early morning of November 1, we reached Pocatello (such a strange name), where Idaho State University is located. We passed the famous American Falls Reservoir and arrived in Minidoka. I had heard that the Hunt Relocation Center was located here.[2] Of course, we were not able to stop and look at the camp.

Here the plains extended to the horizon with not a human in sight. We proceeded along the Snake River, which on a map winds like a snake, but up close is as wide as a lake, so that you cannot see the curves of the river.

We crossed the Oregon border at about two o'clock in the afternoon and arrived in Huntington, by way of the Idaho towns of Twin Falls, Mountain Home, Nampa, and Weiser. We passed through mountain ranges and gorges that emerged before us, one after the other. Most of the foliage had begun to turn red amid the evergreens, creating a beautiful scene.

Darkness fell as we approached Baker, Oregon. The train crossed a long bridge spanning the Columbia River near Portland and entered the state of Washington on the morning of November 2. Through the thick fog, I saw what appeared to be a somewhat tropical land of dense green grass. I learned that this was because of the warm current that ran along the coastline.

We passed through Tacoma at nine-thirty in the morning and finally arrived at Seattle Station. I wondered what was going to happen next. After a while, buses arrived and took us to a large building that looked like a hotel. It turned out to be the INS building. Half of our group remained in the building, while the rest, myself included, were taken to the seaman's club located on the northern shore. Buses took us to the INS building for meals, and we enjoyed the ride like tourists as we were driven through the busy streets of the city.

The City of Seattle

Our quarters were located on a scenic point with a commanding view of Puget Sound. The seaman's club was equipped with pool tables, and the doors of our rooms were kept unlocked. Since we were not allowed to wander freely, we looked forward to the mealtime drives to the INS building.

It was not only the Santa Fe group who took their meals there, but also internees from the Amache Relocation Center and parolees from New York and Chicago, such as Yoichi Hata, Ryuten Kashiwa, Taichi Sato, Hajime Nishimoto, Usaku Morihara, Aisuke Kuniyuki, and Shigeki Yamada. We exchanged stories about our experiences after having parted. They bought *matsutake* mushrooms and Yakima apples from the vendors in town and shared them with us. I enjoyed juicy Yakima apples again for the first time since tasting them two years earlier in Missoula. Enjoying treats provided only by some from among their INS group pricked the conscience of the others, and so everyone chipped in two dollars and asked Mr. Nishimoto to buy prawns, fish cake, raw oysters, and Japanese pickles. They enjoyed a Japanese meal once a day, but those of us who were staying at the seaman's club were left out of the feast. I guess a good thing never happens twice.

On Monday, November 5, the district chief of the INS handed out our embarkation permits. In addition, Santa Fe internees were given the balance of their savings in brand new bills. It totaled some $75,000. Individual payments ranged from as much as $1,300 to as little as forty cents. The majority of us received $200 to $300. An INS inspector, curious about how internees had managed to save such large sums of money, asked Spokesman Kawasaki for an explanation.

"Most of the money was sent by our families," he replied. Apparently the inspector still appeared puzzled.

Perhaps Japanese and Caucasians would behave differently in a situation like ours. Caucasians seemed unable to understand how we had managed.

Boarding the Military Transport Ship *Yarmouth*

On November 7, a light snowfall covered the grass on the shore. Snow was piled on the roofs of cars that approached from further inland. At eleven-thirty in the morning, we boarded the *Yarmouth*, a military transport vessel. As usual, we were put through various inspections, and the ship left port at about four o'clock.

The distance to Honolulu was 2,500 nautical miles. On board the ship with us were about three hundred internees from various camps, as well as soldiers returning to Hawai'i. Among them was Master Sergeant Takanishi, the son of Kazuichi Takanishi of Kekaha, Kaua'i, who had been interned for four years and was going back to Hawai'i along with us. It was a very emotional reunion. The sight of a grown man tearfully hugging his elderly father was so heartwarming that even those of us watching became a little teary.

Surprised by the Bounty of Food Onboard Ship

For nine days, from the time we left Santa Fe on October 30, we had been treated like hotel guests, as far as meals were concerned. But now, because we were on a military ship, we were placed under supervision once again. Cooking, KP, and cleaning became our responsibilities once more.

Since the beginning of 1945, our camp meals had been quite meager. The quality of the rice and fresh vegetables had grown poorer, and meat had been available only once a week, with ox brains sometimes substituted for beef. We had presumed that America was suffering from a shortage of food. However, the situation was entirely different on the military ship. We were provided with unopened one-hundred-pound bags of sugar and generous supplies of meat, cream, and other staples. Leftover food was simply thrown into the ocean. The United States is indeed a wealthy country, I thought to myself.

Since smoking was not allowed in the mess and the cabins, we all went out in the cold onto the deck to smoke. Some men fixed their gaze on Puget Sound, which was said to have seventy-seven inlets. But the real reason for their interest may have been because victory believers had spread the rumor that Japanese warships were anchored in Seattle harbor. Naturally, they were unable to find any ships flying Japanese flags.

Although they were very confident that the truth of Japan's victory would be revealed upon our arrival in Honolulu, they nevertheless looked somewhat dispirited.

On board with us were Manzuchi Hashimoto, Sueji Iwasa, Koichiro Nakamura, Tetsuo Toyama, and Shozaemon Masaki, all of whom had been paroled earlier. We grasped each other's hands and congratulated one another on our safe return. On the passenger list was Rev. Masahiro Himeno, who had been paroled and admitted to Harvard University. He had been my English teacher and a good fishing companion while we were in Missoula, and I had hoped to see him. But for some reason, he was not onboard, and I was disappointed.

Soon after reaching the open ocean, most of us became seasick. Hardly anyone could work at KP duty, but the kitchen workers worked very hard to cover the labor shortage. I appreciated their efforts very much. Ladies and children from the free zones and the Family Camp were assigned to cabins and a separate mess. When mothers became seasick and remained in bed, their children happily played among themselves. We, men, may have become sick, but our vigor was not lost, for the joy of returning to Hawai'i.

On ship we could buy cigarettes very cheaply like the servicemen could. The price for a carton of Camel cigarettes was only sixty cents and other brands were fifty cents, whereas it would cost fifteen cents a pack in town. Smokers were so happy, and they rushed to buy cigarettes, even though there was a limit of three cartons per person.

Dear Old Honolulu

On the fourth day, the sea became a little calmer as we sailed southward. Some passengers got out of bed and went onto the deck. It was announced that we were seven hundred nautical miles to Honolulu and that our estimated arrival was at two-thirty in the afternoon of November 13, as originally scheduled.

Tuesday, November 13. This was the day when we were to arrive in Honolulu. I rose early and went to the deck and looked toward the southwest. Although I could not see anything, I noticed that the color of the ocean had changed to a deeper blue, and I realized the ship was nearing Hawai'i.

At ten-fifty in the morning, we finally saw the silhouette of an island on the horizon. Oh, Hawai'i. We had yearned for you for four long years. Our faint hope had become reality. The hours dragged on as the ship inched its way toward the lush green island where our families waited. As the news spread, the deck filled with passengers. We behaved like people on a ship heading for Japan, rushing to the deck when they hear that Mount Fuji can be seen.

Several warships and steamships were visible in the waters near O'ahu. Someone said he saw a flag that looked like the Hinomaru[3] flying from one of the ships. Impossible, I thought. But I was unable to remain indifferent, and I looked about with my eyes wide open. I wondered if a trace of wishful thinking was still somewhere deep in my heart.

The ship sailed past Makapu'u Point and Koko Head on the right, as it made its way toward Honolulu Harbor. At a little after two o'clock, we finally docked at Pier 26, from where we had left for the Mainland four years earlier. Swedish Consul Olson and his staff, INS inspectors, and Emergency Service Committee members Isao Murai, Masatoshi Katagiri, Katsuro Miho, and others came aboard to help with the landing procedures. As usual, gangway passes were distributed in alphabetical other. We also were given release orders typed in an official format, instead of the temporary ones that we had been carrying.

Thus, we were finally cleared of all the charges against us.

Back Home with Our Families after Four Years

With the disembarkation taking place alphabetically, I was able to get off the ship quickly. Among the crowd who had come to greet us, the first people I saw were my wife and youngest daughter, Yoko. The daughter, who I had worried might forget me, had grown, and she rushed to me and hugged me tightly. She put lei over me, calling happily, "Papa, Papa." Relief and pent-up emotions brought tears to my eyes, and I was left speechless. My wife, Jun, appeared exhausted, having gone through the difficulties of the last four years. I was greatly relieved to see that our sons, Hanzo, the eldest; Seizo, the third; Keiichi, the fourth; and Tomochi, the fifth, had grown up respectably.[4]

After exchanging firm handshakes with my friends, we headed for home with Hanzo driving the car. Words cannot describe my happiness that night as I sat down to dinner at a table decorated with flowers, looking upon the faces of my family after so long.

A Taste of Home

After dinner, there was so much to talk about that I had no idea where to start, so we decided to let my wife ask the questions. Once I started, I talked endlessly. It was past midnight, and so we agreed to end the first chapter of the story and go to bed.

I woke up the next morning after a sound sleep. Bright morning sunlight was shining through the windows of my bedroom. I turned to my side but there were no beds of my barracks mates. Oh, yes, this is my home.

For breakfast, I had papaya and fragrant Kona coffee, bacon and eggs, and hotcakes. I was overcome by a feeling of gratitude to no one in particular.

I stepped out into the garden and saw the blooming hedge of hibiscus. In the hothouse out in the back, winter-blooming orchids were in their glory.

My children were healthy and so happy to have their father back home. Be it ever so humble, there is absolutely no place like home.

I have added here some of my haiku written in Santa Fe as a record of my life there.

Haiku from Santa Fe

1944
SPRING

Row upon row of barracks
Engulfed
In a thick cloud of yellow dust
天地ただ黄塵バラックの並んだ風景

On green branches
We all dry our cups
Spring is in the air
青む枝へみんながカップを干すので春

Butterflies and leek flowers
Signs of spring
I, too, changed into spring clothes
蝶々葱坊主わたしも着物を更へた

Tips of cucumber vines
Reach for the sun
Becoming flowers
陽へ手をのばした胡瓜が花になる

Beneath a clear sky
Buffeted by the winds
On the hill
The flagpole stands
吹いて吹いて晴れきった丘の旗棹

SUMMER

On this cool evening
A grown man studies
A busy ant nest
夕べは涼しく大の男が蟻の巣を見ている

Thundering Pueblo festival drums
Welcome the rising moon
月の出頃のプエブロの祭の太鼓

Thrown from the dark clouds below me
A lightning bolt strikes the earth
眼下一帯の黒雲から電光地を刺す

Early flowers bloom on the hill
Encouraged by the closeness of the sun
丘は陽が近くて土には花が咲いている

In the cool of the morning
Sparrows edge close to me
朝は涼しく雀らわたしに近よる

AUTUMN

Color on the mountain slopes
Autumn is around the corner, it seems
秋がそこまで来たらしい山腹の色です

Endlessly
Hills of young pines
Under the clear skies
どこまで行っても小松の丘で晴れきった空

Under the autumn sky
Internees leave camp
Paroled
秋空、パロールで出て行く人々

Done with KP duty for today
The mountains in their autumn splendor
今日のKPもすんだ、山は秋晴れ

Smoke from my cigarette drifts
Into the depths of the sky
わたしの煙草のけむりの空の深さである

Blooming dahlia and cosmos
Even in our camp on the plateau
Autumn
ダリア、コスモス高原の配所も秋です

Is this how we enter our declining years
Like the evening clouds?
ここでかうして晩年に入るのか、夕雲

How many more years
Walking along the fence?
Leaves fall again
柵に沿うて歩く暮しも何年か木の葉散る

WINTER

Packs of wailing coyotes pass by
The Big Dipper looms in the deep night
カヨテ啼き過ぎて夜更の七つ星

The moon and a few stars
Frozen in the sky
月と、星が三つ四つ凍っている

The moon and Venus align and shine
Is this a sign of peace?
はたして平和の兆しか月星並びかがやく

1945

Snow disappears and breezes begin
Butterflies might as well be back
雪もなくなると風、蝶でもとんで来さうな

Spring breezes
Even rocks are sprouting
はるかぜ、石も芽ぐんでいる

Birds chirping here and there
One even perches on the barbed wire
囀りあちこち一羽はバブワイアに来ている

A dirt-covered sparrow
Bathes in the spring rain
煤け雀よい春雨で浴びている

My flower garden is lush
Butterflies come visiting today
繁って私の花畑けふは蝶々が来た

A cool breeze fans the flowers
Three hummingbirds visit
花に涼しい風が出て蜂雀が三つも来た

From inside the fence
We watch the victory fireworks
柵の中から戦勝の煙火あがるを見ている

A message that peace has come
A fine, yet empty, autumn day
平和が来たといふ空はうつろな秋晴るるばかり

VOYAGE HOME

The color of the sea
The flying fish
We are nearing Hawai'i
海の色や飛魚やハワイへ近づく

The blue of the sea deepens
I may soon see my islands
海が更に碧くなり島が見えさうな

Among the many to welcome me home
My wife and children surround me
出迎えの人のなか妻子にかこまれている

THE RETURN HOME

Flowers, even in the hedges,
I enjoy my meal in my dear old home
外の垣にも花の我家でご飯をいただく

I awaken from sleep
I am really home
目ざめてみてもわが家

The Rest of Our Group Returns

I have told my story up to the day when I came home. However, I would be at fault if I did not write about the forty-two internees who stayed behind in Santa Fe. Before I finish this work, I would like to write down what happened to them and what I know of the Family Camp.

I heard that some members of the group had become so discouraged about being left behind and the uncertainty of their release that they suffered nervous breakdowns. I would have felt that same way if I had been in their position.

At the end of November, the forty-two internees and the three who had reconsidered their requests for repatriation—a total of forty-five people—were notified that they were to return to Hawai'i. There were scheduled to leave Santa Fe on December 2. The officers of the group were:

Spokesman	Hatsuichi Toishigawa
Vice Spokesman	Tsuneichi Yamamoto
Accountant	Katsuichi Kawamoto
Secretary	Yoshio Yoshioka

These four men took on leadership roles in the group and finally began making their way home. In contrast to the northwesterly route we had taken, this group went south. They boarded their ship in Los Angeles and arrived in Honolulu on December 8, twenty-five days after we did. Their trip was shorter and the ocean calmer because of the route they took. Things cannot go wrong twice, I thought.

The Family Camp

The Family Camp was built to house internees who had expressed their desire to return to Japan with their families. The camp was located in Crystal City at the southern tip of Texas. It was originally meant for Mexican seasonal laborers, so cottages for families were added later.

In August 1942, 137 dependants of Hawai'i internees were moved to the Mainland, escorted by Dr. and Mrs. Isao Murai. They first stayed at the Grove Park Inn in North Carolina for eight months. Then, they were transferred to the Assembly Inn for another four months. Because Americans are respectful of women, they received first class treatment on the ship and trains, and they stayed at the best hotels.[5]

They were transferred to the Family Camp in Crystal City in August 1943. Some joined husbands or fathers who had arrived at Crystal City earlier. On September 1, some of the families departed from New York aboard the SS *Gripsholm* for repatriation to Japan. Those families who were unable to board the second exchange ship had no choice but to stay in the Family Camp for the duration of the war.

Male internees who had lived in the other camps moved to the Family Camp and now lived happily together with their families. They enjoyed a semi-free life in the camp and lived independently. They were able to buy food and other daily necessities with coupons provided by the camp administration. The amount was so generous that they could even buy expensive suits and hats and even some accessories for the ladies.

There was a public school within the camp, where not only Japanese and English were taught, but also handicrafts. The Japanese language teachers were selected from among the internees. It was said that life in the Family Camp was better than that in the relocation centers.

Internees from the Family Camp returned to Hawai'i a month after us, on December 10, 1945.

And so, in 1946, most of the internees were able to celebrate New Year's Day at home with their families, enjoying *toso* and *zōni*.[6]

The New Year has arrived,[7] and in our hearts we are at peace.

Postscript

The bombing of Pearl Harbor, which marked the beginning of the war between the United States and Japan, prompted the detention of most of the influential Japanese in Hawai'i. Incarcerated on the Mainland, they were moved from camp to camp.

Keiho Soga has already published a book, *Tessaku Seikatsu*, about his internment experiences. However, because Mr. Soga was sent with the fifth group of internees, his book does not cover the very early days of the Mainland internment.[1]

I was sent to the Mainland with the first group and spent time in camps as far north as Wisconsin and Montana and as far south as Tennessee, New Mexico, and Louisiana. Mr. Soga and I did not live in the same camp until I moved to my last camp in Santa Fe, where I spent many days with him. Because my experiences differed from Mr. Soga's, I decided to write a series of articles about it for *The Hawaii Times*. The series ran for a period of two years.

My original intention was to write essays on topics that might interest my readers. However, many readers asked me to provide a detailed record of my experiences. It would please me greatly if my writing helps to enrich the history of the Japanese in Hawai'i.

While in camp, I did not plan to write a book, and I did not keep any record of my incarceration other than my haiku. By referring to works like Mr. Soga's *Tessaku Seikatsu*, the *Santa Fe Jihō*, camp directories, Ensign Sakamaki Kazuo's *Horyo dai-ichigo*, and Private First Class Obinata Aoi's *Makkoi byōin*, I was able to write the stories fairly accurately.[2]

Totaro Matsui, Rev. Joei Oi, Tomoaki Nakamura, and Soichi Obata kindly provided documents and photographs. Some readers corrected errors of fact and others provided suggestions, which I have incorporated.

I would like to express my sincere appreciation to Rev. Joei Oi, Rev. Masahiro Himeno, and Totaro Matsui, who provided the forewords for this
book, and also to Bunshiro Furukawa who illustrated the cover.[3]

Suikei Furuya
May 1964

Author's Profile

Kumaji Furuya 古屋熊次   Suikei Furuya 古屋翠渓 (pen name)

Born   February 22, 1889

        Kawaguchi village, Kawaguchi lakeshore

        Minami Tsuru district, Yamanashi prefecture[1]

        Second son of Furuya Iwakichi and Nobu

Graduated from elementary school; moved to Hawai'i at age eighteen.

Worked for plantations and stores for five years.

1919 to 1963: managed furniture stores, held various positions, including:

        Chairman of the Board, Palama Youth Association
        Chairman of the Board, Kalihi Education Foundation
        President, Honolulu Japanese Merchants Association
        Vice President, Hawai'i United Japanese Society
        President, Honolulu Japanese Chamber of Commerce and
            Industry
        President and owner, Fuji Furniture, Inc.
        Chairman of the Board, Kuakini Hospital and Home
        Chairman of the Board, Central Kalihi Neighborhood Friendship
            Association
        Chairman of the Board, Yamanashi Club of Hawai'i

December 7, 1941, 4 p.m.: Arrested by the FBI

For four years, until November 1945: interned in various Mainland camps

Currently,[2] president of Hawaiian State Enterprises, Inc. (State Furniture) and executive vice president of Pacific Suppliers, Inc.

Other positions include:

> Member of the Board of Directors, The Hawai'i Times, Inc.
> Member of the Board of Trustees, Honolulu Japanese Chamber of Commerce
> Chairman, Central Kalihi Scholarship Foundation
> Advisor, Yamanashi Club of Hawai'i

Interests include: writing, reading, the theater, sports, Noh songs, the game of *go*; haiku writing for many years; authored a book of poems titled, Ruten.

* * *

Kumaji Suikei Furuya died on November 4, 1977, in Honolulu at the age of eighty-eight.

Moon over the Camp
(a short song)

Leaving green islands to travel thousands of miles
Across oceans and mountains
We arrive in America, far, far north,
The land buried in snow.

Surrounded by high barbed wire,
Without even a penny,
A summer hat in the snow,
Canadian winds penetrate my soul.

A bright moon, a clear evening sky
Thinking of my beloved family
Left behind in a faraway place
Who knows my aching heart?

Yet, when I think of the thousands in the world
Suffering more than I
The snow on my shoes feels lighter
As I wait for peace to return.

小曲　配所の月

緑の島を後にして
海山越ゆる幾千里
着いた所はアメリカの
雪にうもれし北の果て

鉄柵高く囲む中
身に一仙の金もなく
夏帽かぶる雪の中
カナダ嵐が身にしみる

月皎皎と冴ゆる空
想いは遠く残したる
愛しきものの上に馳す
ああ誰か知るこの心

されども世界幾万の
人の特牲を思う時
わが身に軽し靴の雪
待つは来服平和の日

Appendix A

In the Case of Kumaji Furuya

RECORD OF THE HEARINGS OF A BOARD OF OFFICERS AND CIVILIANS CONVENED PURSUANT TO PARAGRAPH 33, SPECIAL ORDERS NO. 320, HEADQUARTERS, HAWAIIAN DEPARTMENT, DATED AT FORT SHAFTER, T.H., 19 DECEMBER 1941.*

IN THE CASE OF

KUMAJI FURUYA

[signed, Kumaji Furuya]

ISN-HJ-188-CI

REPORT OF PROCEEDINGS OF A BOARD OF OFFICERS AND CIVILIANS

Proceedings of a Board of Officers and Civilians which convened at Honolulu, T.H., pursuant to paragraph 33 of Special Orders No. 320, Headquarters, Hawaiian Department, Fort Shafter, T.H., 19 December, 1941, as amended by paragraph 6 of Special Orders No. 326, Headquarters, Hawaiian Department, 25 December, 1941, as amended by paragraph 26, Special Orders No. 332, Headquarter, Hawaiian Department, Fort

---

* Kumaji Furuya, Alien Case File, A002-426-398, Accession 085-12-001, Box 163, Immigration and Naturalization Service, National Archives and Records Administration, College Park, Maryland. Furuya's Case File was scanned by Adriana Marroquin of the Angel Island Immigration Station Foundation and generously shared with JCCH for the purposes of this book.

Shafter, T.H., 31 December, 1941, copies of which are attached hereto as Exhibit A, A-1 and A-2.

The Board met pursuant to the foregoing order at 9:30 a.m., at Honolulu, T.H., on 24 January, 1942.

Members present:

> Mr. Edward N. Sylva, President
> Mr. David Y. K. Akana
> Mr. Mark A. Robinson
> First Lieut. Blaine E. Anderson, FA., Executive and Recorder

The Board Recorder and Reporter were sworn; the Board was sworn.

PURPOSE: The hearing of evidence and making recommendations as to internment of enemy aliens, dual citizens and citizens.

KUMAJI FURUYA, the internee, appeared without counsel.

The order appointing the Board and the substance of the regulations under which it was convened were read aloud by the Recorder.

Warrant of Arrest was received and read in evidence and is hereunto appended as Exhibit B.

Except when Government witnesses were being heard, the internee, KUMAJI FURUYA, was present during all open sessions of the Board, was afforded full opportunity to present evidence in his own behalf, have counsel, to testify in person or submit a written statement, and to submit a brief.

RECORDER: The Board is prepared to hear the Government's testimony in this case.

JOHN HAROLD HUGHES, Special Agent, Federal Bureau of Investigation, was called as a witness, and being first duly sworn, testified as follows:

Q   (By Recorder) State your full name, official capacity, and from what Government agency you are submitting evidence.
A   John Harold Hughes, Special Agent, Federal Bureau of Investigation.

Q   Is your evidence given from official records of that bureau?
A   Yes.

Q   Will you present the Government's case in the matter of Kumaji Furuya?
A   Kumaji Furuya, 811 Gulick Avenue, Honolulu.

He is vice-president of the United Japanese Society of Honolulu, which is predominantly an alien organization and pro-Japanese in sympathy and the most influential Japanese organization on the island of Oahu. He is also vice-president of the Honolulu Japanese Chamber of Commerce, an organization linked with the Japanese United Society and having similar aims and purposes

He was elected president of the Kalihi Educational Foundation, Honolulu, on September 28, 1940. This organization sets the policies and acts as a member of the Kalihi Japanese School. He was on the list furnished by the Japanese consul-general of Honolulu of prominent Japanese who were invited to a tea given by the Officers Club at Pearl Harbor in honor of vice-admiral Zengo Yoshida.

In 1936 he was appointed to the headquarters committee and general affairs committee for the squadron reception of the Japanese Naval Training Squadron Iwate-Yakumo. He appears in a photograph of the United Japanese Society and again at the Japanese consul-general's quarters on April 27, 1937.

At this time he was auditor for the United Japanese Society. He was elected second vice-president of the Japanese Chamber of Commerce on February 12, 1939. He is treasurer and manager of the Fuji Furniture Company, Limited. That was as of 1940. He is very prominent in Japanese circles.

Q   (By Recorder) Is he an alien Japanese?
A   Yes. I do not have the date of his birth here; I don't have his age. He is from Yamanashi-ken, Japan.

That is the substance of the Government's information on this case.

RECORDER: This case is recessed.

(24 January, 1942, 9:35 a.m., this case was recessed)

———————————

(24 January, 1942, 10:43 a.m. All members of the Board being present, the recorder and reporter being present; the Board, recorder and reporter having been previously duly sworn, the following proceedings were had:)

(Forrest Garnett was duly sworn as Japanese interpreter.)

KUMAJI FURUYA, internee, was called as a witness, and testified through the Japanese interpreter as follows:

Q   (By Recorder) What is your name?
A   Kumaji Furuya.

Q   Spell it.
A   K-u-m-a-j-i F-u-r-u-y-a.

Q   This is your Japanese name?
A   Yes.

Q   Do you have a haole (American) name?
A   No.

Q   Were you served with this warrant of arrest this morning?
A   Yes.

Q   This military hearing is accorded you as a matter of justice. You may testify for yourself under oath, without being placed under oath, or you may submit a written statement as to your feelings or actions. Which do you choose?
A   I will take oath.

(At this point the internee was duly sworn as a witness through the Japanese interpreter and testified as follows:)

Q   (By Recorder) Your character is not at issue in this hearing, but if you desire you may call witnesses to testify as to your feelings or actions. Do you want any witnesses?
A   Yes, I would like to call a witness.

Q   Do you want an attorney, at your own expense?
A   No need.

Q   What is your occupation?
A   Manager, Fuji Furniture Company, Limited.

Q   What is your citizenship?
A   Japanese.

Q   Are you married?
A   Yes.

Q   Do you have any children?
A   Yes.

Q   How many?
A   Four boys, one girl.

Q   Are they here or in Japan?
A   All here.

Q   Are they dual citizens?
A   The first child is expatriated.

Q   The rest of them are dual?
A   The other two have not been registered at the Japanese consul, they are full American citizens. My oldest son is at the University of Hawaii now and in the R.O.T.C.

RECORDER: The president of the Board has some questions he would like to ask you.

Q   (By Board) Have you ever served with the Japanese armed forces?
A   No.

Q   Have you any relatives or friends now serving with the Japanese armed forces?
A   No, I have no relatives in the armed forces. I have only a sister.

Q   A sister in the United States?
A   She is in Japan.

Q   Is she with the armed forces?
A   No.

Q   Have you any friends with the armed forces?
A   No.

Q   Have you ever occupied any position, official or semi-official, with the Japanese Government?
A   No connection whatsoever with the Government.

Q   Have you ever given "imonbukuro"?
A   I have not given comfort kit.

Q   Any members of your family give any comfort kit?
A   My wife gave one three or four years ago.

Q   Who solicited this comfort kit?
A   I don't know.

Q   Have you ever given any money toward the Japanese cause, such as money for sick soldiers, money for families of deceased soldiers, or what like?
A   I donated about $25.

Q   For what particular purpose?
A   For the families of soldiers, comfort.

Q   Who solicited this offering?
A   The Kenjin-kai.

Q   What organization is that and where is it's offices or headquarters?
A   They do not have any office. It is a society for Japanese and we meet about once a year.

Q   Where do they hold their meetings?
A   Sometimes in the tea house and sometimes in the restaurant.

Q   You are a member of this organization?
A   Yes, I am.

Q   Do you ever entertain personnel from the Japanese warships, tankers, passing through Honolulu?
A   I am a member of the—I am on the welcoming committee for ships and I go down to welcome them in. I have not entertained any of the members.

Q   What is the name of this committee?
A   It is a temporary committee composed of when any ships come in.

Q   Who are the officers of this Kenjin-kai?
A   Yoda is the president this year.

Q   How do you spell his name?
A   Y-o-d-a.

Q   What is his first name?
A   Seiji.

Q   What does he do?
A   He runs the City Grill.

Q   Who are the other officers?
A   I don't know.

Q   Have you ever purchased any Japanese war bonds, emergency bonds?
A   No, I have not. I do not own any Japanese bonds.

Q   Do you ever listen to Japanese broadcasts from Japan?
A   Yes, I have listened before.

Q   What is the nature of those broadcasts, talks about the Japanese-Chinese War, about the Japanese side of their expansion in the Pacific?
A   Sometimes I listen to news, sometimes to the music.

Q   The news, what does that consist of, propaganda?
A   Yes, it is news about the war.

Q   News about the Japanese expansion in the Pacific?
A   I have only heard about the Chinese and Japanese War.

Q   And this news broadcast is giving the Japanese side, Japanese justification for their march into China?
A   No. It is about the same as the news which you read in the papers here.

Q   Have you a picture of the Japanese Emperor and Empress in your home?
A   I do not.

Q   Do you have a Japanese flag in your home?

A   Before I had a toy flag.

Q   Where is it now?

A   We have not got it any more.

Q   Japan is now at war with the United States; what side would you like
     to see win this war or which side would you like to see lose it, or you
     have no views on the matter so long as peace is restored?

A   I came here 18 years before and expect to die here; all of my children
     were born here and they are American citizens; they have no connec-
     tion with Japan. I do not possess an American citizenship, but I have
     the same feelings as an American. I have lived here so long that I feel
     it is my country. I have lived here so long and thought of my children's
     future here and I have tried to follow the situation but my brain, as
     you know, was tired and I am so confused mentally about the whole
     thing that I can't say which side I want to see win. All I can hope for
     every day is that there will be peace as soon as possible and former
     conditions will be resumed.

Q   Peace irrespective of which side wins?

A   Since America was—since Japan was first opened by America to for-
     eign trade we have always hoped only for peace, and we simply cannot
     think about which side we want to win. We can only hope that we will
     have peaceful relations.

Q   Is there anything further you would like to say to this Board? Any
     further statement you would like to make to this Board?

A   I have talked with many people since living in this country and I have
     always said that if we are living here that we should follow American
     laws and be law-abiding and be loyal to this country and do the best we
     can to be good citizens of this country, even though we are Japanese.

     Since I have been on Sand Island I received a letter from my two small
     children the other day, and they said that we are at home alone, only
     with our mother and our brother, who is with the R.O.T.C. at the Uni-
     versity of Hawaii, and we wish that you could soon come home to us.

Q   Have you been well treated since you have been here in internment?

A   No one so far has really mistreated us, but in the beginning—now it is
     much better; in the beginning it was a little difficult.

BOARD: I have no further questions.

RECORDER: The internee is excused.

INTEPRETER: He says he has something else he wants to say.

Q (By Board) Do you have anything further you want to say?
A My children are 100 per cent American. As my children are 100 Per cent Americans and they now see their father interned here on Sand Island. I am worried that it might put a cloud in their minds and sort of weaken their loyalty to America.

RECORDER: The internee is excused.

(The internee was excused.)

RECORDER: This case is recessed.

(24 January, 1942, 11:06 a.m. The case was recessed.)

(24 January 1942, 9:05 a.m. All members of the Board being present, the Recorder and Reporter being present; the Board, Recorder, and Reporter having been previously duly sworn, the following proceedings were had:)

RECORDER: Let the record show request by the internee of Eugene Valentine to appear as a witness on his behalf before this Board.

EUGENE VALENTINE was called as a witness on behalf of the internee, KUMAJI FURUYA, and being first duly sworn, testified as follows:

Q (By Recorder) Will you give us your name, address and occupation please?
A Eugene Valentine, 4249 Sierra Drive; business address 647 Kiawe Street, wholesale and general merchandise jobbers.

RECORDER: The President of the Board has some questions he would like to ask you.

Q   (By Board) Do you know the internee, Mr. Furuya?
A   Yes, I do.

Q   How long have you know him?
A   About seventeen or eighteen years.

Q   From what you know of him, your contacts and associations, and so on, have you any statement to make to this Board as to where you believe his loyalty and sympathies lie?
A   Well, that is—

Q   If you have none, that is all right.
A   What I mean, you gentlemen understand that I want to be honest with my country and I want to be honest with Mr. Furuya.

Q   We appreciate that.
A   I would like to elaborate on that, if I could talk to you gentlemen here, but if I have to talk like I were in court, then it would be yes or no. I will explain just the way I feel.

Q   Yes?
A   I think that the man, being Japanese, and so forth, naturally he is Japanese. However, I thought he was loyal to this country, and his actions as I have known them over the last seventeen years, as I say, I think that he is. I do not think that he would do anything against this country. I know in these welfare drives and all those other community activities, he has taken an active part. I do not know anything that would lead me to believe that he would be anything but a loyal citizen, as any other alien might be.

BOARD: We appreciate it very much. Thank you for coming. I have nothing further.

RECORDER: You are warned that the proceedings before this Board are confidential and are not to be divulged to anyone under the severe penalties provided under the Enemy Alien Act of 1917.
You are excused.

BOARD: Thank you for coming.

    (The witness was excused.)

MASAJI MARUMOTO was called as a witness on behalf of the internee, and having been first duly sworn, testified as follows:

RECORDER: Let the record show that the internee requested MASAJI MARUMOTO to appear before this Board as a witness on his behalf.

Q   (By Recorder) Will you give us your name, address and occupation?
A   Masaji Marumoto, 218 Sumitomo Bank Building, Honolulu, T.H.; occupation, attorney-at-law, practicing in Honolulu, T.H.

Q   Your citizenship?
A   Citizen of the United States.

RECORDER: The President of the Board has some questions he would like to ask you.

Q   (By Board) Mr. Marumoto, how long have you known Mr. Furuya?
A   Since 1930.

Q   From what you know of Mr. Furuya, your contacts and your association with him, have you any statement to make to this Board as to where you believe his loyalties and sympathies lie?
A   As far as his loyalty is concerned, being a Japanese subject, I would say that his allegiance is towards Japan. As far as sympathies are concerned, I don't know where the sympathy would be. However, he has been law-abiding all the time that I have known him and his statements have not been anti-American.

BOARD: I have nothing further.

RECORDER: Thank you, Mr. Marumoto, for coming. You are warned that the proceedings before this Board are confidential and are not to be divulged or revealed to anyone under the severe penalties of the Enemy Alien Act of 1917.
You are excused.

(The witness was excused.)

RECORDER: Let the record show that the internee requested Beatrice M. Arita to appear before this Board as a witness on his behalf.

BEATRICE MATSUI ARITA was called as a witness on behalf of the internee, and being first duly sworn, testified as follows:

Q   (By Recorder) Will you state your name, address and occupation please?
A   My name is Mrs. Beatrice Matsui Arita; my address is 951 North King Street. I am bookkeeper for the Fuji Furniture Company.

RECORDER: The President of the Board has some questions he would like to ask you.

Q   (By Board) How long have you known Mr. Furuya?
A   I have know him, worked for him for almost fifteen years.

Q   From what you know of Mr. Furuya, your contacts and your association, and so on, have you any statement to make to this Board?
A   Mr. Furuya is a very good man. I have known him for all those [years] and I have worked for him.

Q   Have you any statement to make as to where you think his loyalties lie, whether he is loyal to the United States or loyal to Japan, or sympathetic towards our cause or the Japanese cause?
A   I think he is very loyal to his American cause. He has helped with everything that is possible for the people.

Q   (By Recorder) Will you state your citizenship, please?
A   I am an American citizen.

Q   You are warned that the proceedings before this Board are confidential and not to be revealed to anyone. The Enemy Alien Act of 1917 provides severe penalties for any violation of this confidence.
A   Yes.

RECORDER: You are excused.

(The witness was excused.)

FINDINGS:

The Board, having carefully considered the evidence before it, finds:

1. That the internee, KUMAJI FURUYA, is a subject of the Empire of Japan;

2. That he is loyal to Japan;

3. That he is not engaged in subversive activities.

RECOMMENDATIONS:

In view of the above findings, the Board recommends that the internee, KUMAJI FURUYA, be interned.

The Board adjourned at 9:20 a.m., on 26 January, 1942.

[signed, Edward N. Sylva]
(President)

[signed, Blaine E. Anderson]
First Lieut., FA., U.S. Army
(Recorder)

[signed, David Akana]
(Member)

[signed, Mark A. Robinson]
(Member)

Appendix B
The Mott Bill
May 9, 1944

"A bill to provide for the deportation of Japanese aliens"*

Sec. 1. That all persons in the United States who on the 7th day of December 1941 were subjects of the Government of Japan and who became enemy aliens of the United States by reason of the declaration of war between the United States and Japan are hereby defined and declared to be undesirable aliens and subject to deportation under the statutes of the United States providing for the deportation of undesirable aliens.

Sec. 2. Within thirty days after the approval of this Act the Attorney General of the United States shall proceed to prepare warrants for the deportation of all undesirable aliens as defined in section 1 of this Act. Such warrants shall be executed and such aliens deported immediately upon the cessation of hostilities between the United States and Japan.

Sec. 3. No undesirable alien as defined in this Act, who has been interned as an enemy alien in the United States, shall be released from internment except for the purpose of deportation under warrant as herein provided.

---

* "A bill to provide for the deportation of Japanese aliens," HR 4779, 78th Congress, 2nd Session, (May 9, 1944).

Appendix C
Letter from Ivan Williams, Officer-in-Charge*
Santa Fe Internment Camp

U.S. Department of Justice
Immigration and Naturalization Service
Santa Fe, New Mexico

March 15, 1945

To Each Internee, Santa Fe Internment Camp, Santa Fe, New Mexico

The purpose of this Memorandum is to dispel any misunderstanding there may exist concerning the position of the Immigration and Naturalization Service and the Administration of this Camp with regard to the activities of certain discordant elements recently transferred here from Tule Lake.

The background of the situation as it pertains to the former Tule Lake residents and the general welfare of this Camp can be summed up briefly as follows:

Since December 30, 1944, 366 persons, all former members of the "Sokuji Kikoku Hoshi Dan" and the "Hokoku Seinen Dan", Japanese organizations at Tule Lake with whose objectives I think you are all familiar, were transferred to this Internment Camp. Prior to the departure from Tule Lake of the first group, the heads of these two organizations were

_____

* Ivan Williams to Each Internee, Santa Fe Internment Camp, 15 March 1945, National Archives, Record Group 85, Entry 308, Box 1300/C, Washington, D.C.

informed by Mr. John Burling, representing the Attorney General, that certain activities of members of this group would no longer be tolerated. Mr. Burling's statements were confirmed by the Attorney General himself.

Upon arriving at this Camp, each internee from Tule Lake was told that militaristic drills and other militaristic demonstrations, including the display of nationalistic emblems would not be permitted. It may be well at this point to state briefly the reasons for this Service's objections to a continuation of the activities mentioned.

The reason for our prohibiting Japanese military training in this Camp should be so obvious as to require no explanation. What do these people take us for!

The wearing of the insignia which adorned the sweatshirts of the Tule Lake group would appear to be harmless enough in itself. However, this emblem has become, as a result of the acts of hoodlumism and worse that have been carried on by at least some of the more rabble rousing members of this group, a symbol of such intolerable activities. We therefore did not propose to permit the flaunting of this symbol any longer. Furthermore, we have been unable to perceive any necessity for these internees to wear or possess these so-called "Rising Sun sweatshirts." If the wearing of this emblem is intended to be a demonstration of loyalty toward Japan staged for the benefit of this Service, it is totally unnecessary. The United States Government has permitted these people to renounce their U.S. citizenship and has formally recognized their loyalty to Japan.

In this connection, it should be observed that the United States was not compelled to take this action. The Government could have continued to regard these people as United States citizens and could have criminally prosecuted many of them for treasonable or seditious acts.

Incidentally, we do not regard loyalty as something than can be worn on a sweatshirt to be taken on and off at will, although this may very well be true of some of the recent wearers of this insignia. We think that loyalty is a quality of entirely different nature and are willing to assume that all internees in this Camp are loyal to their country. We respect that loyalty. However, since it appears to us that insistence upon having and wearing these emblems is not a true demonstration of loyalty but, on the contrary, a manifestation of a trouble making intent, we naturally will not tolerate it. To put it bluntly, if these men have come to this Camp looking for trouble, they have come to a bad place as far as they are concerned.

To continue regarding the events from which the present situation has developed: when the last group of internees arrived from Tule Lake, certain internees in this Camp, possibly feeling the need of trying to prove to the new arrivals that they had not changed their national loyalties within the preceding few weeks, demonstrated in these so-called "Rising Sun sweatshirts", in willful disobedience of the instructions which had been issued. They were accordingly instructed to turn them in, where upon certain members of the group had the effrontery to appear at my office and informed me that the order would not be obeyed. At the same time, they made deliberate misrepresentations in that they stated that what they had to say reflected the attitude of the entire Tule Lake group. Upon investigation, it was ascertained that Mr. Zenshiro Tachibana, with whose trouble-making propensities we were already well acquainted, was at the bottom of the agitation to disobey the order and create a disturbance. Therefore, Mr. Tachibana was removed to another place of detention where he will cause no further trouble.

Immediately following Tachibana's removal from the Area, approximately 250 internees formerly of Tule Lake appeared in riotous and disorderly manner at the main gate in this Camp. Some of these hoodlums, presumably in protest against the action taken in Tachibana's case, hurled stones and insults in the direction of this Administrative building. They refused to carry out the order to disperse and it became necessary for us to disperse them forcibly. I want to state here and now, it was only the cool-headedness of the Officers engaged, and not actions of certain members of this mob, which prevented much more serious consequences.

Yesterday, as I believe you all know, most of the internees from Tule Lake were moved to the Barracks within a Stockade in the Lower Area. We intend to take appropriate action against the chief offenders. I assure every internee here as emphatically as I can that the action taken will be directed toward the permanent restoration of peace and order in this Camp.

We regret exceedingly that this unpleasant situation has arisen. I think that every sensible internee realizes that from the inception of this Service's connection with the internment program, we have shown a desire to establish between us and the internees a relationship of mutual respect and cooperation to the end that the burdens of internment shall be as light as it is possible to make them. As for us, we have enjoyed that relationship and we greatly deplore incidents such as have occurred in the past few days. Unfortunately, the situation has not yet returned entirely to normal. We know that there are a few internees in Camp who are still intent upon stirring up trouble. We can only guess as to their motives. It may be that they are in the grip of a hysteria which has grown upon them as the result of their own past stupid or wrongful acts. A few of them may have the idea that a continually disturbed atmosphere may serve as a sort of cloak of protection for them personally. Some of them may be merely stupid and incorrigible. We will take care of them and "Them" includes the members (whom we shall identify) of that heroic group which slinks around the Camp sending threats from the rat hole of anonymity, and courageously calls itself the "Suicide Squad".

I wish to make it clear that no internee need have anything to fear from the "Suicide Squad". Its members will not be here very long. And where they are going, they will not be together.

As to the majority of the internees who came from Tule Lake, we suppose that fundamentally they are reasonable and decent people. It is time for each one of them to do some serious independent thinking concerning his own present and future welfare. We do not intend to maintain a permanent Segregation Camp in this Area and we think if each will carefully consider his own individual problems, he will not only be helping himself, but all his fellow internees.

I trust that in the future, wisdom and common sense will prevail in order that present conditions will quickly be corrected.

Ivan Williams
Officer-in-Charge

Appendix D
Excerpt from "A Note to Roosevelt"[*]
March 1945

Though you may use the surprise attack on Pearl Harbour as your primary material for propaganda, I believe you, of all persons, know best that you left Nippon no other method in order to save herself from self-destruction....Judging from your actions, white races especially you Anglo-Saxons at the sacrifice of the coloured races are monopolizing the fruits of the world.

In order to attain this end, countless machinations were used to cajole the yellow races, and to finally deprive them of any strength. Nippon in retaliation to your imperialism tried to free the oriental nations from your punitive bonds, only to be faced by your dogged opposition. You now consider your once friendly Nippon an harmful existence to your luscious plan, a bunch of barbarians that must be exterminated. The completion of this Greater East Asia War will bring about the birth of the East Asia Co-Prosperity Area, this in turn will in the near future result in the ever-lasting peace of the world, if, of course, it is not hampered upon by your unending imperialism.

Why is it that you, an already flourishing nation, nip in bud the movement for the freedom of the suppressed nations of the East. It is no other than to return to the East that which belongs to the East.

It is beyond our contemplation when we try to understand your stinted narrowness. The existence of the East Asia Co-Prosperity sphere does not in anyway encroach upon your safety as a nation, on the contrary,

---

[*] Toshinosuke Ichimaru to Franklin Roosevelt, March 1945, seventeen pages Japanese with cover, ten pages English translation, U.S. Naval Academy Museum.

will sit as a pillar of world peace ensuring the happiness of the world. His Imperial Majesty's true aim is no other than the attainment of this everlasting peace....

It is beyond my imagination of how you can slander Hitler's program and at the same time cooperate with Stalin's 'Soviet Russia' which has as its principle aim the 'socialization' of the World at large.

If only brute force decides the ruler of the world, fighting will everlastingly be repeated, and never will the world know peace or happiness.

Upon the attainment of your barbaric world monopoly never forget to retain in your mind the failure of your predecessor President Wilson at high heights.

Notes

Introduction to the Translation

1. Many have undoubtedly learned of these events in the last decade, when concerns about the abuse of civil liberties in the arrest and detention without charge of "enemy combatants" and others in the aftermath of the 9/11 terrorist attacks drew much attention and caused many to draw comparisons with the somewhat analogous events of World War II. The last decade-and-a-half has also seen the rise of numerous state and federal programs to commemorate aspects of this history, ranging from the establishment of "Fred Korematsu Day" in California, federal recognition and preservation of several Japanese American confinement sites, and grant programs that have funded a flood of documentary films, plays, oral history projects, and a wide range of other media. School districts throughout the country have also added the general topic to lists of benchmarks for their middle and high school social studies teachers. For more on these various projects, see Alexandra L. Wood's "After Apology: Public Education as Redress for Japanese American and Japanese Canadian Confinement" (Ph.D. dissertation, New York University, 2013) and Abbie Lynn Salyers' "The Internment of Memory: Forgetting and Remembering the Japanese American World War II Experience" (Ph.D. dissertation, Rice University, 2009), along with Wood's contributions to the online *Densho Encyclopedia* on K-12 Education and WWII Incarceration (http://encyclopedia.densho.org/K–12%20Education%20and%20WWII%20Incarceration/), the California Civil Liberties Public Education Fund (http://encyclopedia.densho.org/California%20Civil%20Liberties%20Public%20Education%20Program/), and the Washington Civil Liberties Public Education Fund (http://encyclopedia.densho.org/Washington%20Civil%20Liberties%20Public%20Education%20Program/).

2. Tetsuden Kashima, "Introduction," in *Life behind Barbed Wire: The World War II Internment Memoirs of a Hawai'i Issei* by Yasutaro Soga, translated by Kihei Hirai (Honolulu: University of Hawai'i Press, 2008), 1–16. See also Kashima's *Judgment Without Trial: Japanese American Imprisonment during World War II* (Seattle: University of Washington Press, 2002) and Gary Y. Okihiro's *Cane Fires: The*

Anti-Japanese Movement in Hawai'i, 1865–1945 (Philadelphia: Temple University Press, 1991).

3. Roger Daniels' *The Politics of Prejudice: The Anti-Japanese Movement in California and the Struggle for Japanese Exclusion* (1962; 2nd edition, Berkeley: University of California Press, 1977) is generally viewed as the definitive work on anti-Japanese agitation on the West Coast while Okihiro's *Cane Fires* tries to make similar case for Hawai'i. Other useful studies on Japanese migration to Hawai'i include Alan T. Moriyama's *Imingaishi: Japanese Emigration Companies and Hawaii, 1894–1908* (Honolulu: University of Hawai'i Press, 1985) and Yukiko Kimura's *Issei: Japanese Immigrants in Hawai'i* (Honolulu: University of Hawai'i Press, 1988).

4. The definitive study of Issei on the continental U.S. is Yuji Ichioka's *The Issei: The World of the First Generation Japanese Immigrants, 1885–1924* (New York: The Free Press, 1988). See also Ichioka's *Before Internment: Essays in Prewar Japanese American History* (edited by Gordon H. Chang and Eiichiro Azuma; Stanford: Stanford University Press, 2006).

5. The term "Little Tokyo" was largely a misnomer, since the great majority of Japanese immigrants came from rural prefectures in the southern and western parts of Japan.

6. For ethnic communities, see, for instance, John Modell's *The Economics and Politics of Racial Accommodation: The Japanese of Los Angeles 1900–1942* (Chicago: University of Illinois Press, 1977), Brian Masaru Hayashi's *'For the Sake of Our Japanese Brethren': Assimilation, Nationalism, and Protestantism among the Japanese of Los Angeles, 1895–1942* (Stanford: Stanford University Press, 1995), and Michael M. Okihiro's *A'ala: The Story of a Japanese Community in Hawai'i* (Honolulu: Japanese Cultural Center of Hawai'i, 2003); there are many other studies of specific Japanese American communities. For the Nisei, see Eileen Tamura's *Americanization, Acculturation, and Ethnic Identity: The Nisei Generation in Hawai'i* (Urbana: University of Illinois Press, 1994), Jere Takahashi's *Nisei/Sansei: Shifting Japanese American Identities and Politics* (Philadelphia: Temple University Press, 1997), David Yoo's *Growing Up Nisei: Race, Generation, and Culture among Japanese Americans of California, 1924–49* (Urbana: University of Illinois Press, 2000), and Valerie Matsumoto's *City Girls: The Nisei Social World in Los Angeles, 1920–1950* (New York: Oxford University Press, 2014).

7. Ichioka, *The Issei* and *Before Internment*; Eiichiro Azuma, *Between Two Empires: Race History, and Transnationalism in Japanese America* (New York: Oxford University Press, 2005).

8. For Japanese Associations, see Ichioka, "Japanese Associations and the Japanese Government: A Special Relationship, 1909–1926," *Pacific Historical Review* 46.3 (Aug. 1977): 409–38, much of which reappears in chapter 5 of Ichioka's *The Issei*. For *toritsuginin* in Hawai'i, see Alan Rosenfeld, "'An Everlasting Scar': Civilian Internment on Wartime Kaua'i," *The Hawaiian Journal of History* 45 (2011), 125 and *Personal Justice Denied: Report of the Commission on Wartime Relocation and Internment of Civilians* (Washington, D.C.: Government Printing Office, 1982; Seattle: University of Washington Press, 1997), 278–79.

9. Eiichiro Azuma, "'Pioneers of Overseas Japanese Development': Japanese American History and the Making of Expansionist Orthodoxy in Imperial Japan," *Journal of Asian Studies* 67.4 (Nov. 2008): 1187–226 and Ichioka, "Japanese Immigrant Nationalism: The Issei and the Sino-Japanese War, 1937–1941," *California History* 69.3 (Fall 1990): 260–75, 310–11, which is also chapter 8 of *Before Internment*.

10. John Stephan, *Hawai'i under the Rising Sun: Japan's Plans for Conquest after Pearl Harbor* (Honolulu: University of Hawai'i Press, 1984), 48–54; Ichioka, *Before Internment*, 194–99; and Azuma, *Between Two Empires*, 107–09.

11. See, for instance, Yuji Ichioka, "A Study in Dualism: James Yoshinori Sakamoto and the Japanese American Courier, 1928–1942," *Amerasia Journal* 13.2 (1986–87): 49–81, which is also chapter 5 in Ichioka's *Before Internment* and Eriko Yamamoto, "Miya Sannomiya Kikuchi: A Pioneer Nisei Woman's Life and Identity," *Amerasia Journal* 23.3 (Winter 1997): 72–101.

12. Jack Y. Tasaka, "Hawai o irodoru Nihonjin: Furuya Suikei-shi no koto" [A Japanese who has influenced Hawai'i: Suikei Furuya], *East-West Journal*, 1 June, 15 June, 1 July 1995; Kei Suzuki, "Media: Kumaji Furuya," *The Hawai'i Herald*, 17 October 2008; Tsuneichi Yamamoto, ed., *The Rainbow, a Bridge: A 70-Year History of the Honolulu Japanese Chamber of Commerce* (Honolulu: Honolulu Japanese Chamber of Commerce, 1970), 153; Suikei Furuya, *Imin no rakugaki* [The scribblings of an immigrant] (Honolulu: Hawaii Times, 1968), 81–82.

13. Furuya, *Rakugaki*, 8, 81–82; Federal Bureau of Investigation Report by F. G. Tillman, 30 January 1942, Kumaji Furuya, Alien Case File, A002-426-398, Accession 085-12-001, Box 163, Immigration and Naturalization Service, National Archives and Records Administration, College Park, Maryland. Furuya's Case File was scanned by Adriana Marroquin of the Angel Island Immigration Station Foundation and generously shared with JCCH for the purposes of this book. Some sources suggest that he also may have worked as a sharecropper, most likely on Maui. Tomio Sakamoto, "Furuya Kumaji-shi: Oi o shiranu iyoku," [Kumaji Furuya: A will that does not know old age], *Hawai jinbutsu tenkizu* (Honolulu: n.p., 1957?), 10; Tasaka, "Hawai o irodoru Nihonjin;" Suzuki, *The Hawai'i Herald*.

14. Tillman report, 1942; Tasaka, June 1, 1995; Hanzo Furuya, "Oral History Interview with Hanzo Furuya," 29 April 1998, Tape No. 28-36-1-98, interview by Michiko Kodama-Nishimoto, University of Hawai'i Center for Oral History.

15. Jun Furuya, "Oral History Interview with Jun Furuya," 20 May 1998, Tape Nos. 28-37-1-98J, 28-38-1-98J, interview by Michiko Kodama-Nishimoto, University of Hawai'i Center for Oral History.

16. Hanzo Furuya Oral History; Okihiro, *A'ala*, 11–25; Tasaka, "Hawai o irodoru Nihonjin."

17. Bob Sigall, *et al.*, *The Companies We Keep: Amazing Stores About 450 of Hawaii's Best Known Companies* (Honolulu: Small Business Hawai'i, 2006), 318; Suikei Furuya, "Nihongo hōsōkai" [The world of Japanese broadcasting], *Hawai Nihonjin iminshi* [A History of Japanese Immigrants in Hawai'i], 2nd ed. (Honolulu: United Japanese Society of Hawai'i, 1977), 510.

18. Tasaka, "Hawai o irodoru Nihonjin;" Jun Furuya Oral History; Furuya, "Nihongo hōsōkai," 511; Furuya, *Rakugaki*, 54, 221–22.

19. HJCC, *The Rainbow*, 70, 71, 161, 191, Japanese section, 66; United Japanese Society of Hawai'i Publication Committee, ed., *A History of Japanese in Hawai'i* (Honolulu: United Japanese Society of Hawai'i, 1971), 239.

20. Tillman report, 1942.

21. HJCC, *The Rainbow*, 161; Furuya, *Rakugaki*, 338; "Mrs. Furuya's Interview," notes 2pp, Patsy Saiki Collection, AR 18, Box 1, Folder 12, Japanese Cultural Center of Hawai'i, Honolulu, Hawai'i.

22. Noriko Shimada, "Haiku to haiku kessha ni miru Hawai Nihonjin imin no shakai bunkashi" [The social and literary history of Hawai'i Japanese immigrants as seen in their haiku and haiku societies], in Noriko Shimada, ed., *Haiku, tanka, senryū ni miru Hawai Nihonjin iminshi* [History of Japanese immigrants in Hawai'i seen through their haiku, tanka, and senryu] (Tokyo: privately printed, 2009), 14–21.

23. Kempu Kawazoe, "Bungei" [The literary arts], *Hawai Nihonjin iminshi* [A history of Japanese immigrants in Hawai'i] (Honolulu: United Japanese Society of Hawai'i, 1964), 506; Shimada, "Haiku to haiku kessha," 11–13, 16–17.

24. Shimada, "Haiku to haiku kessha," 15–16.

25. Shimada, "Haiku to haiku kessha," 19; Furuya, *Rakugaki*, 207–208; Suikei Furuya, *Ruten* [Vicissitudes] (Kamakura: Sōunsha, 1958), 160.

26. Furuya, *Rakugaki*, 33, 49–51; Furuya, *Ruten*, 159; Shimada, "Haiku to haiku kessha," 19–20; Kawazoe, "Bungei," 506.

27. Kawazoe, "Bungei," 506; Shimada, "Haiku to haiku kessha," 22.

28. Furuya, *Ruten*, 161; Furuya, *Rakugaki*, 9.

29. Louis Fiset, *Imprisoned Apart: The World War II Correspondence of an Issei Couple* (Seattle University of Washington Press, 1997), 46–51 and Kashima, *Judgment Without Trial*, 58–64, 73–74.

30. Furuya, Alien Case File.

31. A small library could be filled with works analyzing how the decision to remove West Coast Japanese Americans came to be. Key works include Roger Daniels' *Concentration Camps, U.S.A.: Japanese Americans and World War II* (New York: Holt, Rinehart and Winston, 1971); *Personal Justice Denied*; Peter Irons' *Justice at War: The Story of the Japanese American Internment Cases* (New York: Oxford University Press, 1983, Berkeley: University of California Press, 1993); and Klancy Clark de Nevers' *The Colonel and the Pacifist: Karl Bendetsen, Perry Saito and the Incarceration of Japanese Americans during World War II* (Salt Lake City: University of Utah Press, 2004).

32. Both Fiset's *Imprisoned Apart* and the second volume of the JCCH internment trilogy, *Family Torn Apart: The Internment Story of the Otokichi Muin Ozaki Family*, edited by Gail Honda (Honolulu: Japanese Cultural Center of Hawai'i, 2012) consist in large part of correspondence between husbands and wives imprisoned separately in the two programs.

33. On renunciation, see Michi Weglyn's *Years of Infamy: The Untold Story of America's Concentration Camps* (New York: William Morrow & Co., 1976; updated

edition, Seattle: University of Washington Press, 1996) and Donald Collins' *Native American Aliens: Disloyalty and the Renunciation of Citizenship by Japanese Americans During World War II* (Westport, Conn.: Greenwood Press, 1985).

34. Hanzo Furuya Oral History.

35. Hanzo Furuya Oral History.

36. Hanzo Furuya Oral History.

37. Jun Furuya Oral History.

38. Hanzo Furuya Oral History.

39. Furuya, *Rakugaki*, 21, 331–32; HJCC, *The Rainbow*, 153.

40. Sakamoto, 11; Suzuki, *The Hawai'i Herald.*

41. Furuya, *Ruten*, 5; Yukio Itō, ed., *Sōun hitori jikkushū* [A collection of *Sōun* poets and their ten haiku] (Kamakura: Sōunsha, 1961).

42. John A. Rademaker, "Hawaii Will Never Be Quite the Same Again: A Sociologist's View of the Island Situation," *Pacific Citizen*, Dec. 22, 1945, III-17, III-24. http://pacificcitizen.org/digitalarchives/assets/images/full/PCN_19451222_017.jpg, http://pacificcitizen.org/digitalarchives/assets/images/full/PCN_19451222_024 .jpg; Franklin S. Odo, *No Sword to Bury: Japanese Americans in Hawai'i during World War II* (Philadelphia: Temple University Press, 2003); Ellen Wu, *The Color of Success: Asian Americans and the Origins of the Model Minority* (Princeton: Princeton University Press, 2014).

43. Seigai Shinjo, "Zatsudai zatsuwa" [Idle talk on miscellaneous topics], *The Hawaii Times*, Sept. 28, 1963, translated by Tatsumi Hayashi.

44. Yuji Ichioka, "A Historian by Happenstance," *Amerasia Journal* 26.1 (2000): 46, 50–52.

Forewords

1. Joei Oi was a priest of the Nichiren Buddhist sect and a teacher at the Rissho Japanese Language School in Honolulu.

2. In the 1960s, Furuya wrote a series of articles for *The Hawaii Times* about his wartime internment experiences. The series was called *"Haisho Tenten."*

3. The Sand Island Detention Camp in Honolulu Harbor.

4. *Ruten*. Furuya was a prolific writer of the modern form of freestyle haiku, which was developed at the turn of the twentieth century. An entirely new genre, freestyle haiku broke from the traditional format of seasonal themes and the seventeen-syllable structure.

5. This poem, as remembered by Joei Oi, is very similar to the one that appears in Chapter 5, which, in turn, is much like the poem in *Ruten*, 4. That one poem can exist in several different versions is largely due to the fact that in the early days of the internment, internees would compose poems and, deprived of paper and pencil, preserve them through memory. See also the different versions of Shoichi Asami's "Wandering Internees" on page 82.

6. Masahiro Himeno was a Christian minister in Honolulu.

7. Totaro Matsui was president of Pacific Bank in Honolulu.

8. Keiho Soga is the poetry name of Yasutaro Soga, author of *Tessaku Seikatsu*.

9. Matsui is probably referring to the Kalāheo Stockade on Kaua'i, the Ha'ikū Detention Camp on Maui, and the Kīlauea Military Camp on Hawai'i Island, besides Sand Island, the most well-known of the detention sites. There were other detention sites throughout the islands, but because they were smaller or of shorter duration, Matsui may not have been aware of them at the time of *Haisho Tenten*'s publication. Other sites include Waiākea Prison on Hawai'i Island; Līhu'e Plantation, Wailua County Jail, and Waimea Jail on Kaua'i; Wailuku County Jail on Maui; Kaunakakai Jail on Moloka'i; and Lāna'i City Jail on Lāna'i.

Chapter 1

1. By late 1941, preparations for conflict between the United States and Japan had become daily occurrences, including territory-wide blackout practices, simulated military maneuvers, and disaster preparedness meetings. The 1,200-seat Kokusai Theater was located in the 'A'ala area, only several miles from Pearl Harbor. The theater's owner, Sanji Abe, was a Nisei territorial senator from Hilo who was later arrested and interned at Sand Island and Honouliuli. For a description of war preparations, see *A History of Japanese in Hawaii*, 258.

2. In the hours after the Pearl Harbor attack, Reserve Officers' Training Corps units from the University of Hawai'i and Honolulu high schools were called into service. These ROTC units would subsequently comprise the core of the voluntary Hawai'i Territorial Guard, which was tasked with guarding sensitive sites throughout Honolulu.

3. Kumaji is Furuya's given name. His writings, including *Haisho Tenten*, were published under his pen name, Suikei.

4. Fort Shafter was the headquarters of the U.S. Army in Hawai'i. When Governor Joseph B. Poindexter relinquished his executive powers to the U.S. military some three hours after the Pearl Harbor attack, the commander of the army's Hawaiian Department became the territory's new military governor and martial law was established in the islands. With its underground command post in Āliamanu Crater, Fort Shafter became the military headquarters of the Hawai'i Military Government until martial law was lifted in October 1944. Kashima, *Judgment without Trial*, 70; James C. McNaughton, "The Hawaiian Department, 7 December 1941," United States Army, Pacific (November 20, 2001), http://www.usarpac.army.mil/history2/dec7th.asp.

5. The Honolulu United Japanese Society was the largest Japanese organization in the islands. It served as an umbrella agency for business organizations, prefectural clubs and other similar groups with ties to Japan and Hawai'i's Japanese population. Highly influential within the territory's Japanese community, the organization was rendered inoperable with the arrests of most of its leaders following the Pearl Harbor attack. Furuya also was a vice president of the UJS at this time. The organization was re-established as the United Japanese Society of Hawaii in 1958. *A History of Japanese in Hawaii*, 356.

6. Shinto priests practice the native religion of Japan. Beginning in the Meiji Era (1868–1912), Shinto became increasingly nationalistic, with its doctrine of the emperor's divine status taught in schools and a system of government-supported national shrines instituted throughout Japan. The Kato Shrine was built on Hall Street in the ʻAʻala district of Honolulu in 1911. In 1965, it was absorbed by the Ishizuchi Shrine in Mōʻiliʻili.

7. The Honolulu office of the Justice Department's Immigration and Naturalization Service was located on Ala Moana Boulevard, between Honolulu Harbor and Waikīkī. Arrests in Honolulu were made by officers of the FBI, the army's military intelligence, and the local police. Prisoners were then turned over to the military police at the INS office, which served as a temporary detention station. Kashima, *Judgment without Trial*, 69–71.

8. The *Hokke-kyō*, or the Lotus Sutra, is an important element in Japanese Buddhism, especially in the Nichiren sect. It is frequently recited at funerals.

9. In response to the Japanese occupation of southern French Indochina, President Franklin Roosevelt issued in July 1941 an executive order freezing all Japanese and Chinese assets in the United States. The move came a month after a similar order that froze the assets of various European countries and was designed to staunch the outflow of U.S. dollars that could be used to aid America's adversaries. News of the order spread anxiety within the Japanese community, causing a run on the Japanese banks. *A History of Japanese in Hawaii*, 260.

10. These were among the most powerful government and business officials in Hawaiʻi. The territorial governor at the time was Joseph B. Poindexter. On the afternoon of December 7, under pressure from the military, Poindexter ended civilian administration of the territory and placed Hawaiʻi under martial law. The mayor of Honolulu in 1941 was Lester Petrie. Robert L. Shivers was appointed by FBI Director J. Edgar Hoover to head the department's Honolulu office. Arriving in 1939, Shivers was tasked with compiling a custodial detention list of potentially dangerous Japanese, primarily Issei, on which the arrests of December 7 were based. He also has been credited with having formed friendships with key members of Hawaiʻi's Asian American community, which contributed to preventing a mass incarceration of the territory's Japanese population. Samuel Wilder King, a retired naval commander, had been since 1935 a Republican delegate to the U.S. Congress from the territory of Hawaiʻi. In 1942, King withdrew his candidacy for another term in favor of a new naval commission in the Pacific theater. After his retirement as commanding general of the U.S. Army's Hawaiian Department, Briant H. Wells became an executive with the Hawaiian Sugar Planters' Association, which comprised the majority of the territory's sugar plantations, including those belonging to Hawaiʻi's Big Five mercantile firms. Furuya uses the term "the Caucasian Chamber of Commerce" to distinguish the Chamber of Commerce of Hawaiʻi from the Honolulu Japanese Chamber of Commerce. George S. Waterhouse was then head of the Chamber of Commerce of Hawaiʻi.

11. The expression is "*tsūchi more*," to go unnoticed.

12. Hawaiian: mesquite.

Chapter 2

1. Located in Honolulu Harbor, the man-made Sand Island originated from two small natural islands. Beginning in the mid-nineteenth century, the smaller of the two islands served as a quarantine station to guard against small pox. In 1940, the U.S. military dredged the harbor, pumped the debris onto the two small islands, and transformed them into the 640-acre Sand Island.

2. Kazuo Sakamaki navigated one of five mini-submarines that slipped into Pearl Harbor on the eve of the Japanese attack. His memoir is *Horyo dai-ichigo* [POW No. 1] (Tokyo: Shinchōsha, 1949).

3. Koichi Iida was the owner of the Japanese housewares store that bore the name of its original propietor, Suisan Matsukichi Iida. Rev. Kyokujo Kubokawa was a priest of the Jodo, or Pure Land, sect of Japanese Buddhism. The prominent sects of Jodo, Shin-Jodo (also known in Hawai'i as Honpa Hongwanji), Soto, Shingon, and Nichiren were brought to the islands in the late-nineteenth century by priests who followed the immigrant laborers to Hawai'i's sugar plantations. They established missions in the islands to minister to the growing Japanese communities. Kenji Kimura was a manager for Nippon Yūsen Kaisha, the worldwide shipping company known as the NYK Line.

4. This wife of the sixteenth-century lord Yamanouchi Kazutoyo was known for her unselfish devotion to her husband.

5. Sei Soga was the wife of Yasutaro Soga, publisher of the *Nippu Jiji* newspaper. Furuya's wife and Sei Soga were cousins.

6. Matsujiro Otani, a businessman who had started out as a fishmonger in Honolulu's Chinatown district, was the owner of 'A'ala Marketplace, which in 1941 housed some fifty-five tenant businesses, the majority of them Japanese. William Heen, a prominent Honolulu attorney, who had defended four local men in the infamous Massie Case, served as president of Otani's companies. After the war, Heen would become president of the territorial Senate and Otani would be instrumental in the revival of Hawai'i's fishing industry.

7. Japanese fishermen aboard four sampans were into the fourth day of a week-long search for tuna in the waters off of O'ahu when they learned of the Pearl Harbor bombing. On December 8 they set a return course for their home port of Kewalo Basin. Two miles from Barber's Point, American P-40 fighters swooped low, strafing the fishing boats that were suspected of rendezvousing with ships from the Japanese Imperial Navy. The attack left six of the fishermen dead and seven injured. Saiki, *Ganbare!*, 1–10.

8. People of Japanese lineage, especially those born outside of Japan. In the 1940s, most American Nikkei were second-generation Japanese Americans, or Nisei, as distinct from those whom Furuya refers to as "Japanese," or first-generation Japanese immigrants (Issei), who were prohibited from becoming American citizens.

9. Louis F. Springer later became commander of the Sand Island camp.

10. *Shaba* was a slang term used by inmates to refer to the world outside of

prison. During the internment, Japanese internees often used the term in reference to the world outside the barbed wire from which they were cut off, as if criminals or unwanted members of human society.

11. A priest at Izumo Taisha, a Shinto shrine in Honolulu.

12. Seigi Yamane's wife was Tsuta Yamane.

13. Leaders in the Issei community often served as voluntary agents of the Japanese Consulate, assigned to liaise with the Japanese residents of their districts. They helped to fill out various official documents, usually involving the reporting of births, marriages, and deaths.

14. 'Ōla'a is a plantation community near Hilo on the island of Hawai'i. Shoten Matsubayashi was from Wailuku, Maui. Both Shushin Matsubayashi and Shoten Matsubayashi were Buddhist priests.

15. This is Carl F. Eifler, whose military police company was assigned to guard the Sand Island detainees. He served at Sand Island for only three months but left an indelible impression on the internees. See Saiki, *Ganbare!*, 32–37; Soga, *Life behind Barbed Wire*, 30–31; Honda, ed., *Family Torn Apart*, 21–22. Eifler's autobiography is Thomas N. Moon and Carl F. Eifler, *The Deadliest Colonel* (New York: Vantage Press, 1975).

16. A board game known as Japanese chess, which uses flat wooden pieces with Japanese characters written on each side.

17. This incident involving Rev. Ryoshin Okano is also described by Soga, *Life behind Barbed Wire*, 30–31.

18. Bishop Gikyo Kuchiba was head of the Honpa Hongwanji Mission in Honolulu; Yasutaro Soga was publisher of the *Nippu Jiji* newspaper; and Uyemon Inokuchi was principal of the Manoa Japanese Language School.

19. Sumida, Iida, and Sato were prominent businessmen in the Japanese community. Sumida was the proprietor of the Honolulu Sake Brewery and Ice Company, the first *sake* brewery established outside of Japan. Iida was owner of the popular Japanese housewares store, Iida Suisando. Taichi Sato found success with his apparel shop, Sato Clothiers, which specialized in small-sized suits that fit Asian men. He also was president of the United Japanese Society at the time of the Pearl Harbor attack. Okihiro, *A'ala*, 15–16.

20. Norizane Tsuha 津波憲実, a lay priest of the Okinawan Jikoen Hongwanji Mission in Kalihi, has been identified variously as Kenjitsu (Soga), Jitsushige (Kashima), and Norizane (JCCH Hawai'i Internee Database). Norizane is the *kun* (Japanese) pronunciation and Kenjitsu is the *on* (Chinese) pronunciation of the *kanji* characters for his given name. In Japan, and in Hawai'i as well, names tend to be read with the *on* pronunciation because it is easier to do so. Generally, Buddhist names are read with the *on* pronunciation. However, U.S. government documents render Tsuha's name as Norizane.

21. Iga Mori (1864–1951) arrived in the islands in 1890, hired by the Hawaiian government to treat Japanese sugar plantation laborers on Hawai'i Island. He played a leadership role in the 1900 bubonic plague crisis and then served as the first director of the Japanese Hospital built in the wake of the epidemic. His son,

Motokazu, also became a prominent Honolulu physician and was interned along with his wife. Yasutaro Soga (1873–1957) was the publisher of Honolulu's *Nippu Jiji*, the largest Japanese-language newspaper in the pre-WWII United States. He was jailed for his leadership role in the Great Oʻahu Strike of 1909 and for the first half of the twentieth century served as one of the most influential voices in Hawaiʻi's Japanese community. Seiha Asami was the pen name of Shoichi Asami (1896–1945), the editor-in-chief of the *Nippu Jiji*. Asami was initially in the same internee group as Furuya and was transferred from camp to camp, while his wife and five children were housed in Mainland hotels with the families of other repatriating internees. The Asamis were eventually reunited in Crystal City, Texas, in May 1943, where they stayed until their departure several months later aboard the second repatriation ship. Iga Mori Archival Collection, Japanese Cultural Center of Hawaiʻi Resource Center; James C. Mohr, *Plague and Fire: Battling Black Death and the 1900 Burning of Honolulu's Chinatown* (New York: Oxford University Press, 2005). Soga's account of his internment, *Tessaku seikatsu*, was published in Honolulu in 1948; its English-language translation is *Life behind Barbed Wire*. His autobiography, *Gojūnen no Hawai kaiko*, was published in 1953. Brian Niiya, "Yasutaro Soga," *Denshō Encyclopedia*, http://encyclopedia.densho.org/Yasutaro%20Soga/ (accessed July 11, 2013).

22. The Matson Navigation Company's fleet of luxury ships transported travelers from the American West Coast to the shores of Hawaiʻi. Its signature passenger vessel was the *Lurline*, one of its four "white ships" that christened Matson's entry into the cruise liner era. With the outbreak of World War II, the white ships, including the *Lurline*, were painted gray and converted into troop transport vessels.

23. The FBI's offices were located on the second floor of the Dillingham Transportation Building on Bishop Street.

Chapter 3

1. FBI special agent F. G. Tillman was assigned to exclusively investigate matters involving the Japanese. He handled a case concerning Japanese consul official Yoshikawa Takeo (also known as Morimura Tadashi), who was suspected of collecting U.S. military intelligence in preparation for Japan's attack on Pearl Harbor. Yoshikawa Takeo, *Higashi no kaze, ame* [Easterly wind, rain] (Tokyo: Kodansha, 1963); Seki Yokichi, *Beikoku yokuryūki* [Internment in the United States] (Tokyo: Kashima Kenkyūsho Shuppankai, 1971).

2. The Yamanashi Club was a *kenjinkai*, an association made up of people from the same prefecture—in this case Yamanashi, a prefecture north of Tokyo and Furuya's birthplace. Initially organized by early immigrants to provide mutual aid, *kenjinkai* evolved into clubs that provided opportunities to socialize with individuals possessing similar dialects and customs. In Hawaiʻi, there were dozens of *kenjinkai*.

3. Tomoaki Nakamura

4. Dumplings made from sweet, sticky rice.

Chapter 4

1. Furuya is referring to individuals on the custodial detention lists compiled by the FBI and other government agencies, in order to identify those deemed "dangerous" in the event of war. See Tetsuden Kashima, "Custodial detention / A-B-C list," *Densho Encyclopedia*, http://encyclopedia.densho.org/Custodial%20detention%20/%20A-B-C%20list/(accessed September 23, 2014).

2. Bernard Julius Otto Kuehn, a member of the Nazi Party, was said to have had close ties to propaganda minister Joseph Goebbles. It was through Goebbles that Kuehn obtained work as an agent of Japanese intelligence in Hawai'i. He moved his family to Honolulu in 1935, was arrested in February 1942, and was subsequently found guilty of spying. Besides Kuehn, the only other individual in Hawai'i believed to have engaged in spying for the Japanese was consulate official Yoshikawa Takeo. For a first-hand account of Kuehn's activities, see Yoshikawa's memoir, *Higashi no kaze, ame*, 79–83.

3. Frederick Kinzaburo Makino (1877–1953) was the Issei publisher of Honolulu's *Hawaii Hochi*, the rival newspaper of the *Nippu Jiji*. While Soga and most of the *Nippu Jiji* staff were interned, Makino remained free and continued as editor of the *Hochi*, which published during the war under the banner, the *Hawaii Herald*. Historian Kelli Y. Nakamura, writing for the online *Densho Encyclopedia*, reviews the various published explanations for Makino's having "slipped through the net": government fear of a lawsuit, lack of evidence of a clear link between Makino and the Japanese government, and purported clandestine meetings between FBI head Robert Shivers and the newspaper publisher. In 1952, Makino's newspaper reverted to its original name, and today it continues as the only Japanese-language weekday newspaper in the islands. Zenkyo Komagata was the head of the Soto Buddhist temples in Hawai'i. Tetsuo Oi was the UJS director. *Shōgyō Jihō* newspaper president Seiichi Tsuchiya was Makino's half-brother. Kelli Y. Nakamura, "Hawaii Hochi (newspaper)," *Densho Encyclopedia*, http://encyclopedia.densho.org/Hawaii%20Hochi%20(newspaper)/ (accessed July 11, 2013); Roland Kotani, *The Japanese in Hawaii: A Century of Struggle* (Honolulu: Hawaii Hochi, Ltd., 1985), 39–45, 56–66.

4. Tsunoda was the son of Ryusaku Tsunoda, a prominent scholar of Japanese studies in the United States. For more information on the senior Tsunoda, see page 328n41. The Japanese Charity Hospital started out as a two-story wooden structure built in the aftermath of the city's bubonic plague crisis and 1900 Chinatown fire. By 1941, it was a modern facility with a care home for retired, unmarried plantation workers. With Japanese descendants on its board of trustees, the hospital became the only medical facility in the United States to be occupied by the U.S. Army during World War II. Today, it is known as Kuakini Medical Center and is the only hospital remaining in the United States to have been established by Japanese immigrants. Sigall, *The Companies We Keep*, 201–202.

5. Japanese Consul General Toyokichi Fukuma.

6. Not to be confused with Takaichi Saiki, the Hilo branch manager for Bank of Hawaii.

7. Hawaiian: crazy.

8. Kazuo Miyamoto (1897–1988) was a Nisei physician and author from the Big Island, whose Japanese education and authorship of an account of his travels in China during the Japanese occupation aroused U.S. government suspicions. Among his many works is the fictionalized history of the islands' Japanese immigrants, *Hawaii, End of the Rainbow.* "Oral History Interview with Dr. Kazuo Miyamoto," 1980, Japanese Cultural Center of Hawai'i; Kelli Nakamura, "Kazuo Miyamoto," *Densho Encyclopedia,* http://encyclopedia.densho.org/Kazuo%20 Miyamoto/ (accessed December 3, 2013).

9. Hawaiian: friend.

10. Siegfried Spillner, later commander of the Honouliuli Internment Camp.

11. A malfunctioning gyrocompass prevented Sakamaki's mini-submarine from entering Pearl Harbor, and he instead spent several hours attempting to navigate the craft before it ran aground. The vessel was salvaged and sent to the Mainland, where it was a featured attraction during war bond drives.

12. Motoichi Matsuda was the Honolulu branch manager of the Yokohama Specie Bank. Matsuda and other bank employees were arrested for having played golf at the Wai'alae Country Club on the morning of December 7. The Specie Bank was established under the auspices of the Japanese government and acted as its financial agent through its branches around the world. The bank's Honolulu property was confiscated during the war and all of its assets liquidated and impounded by the U.S. government. Yokohama Specie Bank in Japan was later dissolved by American occupation forces and reorganized as the Bank of Tokyo.

13. Fearing that Latin America—especially the Panama Canal—was vulnerable to conquest by the Axis powers, the United States, in cooperation with Panamanian officials, embarked on an internment program that targeted individuals living in the canal area. The U.S. subsequently reached agreements with more than a dozen Latin American countries, including Peru, Bolivia, and Ecuador, that called for the arrest and expulsion of Japanese, German, and Italian nationals deemed "dangerous" to the security of the region. Those arrested were sent to the United States and confined at the Justice Department's camp in Crystal City, Texas. A plan then evolved to use the Japanese Latin Americans in a prisoner exchange program, creating what has been called a "curious wartime triangle trade." In all, some three thousand Japanese Latin Americans, both resident aliens and citizens, were deported. Robinson, *A Tragedy of Democracy: Japanese Confinement in North America* (New York: Columbia University Press, 2009), 6, 148–52; Kashima, *Judgment Without Trial,* 94–95; Commission on Wartime Relocation and Internment of Civilians, *Personal Justice Denied: Report of the Commission on Wartime Relocation and Internment of Civilians* (Seattle: University of Washington Press, 1997), 305–14; Stephen Mak, "Japanese Latin Americans," Densho Encyclopedia, http://encyclopedia.densho .org/Japanese%20Latin%20Americans/ (accessed December 18, 2013).

14. This is the poetry name of Tokuji Adachi, a Japanese language school principal from Honolulu.

15. Japanese Consul General Hachiro Arita.

16. Zensuke Kanashiro was likely released from Honouliuli before the war's end. Twenty-one Japanese civilian internees did remain confined there until September 1945. However, Kanashiro is not listed among them, nor is he among those who were sent to Tule Lake. See JCCH Internee Database. Honouliuli was the largest civilian confinement site and POW camp in the islands. The majority of its civilian prisoners were Nisei men. For more on Honouliuli see JCCH, *The Untold Story: Internment of Japanese Americans in Hawaii*, http://hawaiiinternment.org/; Alan Rosenfeld, "Honouliuli (detention facility)," *Densho Encyclopedia*, http://encyclopedia.densho.org/Honouliuli%20(detention%20facility)/(accessed July 11, 2013).

17. The respected Honolulu attorney may have been visiting the internees in his role as chairman of the Emergency Service Committee, which had been established as a vehicle for stabilizing race relations in the aftermath of the Pearl Harbor attack. Believing in the need for deeper U.S. military understanding of Hawaiʻi's Japanese community and recognizing that this would only be possible through personal relationships between Japanese and Americans, Marumoto forged friendships with officials in U.S. military intelligence and most especially with the FBI's Robert Shivers. These relationships have been credited with helping to prevent the mass incarceration of the Japanese in Hawaiʻi. After the war, Marumoto served as a Hawaiʻi Supreme Court justice. Dennis M. Ogawa, *First Among Nisei: The Life and Writings of Masaji Marumoto* (Honolulu: Japanese Cultural Center of Hawaiʻi, 2007); Dennis M. Ogawa and Claire Marumoto, "Masaji Marumoto," *Densho Encyclopedia*, http://encyclopedia.densho.org/Masaji%20Marumoto/(accessed November 11, 2012).

18. Harry (Ludwig Victor) Tauber, a native of Austria, was a part-time lecturer at the University of Hawaiʻi. In Hawaiʻi, ethnic German and Italian civilians were arrested, and, as was also the case on the mainland, individuals from countries that had been occupied by Nazi Germany were targeted as well, including those from Austria, Denmark, Finland, and Norway. Also arrested were a number of Jewish civilians. Alan Rosenfeld, "German and Italian detainees," *Densho Encyclopedia*, http://encyclopedia.densho.org/German%20and%20Italian%20detainees/ (accessed October 30, 2012). In *Behind Barbed Wire*, this individual's name has been rendered as "Professor Tower." The translator is grateful to Alan Rosenfeld for his identification of Harry Tauber.

19. *Botamochi* is a rice dumpling covered with a jam of red bean.

20. All internees were subject to a hearing conducted by a board of officers and civilians impaneled by the Hawaiian military government to determine their confinement status. According to Furuya's INS Alien Case File, his hearing took place on January 24, 1942. It was carried out by a four-member panel that included Edward N. Sylva, who would serve as a Republican attorney general for the territory after the war, and territorial Senator David Y. K. Akana. Furuya's testimony lasted for twenty minutes. On January 26, 1942, Eugene Valentine, attorney Masaji Marumoto, and Beatrice Matsui Arita, who worked at Fuji Furniture, stood as Furuya's witnesses. For an excerpt of the government's record of this hearing, see Appendix A: In the Case of Kumaji Furuya.

21. The Hawai'i Territorial Guard was formed within several hours of the Pearl Harbor attack and placed under direct command of the army. Comprised of University of Hawai'i and high school ROTC units, the HTG was voluntary and largely Nisei. Its duties involved guarding sensitive positions in and around Honolulu, including the governor's residence and the FBI office, courthouses, electric substations, bridges, reservoirs, water tanks, gas storage sites, and the pineapple cannery. Unaware that his father had been arrested, Hanzo Furuya carried out his assignment to guard Farrington High School, which, along with Punahou School, had been converted into an emergency hospital. In January 1942, six weeks after its formation, Military Governor Delos Emmons disbanded the HTG, reorganizing the unit the next day minus its 317 Nisei. Odo, *No Sword to Bury*, 117–41; Kotani, *The Japanese in Hawaii*, 94–95.

22. Furuya may be referring to the December 17 arrest of Yokohama Specie Bank employees who had been playing golf at the Waialae Country Club in east Honolulu on the morning of the Pearl Harbor attack. In a letter dated December 17, 1941, to FBI Director J. Edgar Hoover, the head of the FBI's Honolulu office, Robert Shivers, writes:

> Seven individuals were apprehended today and placed in internment, as a result of investigations by this office. Investigation indicated that these seven individuals are all employed by the Yokohama Specie Bank and that on or about December 1, 1941, they had arranged for permission to play golf at the Waialae Country Club at eight o'clock Sunday, December 7, 1941. These people had not played golf, so far as we were able to ascertain, before this time as far back as April of this year. The indications are that they probably knew of the air raid which was to come on Sunday morning and for that reason were trying to arrange alibis for their presence.

Robert L. Shivers to Director, Federal Bureau of Investigation, Washington, D.C., 17 December 1941.

23. Thirty-five Japanese fishermen were interned. Among them was Minosuke Hanabusa, whose granddaughter, Colleen Hanabusa, would later be elected to the U.S. Congress from Hawai'i. Before the war, Japanese fishing vessels were frequent targets of investigation by Honolulu FBI agents, who suspected the Japanese fishermen of espionage. None of those investigated were ever found guilty. With the outbreak of the war, all vessels belonging to Issei fishermen were confiscated, and the Japanese fishing industry came to a halt. Odo, *No Sword to Bury*, 247; Kimura, *Issei*, 120–21; Okihiro, *Cane Fires*, 207.

24. Yaroku Tanaka was the publisher of a Japanese language newspaper, the *Kazan Shimbun* [*Volcano Times*], in the town of Hilo on the island of Hawai'i. Furuya was of the first group of internees, all of whom were from Honolulu. Those from the islands of Hawai'i, Maui, Moloka'i, and Kaua'i were in the second group, which did not arrive on Sand Island until February 21, 1942.

25. Japanese Americans born in the United States, who received an education in Japan and then returned to America.

26. The Honpa Hongwanji Betsuin, located in Nuʻuanu Valley, is the Honolulu headquarters of the Shin-Jōdo sect. In 1910, the Hongwanji Betsuin established the Hawaii Japanese Language Middle School (Hawaii Chūgakkō), of which Rev. Genshin Tatsutani was the principal.

27. Mary Lou Eifler

28. Furuya has altered somewhat the usual meaning of this phrase. The actual expression is *"Oni no nyōbō ni wa kijin ga naru,"* a man who behaves like a devil will likewise have a wife who is a devil.

29. This is Motokazu Mori (1890–1958), son of Iga Mori. Motokazu was born and educated in Japan before becoming a surgeon at Honolulu's Japanese Hospital. He was summoned to the hospital on December 7 to attend to victims of the Pearl Harbor attack, but upon his return home that evening was arrested along with his father. His wife was the physician Ishiko Mori. Motokazu was a prolific writer of *tanka*; translations of his poems appear in Keiho Soga, Taisanboku Mori, Sojin Takei, and Muin Ozaki, *Poets Behind Barbed Wire*, ed. and trans. by Jiro Nakano and Kay Nakano (Honolulu: Bamboo Ridge Press, 1983). See also Victor M. Mori, *East Meets West: A Family History* (Honolulu: privately printed, 2010), 32; Soga, *Life behind Barbed Wire*, 39.

30. Ishiko Shibuya Mori (1899–1972) was an Issei physician who married the widower Motokazu. In 1934, Ishiko Mori became the Hawaiʻi correspondent for the major Japanese newspaper *Yomiuri Shimbun*. Two days before the Pearl Harbor attack, with Honolulu FBI agents listening in, Ishiko engaged in a telephone call with the *Yomiuri* office in Tokyo. She was arrested immediately after the bombing and accused of spying. Furuya notes that Iga Mori was released shortly after his arrest because of his poor health, but both Ishiko and Motokazu were interned for the duration of the war. At Crystal City, they established a camp hospital, with Ishiko serving as a general physician and her husband as the chief surgeon. Soga, *Life behind Barbed Wire*, 39; Mori, *East Meets West*; Taniguchi Susumu, *"Shinbun kisha futari no unmei o kaeta Shinjuwan"* [The Pearl Harbor attack that changed the destinies of two newspaper correspondents], *This is Yomiuri* (December 1998): 160–64; Barbara Bennett Peterson, ed., *Notable Women of Hawaii* (Honolulu: University of Hawaiʻi Press, 1984), 274–77.

31. Tekisui was the pen name for Takasuke Tanaka, the principal of the Wahiawa Japanese Language School. When he died in 1928, Haru succeeded him. For an account of the war years based on interviews with Haru Tanaka and her daughter, Muriel Tanaka Onishi, see Tomi Kaizawa Knaefler, *Our House Divided: Seven Japanese American Families in World War II* (Honolulu: University of Hawaiʻi Press, 1991), 59–74.

32. Konkōkyō is a sect of Japan's native Shinto religion.

33. The identities of the women in this section need some clarification. First, although listed as if they are two separate individuals, Shinsho Hirai and Ryuto Tsuda are in fact the same person. Shinsho Hirai was born Kiyome Hirai and took the name Shinsho when she became a Buddhist nun. She later wed an individual named Tsuda and became known by her married name, Ryuto Tsuda. When

she divorced after the war, she reverted to the name Shinsho Hirai. The wife of Kosaku Horibe is Kiku Horibe. She was a Konkōkyō priest. Kanzen Ito was a nun at the Mantokuji Temple in Pāʻia on Maui. She was suspected of espionage and repatriated to Japan aboard the second exchange ship in September 1943. Irene Umeno Harada's husband was involved in the 1941 Niʻihau Incident, in which a Japanese fighter pilot, after participating in the Pearl Harbor attack, crash-landed on the tiny, privately owned island. The pilot and Harada's husband, the Nisei caretaker of the island's ranch, became embroiled in a violent dispute with several residents. The pilot was killed and Harada's husband shot himself. In the aftermath, Irene Umeno was jailed on Kauaʻi and later sent to Sand Island before being interned at Honouliuli. Teruchiyo Suzuki was the stage name of Yasuye Takahashi, a *rōkyoku-shi*, or Japanese minstrel. Furuya lists both names, Teruchiyo Suzuki and Yasue Takahashi separately, although this is the same individual. These women were arrested and interned because of their own individual status and should not be confused with those who would later voluntarily enter the confinement system in order to join their husbands. Eight were confined on the Mainland: Kiku Horibe, Kanzen Ito, Miyuki Kawasaki, Yuki Miyao, Yoshie Miyao, Ishiko Mori, Haru Tanaka, and Tsuta Yamane. Six were interned at Honouliuli: Masako Fujimura, Umeno Irene Harada, Shizuko Nakagawa, Haruko Takahashi, Yasuye Takahashi, and Ryuto Tsuda. For Soga's discussion of the women internees, see *Life behind Barbed Wire*, 45–47. Information on these internees is also from *History of the Soto Sect in Hawaiʻi* (Honolulu: Hawaiʻi Sōtō Mission Bishop's Office, 2002), 116–17; Saiki, *Ganbare!*, 49–59; JCCH Internee Database. Information about Shinsho Hirai was provided to the translator by Rev. K. Hirai, niece of Shinsho, and the current religious leader of the Todaiji Hawaiʻi Bekkaku Honzan in Honolulu.

34. Hawaiian: An area west of Honolulu, also used to indicate a westerly direction.

35. The Emergency Service Committee was one of several morale committees established shortly after the Pearl Harbor attack to bolster the war effort and ensure racial cohesion in Hawaiʻi. A predominantly Nisei organization, the ESC sought to demonstrate the loyalty of the Japanese community by recruiting volunteers for the 442nd Regimental Combat Team and organizing other patriotic efforts. Historians have pointed to the ESC's success in stepping into the leadership void created by the internment of the Issei, as many committee members rose to prominence in the territory's postwar order. Hawaiʻi, Office of the Military Governor, Morale Section, Emergency Service Committee, *Report of the Emergency Service Committee* (Honolulu: n.p., 1944); Kelli Y. Nakamura, "Emergency Service Committee," *Densho Encyclopedia*, http://encyclopedia.densho.org/Emergency%20 Service%20Committee/(accessed November 2, 2012).

36. Masatoshi Katagiri was an insurance executive from Honolulu. Isao Murai was also known as Ernest Isao Murai, a Honolulu dentist. After the war, he would become a close political ally of future governor John A. Burns and play a prominent role in the establishment of the Hawaiʻi Democratic Party. Katsumi Kometani was a Honolulu dentist and an owner of the Asahi, Hawaiʻi's preeminent, semi-profes-

sional Nikkei baseball franchise prior to the war. Kometani volunteered for military service and, in order to prevent confiscation of his Asahi franchise, turned over ownership of the team to his friend John A. Burns. As morale officer for the 100th Infantry Battalion, he organized baseball games among the Nisei soldiers and spearheaded goodwill baseball tours through towns near the 100th's training grounds. He was decorated for bravery during fighting in Italy. Yasuo Goto, also known as Y. Baron Goto, volunteered for military duty during World War II. He later became the director of the University of Hawai'i's Agricultural Extension Service and a vice-chancellor at the East-West Center. A gifted orator and writer, educator Shigeo Yoshida was instrumental in the establishment of the ESC. His encouragement of Japanese American displays of patriotism and cooperation with the government were seen as critical in preventing the mass incarceration of Hawaii's Japanese. Michael Markrich, "Katsumi Kometani: A Man for All Seasons," 100th Infantry Battalion Veterans Education Center, http://www.100thbattalion .org/history/veterans/officers/katsumi-doc-kometani/; Dennis M. Ogawa, *Kodomo no tame ni—For the sake of the children: The Japanese American Experience in Hawaii* (Honolulu: University of Hawai'i Press, 1978), 351–52, 364–65; Hawai'i Nikkei History Editorial Board, ed., *Japanese Eyes, American Heart: Personal Reflections of Hawaii's World War II Nisei Soldiers* (Honolulu: Tendai Educational Foundation, 1998), 269–71; "Yasuo Baron Goto Honorary Album, 1903-ca. 1962," University Archives, University of Hawai'i-Mānoa; Tom Coffman, "Shigeo Yoshida," *Densho Encyclopedia* http://encyclopedia.densho.org/Shigeo%20Yoshida/ (accessed November 28, 2012); Odo, *No Sword to Bury*, 119–21, 244–51.

Chapter 5

1. Hawaiian: blue denim.
2. Shigenari Hattori
3. This is the poetry name of Tsunetaro Harada, an innkeeper from Honolulu.
4. India ink painting.
5. Furuya published a very similar poem in his 1958 haiku collection: 暗い中の声が知人の声で監禁されている. See *Ruten*, 4.
6. Angel Island in San Francisco Bay was the site of a U.S. Army post and a station run by the Immigration and Naturalization Service. The INS station served as a processing center for all immigrants entering through San Francisco, as well as a detention facility, with its island location making it as escape-proof as nearby Alcatraz. In 1940, the army gained control of the INS site, and with the beginning of World War II, it became a POW processing center where German and Japanese prisoners—including those classified as enemy alien internees—were sent before being transferred to camps in the interior. Him Mark Lai, Genny Lim, and Judy Yung, *Island: Poetry and History of Chinese Immigrants on Angel Island, 1910–1940* (Seattle: University of Washington Press, 1980), 8–25; "United States Immigration Station (USIS)," Angel Island Conservancy, http:// angelisland.org/history/united-states-immigration-station-usis/; Erika Lee and

Judy Yung, *Angel Island: Immigrant Gateway to America* (New York: Oxford University Press, 2010).

Chapter 6

1. Folded-paper crane.
2. A miniature Japanese garden displayed on a tray.
3. Some 175,000 Chinese immigrants were processed through the Angel Island Immigration Station at the turn of the twentieth century. Confined at the station barracks, sometimes for months, detainees carved poems into the walls of the wooden two-story building. Subsequently hidden under years of paint, the poems were discovered in 1970 as the barracks were slated for demolition. Since then, some 130 poems have been recorded and translated, and the Angel Island Immigration Station has been preserved as a museum. Lee, Angel Island, 299–314; Lai, Island, 8–25. This first poem is reproduced here as it appears in Lai, *Island*, 162. © 1991. Reprinted with permission of University of Washington Press.
4. Furuya is providing a Japanese interpretation of the Chinese characters 番奴. The actual Chinese meaning of these characters is not "guards," or by Furuya's interpretation, "guys on watch," but rather "barbarians." See Lai, *Island*, 162.
5. Furuya mistakenly rendered the last two poems as one long poem. Reproduced here are the two separate poems as they appear in *Island*, 153, 160. © 1991. Reprinted with permission of University of Washington Press.
6. Katsuichi Kawamoto
7. Yujiro Nada

Chapter 7

1. The Golden Gate International Exposition was held in 1939 and again in 1940.
2. In 1933, the U.S. Army's Camp McCoy became a supply base for the Depression-era public works program known as the Civilian Conservation Corps. Both the National Park Service and the army administered the CCC, which employed men in conservation and reforestation work.
3. This is actually Barracks 3. See Chapter 7.

Chapter 8

1. Furuya likely has erred in identifying this individual. This is probably one of the Isobe brothers, Shigemi or Misao, Shinto priests from Honolulu who were sent to the Mainland along with Furuya in Group 1. No one named Tanehiro Isobe was interned from Hawai'i. Furuya may have been thinking of Hirotane Isobe, a Buddhist priest from Honolulu, but he was in Group 10 and was not transferred to the Mainland until 1943.
2. Hawaiian: Caucasian.

3. This is Charles Ichitaro Hasebe.

4. Only forty names are listed.

5. In 1943, after all Issei internees had been transferred to various Department of Justice camps, McCoy was turned into a prisoner of war camp, becoming the largest permanent facility for Japanese POWs in the continental United States. Japanese POWs at the end of the war numbered some 2,762. About 3,000 German and 500 Korean POWs were held here as well. Brandon Jeffery Scott, "The Untold Story of Camp McCoy: Japanese Prisoners of War in the Heart of Wisconsin during the Second World War," (bachelor's thesis, University of Wisconsin-Eau Claire, 2010), Minds@UW, http://digital.library.wisc.edu/1793/44611; Fort McCoy, U.S. Army, "Fort McCoy: History & Heritage," http://www.mccoy.army.mil/AboutUs/History/FMCHistHrtg.pdf.

6. "The Pacific March" (*"Taiheiyō kōshinkyoku"*), "The March of the Flag of the Rising Sun" (*"Hi-no-maru kōshinkyoku"*), "The Song of the Yalu River" (*"Ōryokko-bushi"*), and similar *gunka*, or war songs, were composed in the late 1930s, when major Japanese newspapers sponsored competitions for the composition of patriotic songs. War songs of this sort, incorporating Western musical styles with Japanese military marches, originated in the Meiji era and continued during the period of the Sino-Japanese (1894–95) and Russo-Japanese (1904–05) wars. Songs glorifying the exploits of the Japanese military became even more popular during the war years.

7. The gods. The term is often associated with Japan's Shinto religion.

8. *Umakata-bushi*, also known as *mago-uta* (songs of the packhorse drivers), are a type of folk song sung by the drivers of packhorses that transported freight and passengers throughout Japan. *Izumo-bushi* are folk songs from the Izumo area in Shimane Prefecture, near Reverend Okano's hometown. *Obako-bushi* (songs of young, unmarried ladies), also called *Akita obako*, are folk tunes with humorous lyrics from Akita Prefecture.

9. The 'Ewa Plantation Company was one of the most prosperous sugar plantations on Oʻahu and an employer of thousands of Japanese contract laborers at the turn of the twentieth century. The plantation was one of six embroiled in the 1920 Oʻahu-wide strike by twelve thousand Japanese and Filipino sugar workers.

10. In a script for a radio broadcast made in Honolulu during the 1950s, Otokichi Ozaki noted:

> We were only allowed to write letters in English in the early days [of the internment]. At the time it was hard for me to write in English, as it seemed I had already forgotten how. Nevertheless, with great difficulty I wrote letters in English to my family and also did so for my fellow internees. English also was a must for the letters from our families. When we spoke amongst ourselves, we naturally spoke in Japanese, but we avoided doing so when there were guards nearby. On the morning of December 8, when we were sent to the camp mess hall, we were told that no Japanese was to be spoken and no finger-pointing would be allowed. Orders were announced in May 1942 that allowed those

who could not write in English to write in Japanese. The letters were supposed to be written within twenty-four lines and in plain language. We could only mail up to two letters a week. These letters were first sent to a censor bureau somewhere in New York and then sent on to Hawai'i. Usually it took a few months before they reached the address.

Translation by Tatsumi Hayashi, from Otokichi Ozaki, "Internees and Japanese Language," Radio Script 7, n.d., Otokichi Ozaki Collection, AR1, Box 4, Folder 13, Japanese Cultural Center of Hawai'i Resource Center, Honolulu.

11. A short-sleeved man's shirt sewn of fabric with a Hawaiian-themed design.

12. This Japanese saying, *"Ame futte, chi katamaru,"* means that good can often come from bad.

13. *"Kachūsha no uta"* (Katyusha's song) was written for a dramatization of the Leo Tolstoy novel, *Resurrection*. The play was produced by Shimamura Hōgetsu, who brought to Japanese audiences modern social dramas by Western playwrights such as Tolstoy, Anton Chekov, and Henrik Ibsen. Matsui Sumako's recording of "Katyusha's Song" was an enormous popular success.

14. The Group that Supports the 100-Year War (*Hyaku-nen sensō kiseikai*); The Group that Supports the Twenty-Five-Year War (*Nijūgonen chōkisen shijikai*).

15. Spain was the protecting power for Japanese citizens in the United States during World War II. It was through the Spanish Consul that internees made requests of the U.S. State Department for redress of their grievances, as was allowed by the Geneva Convention. A formal meeting took place between the Spanish Consul and internee representatives at Fort Missoula in December 1943. Furuya discusses this meeting in Chapter 11.

16. The Swedish ocean liner the MS *Gripsholm* sailed under the aegis of the International Red Cross, exchanging American and Japanese POWs and repatriates. It made two trips. The first involved some 1,400 Japanese nationals and family members, including members of the Japanese diplomatic corps, as well as U.S. and Latin American citizens, who were exchanged for passengers aboard the NYK Lines passenger ship *Asama Maru* at what is today Maputo, Mozambique. The second exchange of Japanese repatriates and American citizens took place a year later at Goa, India, then a territory of Portugal. See Kashima, *Judgment Without Trial*, 280n75.

17. Having transferred to a Japanese ship at the neutral port of Goa, the Asamis were headed back to Japan, when the vessel made a stop in the captured Japanese territory of Singapore. His English-language skills in demand, and finding Singapore's climate favorable for his asthma, Asami disembarked. The family lived in Singapore until the waning days of Japan's control, when all civilians were evacuated from the peninsula. Asami and his son left aboard the *Awa Maru*, which sailed under a U.S. safe-conduct pass because of the supplies it carried for prison camps holding Allied POWs. Near midnight on April 1, 1945, the *Awa Maru* was torpedoed and sunk in the Taiwan Strait by the American submarine, the USS *Queenfish*. All but one of the ship's more than two thousand passengers and crew

were killed. The sinking of the *Awa Maru* was the third worst maritime disaster in history and became a significant issue in post-war diplomatic relations between the United States and Japan. Yasutaro Soga in his autobiography, *Gojūnen no Hawai kaiko*, recounts the news of Asami's death:

> On November 13, 1945, the year the war ended, the ship from Seattle that carried us internees from the mainland arrived in Honolulu. Upon our arrival, we heard the very shocking news: the wife of the chief editor of the *Nippu Jiji*, Shoichi Asami, and their youngest child, Ryozo, had been killed in the seas off of Taiwan when the *Awa Maru*, carrying them from Singapore to Japan, was sunk by an American battleship. Soon after, we were surprised again to learn that one of the victims was not Asami's wife but Shoichi himself.... He was fifty-one years old. Asami was a tanka poet and one of the founders of the Choonshisha poetry society. On December 23, 1945, a memorial service was held by his friends at the Honpa Betsuin in Honolulu.

This translation is courtesy of Emi and George Oshiro. For more on Asami, see Soga, *Gojūnen no Hawai kaiko*, 683; Knaefler, *Our House Divided*, 46–58; Honda, *Family Torn Apart*, 23–25, 74–75. For information on the sinking of the *Awa Maru*, see Roger Dingman, *Ghost of War: The Sinking of the Awa Maru and Japanese-American Relations, 1945–1995* (Anapolis: Naval Institute Press, 1997).

18. The Crystal City Internment Camp in Texas, known as the "Family Camp," was the only Immigration and Naturalization Service camp to hold the families of internees. The Jerome Relocation Center in Arkansas, which closed in 1944, and the Tule Lake Relocation Center in California were under the jurisdiction of the War Relocation Authority (WRA) and also confined internees and families wanting to repatriate. Families of Hawai'i internees incarcerated on the Mainland voluntarily entered the internment system for the sake of family reunification or repatriation to Japan. For a depiction of one Hawai'i family's efforts to reunite, see Honda, *Family Torn Apart*.

19. Asami titled his song, "*Intānī Dōchū*," basing its melody and lyrics on the popular 1935 ballad, "*Tabigasa Dōchū*" [Journey of a wanderer]. Another version of Asami's lyrics appears in Honda, *Family Torn Apart*, 24.

20. *Sumō*, or Japanese wrestling, is a two-thousand-year-old sport. *Sumō* songs (*sumō jinku*) were originally sung by wrestlers to entertain the audience.

21. Rice balls, grilled beef, and vegetables stewed in soy sauce.

22. The Sanka were a group of nomadic people living in the mountains of Japan. Their numbers declined during World War II, and little is known of them today.

23. A U.S. Army post, Schofield's population of fourteen thousand made it the second largest city in the territory during World War II.

Chapter 9

1. Using the authority granted by the Alien Enemy Act of 1798, which gave presidents the power to apprehend and restrain resident enemy aliens during times

of war, the Justice Department investigated and arrested some 6,300 Germans during World War I. Two thousand individuals were interned, laying a precedent for the government's program of investigation and incarceration of resident aliens two decades later. Rosenfeld, "German and Italian detainees," *Denshō*.

2. This is Taichi Sato.

3. Castner Village, as it was informally called, is the U.S. Army post of Schofield Barracks in central Oʻahu.

4. Sakamaki recalls this mission and capture in his memoir, *Horyo dai-ichigo*. Several items in Furuya's account are worth pointing out. He identifies Sakamaki's vessel as an I-24 mini-submarine. The I-24 was actually the mother submarine that carried Sakamaki's HA-19 mini-submarine, which was released off of Pearl Harbor. The fumes that Furuya describes were likely caused when leaking battery acid came into contact with seawater, creating a deadly chlorine gas that consumed the mini-sub. Sakamaki notes that his mini-submarine was stranded near the Kāneʻohe airfield; however, it is more likely that he beached near Bellows Air Field in Waimānalo. See the U.S. Navy's official naval history website containing photographs and descriptions of Sakamaki's midget submarine taken on the morning of December 8, 1941, "Japanese Navy Ships: HA-19 (Midget Submarine, 1938–41)," Naval History and Heritage Command (May 3, 2009), www.history .navy.mil/photos/sh-fornv/japan/japsh-h/ha19.htm.

5. One *ri* is equivalent to about two-and-a-half miles.

6. Kobayashi Issa was a poet and devotee of the Shin-Jōdo sect. He is said to have written this poem during a period of financial difficulty, at the end of the year, when all debts should have been paid off. This translation is from D. T. Suzuki, *Buddha of Infinite Light: The Teachings of Shin Buddhism, the Japanese Way of Wisdom and Compassion* (Boston and London: Shambhala Publications, 1997), 65. Reprinted by arrangement with The Permissions Company, Inc., on behalf of Shambhala Publications Inc., Boston, MA. www.shambhala.com.

Chapter 10

1. The Army-run Livingston Internment Camp was located in Alexandria, north of Baton Rouge, in central Louisiana.

2. This U.S. Army internment camp was located southwest of Oklahoma City, in an area known for its severe dust storms and scorching heat. For a description of Fort Sill by a Hawaiʻi internee, see Otokichi Ozaki, *Family Torn Apart*, 65–67.

3. Internee accounts depict Oshima as having been under great strain, burdened by concerns for his large family (he had eleven children) and his mounting business obligations back in Hawaiʻi. Oshima's killing took place on May 12, 1942. For a description of this event, see Honda, *Family Torn Apart*, 68–69.

4. This is Takaichi Saiki, manager of the Hilo branch of Bank of Hawaii, not to be confused with Takaichi Sakai of the Japanese Consulate, who is mentioned in Chapter 4.

5. Japanese fencing based on sword-fighting techniques, in which practi-

tioners use a length of split bamboo. Because it was seen to have promoted militarism within Japanese society, the practice of kendō was viewed with suspicion in the United States and banned in Japan during the American Occupation.

6. From the Japanese proverb, "*Tanin no gobō de hōji o suru*," to use the burdock brought by someone else for the vegetarian meal at one's own Buddhist funeral. In other words, to benefit at someone else's expense.

7. A play on the expression "*honemi o kezuru*," meaning to scrape off one's flesh from one's bones. In other words, to work without sparing oneself.

8. A dish of thinly sliced meat, usually beef, vegetables, and tofu cooked in a seasoned broth.

9. A five-holed bamboo flute.

10. Michio Ito, a dancer and choreographer, has been called "the forgotten pioneer of American modern dance." He attempted to create a fusion of eastern and western dance styles, something wholly new at the time. A successful Hollywood choreographer before the war, Ito repatriated in 1943. Mary Jean Cowell, "Michio Ito Study Guide: History of Michio Ito," Repertory Dance Theatre, Salt Lake City, Utah, 2009–10 Season, http://www.rdtutah.org/artsedu/study%20 guide%20michio%20ito.pdf; "Michio Ito," *Encyclopedia of Japanese American History: An A-to-Z Reference from 1868 to the Present*, updated ed. (New York: Checkmark Books, 2001), 215–16.

11. "*Gunkan Māchi*" is the most famous of the genre of Western-style military songs that were popular in Japan during the first half of the twentieth century. After the disarmament of Japan at the end of the World War II, things military were ostracized for a time, including music of this type. Today, this march is again played at official ceremonies of the Japanese Maritime Self-Defense Forces.

12. This is the traditional folk music of the Yagi area, near the Tochigi and Gunma prefectural border. The hallmark of this Bon dance song is its driving beat, performed on hand-gongs, various drums, and most distinctly on over-turned sake barrels.

13. Also known as *rōkyoku*, this is a type of musical ballad in which the narrator traditionally is accompanied by a shamisen player. Most items in the repertoire are well-known stories that deal with the perennial Japanese dilemma of love versus duty. *Naniwa-bushi* were very popular during the 1920s and 1930s.

14. "Spring Rain" or "*Harusame*" is a *ha-uta*, a type of short popular song, usually performed to the accompaniment of a shamisen. *Ha-uta* derived from *naga-uta*, or long epic songs, which were developed during the Edo period as the accompanying music for kabuki performances.

15. These holes were probably similar to foxholes, dug in the ground under the floorboards of the raised barracks.

16. Stiff iron fans were carried into battle by samurai who used them to deflect the strokes of swords.

17. Hisahiko Kokubo was a storeowner from Waimea on the island of Kaua'i. His sudden death during the early days of confinement at Sand Island had a profound impact on the Hawai'i internees. Yoichi Kagimoto was a forty-eight-year-

old fisherman from the Kaka'ako district of Honolulu who was confined at Sand Island. Suffering from severe stomach pain, Kagimoto was aided at the camp dispensary, but subsequently died. Kanesaburo Oshima's killing has been previously discussed. Gosaku Masuda, who died in December 1942, was the owner of the Masuda Shokai trading company in Lāhainā, Maui. Concern about Masuda's personal effects is brought up during a formal meeting in December 1943 between the Spanish Consul and internee representatives at Fort Missoula. Furuya discusses this meeting in Chapter 11. For descriptions of these deaths, see Soga, *Life behind Barbed Wire*, 59–60; Honda, *Family Torn Apart*, 44–45; and Saiki, *Ganbare!*, 56, 95–97, 167.

18. Saint Nichiren was the founder of the Nichiren sect of Japanese Buddhism, one of the major sects to become established in the islands.

19. Tokuichi Niimi was a storekeeper from Wahiawā.

20. By early 1942, seventy to eighty German and Italian internees were being held at Sand Island. Some were soon sent to various Mainland camps, but then on April 28, 1942, thirteen of the internees, who were American citizens, were returned to Sand Island. According to Yasutaro Soga, a new rule had been instituted prohibiting the Mainland transfer of U.S. citizens. Soga, *Behind Barbed Wire*, 49.

21. These nineteen Nisei were again transferred back to internment on the Mainland and not allowed to return to Hawai'i until after the war. Lordsburg was a U.S. Army internment camp located in southwest New Mexico.

22. *Sanga Ari* (Hills and rivers remain) was made in 1962 and tells the tale of Japanese migration to Hawai'i. The title is from the expression, *"Kuni yaburete sanga ari,"* which means that although the country lies in ruins, hills and rivers remain. The movie featured the popular actress Takamine Hideko and was directed by her husband, Matsuyama Zenzo. Takamine and Matsuyama later lived in Hawai'i.

23. Japanese wooden clogs.

24. Oiwake is a type of traditional folk song originating in the melancholy ballads of the packhorse drivers from the Shinano-Oiwake region in today's Nagano prefecture.

25. An elevated ring, about twenty-one inches high and fifteen feet in diameter, used in sumō wrestling.

26. Furuya himself owned a retail furniture store in Honolulu called Fuji Furniture, which was a different establishment from Fujii Store.

27. Hirotatsu Kimura was engaged in a law-related business in Los Angeles. His poetry name was Shonan.

28. Seiha was Shoichi Asami's poetry name, and Koran was the poetry name of Minoru Murakami, the Hilo bureau chief of the *Nippu Jiji*. Asami and Murakami also conducted broadcasts while they were together at Fort Sill in the spring of 1942. Broadcasting the news began early in the internment and eventually became common to all the camps. *Family Torn Apart*, 71–73.

29. *Shuryūdan* 手榴弾: hand grenade; *shōsai* 詳細: detail; *oboegaki* 覚書: memorandum; *kakudai* 拡大: to extend; *zenpukuteki* 全幅的: wholeheartedly; *tachiba* 立場: position; *sūjikukoku* 枢軸国: the Axis powers.

30. The expression is from a Chinese proverb meaning, "A rod that extends one hundred feet." Thus to advance a step further or to extend one's reach.

31. Meaning, "Working hard every day, eh?" *Janjan* is a slang term meaning very often, very fast, or very much, so in this case, working hard.

32. Shigeo Joe Takata (1919–43) was a highly regarded amateur baseball player with the championship Honolulu club the Asahi. He also was a member of the 100th Infantry Battalion's Aloha Team, organized by its recreation officer, Katsumi Kometani, owner of the Asahi. The Aloha played "friendship games" against community teams, as well as at nearby internment camps, including a 1943 Fourth of July series at the Jerome Relocation Center in Arkansas. Takata was killed the following September, just a week after his unit landed in Italy, and was posthumously decorated for heroism. Although Furuya describes him as a pitcher, published accounts identify Takata as an outfielder and a shortstop. See Samuel Hideo Yamashita, "The Aloha Team, 1942–1943" in *More than a Game: Sport in the Japanese American Community*, edited by Brian Niiya (Los Angeles: Japanese American National Museum, 2000), 162–73; Michael M. Okihiro, *AJA Baseball in Hawaii: Ethnic Pride and Tradition* (Honolulu: Japanese Cultural Center of Hawai'i, 1999), 40–41; Hirai Ryuzo, *Kakedashi kisha gojyunen: Ashi de kaita hawai nikkeijinshi* (Tokyo: Hirai Ryuzo Shuppan Jikkō Iinkai, 1990), 107.

33. For two years in the early 1960s, Furuya wrote a series of articles for *The Hawaii Times* about his internment experiences. Furuya used those articles as the basis of his book.

34. The Japanese dictionary *Daijiten* was published in twenty-six volumes from 1934 to 1936 by the prominent Tokyo publishing house Heibonsha, Ltd. The linguist Kindaichi Kyōsuke edited *Jikai*, which was first published by Sanseidō in 1952.

35. A type of cicada known for its irritating chirp.

36. Evening cicadas, more commonly known in Japan as *higurashi*.

37. The phrase, meaning to walk while looking upward, comes from the 1960s Japanese hit song of the same name. Translated into English and renamed "Sukiyaki" in order to make it more appealing to non-Asian audiences, the love song gained worldwide popularity.

38. Named "Mizora" or "Misora" because of its phonetic similarity to "Missoula."

39. Fort McDowell was the U.S. Army post on Angel Island. It included a processing center for Japanese and German prisoners of war, who were then shipped to permanent prison camps in the interior of the Mainland.

40. Toka Ida was the pen name of Taira Ida, an art dealer from Honolulu.

41. A monetary offering presented at a funeral to the family of the deceased.

42. Murai, a member of the Emergency Service Committee, and his wife were called upon by the U.S. Army and the Red Cross to accompany the first group of repatriating family members to the Grove Park Inn in Asheville, North Carolina. During World War II, a number of Appalachian resorts, including the

Grove Park Inn, housed Axis diplomats and corporate executives and their families as they awaited repatriation. The family of Shoichi Asami was among those housed at Grove Park. For more on the Asami family, see Knaefler, *Our House Divided*, 46–58; also Kashima, *Judgment without Trial, 180–82* for more on the "internment hotels." Shigeo Yoshida, "Emergency Service Committee, Club 100 30th Anniversary Reunion, June 1972," 100th Infantry Battalion Veterans Education Center, http://www.100thbattalion.org/archives/puka-puka-parades/wartime-hawaii/emergency-service-committee/.

43. (Henry) Toyosaku Komai helped establish the *Rafu Shimpo* (L.A. Japanese Daily News) in Los Angeles in 1903. When Komai and his editorial staff were arrested following Pearl Harbor, the newspaper shut down. It resumed publication in January 1946, the first ethnic press to do so on the West Coast.

44. Takeda Shingen was a military lord of the sixteenth century Warring States period, whose domain comprised territory in present-day Yamanashi, Furuya's home province. Shingen was supported by twenty-four generals who guarded his territory from enemy invasion.

45. This is likely Galen M. Fisher, who headed the YMCA in Japan for twenty years. Living in California at the time of the West Coast mass evacuation, Fisher became an active opponent of the internment. See Robert Shaffer, "Galen Fisher," *Densho Encyclopedia*, http://encyclopedia.densho.org/Galen%20Fisher/ (accessed November 12, 2012); Yoshiko Uchida, *Desert Exile: The Uprooting of a Japanese-American Family* (Seattle: University of Washington Press, 1982), 85.

46. This Justice Department facility was located in Bismarck, *North* Dakota, and was officially known as Fort Abraham Lincoln Internment Camp. For more on this camp, see Kashima, *Judgment without Trial*, 109.

47. The remaining internees left the camp for Santa Fe on June 4, 1943.

48. Located in the prefecture from where Furuya hailed, Shōsenkyō is considered one of the most beautiful gorges in Japan.

Chapter 11

1. Also known as Kōfu Basin and located in central Yamanashi prefecture. The prefectural capital, Kōfu city, is located in this basin. Furuya's hometown is nearby.

2. In 1560, in the narrows of Okehazama, close to the city of Nagoya, the military lord Oda Nobunaga defeated his powerful neighbor, Imagawa Yoshimoto, with a force one-tenth that of his rival's and so took the first step in his domination of Japan.

3. *Mizora* means "beautiful sky."

4. Along with individuals from countries like Panama, Bolivia, and Ecuador, Peruvian Japanese were subjects of a U.S.-sponsored plan that involved the deportation of three thousand Latin American resident aliens and citizens to be used in a prisoner exchange program with Japan. Scholars have pointed to the Peruvian government as the "chief culprit" in the scheme for its role in providing more than

eighty percent of all the Japanese Latin American deportees. Robinson, *A Tragedy of Democracy*, 6, 148–52; Kashima, *Judgment Without Trial*, 94–95; *Personal Justice Denied*, 305–14; C. Harvey Gardiner, *Pawns in a Triangle of Hate: The Peruvian Japanese and the United States* (Seattle: University of Washington Press, 1981); Stephen Mak, "Japanese Latin Americans," *Densho Encyclopedia*, http://encyclopedia.densho.org/Japanese%20Latin%20Americans/(accessed December 18, 2013).

5. Bert H. Fraser was the officer-in-charge of this Justice Department camp.

6. This is the Charles Ichitaro Hasebe who was involved in the "Empty Can Incident" at McCoy and who shook hands with a general at Camp Forrest. While at Missoula, Hasebe wrote a letter to the Office of the Military Governor of Hawaii petitioning for his early release; see *Family Torn Apart*, 64–66. He was later paroled to Denver.

7. Furuya may be mistaken. This is likely Saburo Uyehara, a waiter from Honolulu. While there were six individuals named Uyehara (or Uehara) among the Hawai'i internees, only Saburo was interned at Missoula. JCCH Internee Database.

8. National Geographic Society, *The Book of Fishes: Game Fishes, Food Fishes, Shellfish and Curious Citizens of American Ocean Shores, Lakes and Rivers; with 134 illustrations, color plates of 92 familiar salt and fresh-water fishes, color plates from life by Hashime Murayama* (Washington, D.C.: The National Geographic Society, 1924). Although the illustrator's first name is romanized as "Hashime," his name was more likely correctly pronounced "Hajime."

9. Chinese characters.

10. The pronunciation of his first name is the *on*, or Chinese reading, of the characters 林長.

11. In the early days of the internment, the Department of Justice's Kenedy Internment Camp, located southeast of San Antonio, confined civilians from Latin America—some 450 Germans, 150 Japanese, and a dozen Italians—to be used in the U.S. government's prisoner exchange program. By late 1943, more than 1,100 Germans and 700 Japanese were held there; and beginning in 1944, it became primarily a prison for German and Japanese POWs. Onaga was a barber from Hanapepe, Kaua'i. He may have been sent to Kenedy because his barbering skills were needed there. *Confinement and Ethnicity*, 386–87; Stephen Mak, "Kenedy (detention facility)," *Densho Encyclopedia*, http://encyclopedia.densho.org/Kenedy%20(detention%20facility)/ (accessed December 4, 2013).

12. Furuya renders these names using the Japanese syllabary *katakana*. He does not include the kanji for them, but they are provided here because they are unusual: Mende 免出, Deki 出来, Deme 出面, Kanja 神社, Kokuzo 穀蔵, Akegarasu 暁鳥, Kurotobi 黒飛, Ganyoko 我如古, and Doita 土居田.

13. In *kana*, the Japanese phonetic alphabet, the name "Chikuma" is written as チクマ and provides no meaning to a Japanese speaker. When rendered in kanji as 竹間, it can mean "a room of bamboo" or "in between the bamboo."

14. A form of fortune telling based on the number of strokes in the Chinese characters that make up one's name.

15. The well-known theater was modeled on a shrine to the Japanese ruler

Tokugawa Ieyasu. Along with the Kokusai and other theaters of the 'A'ala district, it showed movies and provided live entertainment for its Japanese-speaking audiences. *A'ala*, 32–36.

16. Established in 1908, this Shinto shrine was located on the corner of South King and Sheridan streets. In 1992, it was absorbed by Izumo Taisha, a shrine in downtown Honolulu.

17. *Kōdan* (historical storytelling) and *rakugo* (comic storytelling) performances in variety theaters in the big cities of Edo (today Tokyo) and Osaka became popular during the Tokugawa era. Even now, they are among the most popular TV programs in Japan.

18. A member of the internee administration's Missoula Office of Japanese Internees, Sawajiro Ozaki held the post of Detail Supervisor, which meant that he was probably in charge of logistics—that is, clean up. For a list of those in the Missoula internee administration and their positions, see *Family Torn Apart*, 53–56.

19. Furuya has written this title in English, meaning a *toritsuginin*.

20. Sokan Ueoka was the resident minister of the Soto sect's Mantokuji temple in Pā'ia on the island of Maui. En route back to Japan, he disembarked in Singapore, where he served as a priest in the Japanese army. Ueoka returned to Maui in 1954 and resumed his position as resident minister of the Mantokuji. *History of the Soto Sect*, 116–17; "History of Paia Mantokuji Soto Mission, 1906–2006," in *Paia Mantokuji Soto Mission Centennial Celebration, 1906–2006* (Pā'ia, Hawai'i: Pā'ia Mantokuji Sōtō Mission, 2006), 14–19.

21. Jinshichi Tokairin was an innkeeper in Honolulu.

22. It is very likely that Banba does appear in this annual directory of Japanese residents. The 1940 and 1941 editions list a "Kuromitsu Kobayashi," no doubt one of Banba's several aliases. The last directory came out in 1941, when the newspaper was shut down following the Pearl Harbor bombing. See *Hawai nenkan: Jinmei jūshoroku, 1941* [The Hawaii Japanese Annual and Directory, 1941] (Honolulu: Nippu Jiji Co., 1941).

23. Japanese laborers buried in the cemetery were members of railroad gangs brought to Montana beginning in 1898 by the Issei-run Oriental Trading Company to build the Great Northern Railway that stretched from Minnesota, through Montana, to Seattle, Washington. The contracting company provided the supervisors, translators, and middlemen who negotiated the labor recruits' working conditions with their railroad employer. Most laborers were bachelors and many died from illnesses related to overwork and malnutrition. Yuji Ichioka, *The Issei: The World of the First Generation Japanese Immigrants, 1885–1924* (New York: The Free Press, 1988), 58, 72–77; Noriko Asato, "Japanese," *Encyclopedia of the Great Plains*, edited by David J Wishart, University of Nebraska-Lincoln, http://plainshumanities.unl.edu/encyclopedia/doc/egp.asam.014.xml.

24. Furuya has written this last group of names in Roman letters. All other names appear in kanji.

25. Masao Sogawa was president of the *Shūkan Hawai Shimpō*, a Japanese-

language weekly that was published in Honolulu until it was shut down in 1941. It should not be confused with its predecessor, the very conservative newspaper, the *Hawai Shimpō*, which supported the position of the sugar planters in the 1909 strike. The conservative *Hawai Shimpō* ceased publication in 1922. Kotani, *The Japanese in Hawaii*, 40–44.

26. A verse form more than 1,200 years old, tanka is made up of thirty-one syllables in five lines in a pattern of 5-7-5-7-7 syllables. It often employs metaphor and other figurative language.

27. Thick Japanese noodles.

28. Japanese-style bathtub.

29. "Business Girls." Today called "OLs" or "Office Ladies."

30. A Japanese-style bathtub made of cast iron and heated directly from below. Its name is associated with Ishikawa Goemon, a notorious sixteenth-century thief rumored to have been executed in this type of vessel.

31. Hawaiian: candlenut tree.

32. Furuya no doubt means the University of Montana, which is located in Missoula.

33. The annual lighting of the "M" is a University of Montana ritual. In Kyoto, the mountain Daimonjiyama is the scene of an annual ritual marking the culmination of the Buddhist Bon Festival, when fires are lit to bid farewell to ancestor spirits. After Daimonjiyama, fires in the shape of other characters are lit on several surrounding mountains. *Dai* 大, meaning large or great, is the first character in Daimonjiyama 大文字山.

34. In Japan, wild duck is often cooked with leeks. Thus the duck has brought along the very ingredients needed to make himself into a delicious meal, which is much more than one could even hope for.

35. See his correspondence describing this event, "Letter from Kametaro Maeda, August 4, 1943" in *Family Torn Apart*, 75 -76.

36. "*Tsuchi to heitai*" and "*Aiba kōshinkyoku*," correctly titled "*Aiba shingunka*," were composed in 1939. "*Aikoku kōshinkyoku*" was composed in 1937. Such marches were intended to boost the militaristic mood among Japanese citizens during the Pacific War.

37. *Kanwa daijiten* is a dictionary of Chinese characters with definitions in Japanese. It was edited by Shigeno Yasutsugu and published in Tokyo by Sanseidō in 1903. It remains much used today.

38. This is a type of folk dance music from Tokushima Prefecture on the island of Shikoku, where an annual summer festival attracts thousands of visitors.

39. Hon'imbō is a title of a professional, world-class *go* champion. The successor to the title is determined through annual competition.

40. A system of ranking exists for both amateur and professional *go* players. Amateur rankings range from the ninth *kyū* (degree), the lowest, to the first *kyū*. The next amateur level is of *dan* (grade) and ranges from the lowest at *shodan* (first grade) to *nanadan* (seventh grade), which is a rank nearly as strong as that of a pro-

fessional. *Go* employs a system of handicapping that allows for players of unequal strength to challenge each other. The player using the black stones is considered the weaker opponent and always starts the game by placing the first stone.

41. Ryusaku Tsunoda (1877–1964) was a pioneer in the development of Japanese studies in the United States and the father of Kensaku Tsunoda, whose story of arrest was told in Chapter 4. Born and educated in Japan, Ryusaku Tsunoda went to Hawai'i under the auspices of the Hongwanji Mission at the turn of the century, becoming principal of the temple's Hawaii Chugakko. Later, at Columbia University, he helped to establish its Japanese studies center. One of his students, the scholar Donald Keene, has provided a description of Tsunoda's wartime experiences: "On December 5, 1941, Sensei's lecture took place as usual, but three days later Sensei was taken into custody as an enemy alien. Two months later I joined the Navy. It was not for another four years that I again heard Sensei's lectures. Sensei, after two or three months of detention, was brought to trial, where he was asked among other things if, in view of the fact that he lived near the George Washington Bridge, there wasn't a possibility that he might blow up the bridge." Donald Keene, "Ryusaku Tsunoda: Pioneer of Japanese Studies at Columbia," *Living Legacies: Great Moments and Leading Figures in the History of Columbia University*, 2002, http://www.columbia.edu/cu/alumni/Magazine/Spring2002/AsianStudies.html.

42. Yoshida was a resident of Honolulu.

43. These are traditional New Year dishes: *zōni* is a soup of rice cakes and vegetables, *nishime* is vegetables stewed in soy sauce, and *gomoku-meshi* is rice steamed with various ingredients.

44. Decorative bundles of pine and bamboo used to celebrate the New Year.

45. Although never formally adopted as the national anthem, "*Kimigayo*" (The reign of our majesty) is considered to be so. The Ministry of Education decreed that the song be sung on national holidays in all elementary schools. It also came to be sung at state ceremonies and sports events.

46. The cheer is "*Tennō heika, banzai!*" meaning "Long live the emperor!" It is usually repeated three times.

47. A type of freeze-dried tofu.

48. The Kooskia Internment Camp, located in the Clearwater National Forest in north central Idaho, was formerly a prison and then CCC camp that came under the jurisdiction of the INS during the war. What set Kooskia apart from other INS camps was that it held resident aliens who had voluntarily transferred to the camp to work as construction laborers building the Lewis and Clark Highway (today U.S. Highway 12). Between May 1943 and May 1945, some 265 internees from Alaska, California, Hawai'i, Idaho, Kentucky, Nevada, New York, Ohio, and Texas, as well as from Peru, Mexico and Panama worked at Kooskia. For more, see Priscilla Wegars, *Imprisoned in Paradise: Japanese Internee Road Workers at the World War II Kooskia Internment Camp* (Moscow, Idaho: Asian American Comparative Collection, University of Idaho, 2010); "The Kooskia, Idaho, Japanese Internment Camp, 1943–1945," *Kooskia Internment Camp Scrapbook*, University of Idaho, www.lib.uidaho.edu/digital/kooskia/about.html.

49. This is Tadao Watanabe, a salesman from Makawao, Maui. He was also known as Ittetsu Watanabe.

50. This meeting was held in two sessions on December 17, 1943, in one of the internee barracks. The eight internee representatives met with Capt. A. R. Martin, the honorary Spanish consul in San Francisco, who was the only official in attendance. The internees recorded the minutes of this meeting in English and distributed copies among themselves. What follows is a translation of Furuya's version of the minutes, which he had translated from the original English into Japanese. His appears to be a shortened and edited version of the original. The complete English-language minutes of the meeting appears in Honda, *Family Torn Apart*, "Report of Internee Meeting with Consul of Spain, Capt. A. R. Martin, December 17, 1943," 56–62.

51. Furuya has omitted the last sentence in this answer, which in the English original reads, "The conditions in some other relocation centers are incomparably more miserable." *Family Torn Apart*, 57.

52. Agena and Kakiuchi were internees from Panama. *Family Torn Apart*, 58.

53. The original English version of the consul's response reads, "I did not know about this. (In the afternoon meeting, the Consul reported as follows: Mr. Fraser received instructions [regarding who was to be repatriated] through a cable from the State Department.)" *Family Torn Apart*, 58.

54. The English original reads, "The Japanese government makes the selection by itself. It will compile a new list." *Family Torn Apart*, 58.

55. The English original reads, "I have no idea." *Family Torn Apart*, 58.

56. This is the Crystal City Internment Camp in Texas.

57. Furuya's version of this section has been shortened. The original reads, "Please discuss the following two issues with Mr. Fraser, commander of this camp, Mr. Kelly of the INS in Philadelphia, and Mr. Ennis in the department of Justice in Washington so that we may live together with our families: (1) Transfer internees to the Family Camp; or (2) Reinvestigate and transfer us to relocation centers or free zones. Please emphasize that it is against American humanitarianism to keep us separated from our families, as we have been for more than two years now. Please point out the following: Whereas those in the Santa Fe Internment Camp now enjoy living with their families [at the Jerome Relocation Center] after having been reinvestigated, we in this camp have been forgotten. As for those from Peru and Hawaiʻi who have requested reunion with their families, please arrange for this as soon as possible." *Family Torn Apart*, 59. Mr. Kelly is Willard F. Kelly, assistant INS Commissioner for Alien Control. Mr. Ennis is Edward J. Ennis, director of the Justice Department's Alien Enemy Control Unit, in charge of the detention of all "enemy alien" Japanese, Germans, and Italians following Pearl Harbor.

58. The original reads, "Answer (in the afternoon): The authorities reported that 150 gallons of Shoyu would arrive within a few days and a tofu-making facility has been completed." *Family Torn Apart*, 60.

59. The original reads, "Request from Hawaii internees: Yokohama Specie Bank in Honolulu allows only citizen depositors, not internees, to make withdraw-

als. Please negotiate with the bank so that internees can make withdrawals." *Family Torn Apart*, 61.

60. Internees may be referring to a violent clash that occurred in November 1943 between Tule Lake prisoners and armed security forces. In the aftermath, martial law was declared at Tule Lake. See Barbara Takei, "Tule Lake," *Densho Encyclopedia*, http://encyclopedia.densho.org/Tule%20Lake/ (accessed February 27, 2013).

61. In the original *Haisho Tenten*, this poem appears as "*Tori ni yarō to tsuka-maeru ya, tori hyoi to kuru*" 鳥にやろうとつかまえるや 鳥ひょいと来る. The second 「鳥」 is most likely a typographical error. The translator has corrected it to read 「烏」 *karasu*, or crow.

62. Ogiwara Seisensui was an outspoken proponent of the modern form of freestyle haiku. During a visit to Hawai‘i, he instructed Furuya in the writing of this type of haiku.

63. A goat-like antelope found only in Japan.

Chapter 12

1. Both Furuya and Yasutaro Soga in their Japanese-language memoirs use the terms *shitamachi* and *uemachi*, literally meaning "downtown" and "uptown," respectively. English-language documents from the Santa Fe camp and other official sources refer to these as the "lower area" and the "upper area."

2. In all, some seven hundred Hawai‘i internees, including eight women, were sent in ten groups to Mainland internment camps during the period from February 1942 to December 1943. Internees in Group 10 left Honouliuli Camp on O‘ahu for the Mainland on December 2, 1943. They arrived in Santa Fe on January 9, 1944, after having been held at the Sharp Park Immigration Station in California for about a month.

3. Santa Fe is considered one of the oldest capital cities in the United States.

4. Furuya is suggesting that the name "Vaca" is phonetically similar to the Japanese word, *baka*, meaning "stupid."

5. Hal Lewis was a popular Honolulu radio personality. In the Hawaiian language, *aku* means "bonito" and *pupule* means "crazy."

6. Like *tempura*, they wear a large *koromo*, or batter, to cover what is very little inside.

7. Shikishima is the poetic name for Yamato or ancient Japan. In Santa Fe, Shikishima was Barracks 11. *Uemachi* refers to the upper area.

8. This is very likely Munetaka Sakamoto, a coffee grower from Hōnaunau on the island of Hawai‘i. His name was mistakenly printed as Sakagi.

9. Also, *gidayū-bushi*, a style of musical chanting for the classical puppet theater.

10. Japanese lute.

11. Chinese poetry recitation.

12. Also known as *kūki chōwa hōshiki*, a method of controlled breathing.

13. A comic form of haiku.

14. The *Santa Fe Times* (*Santa Fe Jihō*) is among the group of Japanese-language newspapers published by the internees in camps administered by the Justice and War departments. The papers provided broad coverage of camp life, including daily announcements, vital statistics, news stories, editorials, human-interest items, literary pieces, and sports news. The first issue of the *Jihō* was published on July 1, 1943.

15. Nippon Hōsō Kyōkai, the Japan Broadcasting Corporation, was Japan's sole broadcaster prior to the end of World War II. It remains Japan's national public broadcasting system, although today it exists alongside competing commercial networks.

16. *Dan-no-ura shitone kassen* is an erotic parody of the kabuki play, *Dan-no-ura kabuto gunki* [The battle of Dan-no-ura] about the epic twelfth-century battle between the Genji and Heike clans. *Aikāne* means "friends" in Hawaiian.

17. An appellation for the sixteenth-century lord Toyotomi Hideyoshi, second of the three great unifiers of Japan.

18. This internee's name appears in documents as both Iju Sueoka and Tameshige Sueoka. Iju is the *on* (or Chinese) reading of his name; Tameshige is the *kun* (or Japanese) reading.

19. Third generation Japanese Americans.

20. After serving in World War I, Wilfred Chomatsu Tsukiyama (1897–1966) became one of the islands' first Nisei lawyers and was Honolulu's city attorney at the outbreak of World War II. Tsukiyama applied for reenlistment in 1942, but at forty-five years old was turned down because of his age. After the war, he served as president of the Territorial Senate, and in 1959 became the first chief justice of the Hawai'i State Supreme Court, the first Asian American in the United States to hold such a position.

21. Shiro Kashiwa (1913–98) became the first attorney general of the newly admitted state of Hawai'i. He was born in Kohala on the Big Island and earned his law degree from the University of Michigan. Kashiwa served as state attorney general until 1962 and was thereafter appointed to a number of federal posts, including one with the U.S. Court of Appeals in Washington, D.C. He went on to become the first Japanese American and the first member of the Hawai'i bar to represent the United States before the U.S. Supreme Court.

22. This is Daniel Ken Inouye (1924–2012), a decorated member of the 442nd Regimental Combat Team, who served in the U.S. Senate for fifty years. In 1959, Inouye became the first representative from the new state of Hawai'i and the first Japanese American in the U.S. Congress. He rose to national prominence during the Watergate hearings of the 1970s and the Iran-Contra Affairs hearings of the 1980s. Upon his death, Inouye was the senior member of the U.S. Senate and president pro tempore, the third in line to the presidential succession.

23. Masayuki "Spark" Matsunaga (1916–90) was a congressman and later senator from Hawai'i. Born to immigrant plantation workers on Kaua'i, Matsunaga was a decorated World War II veteran and graduate of the Harvard Law School.

A member of the Democratic Revolution of 1954, he was elected to the Territorial Legislature along with future political leaders Daniel Inouye and George Ariyoshi. In 1962, he was elected to the U.S. Congress. As a senator, he shepherded the passage of the Civil Liberties Act of 1988 that provided a formal apology and redress for the World War II incarceration of ethnic Japanese in the United States.

24. A ranked listing of all players.

25. Jerome Relocation Center in Denson, Arkansas.

26. Julian P. Langston was both the chief of security and liaison chief of the Santa Fe camp.

27. The above is Furuya's shortened version of the original *New York Times* article. The original article reads, "The Japanese Domei agency said yesterday that Emperor Hirohito would observe his forty-third birthday today in 'the very best of health' although 'His Majesty is especially deeply concerned with intensified aircraft production.' The Domei wireless dispatch, as transmitted to Japanese-occupied areas and recorded by the Federal Communications Commission, said there would be a birthday military review for which General Keisuke Fujiye was named commander by the Army Ministry. His chief of staff will be Lieut. Gen. Eiichi Tatsumi. After telling of the 'brilliant results' achieved by Japan's armed forces and asserting that 'the imperial prestige, attributable to the august virtue of His Majesty, is felt the world over,' Domei gave an account of the Emperor's wartime duties." "Hirohito is 43 Today," *New York Times*, April 29, 1944. The Dōmei Tsūshinsha (Domei News Agency) was the only news service allowed to operate in Japan during the war and as such transmitted the official statements of the imperial government. Domei was dissolved by the American Occupation at the end of World War II.

28. Lt. Gen. Robert C. Richardson, Jr. was military governor of Hawai'i at this time. Although Furuya writes only of the effects in Honolulu, curfew and blackout restrictions were imposed over the entire territory. As the war progressed, curfew restrictions were eased and total blackouts became "dim-outs." For more on conditions in Hawai'i during the war, see Gwenfread Allen, *Hawaii's War Years: 1941–1945* (Honolulu: University of Hawaii Press, 1950).

29. Amache was officially known as the Granada Relocation Center, located in southeastern Colorado. The state of Colorado became the destination of many parolees when its Republican governor, Ralph L. Carr, announced that Colorado would welcome the Japanese free of restrictions. For more, see Gil Asakawa, "Resettlement in Denver," *Densho Encyclopedia*, http://encyclopedia.densho.org/ Resettlement%20in%20Denver/ (accessed January 15, 2013); Adam Schrager, *The Principled Politician: The Ralph Carr Story* (Golden, Colorado: Fulcrum, 2008).

30. The proverb goes, *"Tenka wa mawari-mochi,"* meaning that power and fortune go by turns, changing hands from the rich and the poor, the high and the low.

31. Hawaiian: people, individuals; Native Hawaiians.

32. Shortly after Pearl Harbor, the military instituted policies designed to prevent Japanese Americans from serving in the armed forces and did not reinstitute the draft for Nikkei until January 1944. Thus, those serving prior to this

time—most notably in the segregated 100th and 442nd—had volunteered for military service. In January 1944, the draft was reopened to Japanese Americans. Here Furuya is referring to an announcement made to the WRA in April 1944 by Lt. Col. Harrison A. Gerhardt, an executive officer to the assistant secretary of war. A *New York Times* article reported this announcement and said that Gerhardt's statement had been made as "an answer to many requests" by Nisei soldiers wanting to be assigned to the Pacific. The article quoted Gerhardt: "(T)he use of Japanese-Americans in specific units is not based upon any discrimination policy." Rather, he said, "If a Japanese-American unit were present in combat in the Pacific, it would be possible for the enemy Japanese to secure American uniforms from dead soldiers and mingle with our soldiers." "Bars Nisei Fighting against Japanese," *New York Times*, April 27, 1944.

33. It is noteworthy to point out that Japanese Americans did provide military service against Japanese nationals in the Pacific. As part of a secret language-training program known as the Military Intelligence Service, Nisei served as interrogators, translators, interpreters, and propaganda writers in the Pacific theater. Hundreds served on the front lines, risking "friendly fire" from American soldiers who could not tell them apart from the enemy, while attempting to avoid capture by Japanese forces who viewed them as "traitors." Kelli Nakamura, "Military Intelligence Service," *Densho Encyclopedia*, http://encyclopedia.densho.org/Military%20Intelligence%20Service/ (accessed January 9, 2014);

34. Attorney General Francis Beverley Biddle.

35. James Wheaton Mott, a seven-term legislator, introduced in May 1944 a bill before the U.S. House Committee on Immigration and Naturalization that called for the deportation of all Japanese nationals. The bill was one of many similar proposals made by politicians at the national, as well as state, level. For the wording of the bill, see Appendix B: The Mott Bill. "A bill to provide for the deportation of Japanese aliens," HR 4779, 78th Congress, 2nd Session, (May 9, 1944).

36. Furuya wrote his book in the early 1960s. Today, the National Park Service lists thirteen national parks within the state of New Mexico.

37. This is the White Sands National Monument in Alamogordo, New Mexico, home to the largest field of gypsum sand dunes. It also is the location of the atomic bomb test range, where the world's first atomic bomb was exploded at the Trinity Site on July 16, 1945.

38. There are several errors here. Katagiri Shigeru was an army lieutenant general, not a naval officer; he died in a land battle on New Guinea in 1944. The successor to Yamamoto Isoroku was not Toyoda, but Admiral Koga Mineichi. Koga was killed in March 1944 in an aircraft accident resulting from bad weather while heading from the Palau Islands in Micronesia to the city of Davao in the Philippines. Admiral Toyoda Soemu was appointed after Koga's death. Toyoda survived the war and was acquitted at the Tokyo War Crimes Trials.

39. On the morning of June 8, 1944, the wings of two B-25 bombers interlocked in mid-air, sending the aircraft plummeting into houses in the Honolulu neighborhood of Kalihi. In addition to four army airmen, the crash took the lives

of two women and five children who were trapped in their burning homes, and at least ten houses were destroyed. Earl Albert Selle, "Big Bombers Collide over City," *Honolulu Advertiser*, June 9, 1944.

40. *Chonmage sōshi. Sōshi* means a short story, and a *chonmage* is the top knot often worn by samurai.

41. Daisei Obata is the stage name of Soichi Obata; it means "Loud Voice" Obata. Keigetsu Ito is the stage name of Choichi Ito; it means "Beautiful Moon." Taikō Yoshimoto also is a stage name. Taikō is a pseudonym for the military lord Toyotomi Hideyoshi. Thus Taikō Yoshimoto is "Lord" Yoshimoto, the stage name of Asami Yoshimoto, a barber from Honolulu.

42. *Edokko* means genuine Edo boys, i.e., true Edo-ites; Edo being the historical name for Tokyo. The title *Shirai Gompachi* is the name of a fictional handsome samurai. *Osakaya Kihachi* is the name of the main character of this drama. *Kikai no ichiya* is "A night of opportunity." The title *Hatsukago* means the first ride of the year in a *kago* or basket palanquin.

43. Here Furuya seems to be conflating the resisters and those internees deemed "disloyal," who were collected and kept at Tule Lake. Later in this chapter, he discusses in greater detail the defiance and agitation caused by this group at Tule Lake.

44. Furuya records this individual as James Shoichi Kunimoto, but Tetsuden Kashima and Michi Weglyn identify him as Shoichi James Okamoto. For more on the incident, see Tetsuden Kashima, "Homicide in camp," *Densho Encyclopedia*, http://encyclopedia.densho.org/Homicide%20in%20camp/ (accessed March 7, 2013); Michi Weglyn, *Years of Infamy: The Untold Story of America's Concentration Camps* (New York: William Morrow and Co., 1976), 312n2.

45. Interior Secretary Harold L. Ickes.

46. In the aftermath of Pearl Harbor, the military instituted policies designed to prevent Japanese Americans from serving in the armed forces, reclassifying registered Nisei as IV-C, "not acceptable" for service. A year later, however, the army solicited volunteers for a segregated unit that would become the 442nd, and a year after that, in January 1944, it reopened the draft to Japanese Americans. From their confinement within the WRA camps, nearly three hundred Nisei resisted conscription into the army. Poston and Heart Mountain held the greatest number of resisters, with others coming from Minidoka, Amache, and Tule Lake. Most were tried in federal court and served time in the federal prisons. Eric L. Muller, *Free to Die for their Country: The Story of the Japanese American Draft Resisters in World War II* (Chicago: University of Chicago Press, 2001); Muller, "Draft resistance," *Densho Encyclopedia*, http://encyclopedia.densho.org/Draft%20resistance/ (accessed May 1, 2013).

47. The referee of a sumō match. In a real match, the *gyōji* wears the traditional court dress of a fourteenth-century nobleman.

48. The announcer at a sumō match who calls each wrestler to the ring.

49. Traditionally, wrestlers are divided into east and west teams, although the distinction tends to be arbitrary, and wrestlers do not compete as a team. Wrestlers

are ranked in sumō. The top five ranks are: *yokozuna* (the grand champion, of which none is listed here), *ōzeki, sekiwake komusubi,* and *maegashira.*

50. Some internees used their given names, while others went by wrestling names, such as Wakahibiki, Satsumanada, Wakayanagi, Tsuyashima, Mitamadake, Nippudake, Wakaisamu, and Asahigawa.

51. Wrestlers were required to win three or five consecutive matches in order to be victorious.

52. Money wrapped in folded tissue paper.

53. According to Hawaii Nisei and Tule Lake internee Hideo Kaneshiro, rank-and-file members discovered that their leaders had in fact been eating during the hunger strike. Severely criticized by other strikers, the Tule Lake leaders abandoned the strike. See "Oral History Interview with Hideo Kaneshiro," August 15, 2012, Japanese Cultural Center of Hawai'i.

54. Kenedy initially held Germans, Japanese, and Italians deported from Latin America to be used in a prisoner exchange program. At its peak, it held 2,000 internees of various ethnicities and nationalities. Furuya's comments about Kenedy's closure probably refer to the transfer of internees from the camp in the summer and fall of 1944, when the U.S. Army took over its operations and began using it for POWs, including Sakamaki Kazuo. Burton, *Confinement and Ethnicity,* 386–87; "Kenedy (detention facility)," *Densho.*

55. Yokichi Uyehara was a physician from Waipahu, O'ahu.

56. Fukuda also discusses this incident in his memoir, Yoshiaki Fukuda, *My Six Years of Internment: An Issei's Struggle for Justice* (San Francisco: The Konko Church of San Francisco, 1990), 18–22. The book was first published in Japanese in 1957 under the title, *Yokuryū seikatsu rokunen.*

57. *Manzai* is a comedic dialogue. Mukuchi, meaning reticent, is the stage name of Rev. Sokan Ueoka.

58. Tokiji Takei was a Japanese language school teacher from Pā'ia, Maui. His tanka appear under the pen name Sojin Takei in *Poets behind Barbed Wire,* an anthology with Hawai'i internees Yasutaro Soga, Motokazu Mori, and Otokichi Ozaki.

59. Rice crackers.

60. A formal Japanese meal comprised of many courses.

61. Sumida and Sakamoto were part of the group of nineteen Hawai'i Nisei who were interned in Hawai'i, sent to the Mainland, returned to Hawai'i, and then interned in the Mainland once again.

62. According to historian Greg Robinson, this is likely a reference to a press conference held by FDR on November 21, 1944, one the very few times when Roosevelt publicly mentioned the internment. Regarding the return of Japanese Americans to the West Coast, Roosevelt said:

> A good deal of progress has been made in scattering them throughout the country, and that is going on almost every day. I have forgotten what the figures are. There are about roughly a hundred—a hundred thousand Japanese-origin citizens in this country. And it is felt by a great many lawyers that under the

Constitution they can't be kept locked up in concentration camps....After all, they are American citizens, and we all know that American citizens have certain privileges.

Roosevelt noted that while a portion of the internees had "re-placed themselves" throughout the country, the remainder could be dispersed and resettled without "discombobulating" the rest of the population. When asked about the lifting of military orders that had excluded Japanese Americans from the West Coast, "Roosevelt asserted blandly that he knew nothing about it, and made no further comment." In his study of Roosevelt's role in the internment, Robinson contends that FDR remained fundamentally wary of the ability of Japanese Americans to be American and that he continued to view them as a separate and distinct people. Greg Robinson, *By Order of the President: FDR and the Internment of Japanese Americans* (Cambridge: Harvard University Press, 2001), 2–3, 242–49.

63. Association of Eternal Devotion to the Motherland, or literally, the Seven Lifetimes Association 七生会 from the wartime expression, "*Shichishō* hōkoku" 七生報国, meaning to serve one's country for seven lifetimes, in other words, for an eternity. Soga refers to this group as Seinendan Shichishōkai 青年団七生会; *seinendan* means an organization of young men, Soga, *Tessaku Seikatsu*, 280. Its name also has been translated as "the Club of Seven Lives," *Behind Barbed Wire*, 168.

64. An article in the December 12, 1944, *Asahi Shinbun*, "Jūyō gyōsha wa naranu" [Essential workers not allowed to leave], reported on the new evacuation policy of the Tokyo metropolitan government and described the restrictions that Furuya details.

65. On December 17, 1944, the War Department announced the lifting of the West Coast exclusion orders. Release of those not deemed "disloyal" was set to begin on January 2, 1945. See the earlier discussion on questions about what Roosevelt said during his November 1944 press conference and his lingering doubts about Japanese Americans.

66. On December 17, 1944, in anticipation of the Supreme Court's rulings in the cases of *Korematsu v. United States* and *Ex part Endo*, which challenged the government's mass detention of Japanese Americans, the War Department announced the lifting of the West Coast exclusion orders. Release of those not deemed "disloyal" was set to begin on January 2, 1945. For a discussion of Roosevelt's rare public comments regarding the internment made during a November 21, 1944 press conference, see page 335n62. The official repeal of Executive Order 9066, however, was not made until thirty-four years later with the issuance of Proclamation 4417 by President Gerald Ford on February 19, 1976.

67. Beginning in November 1944, the Japanese military launched nine thousand paper balloon bombs across the Pacific Ocean toward the continental United States. More than one thousand of these balloons landed in North America over an area that stretched from the Aleutians to the Mexican border. The balloons killed six Americans, including five children. Hoping to prevent Japan from gaining any information about the bombs' effectiveness, the U.S. government engaged the

American press and radio in a program of cooperative censorship. For more, see J. David Rogers, "How Geologists Unraveled the Mystery of Japanese Vengeance Balloon Bombs in World War II," Missouri University of Science and Technology, http://web.mst.edu/~rogersda/forensic_geology/japenese%20vengenance%20 bombs%20new.htm; Robert C. Mikesh, *Japan's World War II Balloon Bomb Attacks on North America* (Washington, D.C.: Smithsonian Institute Press, 1978), http:// www.sil.si.edu/smithsoniancontributions/annalsofflight/pdf_lo/saof-0009.pdf.

68. This very likely a misidentification of the Tule Lake group Hōkoku Seinendan 報国青年団 (Young Men's Association to Serve the Motherland). In *Tessaku Seikatsu*, Soga calls this group Seinendan Hōkōkai 青年団奉公会, which is very similar to the name Furuya uses, Seinen Hōkōkai 青年奉公会. Instead, this is most likely Hōkoku Seinendan, identified by Ivan Williams in his letter "To Each Internee" and by Soga in subsequent parts of his Santa Fe chapter. For discussions of internment administration concerns about Hōkoku Seinendan and the removal of its members from Tule Lake to camps like Santa Fe and Bismarck, see John J. Culley, "The Santa Fe Internment Camp and the Justice Department Program for Enemy Aliens," in *Japanese Americans, from Relocation to Redress*, rev. ed. by Roger Daniels, Sandra C. Taylor, and Harry H. L. Kitano (Seattle: University of Washington Press, 1991), 64–65; Kashima, *Judgment Without Trial*, 170–71. Soga, *Tessaku Seikatsu*, 283. Ivan Williams to Each Internee, Santa Fe Internment Camp, 15 March 1945, National Archives, Record Group 85, Entry 308, Box 1300/C, Washington, D.C.

69. Tsuha was one of nineteen internees who were twice sent to the Mainland and then back to Hawai'i. Ichiro Hayashi was the oldest son of Rev. Kyushichi Hayashi of Ko'olau, Kaua'i. Zenshiro Tachibana was a green grocer from Los Angeles.

70. Furuya is referring to questions 27 and 28 of the so-called "loyalty questionnaire" that was administered to all WRA camp internees seventeen years and older in the spring of 1943. Through this means, the government hoped to fill the ranks of the newly created 442nd with loyal Nikkei and to facilitate the resettlement of trustworthy internees outside of the barbed wire. Beginning in the fall, those who had answered "no" to either or both of the questions were confined at Tule Lake, which had by then been converted to a segregation center for those deemed "disloyal." Muller, *Free to Die*, 51; Eric L. Muller, *American Inquisition: The Hunt for Japanese American Disloyalty in World War II* (Chapel Hill: University of North Carolina Press, 2007), 31–38.

71. Sokuji Kikoku Hōshikai 即時帰国奉仕会 (Organization for Immediate Return to the Motherland), also called Sokuji Kikoku Hōshidan 即時帰国奉仕団, was a Tule Lake Issei organization. It appears as the group Immediate Return to Japan Services in the English translation of Soga's book, *Life behind Barbed Wire*. Hōkokudan 報国団 was formally known as Hōkoku Seinendan 報国青年団 (Young Men's Association to Serve the Motherland); Furuya and Soga refer to it by its shortened name, Hōkokudan. Soga, *Tessaku seikatsu*, 289; Soga, *Barbed Wire*, 172. Kashima notes the formation of a women's counterpart organization at Tule Lake

called Hōkoku Joshi Seinendan; Kashima, 170. For a portrayal of the many groups at Tule Lake, see Motomu Akashi, *Betrayed Trust: The Story of a Deported Issei and His American-Born Family During WWII* (Bloomington, Indiana: AuthorHouse, 2004).

72. *Zōni* and *toso*, spiced *sake*, are customarily served on New Year's Day.

73. Chikashi Nakayama was vice principal of the Chuo Gakuin Japanese language school that was established in Honolulu by the Christian minister Takie Okumura. After the war, Nakayama sketched from memory maps of the Sand Island and Santa Fe camps.

74. "Serve the Motherland."

75. In 1941, the *Yomiuri* had the largest circulation of any Tokyo-based daily. It merged with the smaller tabloid *Hōchi Shinbun* in 1942 and was known as the *Yomiuri-Hōchi*.

76. Furuya is paraphrasing Roosevelt's speech. The actual speech contained the following: "This new year of 1945 can be the greatest year of achievement in human history. Nineteen forty-five can see the final ending of the Nazi-Fascist reign of terror in Europe. Nineteen forty-five can see the closing in of the forces of retribution about the center of the malignant power of imperialistic Japan. Most important of all – 1945 can and must see the substantial beginning of the organization of world peace. This organization must be the fulfillment of the promise for which men have fought and died in this war. It must be the justification of all the sacrifices that have been made – of all the dreadful misery that this world has endured. We, Americans of today, together with our allies, are making history— and I hope it will be better history than ever has been made before. We pray that we may be worthy of the unlimited opportunities that God has given us." Franklin D. Roosevelt, "State of the Union Address," 6 January 1945, The American Presidency Project, Gerhard Peters and John T. Woolley, http://www.presidency.ucsb.edu/ws/index.php?pid=16595.

77. Furuya is most likely referring to an article written in early May rather than February 1945. Hitler did not die until April 30, 1945 (German time), a fact that was reported by the *New York Times* on May 2, 1945, along with an announcement of the establishment of a new Nazi leadership under Grand Admiral Karl Doenitz.

78. The expression refers to the *udonge*, a fig-like tree believed by Buddhists to bloom only once every three thousand years; thus a rare and joyous happening.

79. The individuals in this section also are listed by Soga, although there are differences in the renderings of a number of the names; *Barbed Wire*, 176. For the variant renderings, see the JCCH Internee Database.

80. A kanji error erroneously rendered Mankichi as Senkichi.

81. Makitaro Tamura was erroneously identified as Shintaro, and Katsuichi Tanaka was incorrectly identified as Seiichi. These were kanji errors.

82. Shigeyoshi Kawabata, a storekeeper from Los Angeles, was incorrectly identified as Jukichi Kawabata.

83. The last Japanese soldier surrendered in the Philippines in 1974.

84. Kuribayashi's letters from Iwo Jima and famous death poem have been widely written about in the years since World War II. For example, Kumiko Kakehashi, *So Sad to Fall in Battle: An Account of War Based on General Tadamichi Kuribayashi's Letters from Iwo Jima* (New York: Presidio Press, 2007) is a translation of the popular Japanese version of this book.

85. Officer-in-Charge Ivan Williams was the INS head of the Santa Fe camp.

86. Willard F. Kelly was INS assistant Commissioner for Alien Control.

87. Noh recitation or song.

88. This event also is described in *Behind Barbed Wire*, 180–81; Culley, "Santa Fe Camp," 64–65.

89. Gontaro Ono 大野権太郎 and Motoo Hirashima 平島元雄 are sometimes identified as Gentaro Ono and Mitsuo Hirashima. See Williams, "To Each Internee;" Culley, "Santa Fe Camp," 65. However, Soga in *Tessaku Seikatsu* provides the kanji and accompanying *furigana* for these names, and Furuya uses the same kanji names as Soga. Thus, the translator provides the names as rendered by Soga and Furuya. See Soga, *Tessaku Seikatsu*, 304.

90. Shortly after the incident, Ono penned a letter to the Spanish ambassador in Washington, D.C., requesting an investigation of the Santa Fe incident. He cited his leadership role in the Sokuji Kikoku Hōshidan as the basis for his request. However, Ono's letter apparently never made it to the Spanish Embassy, having been forwarded instead to the State Department's Special War Problems Division by Alien Control Commissioner Willard Kelly. In his letter to the Problems Division, Kelly notes that "Internee Ono's letter to the Spanish Ambassador entirely misrepresents the incident." Kelly also denies recognition of Ono's role as a representative of "any group of internees," thus presumably disavowing the dispatch of the letter to the Spanish Embassy. Kelly's correspondence also is accompanied by Ivan Williams's March 15, 1945 letter "To Each Internee," which Kelly describes as providing "the essential," and by implication more accurate, details of the incident. See Williams, "To Each Internee," 15 March 1945; Gentaro Ono, Letter to the Spanish Embassy, u.d.; W. F. Kelly to Bernard F. Gufler (assistant chief, Special War Problems Division, Department of State), 19 March 1945, National Archives, Record Group 85, Entry 308, Box 1300/C, Washington, D.C.

91. This is likely Ernest Kinzo Wakayama, the Nisei World War I veteran from Hawai'i and controversial internment dissident, who early on filed suit against the mass evacuation and became a member of the Tule Lake pro-Japan faction. Wakayama later renounced his American citizenship and was deported to Japan. "Ernest Kinzo Wakayama,"*Encyclopedia of Japanese American History*, 407; Peter Irons, *Justice at War: The Story of the Japanese American Internment Cases* (New York: Oxford University Press, 1983), 114–15.

92. This is Furuya's translation of Ivan Williams's letter "To Each Internee," dated March 15, 1945. For the complete English-original version of the Williams letter, see Appendix C: Letter from Ivan Williams, Officer-in-Charge.

93. The team names can be translated as follows: Shikishima is Ancient Japan; Kongō is Herculean Strength; Sankō is Glaring Light; Kyōjin is the Giants.

Yashima is another name for Ancient Japan; Nankai is the South Seas; Taiyō is the Sun; Tōwa is Eastern Asia; Asahi is the Rising Sun; Donkō is the Dim Light; and Sanga is the Mountains and Rivers. The team Donkō (Dim Light) may have been a pun, a nickname of their official title Sankō Junior, which in turn was a play on the fact that the team was comprised of middle-aged players, while the Sankō (Glaring Light) players were younger men.

94. Tsukigata Hampeita is the hero of a samurai play and movie that was popular before the war.

95. Roosevelt died at his private home in Warm Springs, Georgia. Howard G. Bruenn was Roosevelt's physician.

96. Hien is Kurusu's penname. It means Flying Swallow.

97. Taisei Yokusankai (Imperial Rule Assistance Association), established in 1940, was a national organization designed to bring all citizens under government control, ultimately through a one-party political system. In 1945, the political organization Dainihon Seijikai (Great Japan Political Society) was formed of elements that had succeeded Taisei Yokusankai. Hissho-tō can be translated as the Victory Party.

98. Tsuneyoshi Koba, then forty-four years old, was a physician from Baltimore, Maryland. *Santa fe nihonjin shūyōsho jinmeiroku, daisan-pen, October 1, 1945* [Santa Fe camp directory, volume 3, October 1, 1945] (Santa Fe: Nihonjin Jimukyoku, 1945); hereafter *Santa Fe Directory* (1945).

99. Furuya has mistakenly written Ōta Minoru. Rather, it was Cho Isamu who committed ritual suicide with Ushijima on June 23, 1945, marking the end of coordinated fighting in the Pacific theater. Ōta Minoru was dead by this time, having committed suicide on June 13, 1945, during the final battle of Oroku. *Asahi Shinbun*, "Okinawa rikujo no shuryokusen saishū dankai" [Okinawa in final stage of land battles], June 26, 1945.

100. Hawaiian: lazy.

101. Japan's Navy Regional Commands were located in these cities.

102. Ichimaru Rinosuke (1891–1945) was commander of the 27th Naval Air Corps stationed on Iwo Jima, which fell to the United States in March 1945. Ichimaru's letter to Roosevelt was found on the island by American forces. The letter was written in Japanese on paper bearing the imprint of the imperial navy and titled, "A Note to Roosevelt." Along with it was an English-language translation, also written on paper with the navy imprint. In the summer of 1945, both documents were given to the U.S. Naval Academy Museum in Annapolis, Maryland, where they remain archived.

What Furuya read in the July 1945 *Denver Post* was no doubt the English version of Ichimaru's letter. What he included in his book was *his excerpted Japanese translation* of the official English version of the letter. What is provided here is Furuya's version of the message, which is similar in content to the original. See Appendix D: Excerpt from "A Note to Roosevelt" for the portion of the original translation that Furuya summarized.

The full original English translation of the Ichimaru letter has been published in John Toland, *The Rising Sun: The Decline and Fall of the Japanese Empire, 1936–1945* (New York, Random House, 1970), 921–922. The original documents are: Toshinosuke Ichimaru to Franklin Roosevelt, March 1945, seventeen pages Japanese with cover, ten pages English translation, U.S. Naval Academy Museum.

Ichimaru is often misidentified in English language sources as Toshinosuke Ichimaru. This is an incorrect reading of the kanji for Ichimaru's given name. The correct characters are 利之助, the first character of which 利 can be read as either "Toshi" or "Ri." In his case, his name is correctly read as Rinosuke. Moreover, the English translation of Ichimaru's letter to Roosevelt identifies the Japanese admiral as "R. Ichimaru." While Furuya identifies Ichimaru as Rinosuke, he uses an incorrect kanji. For the kanji for Ichimaru's name, see Sankei Shinbun, ed., *Ano sensō: Taiheiyō sensō zenkiroku jōkan* [That war: A record of the Pacific war], vol. 1 (Tokyo: Shueisha, 2001), 90.

103. Imperial Army General Minami Jirō

104. Furuya refers to the group as the *katta-tō*, frequently identified as the *kattagumi*, which means "the group who believes in Japan's victory."

105. On August 11, the *New York Times* reported on a transmission sent by the Dōmei news service in which Japanese leaders were said to be ready to accept the Potsdam ultimatum. The *Times* quoted Dōmei as follows: "The Japanese Government are [*sic*] ready to accept the terms enumerated in the joint declaration which was issued at Potsdam on July 26, 1945, by the heads of the Governments of the United States, Great Britain and China and later subscribed to by the Soviet Government with the understanding that the said declaration does not comprise any demand which prejudices the prerogatives of His Majesty as a sovereign ruler." "Japan Offers to Surrender; U.S. May Let Emperor Remain; Master Reconversion Plan Set," *New York Times*, August 11, 1945.

106. Admiral Chester Nimitz was Commander in Chief of the Pacific Fleet during World War II.

107. Fleet Admiral William Halsey, Jr., commanded the forces of the Western Pacific, fighting the Japanese in the Philippines and Okinawa.

108. Higashikuni Naruhiko was an army general and the only member of the imperial household to become prime minister. His cabinet lasted for only fifty-four days, the shortest in the history of Japan.

109. MacArthur inscribed his name on behalf of the United Nations. Representatives for the Allied powers followed, lead by Chester Nimitz for the United States. Lt. Gen. Jonathan Wainwright, commander of U.S. forces in the Philippines, was witness to the surrender but did not himself sign the document. Wainwright fought the Japanese on Bataan and Corregidor Island before being taken prisoner of war in May 1942. He was freed from a Manchurian POW camp in August 1945, witnessed the signing in Tokyo Bay, and then returned to the Philippines to receive the formal surrender of General Yamashita Tomoyuki. "Japan Surrenders to Allies, Signs Rigid Terms on Warship; Truman Sets Today as V-J Day," *New York Times*, September 2, 1945.

110. After a short speech, MacArthur added the following closing thought,

"Let us pray that peace be now restored to the world and that God will preserve it always." For his full speech, see "Let Us Pray that Peace Be Now Restored to the World," in *A Soldier Speaks: Public Papers and Speeches of General of the Army Douglas MacArthur*, edited by Vorin E. Whan, Jr. (New York: Frederick A. Prager, Publishers, 1965), 148–49.

111. Granada and Amache are one and the same camp. The WRA's Granada Relocation Center was more commonly known by its postal designation, Amache, Colorado. Also, by this time, Jerome no longer existed as a relocation center. It had been converted to a German POW camp in June 1944.

112. General John L. DeWitt was commander of the Western Defense Command. His recommendations to Secretary of War Stimson provided the military justification for the exclusion of ethnic Japanese from the West Coast. According to the congressional Commission on Wartime Relocation and Internment of Civilians, the total number of Japanese Americans and resident aliens incarcerated during the war was 120,000.

113. According to the 1945 *Santa Fe Directory*, Nagamatsu was a native of Hiroshima prefecture and a resident of Las Vegas.

114. Shōki is a mythic god that fights evil and destroys demons. Based on Chinese legend, he bears a fierce countenance with bulging eyes and a full beard.

115. Located on the Colorado River Indian Reservation in Yuma County, in Arizona. Poston occupied more than 71,000 acres and contained a peak population of seventeen thousand internees, making it Arizona's third-largest "city" at that time.

116. Internees in War Relocation Authority camps who had renounced their U.S. citizenship were transferred to the Department of Justice camps of Santa Fe and Crystal City and were unable to return to Hawai'i for several years after the war. See the oral history of Hawai'i Nisei Hideo Kaneshiro, who was at Tule Lake when the war ended. After the war, he was transferred to Crystal City and then worked at Seabrook Farms in New Jersey, a food packing company that employed thousands of Japanese Americans sent from incarceration camps. Kaneshiro was finally allowed to return to the islands in 1947. "Oral History Interview with Hideo Kaneshiro."

117. Although Furuya identifies these individuals as Yoshio Kiino 紀井野芳夫 and Minoru Uyematsu 植松実, there were no internees in Santa Fe with such names. Persons with similar kanji names were Yoshio Kiyama 木山芳雄, a Los Angeles merchant, and Isamu Uyeoka 上岡勇, a merchant from Hanapepe, Kaua'i. *Santa Fe Directory* (1945); JCCH Internee Database.

118. This is Abner Schreiber. For Schreiber's oral history depicting his wartime experiences, including his description of the March 1945 riot at Santa Fe, see "Abner Schreiber," March 19, 1979, *Japanese American World War II Evacuation Oral History Project, Part II: Administrators*, Arthur A. Hansen, ed., California State University-Fullerton, http://www.oac.cdlib.org/view?docId =ft7199p03k;NAAN=13030&doc.view=frames&chunk.id=Abner%20Schreiber& toc.depth=1&toc.id=0&brand=oac4.

119. Kōshū is the ancient name for present-day Yamanashi prefecture.

120. On July 27, 1942, the two Issei internees, both almost sixty years old and physically disabled, were shot and killed by a guard upon their arrival at Lordsburg as they walked to the camp entrance. The guard accused of the killings claimed at his court martial that the two men were running toward the fence in an attempted escape. In the *Densho Encyclopedia*, these men are identified as Toshio Kobata and Hirota Isomura. Kashima, "Homicide in camp," *Densho Encyclopedia*; Soga, *Barbed Wire*, 77–79.

121. Itsuo Inasaki was a post office employee from Spreckelsville, Maui, who died in Livingston on June 18, 1942. His name was erroneously recorded as Fukuzaki.

122. Nizo Nishizaki of the Big Island died in Santa Fe on July 24, 1943. Kinzaemon Odachi, a Tenrikyo priest, died in Santa Fe on October 21, 1943.

123. This is a reference to the phrase, "*haisho no tsuki*," from the famous essay, *Tsurezure gusa*, by Yoshida Kenko. The phrase means "a moon gazed at from a penal settlement."

Chapter 13

1. Located in Nagano prefecture, Kamikōchi is one of the most famous mountain resorts in Japan.

2. This is the Minidoka Relocation Center in Hunt, Idaho. Administered by the WRA, the center held mainly individuals from Washington State and Oregon. It was closed in October 1945.

3. The flag of Japan.

4. The Furuyas' second child was deceased.

5. The Grove Park Inn, located in Asheville, has a history of hosting America's wealthy and famous. The Assembly Inn in Montreat, North Carolina, was originally established as a religious retreat. For the government's use of these luxury resorts as "internment hotels," see Kashima, *Judgment without Trial*, 180–82.

6. The last group of internees to return to Hawai'i—comprised of those who had renounced their American citizenship—is believed to have arrived back in the islands by 1947.

7. Furuya uses the expression, "*ichiyō raifuku*" from the Chinese fortunetelling book, *Ekikyō*. He uses the phrase to convey the following two meanings: "the New Year has arrived" and "bad things have gone, good things have returned."

Postscript

1. Furuya left Sand Island on February 20, 1942, while Soga was not transferred until August 6, 1942. Thus Furuya was some six months on the Mainland ahead of Soga, being moved about from camp to camp. Both men arrived at Santa Fe in June 1943.

2. Obinata also was a POW; his memoir is Obinata Aoi, *Makkoi byōin* [McCoy Hospital] (Tokyo: Kodansha, 1947).

3. Akira (Bunshiro) Furukawa, a photographer for the *Nippu Jiji* in Honolulu, provided the cover illustrations for Furuya's original book.

Author's Profile

1. Kawaguchi-mura, Kawaguchi-kohan, Minami Tsuru-gun, Yamanashi-ken.

2. I.e., June 1964, the publication date of the original Japanese-language edition of *Haisho Tenten*.

Bibliography

Newspapers

(Tokyo) *Asahi Shinbun*
(Honolulu) *Hawaii Times*
Honolulu Advertiser
Honolulu Star-Bulletin
New York Times

Selected Works by Kumaji (Suikei) Furuya

Furuya, Suikei. *Haisho Tenten* [An internment odyssey]. Honolulu: The Hawaii Times, 1964.

———. *Imin no Rakugaki* [The scribblings of an immigrant]. Honolulu: Hawaii Times, 1968.

———. "Nihongo hōsōkai" [The world of Japanese language broadcasting] in *Hawai Nihonjin iminshi* [A History of Japanese Immigrants in Hawaii], 2nd ed. Honolulu: United Japanese Society of Hawaii, 1977.

———. *Ruten* [Vicissitudes]. Kamakura: Sōunsha, 1958.

Itō, Yukio, ed. *Sōun hitori jikkushū* [A collection of *Sōun* poets and their ten haiku]. Kamakura: Sōunsha, 1961.

Archival Sources and Government Documents

Furuya, Kumaji. Alien Case File, A002-426-398, Accession 085-12-001, Box 163. Immigration and Naturalization Service. National Archives and Records Administration. College Park, Maryland.

Ichimaru, Toshinosuke. Letter to Franklin Roosevelt. March 1945. U.S. Naval Academy Museum. Annapolis, Maryland.

Kelly, W. F. Letter to Bernard F. Gufler. 19 March 1945. Record Group 85, Entry

308, Box 1300/C. National Archives and Records Administration. Washington, D.C.

Mori, Iga. Papers. Archival Collection 8. Japanese Cultural Center of Hawaiʻi Resource Center. Honolulu.

"Mrs. Furuya's Interview," notes 2pp. Patsy Saiki Collection, AR 18, Box 1, Folder 12. Japanese Cultural Center of Hawaiʻi Resource Center. Honolulu.

"Oral History Interview with Hanzo Furuya." By Michiko Kodama-Nishimoto. April 29, 1998. Tape No. 28-36-1-98. University of Hawaiʻi Center for Oral History. Honolulu.

"Oral History Interview with Jun Furuya." By Michiko Kodama-Nishimoto. May 20, 1998. Tape Nos. 28-37-1-98J, 28-38-1-98J. University of Hawaiʻi Center for Oral History. Honolulu.

"Oral History Interview with Hideo Kaneshiro." By Florence Sugimoto. August 15, 2012. Japanese Cultural Center of Hawaiʻi Resource Center. Honolulu.

"Oral History Interview with Dr. Kazuo Miyamoto." By Karen Motosue and Pauline Siefermann. 1980. Japanese Cultural Center of Hawaiʻi Resource Center. Honolulu.

Ozaki, Otokichi. "Internees and Japanese Language." Radio Script 7. Undated. Otokichi Ozaki Collection, AR1, Box 4, Folder 13. Japanese Cultural Center of Hawaiʻi Resource Center. Honolulu.

Williams, Ivan. Letter to Each Internee, Santa Fe Internment Camp. 15 March 1945. Record Group 85, Entry 308, Box 1300/C. National Archives and Records Administration. Washington, D.C.

"Yasuo Baron Goto Honorary Album, 1903-ca. 1962." University Archives. University of Hawaiʻi-Mānoa.

Books and Articles

Akashi, Motomu. *Betrayed Trust: The Story of a Deported Issei and His American-Born Family During WWII*. Bloomington, Indiana: AuthorHouse, 2004.

Allen, Gwenfread. *Hawaii's War Years: 1941–1945*. Honolulu: University of Hawaiʻi Press, 1950.

———, ed. *Men and Women of Hawaii: A Biographical Directory of Noteworthy Men and Women of Hawaii*, vol. 8. Honolulu: Honolulu Star-Bulletin, Inc., 1966.

Boylan, Dan and T. Michael Holmes. *John A. Burns: The Man and His Times*. Honolulu: University of Hawaiʻi Press, 2000.

Buchanan, Daniel Crump. *Japanese Proverbs and Sayings*. Norman: University of Oklahoma Press, 1965.

Burton, Jeffery F., Mary M. Farrell, Florence B. Lord, and Richard W. Lord. *Confinement and Ethnicity: An Overview of World War II Japanese American Relocation Sites*, rev. ed. Seattle: University of Washington Press, 2002.

Commission on Wartime Relocation and Internment of Civilians. *Personal Justice Denied: Report of the Commission on Wartime Relocation and Internment of Civilians*. Seattle: University of Washington Press, 1997.

Culley, John J. "The Santa Fe Internment Camp and the Justice Department Program for Enemy Aliens." *Japanese Americans, from Relocation to Redress.* Rev. ed. by Roger Daniels, Sandra C. Taylor, and Harry H. L. Kitano. Seattle: University of Washington Press, 1991.

Dingman, Roger. *Ghost of War: The Sinking of the* Awa Maru *and Japanese-American Relations, 1945–1995.* Anapolis: Naval Institute Press, 1997.

Fukuda, Yoshiaki. *My Six Years of Internment: An Issei's Struggle for Justice.* San Francisco: The Konko Church of San Francisco, 1990.

Hawai nenkan: Jinmei jūshoroku, 1941 [The Hawaii Japanese annual and directory, 1941]. Honolulu: Nippu Jiji Co., 1941.

Hawai Nihonjin iminshi [A history of Japanese immigrants in Hawaii], 2nd ed. Honolulu: United Japanese Society of Hawaii, 1977.

Hawaii, Office of the Military Governor, Morale Section, Emergency Service Committee. *Report of the Emergency Service Committee.* Honolulu: n.p., 1944.

Hawaii Nikkei History Editorial Board, ed. *Japanese Eyes American Hearts: Personal Reflections of Hawaii's World War II Nisei Soldiers.* Honolulu: Tendai Educational Foundation, 1998.

Hirai Ryuzo. *Kakedashi kisha gojyunen: Ashi de kaita hawai nikkeijinshi* [Fifty years as a fledgling reporter: My Hawaii Japanese history]. Tokyo: Hirai Ryuzo Shuppan Jikkō Iinkai, 1990.

History of the Soto Sect in Hawaii. Honolulu: Hawaii Sōtō Mission Bishop's Office, 2002.

Honda, Gail, ed. *Family Torn Apart: The Internment Story of the Otokichi Muin Ozaki Family.* Honolulu: Japanese Cultural Center of Hawai'i, 2012.

Ichioka, Yuji. *The Issei: The World of the First Generation Japanese Immigrants, 1885–1924.* New York: The Free Press, 1988.

Irons, Peter H. *Justice at War: The Story of the Japanese American Internment Cases.* Berkeley: University of California Press, 1983.

Kashima, Tetsuden. *Judgment without Trial: Japanese American Imprisonment during World War II.* Seattle: University of Washington Press, 2003.

Kawazoe, Kempu. "Bungei" [The literary arts]. In *Hawai Nihonjin iminshi* [A history of Japanese immigrants in Hawaii]. Honolulu: United Japanese Society of Hawaii, 1964.

Kimura, Yukiko. *Issei: Japanese Immigrants in Hawaii.* Honolulu: University of Hawai'i Press, 1988.

Knaefler, Tomi Kaizawa. *Our House Divided: Seven Japanese American Families in World War II.* Honolulu: University of Hawai'i Press, 1991.

Kotani, Roland. *The Japanese in Hawaii: A Century of Struggle.* Honolulu: The Hawaii Hochi, Ltd., 1985.

Lai, Him Mark, Genny Lim, and Judy Yung. *Island: Poetry and History of Chinese Immigrants on Angel Island, 1910–1940.* Seattle: University of Washington Press, 1980.

Lee, Erika and Judy Yung. *Angel Island: Immigrant Gateway to America.* New York: Oxford University Press, 2010.

Mohr, James C. *Plague and Fire: Battling Black Death and the 1900 Burning of Hono-lulu's Chinatown*. New York: Oxford University Press, 2005.

Moon, Thomas N. and Carl F. Eifler. *The Deadliest Colonel*. New York: Vantage Press, 1975.

Mori, Victor M. *East Meets West: A Family History*. Honolulu: privately printed, 2010.

Muller, Eric L. *American Inquisition: The Hunt for Japanese American Disloyalty in World War II*. Chapel Hill: University of North Carolina Press, 2007.

———. *Free to Die for their Country: The Story of the Japanese American Draft Resist-ers in World War II*. Chicago: University of Chicago Press, 2001.

Niiya, Brian, ed. *Encyclopedia of Japanese American History: An A-to-Z Reference from 1868 to the Present*, updated ed. New York: Checkmark Books, 2001.

Obinata, Aoi. *Makkoi byōin* [McCoy Hospital]. Tokyo: Kodansha, 1947.

Odo, Franklin. *No Sword to Bury: Japanese Americans in Hawai'i During World War II*. Philadelphia: Temple University Press, 2004.

Ogawa, Dennis M. *First among Nisei: The Life and Writings of Masaji Marumoto*. Honolulu: Japanese Cultural Center of Hawai'i, 2007.

———. *Kodomo no tame ni—For the sake of the children: The Japanese American Expe-rience in Hawaii*. Honolulu: University of Hawai'i Press, 1978.

Okihiro, Gary Y. *Cane Fires: The Anti-Japanese Movement in Hawaii, 1865–1945*. Philadelphia: Temple University Press, 1991.

Okihiro, Michael M., *et al*. *A'ala: The Story of a Japanese Community in Hawai'i*. Honolulu: Japanese Cultural Center of Hawaii, 2003.

———. *AJA Baseball in Hawaii: Ethnic Pride and Tradition*. Honolulu: Japanese Cul-tural Center of Hawaii, 1999.

Paia Mantokuji Soto Mission Centennial Celebration, 1906–2006. Pā'ia, Hawaii: Pā'ia Mantokuji Sōtō Mission, 2006.

Peterson, Barbara Bennett, ed. *Notable Women of Hawaii*. Honolulu: University of Hawai'i Press, 1984.

Robinson, Greg. *By Order of the President: FDR and the Internment of Japanese Amer-icans*. Cambridge: Harvard University Press, 2001.

———. *A Tragedy of Democracy: Japanese Confinement in North America*. New York: Columbia University Press, 2009.

Saiki, Patsy Sumie. *Ganbare! An Example of Japanese Spirit*. Honolulu: Mutual Pub-lishing, 1982.

Sakamaki, Kazuo. *Horyo dai-ichigo* [POW No. 1]. Tokyo: Shinchōsha, 1949.

Sakamoto, Tomio. "Furuya Kumaji-shi: Oi o shiranu iyoku" [Kumaji Furuya: A will that does not know old age], *Hawai jinbutsu tenkizu* [A chart of personages of Hawai'i]. Honolulu: n.p., 1957?

Sankei Shinbun, ed. *Ano sensō: Taiheiyō sensō zen kiroku jōkan* [That war: A record of the Pacific war], vol. 1. Tokyo: Shueisha, 2001.

Santa fe nihonjin shūyōsho jinmeiroku, daisan-pen, October 1, 1945 [Santa Fe camp directory, volume 3, October 1, 1945]. Santa Fe: Nihonjin Jimukyoku, 1945.

Schrager, Adam. *The Principled Politician: The Ralph Carr Story*. Golden, Colorado: Fulcrum, 2008.

Seki, Yokichi. *Beikoku yokuryūki* [Internment in the United States]. Tokyo: Kashima Kenkyūsho Shuppankai, 1971.

Shimada, Noriko. "Haiku to haiku kessha ni miru Hawai Nihonjin imin no shakai bunkashi" [The social and literary history of Hawaii Japanese immigrants as seen in their haiku and haiku societies]. In *Haiku, tanka, senryū ni miru Hawai Nihonjin iminshi* [History of Japanese immigrants in Hawai'i seen through their haiku, tanka, and senryu], Noriko Shimada, ed. Tokyo: privately printed, 2009.

Sigall, Bob, *et al. The Companies We Keep: Amazing Stories About 450 of Hawaii's Best Known Companies.* Honolulu: Small Business Hawaii, 2006.

Soga, Keiho, Taisanboku Mori, Sojin Takei, and Muin Ozaki. *Poets behind Barbed Wire.* Edited and translated by Jiro Nakano and Kay Nakano. Honolulu: Bamboo Ridge Press, 1983.

Soga, Yasutaro. *Life behind Barbed Wire.* Trans. by Kihei Hirai. Honolulu: University of Hawai'i Press, 2008.

———. *Gojūnen no Hawai kaikō* [Fifty years of Hawai'i memories]. Honolulu: The Hawaii Times, 1953.

———. *Tessaku Seikatsu* [Life behind barbed wire]. Honolulu: The Hawaii Times, 1948.

Suzuki, D. T. *Buddha of Infinite Light: The Teachings of Shin Buddhism, the Japanese Way of Wisdom and Compassion.* Boston and London: Shambhala Publications, 1997.

Suzuki, Kei. "Media: Kumaji Furuya." *The Hawaii Herald.* Oct. 17, 2008.

Taniguchi, Susumu. "Shinbun kisha futari no unmei o kaeta Shinjuwan" [The Pearl Harbor attack that changed the destinies of two newspaper correspondents]. *This Is Yomiuri.* December 1998.

Tasaka, Jack Y. "Hawai o irodoru Nihonjin: Furuya Suikei-shi no koto" [A Japanese who has influenced Hawai'i: Suikei Furuya]. *East-West Journal.* June 1; June 15; July 1, 1995.

Toland, John. *The Rising Sun: The Decline and Fall of the Japanese Empire, 1936–1945.* New York: Random House, 1970.

Uchida, Yoshiko. *Desert Exile: The Uprooting of a Japanese-American Family.* Seattle: University of Washington Press, 1982.

United Japanese Society of Hawaii Publication Committee, ed. *A History of Japanese in Hawaii.* Honolulu: United Japanese Society of Hawaii, 1971.

Wegars, Priscilla. *Imprisoned in Paradise: Japanese Internee Road Workers at the World War II Kooskia Internment Camp.* Moscow, Idaho: Asian American Comparative Collection, University of Idaho, 2010.

Weglyn, Michi. *Years of Infamy: The Untold Story of America's Concentration Camps.* New York: William Morrow and Co., 1976.

Whan, Vorin E., Jr., ed. *A Soldier Speaks: Public Papers and Speeches of General of the Army Douglas MacArthur.* New York: Frederick A. Prager, Publishers, 1965.

Yamamoto, Tsuneichi ed. *The Rainbow, a Bridge: A 70-Year History of the Honolulu Japanese Chamber of Commerce.* Honolulu: Honolulu Japanese Chamber of Commerce, 1970.

Yamashita, Samuel Hideo. "The Aloha Team, 1942–1943." *More than a Game: Sport in the Japanese American Community.* Edited by Brian Niiya. Los Angeles: Japanese American National Museum, 2000.

Yoshikawa, Takeo. *Higashi no kaze, ame* [Easterly wind, rain]. Tokyo: Kodansha, 1963.

Yost, Israel A. S. *Combat Chaplain: The Personal Story of the World War II Chaplain of the Japanese American 100th Battalion.* Honolulu: University of Hawai'i Press, 2006.

Online Sources

"Abner Schreiber" (March 19, 1979). *Japanese American World War II Evacuation Oral History Project, Part II: Administrators.* Arthur A. Hansen, ed. California State University-Fullerton. http://www.oac.cdlib.org/view?docId=ft7199p03k ;NAAN=13030&doc.view=frames&chunk.id=Abner%20Schreiber&toc .depth=1&toc.id=0&brand=oac4.

Asato, Noriko. "Japanese," *Encyclopedia of the Great Plains.* David J Wishart, ed. University of Nebraska-Lincoln. http://plainshumanities.unl.edu/encyclopedia/ doc/egp.asam.014.xml.

Clark, John. "Nu'uanu Home: On The Reef." Pacific Worlds: Nu'uanu, Honolulu. http://www.pacificworlds.com/nuuanu/sea/reef.cfm.

Cowell, Mary Jean. "Michio Ito Study Guide: History of Michio Ito." Repertory Dance Theatre, 2009–10 Season. Salt Lake City, Utah. http://www.rdtutah .org/artsedu/study%20guide%20michio%20ito.pdf.

Densho Encyclopedia. http://encyclopedia.densho.org/.

"Densho: Sites of Shame." Densho. http://www.densho.org/sitesofshame/index .html.

Fort McCoy, U.S. Army. "Fort McCoy: History & Heritage." http://www.mccoy .army.mil/AboutUs/History/FMCHistHrtg.pdf.

Hawaii State Legislature. *Hawaii Legislators' Handbook.* "Table of Presiding Officers." Hawaii State Legislature, 1901–1996. http://state.hi.us/lrb/hndbook/ appe.html.

Itoh Mayumi. "Japan's Neo-Nationalism: The Role of the Hinomaru and Kimigayo Legislation." *Japan Policy Research Institute Working Paper,* 79 (2001). http://www.jpri.org/publications/workingpapers/wp79.html.

Japanese Cultural Center of Hawai'i. "Hawai'i Internee Database." http:// hawaiiinternment.org/internee_list.

"Japanese Navy Ships: Ha-19 (Midget Submarine, 1938–41)." Naval History and Heritage Command (May 3, 2009). www.history.navy.mil/photos/sh-fornv/ japan/japsh-h/ha19.htm.

Kakesako, Gregg K. "Former Chief Justice a Proud, Loyal Nisei." *Honolulu Star-Bulletin* (September 29, 1999). http://archives.starbulletin.com/1999/09/29/ news/story8.html.

Keene, Donald. "Ryusaku Tsunoda: Pioneer of Japanese Studies at Columbia." *Liv-*

ing Legacies: Great Moments and Leading Figures in the History of Columbia University (2002). http://www.columbia.edu/cu/alumni/Magazine/Spring2002/AsianStudies.html.

"The Kooskia, Idaho, Japanese Internment Camp, 1943–1945." *Kooskia Internment Camp Scrapbook.* University of Idaho. www.lib.uidaho.edu/digital/kooskia/about.html.

Markrich, Michael. "Katsumi Kometani: A Man for All Seasons." 100th Infantry Battalion Veterans Education Center. http://www.100thbattalion.org/history/veterans/officers/katsumi-doc-kometani/.

McNaughton, James C. "The Hawaiian Department, 7 December 1941." United States Army, Pacific (November 20, 2001). http://www.usarpac.army.mil/history2/dec7th.asp.

Mikesh, Robert C. *Japan's World War II Balloon Bomb Attacks on North America.* Washington, D.C.: Smithsonian Institute Press, 1978. http://www.sil.si.edu/smithsoniancontributions/annalsofflight/pdf_lo/saof-0009.pdf.

"Missoula Cemetery (1884-present)." City of Missoula, Montana. http://www.ci.missoula.mt.us/DocumentCenter/Home/View/412.

Morse, Harold. "Shiro Kashiwa dies at 85; first to serve as isles' attorney general." *Star-Bulletin* (March 19, 1998). http://archives.starbulletin.com/98/03/19/news/obits.html.

"Report of Elwyn J. Eagen on the Hawaiian Islands." Special House Committee Hearings, 76th Congress on the National Labor Relations Act pursuant to H. Res. 258, 12-11-39. May 3, 1940. http://clear.uhwo.hawaii.edu/eagan.html.

Rogers, J. David. "How Geologists Unraveled the Mystery of Japanese Vengeance Balloon Bombs in World War II." Missouri University of Science and Technology. http://web.mst.edu/~rogersda/forensic_geology/japenese%20vengenance%20bombs%20new.htm.

Roosevelt, Franklin D. "Executive Order 8832: Freezing Japanese and Chinese Assets in the United States." 26 July 1941. Gerhard Peters and John T. Woolley. The American Presidency Project. University of California-Santa Barbara. http://www.presidency.ucsb.edu/ws/index.php?pid=16148.

———. "State of the Union Address." 6 January 1945. Gerhard Peters and John T. Woolley. The American Presidency Project. University of California-Santa Barbara. http://www.presidency.ucsb.edu/ws/index.php?pid=16595.

"Schofield Barracks: A Historic Treasure." Tropic Lightning Museum (August 2008). http://www.garrison.hawaii.army.mil/tlm/files/history.pdf.

Scott, Brandon Jeffery. "The Untold Story of Camp McCoy: Japanese Prisoners of War in the Heart of Wisconsin during the Second World War." Bachelor's Thesis. University of Wisconsin-Eau Claire, 2010. Minds@UW. http://digital.library.wisc.edu/1793/44611.

Shivers, Robert L. to Director, Federal Bureau of Investigation, Washington, D.C. 17 December 1941. The Freedom of Information Times: Custodial Detention Files of the FBI of the World War II Era. http://www.foitimes.com/internment/Honolulu1.pdf.

Soennichsen, John. "Historic California Posts: Fort McDowell (Camp Reynolds, Post of Angel Island)." The California State Military Museum. http://www .militarymuseum.org/CpReynolds.html.

"United States Immigration Station (USIS)." Angel Island Conservancy. http:// angelisland.org/history/united-states-immigration-station-usis/.

Wagner, David. "Little Tokyo Community Profiles -2010: Early History of the *Rafu Shimpo*." Discover Nikkei: Japanese Migrants and Their Descendants (May 17, 2010). http://www.discovernikkei.org/en/journal/2010/5/17/early -history-rafu-shimpo/.

Yoshida, Shigeo. "Emergency Service Committee, Club 100 30th Anniversary Renuion, June 1972." 100th Infantry Battalion Veterans Education Center. http://www.100thbattalion.org/archives/puka-puka-parades/wartime-hawaii/ emergency-service-committee/.

Index

A

'A'ala (Honolulu), xxviii, xxix, 7
Abiko, Rev.Yoshitaka, 225
Adachi, Ichiji, 192, 207–208, 238–239
Adachi, Masayuki, 37
Adachi, Tokuji (Ryou), 30, 199
Aka, Ryosei, 201
Akahoshi, Rev. Shingetsu, 225
Akana, Senator David Y. K. (Hawai'i), 34, 280
Akata, Yaichiro, 233
Akino, Kumao, 227
Akizaki, Takeo, 25–26, 74, 106
Alien Property Custodian, xxxv
Ama, Takao, 199
Amache Relocation Camp. *See* Granada Relocation Center

Amino, Inokichi (San Francisco), 119
Anami, Korechika (Japanese prime minister), 234, 247, 252
Ando, Shigeru, 199
Angel Island Immigration Station (California), ii, 50–57, 58; Chinese poetry at, 53–54; haiku about, 55–56; as processing center, xxxiv; transfer to, 43–46, 49–51
Aoki, Rev. Zenyu, 39
Arai, Kazuo, 147, 193, 194, 248
Araki, Kazuma, 26, 69, 74, 105, 106
Arita, Beatrice Matsui, xxxiii, 34, 289–290
Arita, Gentaro, 199
Arita, Hachirō (Japanese consul general and foreign minister), 31, 79, 81, 153

Arita, Nizo, 233
Arita, Takazo, 212
Arita, Tamaki, 26, 69, 75, 131, 155
arrests, xxvi, 8, 9, 15–16, 36–38, 39, 40, 135; of Issei community leaders, xxxii–xxxiii, 22–23, 24–25, 141–142, 274; on December 7, 3–4, 6, 7–10, 36–37, 47–48; of Furuya, 7–9; and those who "slipped through the net," 10, 22, 24, 38–39, 136, 195. *See also* custodial detention lists, Federal Bureau of Investigation (FBI)
Asaeda, Rev. Horyu, 81
Asakawa, Hachiro (San Diego), 119
Asami, Shoichi (Seiha), 18, 26, 28, 30, 74, 80, 99, 107; broadcasting the news, 65, 72–73, 111; repatriation by, 80, 81, 137; "The Song of the Yalu River," 72–73; "Wandering Internees," 82–83. See also *Nippu Jiji* newspaper
Asano, Rev. Kakusho, 113
Asaoka, Rev. Kakuho, 197
Asato, Eishu, 81, 137
Assembly Inn, North Carolina. *See* internment hotels
atomic bombs, 242, 245–246, 248–249, 251
Atsuumi, Noriaki, 26, 65, 74, 106
Azumi, Suimei, 154

B

Baba, Tokuji, 26, 32, 65, 81, 137
Banba, Kuromitsu, 137, 158
bird-watching. *See* passing time in camp

Bismarck Internment Camp. *See* Fort Abraham Lincoln Internment Camp

blacklist. *See* custodial detention lists

blackouts: in camp, 92; in Hawai'i, 200

Board of Officers and Civilians, hearings of, xxxii–xxxiii, 33–36, 279–291. *See also* internee interrogations and hearings

Buddhism: 39, 238, 251; and arrests of priests, xxvi, 9, 16, 24; and celebrations in camp, 70, 74; and funerals in camp, 103–104, 118, 141–142, 241; priests of, 17-18, 32, 38–39, 137, 138, 201–202, 224–225, 238, 249, 253–254

C

Camp Forrest Internment Camp (Tennessee), xxxiv, 88–97, 126; conditions at, 88–89, 91–92; departure from, 96–97; haiku, 97; internee population of, 89–91; passing time, 88–89, 92, 94; repatriation from, 95–96; Sakamaki Kazuo (POW), 27, 93–94; self-government, 89; train transport to, 85–87

Camp Kenedy Internment Camp (Texas), 135, 157

Camp Livingston Internment Camp (Louisiana), xxxiv, 98–127; commanders of, 117–118, 119, 120; conditions at, 102, 107; food and cooking, 100, 113–114; haiku, 123–126; internee population of, 98–99, 105, 113, 115–117, 126; mail, 122–123; news broadcasts, 111–112; Panama internees, 29, 99; passing time, 94, 99, 100–103, 106, 107–108, 108–109, 114–115, 115–116, 117; repatriation from, 118–119; Japanese POWs, 104–105, 116–117; self-government, 99

Camp McCoy Internment Camp (Wisconsin), xxxiv, 42, 56–85, 126; commander Horace Rogers, 65, 70–71, 74, 78–79, 85, 86; food and mess hall, 66–68; haiku, 84–85; internee population of, 65–66, 69–70, 71–72; mail, 64–65, 76; passing time, 72–75, 77–78; repatriation, 79–82; self-government, 57, 64–65, 77; songs about, 72–73, 82–83; train transport to, 56–63

celebrations in camp: 152–153, 216; Christmas, 18, 33, 153–154, 220; emperor's birthday, 200, 214, 237–238; New Year's Day, 153, 221

Chamber of Commerce. *See* Honolulu Japanese Chamber of Commerce

Chikuma, Masayuki, 98, 113, 130, 135, 136, 151, 155, 185, 193, 227

Chikuma, Rev. Takiji, 135

Chinen, Takahiko, 199

Cho, Isamu (Japanese general), 241–242

Christian ministers, xi, xxvi, xxviii, 16, 18, 35, 37, 45, 66, 71, 90–91, 103–104, 203, 220, 249, 253

consular agents (*toritsuginin*). *See* Japanese Consulate

Coughlin, Capt. John G. (Sand Island camp commander), 11

Crystal City Family Internment Camp (Texas), xx, 5, 81, 137, 160, 198, 199, 212, 215–216, 233, 272–273

custodial detention lists, xxvii, xxxiii, 24–25, 36, 77. *See also* arrests; Federal Bureau of Investigation (FBI)

D

Dainihon Seijikai (Japanese political party), 237, 245

deaths in camp (Hawai'i internees), 103–104, 124, 141–142, 208, 241, 251, 261. *See also* Masuda, Gosaku; Oshima, Kanesaburo; Sogawa, Masao

December 7: arrests, 3–4, 6, 7–10, 36–37, 47–48; Japanese fishermen, arrest and killing of, 37. *See also* arrests, custodial detention lists, Pearl Harbor attack

Deki, Ichiro, 193, 195, 212

Deme, Josen, 18, 23, 44, 130, 137, 151, 191, 193

dentists, 32, 91, 191

deportation bill (Mott Bill), 203–204, 292

Dōmei News Agency, 80, 200, 225, 246

draft resistance, 208–209. *See also* Nisei, military service

E

Eifler, Carl F. (Sand Island camp commander), 16–18, 28, 29–30, 31, 37–38, 39–40, 54

Eifler, Mrs. Mary Lou, 39–40

Emergency Service Committee, 41, 76, 196, 267

Endo, Sutematsu, 81

espionage, suspicions of, 24–25. *See also* Kuehn, (Bernard Julius) Otto; Mori, Ishiko

exchange ship. *See* repatriation

F

Family Camp. *See* Crystal City Family Internment Camp (Texas)

Federal Bureau of Investigation (FBI), xxiv, 3, 24–25, 38, 77, 219–220; arrests by, xxvii, 7–8, 14, 16, 36–38; interrogations by, 195. *See also* arrests; custodial detention lists

Fisher, Dr. Galen, 121

fishing in camp. *See* passing time in camp

Florida, internees from, 88, 90

food: aboard ship, 44, 265; aboard trains, 58–60, 86; in camp, 17, 22–23, 66–68, 88, 99–100, 109–110, 113–114, 142–143, 146–147, 152–153, 159; shortages, 32, 66–68, 106

Forrest Internment Camp. *See* Camp Forrest Internment Camp (Tennessee)

Fort Abraham Lincoln Internment Camp (North Dakota), 126, 217, 225, 238

Fort Missoula Internment Camp (Montana), xxxiv, 79, 126, 128–165; commemorative photos of Hawai'i group, 140; description of, 128–129; flu epidemic, 151–153; food, 146–147; haiku, 163–165; internee population of, 129, 143–144, 157–158, 162; Japanese graves in Missoula Cemetery, 138–140; meeting with Spanish consul, 158–159; news broadcasts, 147–148; passing time, 131–134, 137–138, 140–141, 148, 149, 150–151, 156–157, 161–162; repatriation, 136–137; seasons and weather, 145–146, 148–149, 156; self-government, 129–131, 154–156; shopping in town, 144–145, 149–150; train transit to, 126–127

Fort Shafter (O'ahu), 8, 31, 279

Fort Sill Internment Camp (Oklahoma), 99, 104, 126

Fraser, Bert H. (Missoula camp commander), 129, 142, 159

Fuchino, Heigo, 15, 26, 44, 64, 89, 113, 191, 238

Fuji Furniture, xxix–xxx, xxxv–xxxvi, xxxvii, 281, 283

Fujihana, Rev. Kyodo, 113

Fujii, Osamu, 192, 227

Fujii, Seiichi, 44, 69

Fujiie, Rev. Shoho, 29, 44, 45, 65, 72, 137, 147, 193, 214

Fujimoto, Kenkichi, 18, 44, 69, 75, 106

Fujimura, Masako, 40, 314n33. *See also* women internees

Fujino, Rev. Shigeo, 106

Fujisawa, Rev. Hideo, 44, 45, 69, 75

Fujishiro, Rev. Utanosuke, 44, 45, 81

Fujita, Empei, 207

Fujitani, Rev. Kodo, 224

Fukuda, Teiichiro, 44, 69

Fukuda, Rev. Yoshiaki, 213–214

Fukuhara, Hisashi (Getsugaku), 105

Fukuma, Toyokichi (Japanese consul general), 24–25

Fukunaga, Zeichi, 224

Fukutomi, Shinjiro, 39

funerals in camp. *See* Buddhism, Christian ministers, deaths in camp

Furukawa, Akira (Bunshiro), xxxi, xxxvii, 275

Furukochi, Sadakazu, (physician), 191, 209, 258, 259

Furuya, Hanzo (son of Kumaji), xxxv, xxxvi, 7, 35, 267, 283, 286

Furuya, Jun (wife of Kumaji), xxviii–xxix, xxxvi, 8, 81, 145, 267, 283, 284, 286

Furuya, Kaetsu, 199

Furuya, Keiichi, (son of Kumaji), 267, 283

Furuya, Kicho (Peru), 214, 233, 256–257

Furuya, Kumaji (Suikei): after internment, xxxvi–xxxviii; Angel Island, 50–57, 58; arrest of, 4, 7–9, 47–48; as a community leader, xxix–xxx, xxxvi–xxxvii; business interests of, xxix–xxx, xxxv–xxxvii; Camp Forrest, 88–97; Camp McCoy, 62–86; and family, 76–77, 95–96, 206; FBI interrogation of, 18, 19, 20–23; hearing by Board of Officers and Civilians, xxxii–xxxiii, 33–36, 279–291; immigration to U.S., xxvii–xxix; INS office detention, 8–10, 15, 22–23, 40–41, 43; internment history of, xliii; Livingston, 98–127; marriage and family, xxviii–xxix, xxxv; Missoula, 128–165; parole notice, 224; profile, 276–277; repatriation decision, 95–96; return to Hawai'i, xxxvi, 258, 260–273; Sand Island, 46–47, 48–49; Santa Fe, 185–262, 268–271; in transit, 43–47, 49–50, 56–63, 126–127, 165–166; writings, ii, xix, xxxvii, 83–84, 278. *See also* haiku; *Haisho Tenten* (book), "Haisho Tenten" (newspaper series), *Imin no Rakugaki* (book), *Ruten* (book)

Furuya, Seizo (son of Kumaji), 267, 283

Furuya, Suikei. *See* Furuya, Kumaji
Furuya, Takahisa (Peru), 194
Furuya, Tomochi, (son of Kumaji), 267, 283
Furuya, Yoko (daughter of Kumaji), 261, 267, 283

G

German internees: World War I, 89, 141, 201; World War II, xx, xxxii, 32, 33, 89, 105–106, 129, 153. *See also* POWs
Germany, 223, 235–236, 238
Gima, Shimpuku, 191, 195, 212
go (Japanese board game). *See* passing time in camp
golf in camp. *See* passing time in camp
Goto, Baron. *See* Goto, Yasuo (Baron)
Goto, Mankichi, 29, 98, 141, 197
Goto, Rev. Shinpei, 18, 37
Goto, Yasuo (Baron), 41, 196
Granada Relocation Center (Colorado), 201, 208, 219, 252, 264
Grant, USS, 43–47, 49–50. *See also* transport to camps
Grew, Joseph (U.S. ambassador), 80
Gripsholm, SS. *See* repatriation
Group that Supports the Hundred-Year War, The (*Hyaku-nen sensō kiseikai*), 79
Group that Supports the Twenty-Five-Year War, The (*Nijūgonen chōkisen shijikai*), 79, 81
Grove Park Inn, North Carolina. *See* internment hotels

H

haiku: Angel Island, 55–56; arrest, 4, 47–49; Camp Forrest, 97; Camp McCoy, 84–85; clubs in Hawai'i, xxi, xxx–xxxi; funerals, 124, 125; Livingston, 123–126; Missoula, 163–165; on peace, 236; poets and their names, xxi–xxii; return to Hawai'i, 271–272; Sand Island Camp, 48–49; Santa Fe Camp, 268–271; trains, 59, 61, 62; transport ships, 46, 49, 50. *See also* poetry
Haisho Tenten (Furuya): translation, xvii–xxii, xxiii, xxxiv–xxxv; writing and publication in Japanese, xi, xix, xxxvii, xxxviii, 6, 122, 274–275
"Haisho Tenten" (newspaper series), xix, xxxviii, 3, 6, 274
Hamada, Itsuo, 101, 105, 193, 206
Hamada, Kyuichi, 37

Hamada, Noriyoshi, 227
Hamada, Otoshiro, 193, 206, 212
Hamamoto, Katsuo (Peru), 155
Hamamoto, Sadasuke, 15, 29, 47, 98
Hamamura, Kyoichi, 44, 57, 81
Hanabusa, Minosuke, 193, 214
Hanada, Rev. Tessui, 199
Hanamoto, Hitoshi, 158
Hara, Masatoshi, 196
Harada, Nobutaro, 39
Harada, Tsunetaro (Sanko), 45, 57
Harada, (Irene) Umeno, 40, 314n33. *See also* women internees
Hasebe, Charles Ichitaro, 68–69, 78–79, 91, 130, 201
Hasegawa, Haruzo, 207
Hasegawa, Tsuruzo, 102–103, 199
Hashibe, Shinichi, 81
Hashimoto, Manzuchi, 67, 69, 75, 118, 201, 266
Hata, Yoichi, 201, 264
Hattori, Shigenari, 44, 57, 69, 76, 80, 95
Hawai'i: under martial law, xxxii, xxxiv, xxxv–xxxvi, 9, 220, 224, 233; and U.S. global supremacy, xii–xiii. *See also* Honouliuli Internment Camp, Pearl Harbor attack, Sand Island Internment Camp
Hawai'i, internees return to: xxxviii, 241, 262–264, 272; arrival in Honolulu, 266–267; commemorative photographs, 255–257; emotional goodbyes, 258, 260–261; family reunions, 267–268; haiku, 271–272; interviews and baggage inspection, 254–255; aboard USS *Yarmouth*, 265–266
Hawai'i Japanese Language Middle School, 38, 43. *See also* Japanese language schools
Hawaii Times, The, xix, xxxvii, xxxviii, 6, 274
Hawaiians, native, xi, xii, 203
Hayasaka, Shingo, 215
Hayashi, Ichiro, 220
Hayashi, Rev. Kyushichi, 199, 220
Hayashi, Meijiro, 200
Hayashi, Tomoichi, 32, 65, 74
Heen, William, 14, 43, 211
Hida, Rev. Sensho, 199
Hidaka, Suguru, 191
Higa, Kamasuke, 185
Himeno, Rev. Masahiro, xi, xiii, 4–5, 98, 100–101, 105, 134, 142, 156, 191, 192, 207, 266, 275

Hino, Rev. Shuzui, 199
Hino, Rev. Yoshio, 69, 76, 118, 158
Hinoki, Minoru, 225. *See also* Hōkokudan, Tule Lake group (Santa Fe Camp)
Hirai, Katsutoshi, 194
Hirai, Ryuzo, 39
Hirai, Shinsho, 40, 314n33. *See also* women internees
Hirai, Toyo, 192
Hirama, Teruzo, 81
Hirano, Rev. Naogoro, 193
Hirano, Rev. Toshio, 207
Hirashima, Masaichi, 65, 69, 155
Hirashima, Motoo, 228
Hirayama, Rev. Unji, 199, 225
Hirose, Kosuke, 105, 261
Hirose, Magotaro (San Francisco), 119
Hiroshima, bombing of. *See* atomic bombs
Hisatake, Itsuei, 156, 192, 227
Hitomi, Tasaku, 210–211
Hōkoku Seinendan (Young Men's Association to Serve the Motherland), 220–221, 224–225, 228, 230–231, 251, 293–296. *See also* Nisei, Tule Lake group (Santa Fe)
Hōkokudan. *See* Hōkoku Seinendan
Honda, Hiroshi, 65, 74, 77, 106
Honda, Rev. Kaneki, 130
Hongwanji Mission, 30, 39, 45, 80, 91, 241. *See also* Buddhism
Honolulu Japanese Chamber of Commerce (HJCC), xxx, xxxiii, xxxvi, 216, 281.
Honouliuli Internment Camp (Oʻahu), xx, xxxiv, 6, 32, 37, 216
Hori, Rev. Minetaro, 81
Horibe, Mrs. Kosaku (Kiku), 40, 314n33. *See also* women internees
Horikawa, Isuke, 193
Horita, Shigeru, 39
Horiuchi, Mitsutaka, 155
Horiuchi, Norimasa, 20–21
Hotta, Kiyoji, 246
hygiene: 40, 68–69, 85; toilets (latrines), 30, 44–45; laundry, 36, 53

I

Ichikawa, Kiyoshi, 105, 113, 133, 136, 153, 155, 191
Ichimaru, Rinosuke, 244–245, 297–298, 340n102
Ichimaru, Toshinosuke. *See* Ichimaru, Rinosuke
Ida, Taira (Toka), 118

Idemoto, Masao, 39
Ihara, Tamotsu, 65, 106
Iida, Koichi, xxx, xxxvii, 13, 18, 101, 118, 137, 185, 192, 209, 213, 257
Iida, Mrs. Koichi, 14, 118, 125
Iinuma, Toshio, 69, 99, 103, 110, 191, 197
Ikeda, Chiei, 191
Ikeno, Masao, 156, 192, 227
Ikezawa, Rev. Shuntaro, 16, 56, 90–91, 220
Ikuma, Rev. Kinai, 193
illness in camp: 91, 103–104, 109–110, 120–121, 151–152, 257; psychological distress, 29, 36, 44–45, 89, 92–94, 117, 194, 241, 259, 272. *See also physicians*
Imamura, Rev. Teizen, 191, 193, 233
Imamura, Tsutomu, 81, 99, 110, 121
Imin no Rakugaki (Furuya), xxxvii
Immigration and Naturalization Service (INS) (Angel Island). *See* Angel Island Immigration Station (California)
Immigration and Naturalization Service (INS) (Honolulu), xx, 3; detention at, xxxii, 4, 8–10, 22–23, 40–41; haiku about, 4, 49; hearings, xxxii–xxxiii, 25–26, 31, 33–36, 278–291
Immigration and Naturalization Service (INS) (Seattle), 264–265
Imoto, Seiko, 225
Inamine, Kiyoyoshi, 227
Inasaki, Itsuo, 261
Inokuchi, Uyemon, 18, 56
Inouye, Daniel K., xxxviii, 196
Inouye, Ken. *See* Inouye, Daniel K.
INS. *See* Immigration and Naturalization Service
International Red Cross. *See* Red Cross
internee interrogations and hearings, xxxii–xxxiii, 18–23, 26, 33–36, 254–255, 279–291. *See also* Board of Officers and Civilians, Federal Bureau of Investigation, Immigration and Naturalization Service
internee labor in camp, 27–28, 30, 67, 74, 100, 109, 112–114, 131, 201–202, 213
internee self-government. *See* Camp Forrest, Camp Livingston, Camp McCoy, Fort Missoula, Sand Island Internment Camp, Santa Fe Internment Camp
internment, definition and overview, xx, xxiii–xxvii, xxxiii; remembrance and commemoration of, xxxviii–xli
internment camps. *See* Camp Forrest,

Camp Kenedy, Camp Livingston, Camp McCoy, Crystal City Family Internment Camp, Fort Abraham Lincoln (Bismarck), Fort Missoula, Fort Sill, Honouliuli Internment Camp, Kenedy Internment Camp, Kooskia Internment Camp, Lordsburg Internment Camp, Sand Island Internment Camp, Santa Fe Internment Camp

internment hotels, 119, 273

Ipponsugi, Ryuichi, 191

Isa, Kashin, 185

Isemoto, Hisato, 191

Iseri, Torao, 105, 132, 191

Ishida, Kusuro, 57, 99, 110

Ishimoto, Masao, 74, 106

Isobe, Rev. Misao, 81, 119

Isobe, Rev. Shigemi, 32, 74, 81

Isomura, Hirotaro (Hirota), 259

Isomura, Takasuke "Chicken," 195, 216

Issei: arrests of community leaders, xxxii–xxxiii, 22–23; camps, xx–xxi, xxiii, xxxiii–xxxiv; discrimination against, xxiv–xxv; feelings about Japan, xxv–xxvi, 147–148, 153–154; memoirs, xv, xvii, xxxviii–xli; perspectives on Japan's war, 34–35, 206, 218–219, 237–238, 247–248, 249, 250–252, 286; at Tule Lake, 220–221, 225. *See also* Japanese Consulate; Japanese emperor; Japanese immigrants; Japanese military; *kenjinkai* (prefectural associations), United Japanese Society

Italian internees: World War I, 141; World War II, xx, xxxii, 92, 129, 131, 147, 152, 153. *See also* POWs

Ito, Kanzen, 40, 314n33. *See also* women internees

Ito, Choichi (Keigetsu), 193, 206

Ito, Michio, 101

Ito, Tatsuo, 224

Itsuno, Tokio, 113

Iwahara, Taketo, 69, 81, 119, 137

Iwakami, Konosuke, 81

Iwamoto, Masao, 39

Iwasa, Shinzo, 195

Iwasa, Sueji, 162, 266

Iwata, Rev. Masayuki, 32, 191

Iwo Jima, Battle of, 225–226, 240

Izumi, Kiyoto, 194

Izutsu, Ryozo, 224, 241

J

Japan: defeat of, 240, 244–247, 250, 251–252; deteriorating relations with U.S., xii, 25, 38, 185, 187, 195; and emigration, xxi, xxiv–xxvi, 211; government changes, 233–234, 237, 250. *See also* Issei, Pearl Harbor attack, World War II

Japanese Americans. *See* Issei, Kibei, Nisei

Japanese Chamber of Commerce. *See* Honolulu Japanese Chamber of Commerce

Japanese Consulate (Honolulu), xxvi, xxxvi, 16, 21, 22, 24–25, 38; consular agents (*toritsuginin*), xxvi–xxvii, 16, 40, 75, 136, 236, 281; consuls general, 16, 31

Japanese emperor, 7, 200, 214, 237–238, 250, 285

Japanese immigrants, xxiv–xxvi, 104–105. *See also* Issei

Japanese Imperial Navy: receptions for training ships of, xxvi, xxxiii, 24–25, 38, 40, 281, 284; victories of, 205–206. *See also* Japanese military, Pearl Harbor attack

Japanese language schools (Hawai'i), xix, 22, 38, 39, 43, 75, 102, 110, 142, 223–224, 251, 254, 281; arrests of teachers, xxvi, 9, 39, 40

Japanese military, 221–222; balloon bombs, 219–220, 240; losses, 225–226, 233–234, 237, 242, 244–247; songs about, 72, 101, 147–148; victories of, 21, 27, 205–206. *See also* Issei, perspectives on Japan's war; Japanese Imperial Navy, Pearl Harbor attack

Japanese naval training ships. *See* Japanese Imperial Navy

Japanese POWs (prisoners of war), 13, 26–27, 70–71, 77, 78, 80, 104–105, 116–117. *See also* Sakamaki, Kazuo

Japanese Red Cross. *See* Red Cross

Jerome Relocation Center (Arkansas), 198, 200

K

Kabashima, Suijo, 29, 39, 54–55, 65, 74, 137, 155

Kagawa, Takeo, 18, 74, 89, 106

Kagesa, Shikatsu, 39

Kagimoto, Yoichi, 104

Kajiwara, Shigekichi, 192

Kajiwara, Tasuke, 105, 113, 119
Kalihi Japanese Language School, 22, 142, 281
Kamijo, Isamu, 192
Kamioka, Matsutaro, 37
Kan, Buntaro, 197
Kanamori, Shinroku, 246
Kanashiro, Zensuke, 32
Kaneshiro, Hideo, 335n53, 342n116
Kanno, Tomizo, 199
Kano, Rev. Hisanori (Nebraska), 66, 68, 71, 75, 90, 100–101, 108, 259
Kanzawa, Rev. Tsunetaro (San Francisco), 256
Kasai, Yoshihiko (Salt Lake City), 105, 119, 198
Kasajima, Hatsutaro (Mexico), 149–150
Kasamoto, Mitsuji, 201
Kashima, Ryuichi, 74, 129, 154, 226, 238–239
Kashiwa, Rev. Ryuten, 212, 264
Kashiwa, Shiro, 196
Katagiri, Masatoshi, 41, 196, 267
Katagiri Shigeru, 206
Katamoto, Usaburo, 191, 227
Kato, Shu, 212
Kato, Yoshinobu, 195
Katoda, Rev. Tetsuei, 199
Kawabata, Shigeyoshi, 225
Kawahara, Toraji, 106
Kawakami, Shozo, 69, 81, 99, 119, 137
Kawamoto, Katsuichi, 22, 57, 65, 118, 154, 193, 226, 239, 255, 272
Kawamoto, Takuzo, 39, 42, 217
Kawamura, Rev. Shodo, 212
Kawano, Kazuyuki, 212
Kawasaki, Kango, 261, 264
Kawasaki, Rev. Kazoe, 15, 29, 36, 81, 89, 92, 137
Kawasaki, Miyuki, 40, 314n33. *See also* women internees
Kawauchi, Kichitaro, 224, 241
Kawazoe, Zen'ichi, 39
Kayahara, Chosuke, 255
Kelly, Willard F. (INS commissioner), 158–161, 226, 329n57, 339n90
Kenedy Internment Camp (Texas), 135, 157–158, 211, 215
kenjinkai (prefectural associations), xxv, 20–21, 284–285
Kiba, Tsuneyoshi, 155, 239
Kibei (Japanese Americans educated in Japan), xx, xxvi–xxvii, xxxii, xxxiv, xxxix,

208, 217, 220–221, 228, 251; internment memoirs by, xxxixi, xl
Kida, Katsuichi, 195
Kikuchi, Chikyoku, 197
Kimura, Akio (physician), 22, 23, 42, 44, 56, 64, 65, 74, 77, 89, 91, 130, 134, 191, 216, 259
Kimura, Hirotatsu Shonan, 111, 247–248
Kimura, Kenji (shipping company manager), 13, 15, 36, 65, 68, 81, 95, 129, 137
Kimura, Muneo, 156, 191, 193, 214, 227
Kimura, Rev. Tomiji, 130, 151
Kimura, Toraki, 120–121, 199
Kinjo, Chin'yei, 202
Kinoshita, Ichiji, 191
Kinoshita, Takichi, 193, 206
Kirita, Kamekichi, 199
Kishida, Eiichi, 81, 130, 137
Kishimoto, Hirotomo, 215
Kitajima, Masao, 198, 199
Kitajima, Rev. Yoshio, 199
Kiyosaki, Masato, 99, 105, 130, 155
Kiyotsuka, Rev. Tetsuzo, 199
Kobata, Toshiro, 259
Kobayashi, Masaichi, 191, 193, 212, 216
Kobayashi, Motoichi, 81, 105
Kobayashi, Rev. Nisshu, 18, 104, 148, 193
Kobayashi, Tokio, 14, 37
Kobayashi, Rev. Yoshio, 105, 113
Kodama, Rev. Masayuki, 66, 81, 130, 137
Kodama, Yoshiharu, 39
Koga, Masao, 39
Kohatsu, Yukihide (physician), 42, 130, 141, 151–152, 191, 257, 259
Koide, Kiyoichi, 199
Koide, Shoichi, 199
Koike, Haruo, 205, 255
Koike, Yoshio, 192, 214, 227
Koiso, Kuniaki (Japanese prime minister), 221, 222, 233
Kojima, Teikichi, 9, 69
Kokubo, Hisahiko, 104
Kokuzo, Rev. Zenkai, 199
Komagata, Rev. Zenkyo, 24, 39
Komai, Toyosaku (Henry) (Los Angeles), 119, 190, 198, 253, 256
Komatsu, Taiichi, 81, 130, 137
Komeiji, Toshisuke, 20, 21
Kometani, Katsumi, 41, 196
Komeya, Miyotsuchi, 9, 37
Komu, Mannosuke, 191

Kondo, Ichikuro (Salinas, California), 200, 207, 209, 260
Kondo, Kikujiro, 192, 195
Kondo, Shiro, 227
Konkōkyō, 40; priests of, 66, 81, 130, 137. *See also* Shintoism
Konno, Ichiro, 129, 155, 162
Kooskia Internment Camp (Idaho), 158
Kotake, Toshikazu, 37
Koyama, Iwao, 194, 209
Koyama, Takashi, 260
Koyanagi, Kunizo, 193, 206
Kubokawa, Rev. Kyokujo, 13, 18, 29, 32, 56, 81, 103, 119, 137, 256
Kubota, Rev. Ryudo, 199
Kubota, Saichiro, 105, 148, 156, 224
Kuchiba, Rev. Gikyo, 18, 29, 30, 39, 56, 81, 91, 130, 137, 142, 193, 241
Kuehn, (Bernard Julius) Otto, 24, 27, 120. *See also* espionage
Kunimoto, James Shoichi, 208, 334n44
Kuniyoshi, Choshu, 185
Kuniyuki, Aisuke, 195, 212, 264
Kuraishi, Tomomichi, 39
Kurakake, Toraichi, 191, 197, 224
Kuribayashi, Tadamichi (Japanese general), 225–226
Kurisu, Koichi, 158, 195
Kurita, Yasuro, 154, 199
Kuroda, Rev. Keisei, 32
Kurohira, Rev. Hosho, 194, 238
Kurokawa, Tetsuji, 137, 159, 191, 197
Kurotobi, Isamu (Peru), 129, 154, 190, 226
Kurusu, Saburō (Hien), (Japanese ambassador), 80, 236
Kusano, Ishima, 227
Kusao, Takegoro, 191, 194, 233, 260
Kusao, Yugoro, 227
Kuwahara, Gunichi, 105, 197
Kuwatsuki, Fumitaka, 239

L
Langston, Julian P. (Santa Fe camp administrator), 199–200, 213, 221, 223, 225
Latin America, internees from, xx, xxi, 211, 215, 254, 255–256. *See also* Panama, Peru
Life behind Barbed Wire (Soga), xvii, xxi, xxii, xxiv, xxxviii–xxxix, 6
Lordsburg Internment Camp (New Mexico), 137, 206, 233, 259, 260
Lordsburg Jihō, 233

M
MacArthur, Gen. Douglas, 222, 223, 247
Maeda, Rev. Gisei (Fresno, California), 253
Maeda, Rev. Kametaro, 29, 98, 146, 156, 201, 224
Maehara, Teiichiro, 193, 224, 241
Maehokama, Shobun, 192, 209, 215, 227
Maekawa, Shigezo, 65, 199
mail, 13–15, 42, 56, 64, 66, 76–77, 89, 95, 122–123, 130
Mainland internees, 65, 71–72, 88, 90, 99, 107, 119, 129, 134, 135, 190, 211, 217, 253, 255–256
Makino, Frederick Kinzaburo (newspaper editor), 24
Manabe, Tatsuo, 227
Manoa Japanese Language School, 223–224
Martin, A.R. (Spanish consul), 158–161
Marumoto, Masaji, xxxiii, 32–33, 41, 43, 196, 289
Marutani, Matsuo, 190, 191, 197
Maruyama, Gunjiro (Miami), 90, 119, 198, 207
Maruyama Tsurukichi, 153, 154
Masaki, Rev. Jikyo, 29, 32, 74, 81
Masaki, Rev. Shozaemon, 65, 83, 162, 194, 266
Masuda, Gosaku, 103–104, 124–125, 161, 261
Matano, Rev. Konin, 130, 233
Matayoshi, Shinjiro, 224
Matsubayashi, Rev. Shoten, 16, 199
Matsubayashi, Rev. Shushin, 16, 39, 81, 130, 137
Matsuda, Ishichi, 81
Matsuda, Motoichi, 28, 30, 37, 69, 80, 95
Matsuda, Rev. Ryugen, 105, 199
Matsudo, Kinsuke (San Diego), 119
Matsui, Totaro, xxx, 6, 18, 22, 64, 66, 89, 99, 107–108, 129, 130, 137, 142, 151, 153, 154, 158, 162, 207, 216, 259–260, 274, 275
Matsukawa, Kuniharu, 214, 215
Matsumoto, Kazumi, 193
Matsumoto, Kuramatsu, 216
Matsumura, Tamotsu, 81
Matsunaga, Masayuki "Spark," xxxviii, 196
Matsuo, Umesuke, 199
Matsuoka, Tokuzo, 37
Matsuoka Yosuke, 246
Matsushita, Iwao, 129, 158–159
Matsuura, Rev. Gyokuei, 199
Matsuura, Rev. Shuun, 81

Matsuzaka, Shigeru, 217
Mayeda, Yoshihisa, 212
Miake, Rev. Eimu, 81
Miho, Katsuichi, 105, 191
Miho, Katsuro, 267
Mikami, Shuji, 101, 156, 192
Mikami, Yoshiye, 81
Mikuni, Rev. Matagoro, 201
military police. *See* MPs
military service. *See* Nisei, Reserve Officer Training Corps (ROTC)
Minami Jiro, 237, 245
Missoula, Montana, 127, 144–145, 149–150; cemetery, 138–140; Mercantile Company, 145, 149–150. *See also* Fort Missoula Internment Camp (Montana)
Mita, Chumu, xxxi, 107
Miura, Gempei, 105, 119
Miura, Mankichi, 224
Miura, Shin'ichi, 207
Miura, Takeo, 199
Miwa, Seigo, 42, 81
Miyagawa, Shintaro, 137
Miyagi, Genyei, 198, 199
Miyagi, Takeo, 57, 261
Miyaji, Kyohei, 227
Miyamasa, Kaichi, 190, 191
Miyamoto, Rev. Buntetsu, 98
Miyamoto, Kazuo (physician), 26, 31, 32, 65, 72, 77, 89, 92, 105, 106, 259
Miyamoto, Nihei, 37, 67, 69, 81, 137
Miyao, Rev. Shigemaru, 15, 22–23, 39, 69, 75–76, 198. *See also* Shintoism
Miyao, Yoshiye (mother of Shigemaru), 15, 39, 40, 314n33. *See also* Shintoism, women internees
Miyao, Yuki (wife of Shigemaru), 15, 39, 40, 75–76, 314n33. *See also* Shintoism, women internees
Miyata, Kazue, 192
Miyata, Kyoichi, 22, 98, 118, 224
Miyazaki, Hiseki, 105, 199
Miyazawa, Yasutaro, 191, 209, 226
Mochizuki, Rev. Kanryu, 105, 119, 199
Mochizuki, Kohei (California), 256
Mochizuki, Masao, 159, 253 (Peru)
money, 70; and assets of internees, xxxv, 9, 42, 131, 185; difficulty obtaining in camp, 42, 66, 131, 264–265; and freezing of assets, 9, 42, 66, 195
Montana. *See* Fort Missoula Internment Camp (Montana), Missoula (Montana)

Mori, Iga (physician), 18, 37
Mori, Ishiko (physician, wife of Motokazu), 39–40 , 314n33. *See also* espionage, women internees
Mori, Motokazu (physician, son of Iga), 32, 39–40, 198, 216
Mori, Rev. Tenran, 193
Moribe, Ryuichi, 191, 195
Morifuji, Sadato, 18, 22, 189–190
Morihara, Usaku, 212, 264
Morishita, Toshio, 233
Morita, Koetsu, 199
Morita, Takeshi, 129, 154
Morita, Zenkichi, 226, 239
Morrison, Gen. William R. C., 224, 233
Motoki, Moritsugu, 37
Motoshige, Hiroshi, 18, 22–23, 29, 65, 74, 81, 137
Motoshige, Tatsuo, 22–23, 29, 65, 81, 137
Mott Bill, 203–204, 292
MPs (military police), 8, 9, 34, 208
Mukaeda, Katsuma, 190, 208, 214, 221, 223
Murai, Isao, 41, 118–119, 196, 273
Murakami, Jinji, 199
Murakami, Kanami, 39
Murakami, Minoru (Koran), 105, 111, 147, 153, 159, 191, 192, 194, 216, 261
Murakami, Shigeru, 212
Murata, Jitsuma, 191, 209
Murata, Ryuichi, 191
Murata, Yasumasa, 39
Murayama, Hajime, 133
Murayama, Tamotsu, 154
Mutobe, Rev. Ryujun, 69

N

Nada, Yujiro, 57
Nagai, Sekitaro, 130, 155
Nagakura, Eizo, 197, 246
Nagamatsu, Rev. Ikugoro, 192, 193, 253
Nagasaki, bombing of. *See* atomic bombs
Nagasawa, Shukichi, 191
Nagata, Shigeru, 209
Nago, Rev. Ninryo, 29, 56, 77, 78, 99, 191
Nagumo Chuichi, 219
Naito, Rev. Kyojo, 113, 199
Nakagawa, Shizuko, 314n33. *See also* women internees
Nakagawa, Takejiro, 212
Nakahara, Buntaro, 241, 261
Nakaichi, Yuichi, 193, 195, 206
Nakama, Ginpachi, 201
Nakamura, Ichiro, 195, 197, 227, 255

Nakamura, Koichiro, 22, 42, 198, 200, 266
Nakamura, Kokichi, 158
Nakamura, Mitsuru, 37
Nakamura, Sadamu, 192, 209
Nakamura, Tomoaki, 18, 21, 32, 65, 71, 119, 198, 199, 256, 274
Nakamura, Yukio (Peru), 129, 155
Nakamura, Yukiteru, 215
Nakano, Minoru, 199
Nakano, Norikazu, 22, 80, 95
Nakano, Tamejiro, 74, 81, 137
Nakayama, Chikashi, xix, 221, 227; maps by, 12, 186
Nakayama, Dengo, 81
Nakayama, Rev. Hozui, 105, 193, 224
Nekomoto, Shunichi, 81
news broadcasting in camp, 72, 111–112, 147–148, 193–194, 248
newspapers, 14, 24, 27, 194. See also *Nippu Jiji*, *Lordsburg Jihō*, *Santa Fe Jihō*
Niimi, Tokuichi, 69, 74, 105, 106
Nippu Jiji (newspaper), xxviii, xxxi, xxxviii, 40, 255. *See also* Asami, Shoichi; newspapers; Soga, Yasutaro
Nisei, xx–xxi, xxxiv, 105–106, 195–197, 217–218, 238, 248, 249; citizenship of, xxiv, xxv, xxvi, xxxiv; loyalty to America, 34–36, 104–105, 286, 287; memoirs by, xxxix–xl; military service by, xxxviii, 5, 112, 196, 203, 265; ties to Japan, xxvi–xxxii, 218, 251. *See also* Emergency Service Committee, Kibei, Reserve Officer Training Corps (ROTC), Tule Lake group (Santa Fe), Tule Lake Relocation Center
Nishida, Rev. Yoshifusa, 130
Nishii, Rev. Hironori, 199
Nishiki, Kakujiro, 32, 65, 69
Nishimoto, Hajime, 193, 212, 264
Nishimura, Jiro (Seattle), 65, 71
Nishioka, Kuniaki, 217
Nishiyama, Matsujuro, 192
Nishizaki, Nizo, 261
Nishizaki, Shohachi, 193
Nishizawa, Rev. Kozan, 198, 199
Nomura, Giichi, 158, 195
Nomura Kichisaburo (Japanese ambassador), 80, 222, 236
Nonomura, Rev. Yuko, 199
"Note to Roosevelt, A" (Ichimaru), 244–245, 340n102
Nozawa, Yoshinori (Los Angeles), 119

O

Obata, Soichi (Daisei), 18, 30, 65, 71, 74, 153, 155, 193, 200, 206, 214, 274
Obinata, Aoi (*Makkoi byōin*), 274
Ochi, Michikazu, 192, 227
Oda, Rev. Hakuai, 69, 130, 137
Oda, Junji, 233
Odachi, Rev. Kinzaemon, 261
Odate, Rev. Chiko, 199
Odo, Shunichi, 65, 105, 106
Office of Naval Intelligence (ONI), xxiv, 24
Office of Price Administration, xxxvi
Ogata, Kazuhiko, 69, 76, 81, 120–121, 130, 137, 198
Ogawa, Yoshiro, 69, 81, 130, 137
Ogiwara Seisensui, xxxi, xxxvii, 165. *See also* haiku
Ohama, Futoshi, 224
Ohara, Naoyoshi, 136
Ohata, Seiichi (physician), 81, 198
Oi, Rev. Joei, 3–4, 8, 22–23, 32, 65, 130, 138, 140, 142–143, 143–144, 155, 227, 274–275
Oi, Tetsuo, 24
Oikawa, Tokuji, 199
Oka, Suekichi, 69
Okada, Jiro, 198, 199
Okada, Saichiro, 129, 155
Okamoto, Rev. Kakichi, 224
Okamoto, Rev. Nanshin, 193
Okamoto, Shoichi James. *See* Kunimoto, James Shoichi
Okamoto Suemasa, 247
"Okano Incident," 17–18
Okano, Rev. Ryoshin, 17–18, 32, 69, 75, 76, 81, 137
Okawa, Rev. Gendo, 130, 151, 256
Oki, Iwao, 39
Okimoto, Sakazuchi, 195
Okinawa, Battle of, 237, 241–242
Okumoto, Yoshimi, 199
Okuyama, Toyoaki (Peru), 194, 256
Onaga, Rincho, 135
Onishi, Katsuji, 129, 155, 159
Onishi Takijiro, 247
Ono, Gontaro, 228
Ono, Shoroku (San Francisco), 116, 119, 198
Onoda, Torataro, 81, 95, 129, 137
Onouye, Hikohachi, 224
Orimo, Kichitaro, 229
Orita, Isaku, 65, 74, 130, 150, 197
Osaki, Yojiro, 195

Oshima, Kanesaburo, 99, 104, 261
Oshima, Shigeo, 74, 81
Osugi, Akira, 228, 229
Otani, George Genji, 8, 15, 31, 57, 65, 68, 80, 95
Otani, Matsujiro, 14, 43, 207, 211
Otojiro Okuda, 16
Otomo, Rev. Kenju, 191
Otsuka, Hikojuro, 224
Oyama, Shuhei, 185
Ozaki, Otokichi (Muin), xxxix, 105, 107, 199
Ozaki, Sawajiro, 98, 129, 130, 135, 153, 154, 191, 192, 197, 223, 226, 261
Ozawa, Rev. Gijo, 103, 119, 199, 256
Ozawa, Takeo, 154
Ozu, Yoshihiko, 43

P

Panama, internees from, 29, 99–100, 107, 109, 110, 111, 119, 120–121. *See also* Latin America, Peru
Pāpaʻikou Japanese Language School, 223
parole of internees, xxxiii–xxxiv, 162, 198–199, 200–201, 207, 211, 212, 223–224, 226, 255, 256
passing time in camp, 77–78, 92, 99, 102–103, 155–156, 215; bird-watching, 52, 114–115, 140–141, 146, 189, 212, 234–235, 253; classes, 92–93, 94, 100–101, 104, 107–108, 147–148, 227; fishing, 131–134, 149, 156–157, 161–162; fossil collecting, 94, 115–116, 143, 188–189, 202–203; *go* (board game) 29, 76, 77, 88, 100, 150–151, 197–198; golf, 108–109, 137–138, 188; news broadcasts, 72, 111–112, 147–148, 193–194, 248; performances, 101, 191–193, 206–207, 214; *shōgi* (Japanese chess), 17, 71, 88–89, 188–190, 189–190; *sumō* (wrestling), 83, 209–210; singing, 72–73, 75, 101, 107–108; softball, 74–75, 77, 115, 131, 136, 200, 232–233
Pearl Harbor attack: xi, xii–xiii, 7–10, 14, 30, 37, 274; and Japanese fishermen, arrest and killing of, 37; and Japanese mini-submarines, 27, 93. *See also* arrests; December 7; Sakamaki, Kazuo
Peru, internees from, 129, 131, 135, 157–158, 158–161, 193, 211, 214. *See also* Latin America, Panama
physicians, 32, 259. *See also* dentists; illness in camp; Furukochi, Sadakazu; Kimu-

ra, Akio; Kohatsu, Yukihide; Miyamoto, Kazuo; Mori, Ishiko; Mori, Motokazu; Ohata, Seiichi; Takahashi, Tokuye; Tanaka, Masayoshi; Tofukuji, Koshiro; Uyehara, Yokichi; Yoshizawa, Jiro
poetry, 53–54, 83–84, 192, 216; Chinese poetry at Angel Island, 53–54; clubs in Hawaiʻi, xxi, xxx–xxxi; poetry names, xxi–xxii. *See also* haiku, *Ruten* (Furuya)
Poston Relocation Center (Arizona), 254
Potsdam Declaration, 245, 246–247
POWs (prisoners of war), xxxiv, 11, 17, 29, 141; American, 80, 252. *See* also Japanese POWs
Price Administration and Alien Property Custodian, xxxv–xxxvi

R

radio broadcasts: xxix, 48, 72, 123, 147, 194; and arrests, 14, 37; from Japan, 7, 225, 245–246, 250, 285
Red Cross, 29, 76, 121–122, 205
Relief Association for Overseas Japanese, 153–154
release from internment: 241, 254–255; due to health, 37, 40, 43; without internment, 36–38
relocation centers: 160, 219, 252; defined, xx–xxi; parole to, xxxiii–xxxiv, 200, 212. *See also*: Granada Relocation Center (Colorado), Jerome Relocation Center (Arkansas), Poston Relocation Center (Arizona), Tule Lake Relocation Center (California). *See also* internment camps, War Relocation Authority
renunciants, xxxiv, 254
repatriation, 79–82, 95–96, 159–160, 215–216, 226, 256, 273; first exchange ship (1942), 31, 80, 81, 95, 129; second exchange ship (1943), 80, 81, 118–119, 136–137, 140
Reserve Officer Training Corps (ROTC), xxxv, 7, 14, 19, 119, 283, 286
Richardson, Gen. Robert C., 200, 224
Rogers, Horace (McCoy camp commander), 65, 68, 70–71, 74, 78–79, 85, 86
Roosevelt, President Franklin D.: 222; death of, 211–212, 235–236; and internment and mass incarceration, xxiv, xxxiii, xxxv–xxxvi, 217, 219,

335–336n62; and letter from Ichimaru Rinosuke, 244–245
ROTC. *See* Reserve Officer Training Corps (ROTC)
Ruten (Furuya), xxxvii, 4, 277

S
Sado, Takeshige, 209
Saiki, Enichi, 200
Saiki, Patsy, *Ganbare!*, xxii, xxxix
Saiki, Takaichi (banker), 99, 105, 122, 129, 153, 158, 190, 208, 214, 223, 226, 259–260
Saito, Haruto (Fuyo), 105, 119, 191
Sakaguchi, Kuwasaburo, 232–233
Sakaguchi, Toshio, 194, 227, 233
Sakai, Kunisuke, 105
Sakai, Takaichi (Japanese Consulate employee), 25
Sakakibara, Kamenosuke, 154
Sakamaki, George, 35
Sakamaki, Kazuo (Japanese POW): Sand Island, 13, 26–27; in mainland camps, 51, 64, 70, 78, 93–94, 104–105, 116–117, 274. *See also* Japanese POWs
Sakamoto, Masao, 32, 65, 106, 217
Sakamoto, Munetaka, 191
Sakamoto, Sanji, 106
Sakimizuru, Atsuo, 105, 155, 197
Sakurada, Toyokichi, 190
Sand Island Internment Camp (Hawai'i), xx, xxxiv, 3, 10, 11–19, 24–42; commanders of, 11, 16–17, 28, 30, 31, 37–38, 54; conditions at, 11, 13; feelings of isolation in, 32–33; German section, 18, 39; internee leadership, 18, 31, 36; internees released without hearings, 36–38; interrogations and hearings, xxxii–xxxiii, 18–19, 26, 33–36; map of, 12; "Okano Incident," 17–18; as POW camp, 28; as quarantine facility, 11, 27–28; transfer to Mainland from, 41–42; women detainees, 15–16, 39–40. *See also* Eifler, Carl F.
Santa Fe, New Mexico, 187–188, 252, 257–258
Santa Fe Internment Camp (New Mexico), xxxiv, 126, 137, 162–163, 185–262; administrators of, 199, 221, 223, 255; celebrations, 200, 214, 220, 221, 237–238; commemorative photographs, 255–257; deaths at, 241, 251, 256,

261; departure from, 258–262; haiku, 268–271; illness, 257–258; internee population, xx, 185, 189–190, 194–195, 211, 215–216, 217–218, 220–221; map of, 186; news broadcasts and newspapers, 193–194, 233, 247–248, 250–251, 260; parole, 198–199, 207, 212, 223–224, 246; passing time, 191–193, 199–200, 202–203, 206–207, 209–210, 214, 215, 227, 232–233, 243–244; renunciants, xxxiv; return to Hawai'i, 241; rumors of Japanese victory, 248–250, 251, 253–254; self-government, 190–192, 207–208, 226–227, 238–239; softball, 200, 232–233; train transport to, 162–163, 165–166; war news, 205–206, 218–220, 221–222. *See also* Langtson, Julian P.; *Santa Fe Jihō*; Tule Lake group (Santa Fe); Williams, Ivan;
Santa Fe Jihō (Santa Fe Times), 193–194, 211–212, 233, 239, 248, 250, 256, 260, 261, 274
Sarashina, Rev. Shinri, 39, 69, 81, 130, 137, 147, 152, 156
Sasai, Rev. Myoshu, 113, 199
Sasaki, Giichi, 70, 74, 75, 105, 130
Sasaki, Tadao, 69, 199
Sasaki, Yoshinobu, 15, 69, 74, 129, 130, 132, 142, 154, 192, 227
Sato, Eita, 192
Sato, Taichi, xxx, 18, 31–32, 69, 75, 76, 89–90, 118, 130, 162, 198, 199, 264
Sato, Yazo, 130, 201
Sayegusa, Kinzo, 69, 74, 95, 119, 129, 130, 137, 152, 155, 185, 226, 256
Schofield Barracks (Hawai'i), xii, 91
Schreiber, Abner (Santa Fe camp administrator), 255
Seattle, Washington, 264–265; internees from, 65, 71–72
Seike, Takeo, 197
Seinen Hōkōkai. *See* Hōkoku Seinendan
Seki, Hozen, 158
Seki, Shosaburo, 185
Sekiguchi, Masamichi, 192
Sekiya, Kichitaro, 57, 80, 95
Seri, Usuke, 37
Serizawa, Hideyuki, 69, 76, 120–121, 130, 148, 197
Seto, Rev. Naoichi, 227
shaba (outside the barbed wire), 15, 33

Shafter, Fort (Honolulu), 8, 31
Shiba, Rev. Kakuo, 113, 199
Shichishōkai (Association of Eternal Devotion to the Motherland), 218, 251
Shigefuji, Rev. Enryo (Fresno, California), 251, 253
Shigekane, Shigezo (Kasetsu), 105
Shigekuni, Aisuke, 27, 57, 65, 74, 130, 158
Shigemitsu Mamoru, 251
Shigemoto, Osuke, 8, 18, 22, 74, 118, 130, 137, 151, 155, 185
Shigenaga, Kakuro, 110
Shigenaga, Shigeo, 192, 193, 209, 226
Shiio, Yasujiro, 129
Shimamoto, Seiichi, 39, 154
Shimoda, Rev. Hanzo, 8, 29, 56
Shimoda, Shigezo, 224, 241
Shimonishi, Iwataro, 137
Shinagawa, Tetsuo, 217
Shindo, Takuji, 197, 215, 227
Shinoda, Masaichiro, 105, 130, 191, 261
Shintoism, 153, 224; and arrests of priests, 8, 15, 22–23, 135; priests of, 75, 103–104, 223–224. *See also* celebrations in camp, Konkyōkō
Shiotani, Motoi, 113, 199
Shirasu, Rev. Jukaku, 99–100, 198, 199
Shiratori, Rev. Shunjo, 233
Shitanishi, Iwataro, 137
Shivers, Robert (FBI chief, Honolulu), 9
Shoda, Seiichi, 199
shōgi (Japanese chess). *See* passing time in camp
Sodetani, Yukiyasu, 199
softball in camp, 74–75, 115, 131, 136, 200, 232–233
Soga, Keiho. *See* Soga, Yasutaro
Soga, Sei (wife of Yasutaro), xxviii, 14, 81
Soga, Yasutaro (Keiho), (newspaper publisher), xvii, xxviii, xxxix–xli, 18, 28, 29, 33, 120, 189, 213, 218, 233, 274. See also *Life behind Barbed Wire*, *Nippu Jiji* newspaper
Sogawa, Masao, 74, 130, 141–142, 261
Sokabe, Miyuki, 32, 98, 104, 150, 156, 192, 226, 227, 239
Sokuji Kikoku Hōshikai (Organization for Immediate Return to the Motherland), 221, 225, 230–231, 293–296
Sone, Tetsunosuke, 185, 191
songs, 79, 82–83, 101, 147–148, 278; about internment, 72–73; "The Song of the Yalu River," 73; "Wandering Intern-

ees," 82–83; war marches, 72, 101, 147–148
Sonoda, Santaro, 130, 135, 155
Spanish consul, 122, 158–161, 237
Spillner, Lt. Siegfried, 27
Springer, Louis F. (Sand Island camp commander), 15
Sueoka, Iju, 195, 198, 199
Sueoka, Tameshige. *See* Sueoka, Iju
Sueyasu, Rev. Yonezo, 199
Suga, Mamoru, 195
Sugimoto, Seiichi, 106
Sugiura, Yonematsu, 195, 224
Suguro, Shuhei (Peru), 194, 214, 215, 233
Sumida, Daizo, xxxvii, 18, 74–75, 118, 130, 185, 197, 209, 255
Sumida, Shigezo, 223–224
Sumida, Shinzaburo, 18, 29, 65, 74, 106, 154, 217
sumō (wrestling). *See* passing time in camp
Suyetomi, Rev. Koten, 81
Suzuki, Eijiro, 191, 193, 195
Suzuki, Sadaichi, 199
Suzuki, Tajiro, 224
Suzuki, Teruchiyo. *See* Takahashi, Yasuye

T
Tachibana, Zenshiro, 220, 228, 229, 231, 295. *See also* Tule Lake group (Santa Fe)
Tagashira, Yoshio, 195
Tagawa, Shizuma, 105, 198, 199
Tahara, Haruji, 154
Tahara, Hiroshi, 251, 261
Tahara, Rev. Kameo, 199
Takahashi, Haruko, 40, 314n33. *See also* women internees
Takahashi, Rev. Rien, 191, 238
Takahashi, Shozo, 39
Takahashi, Teisuke, 191, 209
Takahashi, Tokuye (physician), 18, 32, 47, 69, 75, 81, 107, 137, 198
Takahashi, Yasuye, 40, 314n33. *See also* women internees
Takahata, Yoshio, 199
Takai, Seigo (Sacramento, California), 185, 209, 213–214, 257
Takaki, Suekuma, 98, 254
Takakuwa, Shujiro, 65, 74, 233
Takamoto, George, 208–209
Takamoto, Wataru, 191, 239
Takanishi, Kazuichi, 207, 265
Takano, Itaro (Panama), 119, 256

Takashima, Shigeto, 185
Takata, Shigeo Joe, 112. *See also* Nisei, military service by
Takata, Toichi, 224
Takechi, Shizuyo, 40, 314n33. *See also* women internees
Takei, Nekketsu, 201, 209
Takei, Tokiji (Sojin), 192, 212, 216
Takemoto, Rev. Hikojuro, 246
Takeoka, Daiichi, 192, 193
Takeoka, Michikazu, 192
Takesaki, Kazuo, 239
Takeshita, Wataru, 193, 194, 214, 233
Takesono, Rev. Seikaku, 199, 225
Taketa, Kazuo, 190, 192, 207, 223, 261
Taketa, Samonji, 209
Taketa, Torao, 199
Tamabayashi, Hiroshi, 226, 239, 255
Tamura, Makitaro, 224
Tamura, Yoshihisa, 193, 195, 214
Tanabe, Sannojo, 246
Tanada, Gihei, 224
Tanaka, Haru, 39, 40, 314n33. *See also* women internees
Tanaka, Hideo, 154, 190, 191, 255
Tanaka, Horyu, 193
Tanaka, Kanji, 195
Tanaka, Katsuichi, 70, 224
Tanaka, Kazuaki, 195, 233
Tanaka, Kyuhachi, 105, 199
Tanaka, Masayoshi, 191, 257, 259
Tanaka, Ryoichi, 189
Tanaka, Tetsuo, Rev. 199, 225
Tanaka, Yaroku, 38, 197
Tani, Shigeki, 193
Tanigawa, Tomizo, 185–186, 187
Tarasawa, Heitaro, 69, 75
Tarumoto, Fukuo, 37
Tashiro, Manabu, 74, 106, 110
Tatsuguchi, Rev. Goki, 65, 74, 191, 197, 209, 210
Tatsuhara, Koshi, 192, 227
Tatsutani, Rev. Genshin, 38–39, 81, 89, 198
Tauber, Harry, 33. *See also* German internees
Terada, Kyuzo, 39
Terada, Shigeji, 224
Tessaku Seikatsu (Soga). See *Life behind Barbed Wire*
Tillman, F.G. (FBI agent), 20–22, 23
Tochio, Taijiro (Peru), 155, 159
Toda, Sosuke, 199
Toda, Yasuo, 65

Tofukuji, Koshiro (physician), 81
Togawa, Riichi, 191, 195, 210, 255
Togioka, Setsugo, 105, 129, 155, 197
Toguri, Makoto (Los Angeles), 119
Toishigawa, Hatsuichi, 192, 195, 227, 255, 272
Tokairin, Jinshichi, 137, 224
Tokutake, Kaichi, 155
Toma, Masaya, 226
Tominaga, Hisashi (Samoa), 52, 66, 69, 72, 96, 207
Tomita, Kazuo, 31, 38, 155, 201
Torii, Tadaharu, 224
Toyama, Takinosuke, 57, 70, 81
Toyama, Tetsuo, 10, 18, 56, 130, 133, 200, 266
Toyofuku, Hatsutaro, 69–70, 75, 194, 224
Toyota, Setsuzo, 130, 136, 185
trains. *See* transport to camps
transport to camps: trains, 56–63, 85–87, 96–97, 126–127, 165–166, 262, 263–264; ships, 43–47, 49–50
Truman, President Harry S., 236–237, 245, 250
Tsuchiya, Seiichi, 24, 39
Tsuda, Ryuto. *See* Hirai, Shinsho
Tsuha, Rev. Norizane, 18, 74, 77, 106, 220, 228, 229. *See also* Tule Lake group (Santa Fe)
Tsuji, Tokuichi, 39
Tsujita, Akira, 129, 227
Tsukiyama, Wilfred Chomatsu, 196
Tsunoda, Kensaku, 15, 18, 24–25, 70, 92, 198
Tsunoda, Ryusaku, 150
Tsushima, Gempachi, 191, 193, 194, 209, 227
Tsushima, Jukichi, 206
Tule Lake group (Santa Fe Camp), 210, 220–221, 224–225, 228–232; and Japan's defeat, 248, 249, 251, 293–296
Tule Lake Relocation Center (California), 6, 216–217, 220–221, 224–225; incidents at, 160–161, 208, 210–211; internees at Santa Fe, 228–232; Nisei, 210, 217–218, 220–221, 224–225, 228–232, 238

U
Uchida, Isamu, 228
Uchida, Suehiro, 239
Uemori, Shigeyuki, 39
Ueno, Hanpei (Seattle), 119

Ueoka, Isamu, 193
Ueoka, Rev. Sokan (Mukuchi), 65, 74, 81, 137, 158, 214 B
Umehara, Shodo, 199
Umezu Yoshijiro, 251
United Japanese Society (UJS), xxx, xxxiii, xxxvi, 8, 9, 21–22, 24, 25, 89–90, 281
Uranaka, Kazusaburo, 192
Uranaka, Wasaburo, 224
Urata, Masaru, 217
Urata, Minoru, 39
U.S. Air Force, 47, 206, 222, 240, 245–246
U.S. Army, camps administered by, xx, xxxiii, xxxiv, 11, 224, 233. *See also* Hawai'i, under martial law; Reserve Officer Training Corps (ROTC)
U.S. citizenship, renunciation of, xxxiv, 225, 254
U.S. Department of Justice, xx, xxxii–xxxiii, xxxiv. *See also* Immigration and Naturalization Service (INS)
Ushijima Mitsuru, 241–242
U.S.-Japan relationship, xii, 25, 38, 185, 187, 195, 204
Uyeda, Tetsusaburo (Missouri), 65, 66, 71, 88, 89, 209
Uyeda, Toraichi, 37, 74, 81, 137
Uyehara, Masao, 217
Uyehara, Masayoshi, 195, 198
Uyehara, Saburo, 158
Uyehara, Tokuya, 130
Uyehara, Yokichi (physician), 191, 209, 213, 218

V

Valentine, Eugene, xxxiii, 34, 287–288
victory believers (*katta-tō*), 248–250, 251, 253–254, 265–266

W

Wada, Ishiro, 155
Wada, Takashi, 81
Wada, Rev. Umeo, 29, 105
Wahiawa Japanese Language School, 39
Wainwright, Lt. Gen. Jonathan, 251
Wakamoto, Giichi, 39
Wakayama, Jitsuji, 113
Wakayama, Rinzo (Ernest Kinzo), 229
War Relocation Authority (WRA), xx–xxi, xxxiii–xxxiv, 203, 321. *See also* relocation centers
Watanabe, Ittetsu (Tadao), 158, 162
Watanabe, Iwaki, 39, 98, 100

Watanabe, Keiichi, 192
Watanabe, Shingo (San Francisco), 119, 256
Watanabe, Tadao, 155
Watanabe, Rev. Tamasaku, 193
Watanabe, Yoshitaka (Seattle), 119
Wells, Gen. Briant H., 9
West Coast mass incarceration, xx, xxiii–xxii, xxxiii, 208, 217, 219. *See also* Roosevelt, President Franklin D.
Williams, Ivan (Santa Fe camp administrator), 226, 228, 230–232, 237, 248, 254, 293–296
women internees, xxxii, 15–16, 39–40, 143–144, 314n33. *See also* Miyao, Yoshiye; Miyao, Yuki; Mori, Ishiko
World War II: atomic bombs dropped on Hiroshima and Nagasaki, 245–246; Battle of Midway, 116–117; Battle for Okinawa, 237, 242–243; Germany surrenders, 238; hope of peace talks after Roosevelt's death, 236–237; Iwo Jima, 225–226; Japan surrenders, 246–248; Japanese military reports, 218–219, 221–222, 225–226; Japanese navy victory reports, 205–206; Potsdam Declaration, 245, 246–247; U.S. bombing raids of Japan, 222, 240, 244. *See also* Japan, Japanese military; Pearl Harbor attack

Y

Yamada, Shigeki, 191, 264
Yamagata, Heiji, 191
Yamamoto, Hiroemon, 195
Yamamoto, Hiroshi, 155, 157, 215, 232–233, 256, 258
Yamamoto, Kizo, 215
Yamamoto, Koemon, 191
Yamamoto, Shinkichi, 37
Yamamoto, Takeo, 39
Yamamoto, Toyosuke, 195
Yamamoto, Tsuneichi, 193, 195, 197, 206, 255, 272
Yamanaka, Heiichi, 81, 137
Yamanashi (Kōshū) prefecture, xxvii–xxviii, 20–21, 90, 105, 119, 126, 128, 253, 255–257
Yamane, Goichi, 81
Yamane, Seigi, 15–16
Yamane, Tsuta (wife of Seigi), 16, 39, 40, 314n33. *See also* women internees
Yamasato, Rev. Jikai, 42, 197, 215, 255
Yamashita, Soen, 154

Yanaga, Katsutoshi, 35
Yanagi, Tokujiro, 191
Yano, Shigeru, 206
Yarmouth, USS, 265–266
Yatsutake, Toraichi, 37–38
Yoda, Kichisuke, 105, 119, 129, 155
Yoda, Seiji, 20, 21–22, 285
Yogi, Jitsuei, 215
Yogi, Seizaburo, 158
Yokohama Specie Bank, 28, 37, 65
Yokomizo, Kaheiji, 227
Yokota, Kazuto, 191
Yonahara, Ryosen, 185
Yonemura, Isamu, 37

Yonemura, Kiyoshi, 193, 195, 206, 214
Yonesaki, Ushitaro, 224
Yoneyama, Fumiya, 256
Yoshida, Naoji, 151
Yoshida, Shigeo, 41, 196
Yoshida Shigeru (Japanese prime minister),
　　　xxxvi–xxxvii
Yoshimasu, Masayuki, 199
Yoshimasu, Shinjiro, 224
Yoshimoto, Asami (Taikō), 206
Yoshioka, Yoshio, 272
Yoshizawa, Jiro (physician), 191
Yoshizumi, Rev. Kogan, 192, 200, 227

About the Translator

Born in Tokyo, **Tatsumi Hayashi** was a management executive for Japan Airlines for four decades, working in such cities as Fukuoka, Frankfurt, New York, and Honolulu. He retired as the president and CEO of the Ihilani Resort & Spa and Ko Olina Golf Club (then a subsidiary of JAL) in Kapolei, Oʻahu. In 1998, he began volunteering at the Japanese Cultural Center of Hawaiʻi. His translation work has appeared in the center's two previous internment publications, *Life behind Barbed Wire* by Yasutaro Soga and *Family Torn Apart: The Internment Story of the Otokichi Muin Ozaki Family* edited by Gail Honda. He also is the author and administrator of JCCH's online Hawaii Japanese Internee Database, which contains information on approximately 2,300 internees and their families. He lives in Honolulu with his wife, Masako.